Revolutionary Passage

In the series

Politics, History, and Social Change,

edited by John C. Torpey

Brian A. Weiner, *Sins of the Parents: The Politics of National Apologies in the United States*

Heribert Adam and Kogila Moodley, *Seeking Mandela: Peacemaking Between Israelis and Palestinians*

Götz Aly and Karl Heinz Roth, translated by Assenka Oksiloff, *The Nazi Census: Identification and Control in the Third Reich*

Immanuel Wallerstein, *The Uncertainties of Knowledge*

Michael R. Marrus, *The Unwanted: European Refugees from the First World War Through the Cold War*

Revolutionary Passage

FROM SOVIET TO

POST-SOVIET RUSSIA,

1985-2000

Marc Garcelon

Temple University Press
PHILADELPHIA

Temple University Press
1601 North Broad Street
Philadelphia PA 19122
www.temple.edu/tempress

⊗ The paper used in this publication meets the requirements of the American
National Standard for Information Sciences—Permanence of Paper for Printed
Library Materials, ANSI Z39.48-1992

Library of Congress Cataloging-in-Publication Data

Garcelon, Marc, 1958–
    Revolutionary passage : from Soviet to post-Soviet Russia, 1985–2000/
Marc Garcelon.
        p. cm.—(Politics, history, and social change)
    Includes bibliographical references and index.
    ISBN 1-59213-361-4 (cloth : alk. paper)—ISBN 1-59213-362-2 (pbk. : alk. paper)
    1. Political culture—Russia (Federation).   2. Political culture—Soviet Union.
3. Perestroæka.   4. Democracy—Russia (Federation).   5. Demokraticheskaëï
Rossiëï (Political party).   6. Intellectuals—Soviet Union.   7. Soviet
Union—Intellectual life—1970–1991.   8. Soviet Union—Politics and
government—1985–1991.   9. Russia (Federation)—Politics and government—
1991– . I. Title. II. Series.

    JN6699.A15G37 2005
    947.086—dc22   2004062087

2 4 6 8 9 7 5 3 1

Contents

List of Acronyms and Russian Terms

aktiv	activists working at the grassroots levels of voluntary associations or political parties
antipolitika	antipolitics
apparati	apparatuses
blat	influence or "pull"
biznes	business
chelovek naroda	a man of the people
CPD-RSFSR	The Congress of Peoples Deputies of the Russian Soviet Federated Socialist Republic
CPD-USSR	The Congress of Peoples Deputies of the Union of Soviet Socialist Republics
CPRF	The Communist Party of the Russian Federation
CPSU	The Communist Party of the Soviet Union
demokratizatsiia	democratization
DPR	The Democratic Party of Russia (Demokraticheskaia partiia Rossii, "Travkin's Party")
DR	Democratic Russia (Demokraticheskaia Rossiia or DemRossiia)
DR fond	The Democratic Russia Fund (Fond Demokraticheskaia Rossiia)
DU	The Democratic Union (Demokraticheskii soiuz)
derzhavnik	advocate of Russia as a "great" or imperial power
derazhavnost'	the quality of being a "great" or imperial power

vii

dvizhenie	a social or political movement
dvoevlastie	dual power
Edinstvo	"Unity," the slate of candidates organized in the fall of 1999 to support then Prime Minister Vladimir Putin
glasnost'	openness or publicity
gorizpolkom	a city executive committee
gorkom	a city (gorodskoi) committee of the CPSU
grazhdanskoe obshchestvo	civil society
intelligent	a member of the intelligentsia
izbiratel'noe sobranie	voter assembly
izbirkomy	voting committees
izbiratel'nye komissii	voting commissions
izpolkom	an executive committee
kluby izbiratelei	voter clubs
Komsomol	CPSU youth organization
kollektivnyi chlen	collective member
Lensovet	The Leningrad City Soviet
mafiia	mafia
mikroraion	microdistrict
Mossovet	The Moscow City Soviet
multipartiinost'	a multi-party, representative political system
narod	"the people"
narodnost'	populism
narodnye fronty	popular fronts
neformaly	informal groups
nomenklatura	the nomenclature
obkom	a regional (oblastnoi) committee of the CPSU
obnovlenie	renewal
oblast'	sub-republican region, roughly equivalent to a state in the United States
obshchestvennia obed"edineniia	social organizations
oikos	economy
orgkomitet	organizing committee
otechestvo	fatherland
partiinost'	"party-spiritedness"

partokraty	partocrats
perestroika	restructuring
propiska	permit
raikom	a district (raionyi) committee of the CPSU
raisovet	a district-level soviet in Moscow
rang	rank
razgosudarstvlenie	de-statization, i.e., dismantling of state control over society and property
RCP	The Russian Communist Party (Kommunisticheskaia partiia RSFSR)
reabilitiroval	rehabilitated
rezhimnye goroda	closed cities
rezhimnye pred'priiatiia	closed enterprises
RFE/RL	Radio Free Europe/Radio Liberty Reports
RSFSR	The Russian Socialist Federated Soviet Republic
samizdat	self-published and unofficial newspapers
shestidesiatniki	the "60ers"
spetsialist	in Soviet terminology, a mental laborer, that is, a professional (from doctors to academics), manager, or technician
shokovaia terapiia	shock therapy
soslovie	social estate, that is, a major social status group in pre modern Russia
sovet	a council
sovety	soviets
uchastok	a precinct
uskorenie	acceleration
vyborshchiki	electors
Yabloko	"The Apple," political party led by Grigorii Yavlinskii in the 1990s
zakonnost'	legality, the rule of law
zastoi	stagnation

Acknowledgments

The author of such a book, representing as it does the culmination of many years of research and reflection, owes thanks to many people. For those I may have overlooked, please forgive me. I owe particular thanks to Ivan Szelényi, Michael Urban, Christian Joppke, John Torpey, and Micah Kleit, who offered key editorial advice in the final stages of the book's writing. I would also like to specially thank Victoria E. Bonnell for her many years of support during the completion of this project, including her service as Chair of my Dissertation Committee. Robert N. Bellah, Veljko Vujacic, Steven Stoltenberg, Jim Stockinger, Ken Jowitt, Thomas B. Gold, and Gail W. Lapidus all deserve my appreciation for their feedback on earlier drafts of the manuscript. Arkadii Beliavev, Ivaylo Petev, Roman Arkhangelskii, and Shana Hansell served as exemplary research assistants at various stages of this project's realization.

A large number of other people provided useful criticisms or helped with research difficulties at various points in completing this book, including Nina Beliaeva, Vera Beliaeva, Donald L. M. Blackmer, Ann Cooper, Andrei Degtiarev, Gregory Freidin, Ted Gerber, Mikhail Gokhman, Rebecca Gradolph, Lev Gudkov, Gavin Helf, Michael Hout, Kirill Ignat'ev, Viacheslav Igrunov, Bill Keller, Lena Korkia, Vera Kriger, Bob McCarthy, Dar'ia Pavlova-Silanskaia, Anatolii Polikarpov, Boris Rakovskii, Svetlana Rogova, Mark Selden, Peter Stavrakis, Marina Tiurina, Yuri Veshninskii, and Victor Zaslavsky.

I would also like to express appreciation to the following organizations, which funded this project at various times as it matured: the Kennan Institute for Advanced Russian Studies, the Social Science Research Council, the Institute on Global Conflict and Cooperation, the Middlebury College Undergraduate Collaborative Research Fund, the Institute of International Studies of the University of California at Berkeley, the Center for Slavic and East-European Studies of the University of California at Berkeley, and the Berkeley Program in Soviet and Post-Soviet Studies.

Finally, I would like to thank Middlebury College and my fellow colleagues in the Department of Sociology and Anthropology for all their help in bringing this project to fruition, as well as Eva, my mother, and my father for the encouragement and support they have given me over the time it took to bring this book to fruition.

Introduction: Passages

I n the 1990s, Russia's experience under its first popularly elected leader, Boris Yeltsin, seemed to follow some inscrutable law of revolutionary entropy. First, Yeltsin launched a program of sweeping policies aimed at dismantling the economic remnants of the old Soviet order, itself destroyed in the political revolution of August 1991. Such "emergency decrees," however, quickly devolved into political strife. As paralysis gripped Russia's infant governing bodies, the next several years brought relentless economic decline, culminating in political fragmentation and the crushing of a motley uprising of extremist legislators by military force in October 1993. On paper, the events of that fall consolidated Yeltsin's presidential rule.[1] In reality, Russian governmental powers remained weak and divided, declining still further in the wake of the President's ill-conceived December 1994 invasion of the Republic of Chechnya on Russia's southern periphery. Although a cease-fire followed Yeltsin's mid-1996 reelection against the unpopular successor of the Soviet Communists, the Communist Party of the Russian Federation, violent conflicts between and among various official, "business" (*biznes*), and "mafia" (*mafiia*) factions reduced the Russian government to a shell. By the time the ruble collapsed in August 1998—mocking earlier promises of rapid transition to a market democracy—Yeltsin's postrevolutionary government appeared an ignominious failure.

Yet in August 1999, an attack by Chechen separatists against Russian troops stationed in neighboring Dagestan—along with Chechnya, one of sixteen Autonomous Republics of the Russian Federation enjoying a high degree of local autonomy from the federal government—gave a seemingly moribund Yeltsin a sudden opportunity to engineer a successor regime. Unlike December 1994, when Russian armed forces appeared the aggressors, now Russian federal figures appeared in national political discourse as victims. This symbolic reversal proved crucial. On August 9, Yeltsin dismissed then Russian Prime Minister Sergei Stepashin and appointed the little-known former intelligence officer Vladimir Putin in his stead.[2] Within weeks, Putin organized a Russian counterattack against Chechen guerillas. Soon after, Yeltsin designated the new

1

Prime Minister his successor and chosen candidate in the presidential elections scheduled for March of 2000.

Yeltsin's August appointment of Putin risked little opposition from the Duma, the parliament established under Russia's 1993 constitution. After all, a conflict between the Duma and Yeltsin over Stepashin's appointment as prime minister in May 1999—just four months earlier—had ended in a failed parliamentary attempt to impeach the president.[3] Renewing conflict over the installation of yet another prime minister just a few months before the December 1999 parliamentary elections would have allowed Yeltsin to exercise the powers granted under the constitution to dissolve parliament if it refused to confirm the president's appointment. Deputies of all political stripes feared such an outcome, as it would have denied sitting Duma members the use of their parliamentary offices, communications equipment, financial resources, and other considerable advantages enjoyed by incumbents in the election process.[4] If such circumstances made a renewal of confrontation between the president and Duma unlikely, the renewed Chechen war rallied the population around Putin and silenced, for the time being, parliamentary opponents.

During Putin's first six weeks as prime minister, escalating warfare triggered a sea change in Russian politics as a whole. Four seemingly random bombings of apartment buildings between the fourth and the sixteenth of September—three in European Russia and one in Dagestan—consolidated the new era. Denouncing the murder of over three hundred Russian civilians, Putin blamed Chechens for the attacks and announced plans for an all-out Russian invasion of that republic. On September 23, Russia began bombing Chechnya in advance of the invasion, as Putin vowed to "catch" Chechen rebels "in the toilet and wipe them out in their outhouses."[5] Exhausted by years of economic and political turmoil, the populace proved an easy target for patriotic appeals to unify behind Putin's fresh political face in defense of the Federation.

With war in defense of the territorial integrity of the Russian Federation now mapping a paradigm of struggle for the future of the "fatherland" (*otechestvo*), the means grew clear for securing Putin's domination of the Russian political field. Given such circumstances, the Yeltsin group organized a new political umbrella, Unity (*Edinstvo*), as a device for electing a plurality of Putin supporters to the Duma. Although the December 19 elections gave Unity only 23 percent of the seats, Putin adroitly arranged a marriage of convenience with Yeltsin's erstwhile archenemy—the Communist Party of the Russian Federation (CPRF)—in exchange for chairmanships of various parliamentary committees.[6] It did not hurt that the CPRF strongly supported the suppression of the Chechen independence movement. Putin's bargain thus cemented a working parliamentary majority committed to giving him maximal maneuverability as a wartime prime minister. Yeltsin's resignation on New Year's Eve of 1999 consolidated the new government, as Putin assumed the presidency and—in his first official act—granted immunity to members of Yeltsin's inner circle from prosecution on corruption charges.[7]

What emerges from all of this is a pattern of Russian high politics remote from the democratic vision that dominated the reform side of the Russian political field in the late 1980s and early 1990s. Indeed, the manner of Putin's rise to the presidency could only develop given the prior political collapse of pro-democracy activists of the late-communist period who helped bring Yeltsin to power.

Consider, for instance, Putin's promotion of his Chechen war policy as "a national example" for solving Russia's myriad problems.[8] During his presidential campaign—waged more as a plebiscite on whether or not citizens of the Russian Federation opposed the idea of Chechen independence than as an attempt to define issues or programs—Putin wrapped perfunctory nods toward the concept of democracy around promises to restore "a powerful state" (*derzhavnnost'*) and "a dictatorship of law" en route to victory in the 2000 presidential election.[9]

From the perspective of democratic hopes that waxed in the years following the onset of reforms under the last General Secretary of the Communist Party of the Soviet Union (CPSU), Mikhail Gorbachev, the ascent of Putin on a tide of war and a promise to rebuild a powerful centralized state seemed a lurch back toward a past of Tsars and Soviet rulers.[10] The term hijacking comes to mind. But, as the old saw goes, appearances may be deceiving, and a more considered assessment of the outcome of Russia's latest revolution requires a careful untangling of the events, movements, and processes leading from the Gorbachev reforms to Putin's election. Let us take a closer look, then, at the heyday of the Russian democratic movement before turning our attention to its intended (and unintended) consequences.

Democratic Russia and Political Revolution in Moscow

The principal organization of the Russian democratic movement between 1989 and 1991—Democratic Russia or *DemRossiia*—stood at the crossroads of *longue durée* and political revolution.[11] Gorbachev's embrace of policies of "restructuring" (*perestroika*), "openness" (*glasnost'*), and "democratization" (*demokratizatsiia*) between his confirmation as General Secretary of the Soviet Communist Party in April 1985 and the events of 1989 in turn aimed to reverse a decade-long decline in Soviet economic and technological capacities relative to the core powers of the global capitalist order, in particular the United States.[12] But the rise of DemRossiia over the course of 1989 forced the Soviet leadership to change course.

At the end of the 1980s, elite "rebels" occupying high positions in the Soviet "party-state"—the fusion of party and state institutions that emerged in twentieth-century communist and fascist dictatorships—backed the formation of DemRossiia to capitalize on the political opportunity created by Gorbachev's calling of semi-free elections to local, regional, republic, and federal-level legislative bodies—the *sovety* or soviets. By uniting under a single umbrella a plethora of voluntary associations, self-proclaimed political parties, pro-reform factions in the CPSU, pro-democracy deputies in various soviets, and opposition candidates, DemRossiia leaders hoped to "seize power at the local level."[13] A networking process emerged from these organizing efforts, which in the end dismantled the Soviet regime itself.

In organizing networks as a "counterpower" to the Soviet Communist Party, Democratic Russia followed the example of nationalist militants who unexpectedly seized the initiative from CPSU leaders in the republics of Armenia and Estonia of the Union of Soviet Socialist Republics (USSR) in 1987 and 1988. DemRossiia here stepped into the breach opened at the very heart of the Soviet party-state by the reform leadership's gamble in tolerating dilution of central control over the federal hierarchy of territorial and ethnic soviets—a devolutionary process subsequently known as "the parade of sovereignties" (*parad suverenitetov*).[14]

The historical significance of DemRossiia thus stemmed from two primary sources. First, Democratic Russia emerged as the key network along which the parade of sovereignties moved from outlying federal territories of the Soviet Union to its geographical and urban core, Moscow. Second, DemRossiia served as the key grassroots vehicle for both Yeltsin's spring 1990 struggle to become chair of the Russian Supreme Soviet and his June 1991 campaign for the newly created post of president of the largest of the fifteen constituent republics of the USSR, the Russian Socialist Federated Soviet Republic (RSFSR). During these campaigns, DemRossiia's drive to seize power from below converged with splits at the top of the Soviet party-state to empower a counterelite in control of the RSFSR Supreme Soviet, creating a viable contender for power just across Moscow from the seat of the all-Union government itself.

Democratic Russia's strategy bore fruit following Yeltsin's spring 1990 rise to Chair of the Russian Supreme Soviet. Now under Yeltsin's command, the government of the RSFSR—ostensibly subordinate to Soviet legal codes—declared sovereignty over Soviet federal law, creating a dual-power situation (*dvoevlastie*) in the Soviet capital and bringing the devolution of power full circle. Thus, when conservative CPSU officials—dismayed by the parade of sovereignties and opposed to Gorbachev's negotiations with Yeltsin over a new union treaty to replace principles first laid down in the Soviet constitution of 1924[15]—attempted to restore centralized party-state control on August 19, 1991, the countervailing power of the Russian Republic served as a rallying point for resistance to the attempted seizure of power. In the days following the coup's collapse, the Russian government used its revolutionary prestige to sweep the CPSU from power—and with it, the Soviet order a few months later.

As the Soviet Union was dismantled in the fall of 1991, however, Yeltsin abandoned any interest in using DemRossiia as a political base or transforming its networks into a political party. Virtually ignoring the movement's leaders and organizers in cobbling together a postrevolutionary administration, the new government concentrated instead on securing autonomy from legislative oversight and putting together an alliance of pro-reform officials and technocrats in single-minded pursuit of a top-down strategy of implementing a transition to a market economy through state decrees. Modeled on the policy preferences of "the Washington Consensus"—the neoliberal policy frame championed by the American-dominated development establishment, from the International Monetary Fund and the World Bank to neoliberal think tanks and the U.S. Treasury Department—these "shock therapy" (*shokovaia terapiia*) reforms cast democracy as a sort of by-product of the creation of a generically understood market economy.[16]

The embrace of macroeconomic policies imported whole from the international development establishment underscored the postrevolutionary Yeltsin government's abandonment of both its grassroots political base and democratic institution building. However, the democratic movement's previous reliance on grassroots "antipolitics"—the notion that if the Soviet power structure could just be dismantled, all would be well—prepared the political ground for acquiescence to Yeltsin's hypercentralized strategy among democratic activists in the fall of 1991. Indeed, the dream of replicating "the West" on Russian territory as quickly as possible animated the formation and spread of the DemRossiia movement between 1989 and August 1991, creating highly favorable circumstances for simply decreeing the standardized discourse of structural adjustment as a ready-made template, an "elaborate contraption" for Russian policymaking.[17] Thus when the Soviet regime fell, the language and jargon spoken among DemRossiia activists had already congealed into a flexible tool kit of semantic resources used habitually by the Yeltsin counterelite to frame the road ahead and delineate "democrats" from "reactionaries."[18]

In so doing, Yeltsin's immediate advisors in fact returned to a pattern seen repeatedly in Russian cultural history. In this pattern, "[e]very new period—whether the Christianization of Russia or of the reforms of Peter the Great—is oriented toward a decisive break with what preceded it."[19] Here, the Soviet period was rejected in toto by a simplified abstraction, "the West." By such circuitous routes did the discursive contraption of IMF-style neoliberalism wind its way from the global to the local level as an imported substitute for the absence of a politically viable ideology of Russian national identity serviceable for democratic politics.[20] From here it was a short step to the enthusiastic embrace of shock therapy as the reform strategy for consolidating Russian democracy at the end of 1991 despite the fact that, like its counterparts elsewhere, shock therapy had little to do with the nuts and bolts of fashioning democratic institutions. Parallels emerge here between archaic Russian cultural patterns of authoritarian politics and the deep appeal of abstract, "totalistic" theories for remaking Russia anew. For these reasons, the symbolic cast given the rebellion in urban Russia by the projection of a reified notion of the West as model and ideal for the Russian future proved of historic significance in the Russian Federation of the 1990s, despite the absence of any real Western control of the process.

The longing to duplicate Western experience on Russian soil helped prepare the DemRossiia movement for self-subordination to the Yeltsin group, which in turn subordinated much of Russian politics to its own reading of economic reform discourse imported from Western academic and policy circles. Thus, in stark contrast to the Bolshevik movement in 1917, members of Democratic Russia's *aktiv* (the movement's leaders and activist core) found themselves quickly shunted aside in the wake of their seeming political triumph of August 1991. In distinction from the strictly economic parameters of neoliberal theory, ongoing grassroots participation in political life (*narodnoe uchastie*), however vaguely conceived, animated the working notion of democracy among the aktiv. Grassroots participation thus drove the networking process throughout the DemRossiia movement as a whole. Indeed, this working understanding of democracy embodied the aktiv's vision of building a Russian civil society (*grazhdanskoe obshchestvo*), a vision convergent with the ethos of similar civil society projects in Czechoslovakia, Hungary, and Poland in the late 1980s and early 1990s.[21]

But unlike their Czech, Hungarian, and Polish counterparts following the 1989 revolutions in Central Europe, DemRossiia activists after August 1991 found themselves on the sidelines of the government they helped bring to power. Cut off by Yeltsin from mooring defense of government policy in grassroots politics—the would-be incubator of DemRossiia's civil society project—the narrowly urban and professional networks of the democracy movement quickly unraveled. In their stead, often opaque networks asserted themselves at the center of struggles to shape the course of shock therapy and its successors in a Russian Federation populated with multiple and overlapping regional sovereignties.

Feudalization in Postcommunist Russia

As a consequence, postrevolutionary reform rapidly became engulfed in a process of "feudalization"—the privatization of law by regional bodies and economic networks and the de facto ceding of sovereign power to local and sectoral notables by nominal national leaders on the basis of personal ties.[22] Eighteenth- and nineteenth-century historians invented the concept of feudalism retrospectively to capture the enmeshing of tributary economic relations in a highly decentralized pattern of "privatized" local sovereignties dominated by local notables who controlled the means of large-scale violence.[23] In this sense, medieval European feudalization entailed "the passing of public power into private hands" as its distinguishing characteristic.[24]

Parallels between premodern, patriarchal forms of political power, and the Stalinist period in the twentieth-century Soviet Union are common.[25] If we follow Weber and distinguish between centralized (patrimonial) and decentralized (feudal) forms of patriarchal authority,[26] then feudalization here simply maps a limited analogy between historical periods of highly decentralized, "localized" forms of sovereignty, and the devolution of control of the means of violence across large swaths of the former Soviet Union in the late 1980s and its successor states in the 1990s. Indeed, feudalization as process does not necessarily entail consolidation of feudalism as a cosmos of social institutions, which can only emerge as an alternative to centralization over many years.

The concept of feudalization captures aspects of the Russian situation in the 1990s missed by more commonly used notions such as privatization, "mafiazation," and state collapse.[27] The devolution of sovereignty, for instance, stems neither from the contracting out of key state capacities like norm enforcement to commercial firms by a central authority that retains ultimate control of the process, nor from the total criminalization or complete disappearance of such capacities altogether. Rather, the implosion of political authority in 1990s Russia resulted in a segmental dissection of sovereignty and the devolution of norm enforcement and control over the means of violence to multiple local and regional networks originating from the Soviet breakup.

Such local and regional networks reorganized "apparatuses" (*apparati*) dominated on a personalistic basis, either coexisting or warring with one another on the basis of arbitrary "deals." These arbitrary arrangements, in turn, shifted relations between local notables, sectoral interests, and the rump of a central state in the major urban areas on an ongoing basis. At the same time, "power dealing" remained constrained by normative and political relations with local populations, upon whom authority depended in differing degrees at different times and places. Vadim Volkov perceptively called this a process of "violent entrepreneurship."[28]

The seeds of feudalization in postcommunist Russia lie deep in Soviet history, as we shall see, but were powerfully augmented by the parade of sovereignties—the dismemberment of central Soviet authority—that made the political revolution of 1991 possible. Over time, the social logic of feudalization relentlessly gutted the administrative capacity of the Russian state, eroded the legitimacy of its officials, starved the coffers of the federal government, and undermined the ruble as a functioning national currency—trends exemplified by two wars in Chechnya and the explosion of barter exchange in the Yeltsin years.[29] Only with Putin's rise did the Russian government regain the capacity to try and reverse such trends.

Framing Political Revolution and Its Consequences in Soviet and Post-Soviet Russia

What, then, happened in the urban social world of Moscow between 1988 and Putin's election? First stands the question of the origins and developmental course of the political revolution of August 1991. As a political revolution, these events entailed the destruction of the institutional foundation, the sovereign backbone, of the Soviet political order.[30] This process in turn shaped patterns of political change and economic devolution in its wake. How, then, to model such processes?

Prominent in accounts of recent Russian events stand notions like "revolution from below" or "revolution from above." Models framing the Soviet collapse in such terms, however, tend to concentrate either on the political elite or popular opposition to it, at times misconstruing the dynamics of how the situation actually unfolded as Soviet oligarchy fragmented and new social forces emerged at multiple levels. Framing Soviet collapse as a revolution from below, for instance, must somehow grapple with the concentration of emergency powers by Yeltsin's entourage in late 1991 and 1992, and the launching of post-Soviet economic decrees in the explicit language of a revolution from above.[31] At the same time, Yeltsin's attempt at revolution from above followed perestroika, the mobilization of Democratic Russia, and the collapse of the Soviet state, rendering the term revolution from above misleading as a characterization of the entire process.[32]

In fact, while grassroots mobilization indeed drove the Soviet collapse, a small number of senior figures in the communist hierarchy encouraged such mobilization from the beginning, rendering problematic accounts which frame events as driven from either "below" or "above." At this point, framing Russian developments in straightforward notions such as revolution from below or revolution from above gives way to more multifaceted accounts. But once again, such accounts at times overlook crucial relations of groups networking across different levels of status as the Soviet order disintegrated, such as the symbiotic relation between the antipolitics of the Russian grass roots and the modus operandi of elite figures around Yeltsin.[33]

Framing multilevel accounts of Russia's latest political revolution, then, presupposes careful analysis of networks across levels in urban Moscow, and by extension, across the Soviet Russian Republic and its successor, the Russian Federation. But it also presupposes awareness of the limits of revolutionary models and terminology. Getting bogged down in definitional arguments about revolution detracts from empirical analysis of the case at hand. Take accounts of earlier revolutions, such as Theda Skocpol's influential 1979 study of *States and Social Revolutions*. In this book, Skocpol differentiates political from what she calls social revolutions in terms of processes that unfolded long after the collapse of autocracies in peasant societies.[34] Moreover, Skocpol herself restricts social revolutions to three cases—France of the late 1700s, Russia in the early 1900s, and China several decades hence—indicating the limitations of the applicability of this model to the political revolution against Soviet power and its aftermath.

Indeed, for good reason, most historical analyses of revolutions tend to be case specific. "Since revolutions are complex social and political upheavals, historians who write about them are bound to differ on the most basic questions—causes, revolutionary aims, impact on the society, political outcome, and even the time span of the revolution itself."[35] Indeed, framings of revolution in late- and postcommunist Russia can easily mislead. Largely absent from accounts of Russia's latest political revolution, for instance, lies a basic question difficult to generalize and requiring careful limitation of the applicability of received models of revolution: how did nascent feudalizing tendencies long at work in the late-communist Soviet Union shape the strategic proclivities and internal morphology of the Russian democratic movement?

Assuming a minimalist definition of political revolution along Tocquevillian lines—the destruction of the institutional backbone of a political order—gives sufficient flexibility to account for feudalization as a process both before and after the political revolution itself. But it also throws back on the observer the need to connect postrevolutionary outcomes—defined here as the consolidation of postrevolutionary institutions—with the genealogy of the political revolution itself.

Political revolutions, after all, involve the breakdown of institutions, and a great deal of confusion results from sloppy use of this latter term. The concept of institution marks forms of social life with an obligatory character, from habits and customs to the "invisible hand" of markets to the formal laws of constitutional states.[36] Institutions are obligatory insofar as failure to conform to established ways of doing things either entails some significant "cost" in resources, time, or status or provokes marginalization, sanctions, or even exclusion from the situation in which given institutions are effective. For these reasons, institutions map both onto geographic and social boundaries, and "naturalize" as "common sense," accepted ways of "getting by and getting along" in stable social fields.[37] Distinctions between tacit and formalized norms mark institutions as either formal or informal, explicit or implicit. In customary situations, no written rules codify expected ways of behaving. Customary knowledge represents instead a tacit dimension of practical knowledge and entails prior socialization in a given way of life and cultivation of an intuitive sense of what's expected, a feel for the game.[38] Formal institutions, on the other hand, involve the explicit codification of expected rules of behavior.

Refusal to publicly acknowledge the legitimacy of CPSU domination—by, for example, refusing to participate in ritual shows of public obeisance to "the leading role of the Communist Party" at obligatory CPSU youth organization (*Komsomol*) meetings held regularly at Soviet universities—could trigger either the application of any number of sanctions available in Soviet legal codes or simply arbitrary repression by party-state officials.[39] We can thus differentiate formal and informal institutions in Soviet life in terms of their genealogical relation to practices of codification and the actual practices of groups in relation to authoritative figures and pronouncements.[40]

Either too much formality expressed in a plethora of rules and regulations—often called simply "bureaucratization"—or too much informality paralyzes modern organizations by rendering the rules of the game highly opaque to all but privileged insiders, an insight highly germane to the Soviet situation. Too much formality in a bureaucratic setting paralyzes bureaucracies by so limiting the discretion of midlevel ranks in the office hierarchy with various rules and regulations. Officials thus become passive and defer to "others" when the application of rules to practical situations appears unclear or when rules seem to directly contradict one another. Too little formality, on the other hand, simply renders the rules a fiction obscuring the social logic of arbitrary decision-making processes. This is the problem of discretion.[41]

While Soviet communism has often been framed as the most bureaucratic of societies in Western commentary, in fact bureaucracy was only partially developed and arbitrarily applied as a method of social control. The principle of formal legality (*zakonnost'*) remained subordinate to "party-spiritedness" (*partiinost'*), the arbitrary *diktat* of party-state functionaries (*apparatchiki*) justified in terms of Marxist–Leninist ideology but in practice more and more serving as an excuse for arbitrary personal rulership.[42] Thus, while excessive promulgation of often contradictory regulations combined with discouragement of discretionary action at lower ranks of Soviet officialdom to repeatedly undermine "efficient" functioning of bureaucracies on their own terms, great latitude to engage in arbitrary rule by fiat was given to higher officials, and all manner of informal trading between enterprise managers and bargaining over planning targets between managers and party-state officials flourished in practice. In this light, the planned economy appears in retrospect as a sort of ideological fiction imposed on a highly informal economic practice.[43]

The consequence was an all-around arbitrariness and authoritarian informality in institutional settings that continues to plague Russian social and political life. As Alena Ledeneva observes, Russian "popular wisdom" expresses this in ironic commonplaces of everyday language:

> "Russia is a country of unread laws and unwritten rules." Or, as they say, "the imperfection of our laws is compensated for by their non-observance" (*nesovershenstvo nashikh zakonov kompensiruetsia ikh nevypolneniem*).[44]

The arbitrariness of apparat domination and the weaknesses of Soviet legality opened Soviet social relations to feudalization, and yet the common trope of overweening Soviet bureaucracy has deeply obscured Westerners' ability to grasp the arbitrary character of institutional practice in late- and postcommunist Russia.[45] The paradigm of ideal behavior promoted in Soviet law and ideology in fact often had a purely arbitrary relation to actual practices in many fields in Russian society, a fact closely related to the Soviet regime's long-range policy of atomizing the population and striving to monopolize all avenues of organizational advancement from above through socially closed and institutionally opaque apparat networks. Such realities have long vexed analyses of Soviet institutions, compromising attempts to map the emergence of social movements in contexts marked by the disintegration of these same institutions.

The principle of party-spiritedness (*partiinost'*)—arbitrary and often highly personalistic domination by party-state functionaries cast in the heroic tones of an impersonal, historical task[46]—captures the dominant principles animating Soviet institutions, as well as noninstitutional networks trying to operate against them in the late 1980s and early 1990s. The political revolution in Russia in August 1991 thus broke the principle of party-spiritedness as an institutional element of daily life in the Soviet Union, precipitating collapse in the ability of high party-state officials to authoritatively command a minimal probability of obedience in the population writ large. From here, the party-state rapidly unraveled, as the Yeltsin counterelite in the Russian Republic "captured" enough obedience from sections of the populace to carry through with the dismantling of the Soviet party-state altogether in the fall of 1991.

But, as we shall see, the Yeltsin group failed to consolidate an institutional alternative to Soviet power, and in fact was dragged into a protracted, paralytic power struggle from which institutional reconsolidation only emerged at the level of the Russian state itself with Putin's rise in the fall of 1999. This protracted interregnum deepened the process of feudalization in Russia proper—a process long at work in Soviet political institutions prior to August 1991.[47] The empirical body of this text explains why and how this happened, framing political revolution in Russia in terms of the process of feudalization. That we only retrospectively see the institutional patterns first destroyed and then—after a protracted interregnum—regenerated during this process, is itself a sign of how difficult it is to model human behavior in the relative chaos of protracted institutional collapse.

Such dynamics underscore how what Pierre Bourdieu called "habitus"— the dispositions, skills, quirks, and other forms of habitual behavior inscribed on bodies by socialization and the routines of everyday life—intersects with institutions and patterns of representation in particular fields. Such fields in turn form sites of disintegrating institutional order and emerging alternative networks at given points in time in a revolutionary process.[48] In a revolutionary situation, networks of contending agents and secular processes of institutional disintegration and reformation shape one another across a social formation, changing the array of fields themselves. The very stakes that regulate contention here alter in mid-game, undermining the "fit" between habitus and field that normally stabilize the political order of things and orient the habitus of agents.

In the Russian political field of the late 1980s and 1990s, tensions between the communist past and visions of a democratic future intersected with tensions between global, regional, and local networks. That agents expressed such tensions in sometimes archaic Russian cultural representations requires some knowledge of Russian history in order to interpret them.[49] In such an everyday context, the global reference of "democracy" took on distinctly local, Russian characteristics. This global–local dynamic altered the back and forth of discourse and the practices it referenced through representative characters like the *demokrat* and the "power-nik" (*derzhavnik*), the *intelligent* and the apparatchik. The prominence of *demokraty* in Russian politics at the end of the 1980s thus remained bound to the ways distinctive circumstances shaped the reception of Western ideas, models, paradigms, and power in late-communist Russia.

The representation of political processes of change in late-communist Russia thus unfolded through "figurational" ("story telling") dynamics of urban social networks. At the center of such narratives lay the interplay of human agency, institutional disintegration, and the genesis of new, proto-institutional networks.[50] "Stories" of how such developments unfolded linked agents to representations of such processes. Indeed, figurations of experience conveyed agentic conceptions of institutional arrays and varied perceptions of the morphology of social fields across networks.[51] Key here stand references to pools of potential support, "audiences," and the role of transnational perceptions in cutting through them.

The concept of "transnational demonstration effect" captures how relative perceptions link the global to the local through vectors of social networks.[52] Outside the West or Japan as contemporary geopolitical centers such effects often map the impact of external organizational and technological practices on behavior among groups perceiving their own society as relatively deprived, "backward," or oppressed in relation to an external reference—even in the case of a global power such as late-Soviet Russia. Such perceptions signal a disposition among peripheral and semiperipheral elites and middle groups to selectively mimic and adapt techniques predominant in core regions in order to build up technological, organizational, and economic capacities and thus realize either greater autonomy or greater integration with "the developed world," or both. By orienting dispositions in this manner, transnational demonstration effects serve institutional isomorphism on a transnational scale—what George Ritzer recently called "grobalization"[53]—as demonstrated in the whole-scale mimicking of Western patterns of industrial organization by Bolshevik leaders in the 1920s and 1930s.[54]

And yet, political constellations, media representations, network relations, and the cultural context in which agents socialize always mediate such transnational perceptions, focusing attention on state–society relations in modeling patterns of revolutionary change. Such processes unfold nationally in reaction to sovereign powers, although local, regional, and transnational dynamics may figure prominently in their development.[55] The national focus stands particularly true of revolutionary processes, which aim at changing the very institutions of state power and thus often challenge received notions of nationhood and citizenship. Here, social movements situate agency and its figurations in relation to fields in which they manifest as patterns of mobilization and networking. Identifying and tracking how such noninstitutional patterns of networking linked pre- and postrevolutionary phases of Russian development from the late 1980s to the late 1990s presupposes careful tracking of the political processes through which such networks formed and developed. So long as we remember that habitus relates to field through both institutional and noninstitutional patterns, some Russian social movements of the late 1980s can be identified as preinstitutional networks capable of developing sustained challenges to Soviet power.

Rethinking Processes of Political Change in the Soviet Order

How, then, to model preinstitutional networks as social movements that generate revolutionary challenges to political authority? Two recent trends in social movement theory have revived "classical" questions of how social movements generated institutional outcomes in the rise of the modern West, and in so doing have offered a way forward for dealing with the Russian situation from the late 1980s through the 1990s. First, the political process approach arose in the last decades of the twentieth century in response to various functionalist, psychologistic, and utilitarian theories of protest and rebellion that emerged in the postwar period stripped of both historicist and Marxian elements, as well as any way of accounting for the semiotic dimension of social mobilization or any sense of the historical contingency of systemic processes of change, according to their critics.[56] At the center of these tensions lies the interplay of human agency and institutional change.

By foregrounding the interaction of agents in networks, questions of how political processes engender social movements intersect with questions rising from the second relevant tendency in social movement theory, namely "identity theories" of such movements.[57] Such theories emphasize the cultural context of agents active in social movements as central to both interpreting and explaining how such agents behave. Conflicts

> are always conflicts of identity: actors attempt to push others to recognize something they themselves recognize; they struggle to attain what others deny. Every conflict which transgresses a system of shared rules concerning the distribution of material or symbolic resources is a conflict of identity. The central question is why has the theme of identity become such a central issue?[58]

Bringing political process and identity models of social movements together means contextualizing political processes in relation to the figurations of historical situations that agents express in order to understand how such movements attempt to change them.[59] Such contextualization begins with identifying two initial conditions of political processes of social movements present in all known historical situations in which movements form:[60]

- changes in political opportunities, which disorganize a previously stable (institutionally secure) political field; and
- a perceptual shift mobilizing a critical mass of oppositionists in such a destabilized political field.

We can now apply this "identity oriented political process model" of social movements to situations of institutional disintegration of political orders. Splits at the top fire perceptual shifts among "outsiders" and trigger the formation of social movements and, by extension, revolutionary processes. Here, use of framing techniques, control of media instruments, access to various audiences, and orchestration of political spectacles—rallies, demonstrations, protests—mediates the course of events, all of which must be historically contextualized.[61] Agents evading, challenging, and defending established political institutions frame processes of mobilization to themselves, to their opponents, and to larger audiences by bringing processes of mediation into play.[62] At this point, representations of political support—such as perceived views among segments of the "Russian people" (*narod*) at the end of the 1980s— may become "virtual" figures in a social movement.[63] Such representations link groups in networks through patterns of identification and interest.

The social geography of networks (mapped in terms of their internal patterns of social closure, their spatiotemporal extensiveness, and their degree of enmeshing in vertical lines of power and status) figures centrally in how the struggle for position feeds back into secular patterns of political change. As we shall see, the ability of Moscow networks to successfully "steer" this complex process figured centrally in the history of Soviet institutional breakdown and the subsequent long interregnum that followed. As polarization and breakdown of authority deepened at the top of the Soviet party-state, the complexity of network interactions increased rapidly. Institutional cohesion thus buckled as organizational controls waned and the fluidity of the situation accelerated in chaotic ways. The "tipping point" into a revolutionary situation appears here retrospectively as the full disintegration of the Soviet party-state as an institutional order during the failed coup of August 19–21, 1991. And with full institutional disintegration, a full chaotic state arrived, determined by the contingent, processual ensemble of a staggering array of factors.[64]

One way of mapping political agency in this chaotic situation is to explain how habitus constrained or "bounded" behavior in relation to widely shared figurations—stories of what it meant to be a Russian—among agents living through such a turbulent experience. The political process of Soviet institutional disintegration here steered the reorientation of habitus to the figurations of political entrepreneurs attempting to organize political alternatives as "proto-institutions." In reconstructing these developmental sequences, we face the twofold task of first tracing how agents framed the experience of state breakdown as they struggled to influence the course of events, and then integrating agentic perspectives into analyses of changing patterns of social closure, latent network resources, and habitus in key institutional domains undergoing disintegration.[65]

Orienting the selection of evidence along two main analytic lines—a change in the array of prior, institutionally stable, political opportunities, and a perceptual shift favoring rebellion—frames the analysis, which can then be contextualized by interpreting identities and their figurations.[66] But that is all it can do. In this sense, a political process approach contextualized in terms of specific historical identities and their figurations maps an initial strategy for going about the reconstruction of how a relatively stable political order might unravel, rather than a predictive theory. It represents a Weberian "ideal type" model par excellence.[67]

Indeed, the identity oriented political process model remains preliminary, as the identification of two necessary conditions for social mobilization to be possible at all is in no way sufficient for explaining either its onset or its subsequent development into a political revolution proper. To do this, the model requires additional analysis of the historically unique conditions in which political revolutions mature, including tracking the contingent relation between agency and historical circumstance through the chaos institutional disintegration begets.

Mapping Perceptual Shifts in Russian Political Processes

Once a political order tips over into the chaos of institutional disintegration, the contingent play of political entrepreneurs and their immediate networks emerge as the causal locus of the revolutionary process. Such an assumption follows from comparative history, as in all known historical situations, some embedded network, or array of networks, emerged out of such processes as the center of some new institution-building project. How agents disposed to act in particular ways and situated in particular networks adjust and improvise in the face of this contingency are thus assumed to eventually settle the outcome, in the sense of stabilizing the formation of some new political order. Perceptual shifts here steer the ways networks both mobilize material resources and orchestrate symbolic displays of power through spectacles of political representation. And analysis of such displays requires accounting for the "double narrativity" of social processes: how the observer frames events in social-scientific terms, while at the same time mapping agentic representations of these same events into the disintegration and eventual reformation of political institutions over time.[68]

How, then, do we organize "interpreting" the double narrativity of semiotic orders and the "meaning" of signs and representations as agents adjust and improvise in relation to the course of events? A whole range of supplementary interpretive strategies may serve here, ranging from the phenomenological analysis of interaction, to the content analysis of texts, to the genealogical analysis of discursive genres, to the objectivistic analysis of interests as "channelers" of agency, and the signs and representations deployed to express and disguise them.[69] Relations between elites and grass roots, on the one hand, and status and class distinctions, on the other, can easily mislead, as a grass roots may appear relatively high in status at the outset of political mobilization and then suffer collapse in economic terms, as in Russia between 1988 and the mid-1990s. Indeed, more initially passive groups may quickly move to the center of political events, with consequences central to grasping the process of change.

The concept of habitus proves crucial here for mapping who "leads" and who "follows" in periods of institutional disintegration. Habitus theorizes behavioral contexts as apparently "given" due to socialization and routine. What happens, then, if institutions disintegrate, if habitually expected routines of getting by and getting along collapse? In effect, the "game" is destroyed because its institutional parameters disintegrate.

In the Soviet Union between Spring 1989 and December 1991, habitual behaviors such as deferring to the Communist Party leadership disintegrated. At some point, agents in Moscow ceased having to worry about "voting" for the CPSU in order to keep their job, attending Party meetings, and so forth. Once a critical mass of people realized they could vote against Communist Party candidates in elections and defy apparat directives in other ways, the Soviet state rapidly disintegrated, that is, disintegrated as a set of political institutions obligatory in everyday life.

Although some Russians may have initially reacted to such institutional disintegration with elation, many others responded only at length, and then with great distress, to this very disintegration. The initial period of denial Bourdieu called "the hysteresis effect"—people continue to behave habitually as if the disintegrated institution is still there.[70] This is one of the reasons habitus is such a stabilizing force in social life. But the disintegration of institutions in fact leaves many individuals confused and highly susceptible to "movement entrepreneurs," those who improvise stopgap solutions in the form of shifting network arrangements to manage the generalized social distress caused by institutional disintegration.

In such situations, those few figures who manage to steer improvised networks that establish alternative behaviors as obligatory begin to spontaneously engineer new, successor institutions by "capturing" habitus and reorienting it in altered directions. This is what happens in a political revolution: the disintegration of previous political institutions generates a chaotic situation, which persists until some networks manage to reestablish alternative, proto-institutions and then consolidate them as such, thus capturing disoriented persons in webs of alternative practices that consolidate as "habituation" of a critical mass of the population to new behavioral contexts. Eventually, this process generates minimally stable alternative political institutions. The whole period in Russia between August 1991 and Putin's assumption of the presidency on December 31, 1999 tracks a very painful process of reinstitutionalization of just such a political establishment.

At times, the concept of interest as a stereotype of disposition and motivation for bracketing interpretive difficulties can be deployed here, in line with precepts used routinely in a broad range of sociological schools.[71] Assuming, for instance, that figures like Mikhail Gorbachev had interests in controlling high political offices in the revolutionary situation that emerged in late-Soviet Russia seems straightforward enough. More "entrepreneurial," proto-institutional behavior, however, demands broadening interpretive frameworks to account for the genesis and developmental history of patterns of networking that appear highly "risky" in relation to disintegrating institutions.

Recognition of the possibility that agents may risk "social death" in relation to extant institutions needs here to be foregrounded. For Bourdieu, social death entails refusal to play the game as institutionalized, as developed in his analysis of artists and novelists in the cultural field of nineteenth- and twentieth-century France, and his conception of the latter as "the economic world reversed."[72] The apparent "irrationality" of behavior in such fields arises from any number of sources, from the reifications of the sociological observer herself to a whole range of agentic dispositions.[73] The possibility of risking social death is homologous in Bourdieu to notions like transcendence, moral responsibility, and ethical principle in a large variety of social thinkers who reject a strictly strategic-determinist vision of human nature. Take Jürgen Habermas' conception of "communicative action," activity oriented to following the unfolding dialectic of argument and its implicit truths for its own sake, regardless of strategic consequences.[74] To pursue the imperative of truth in settings strategically subordinated to maintenance of a field of power, such as the Soviet Academy of Sciences for most of the Soviet period, is to risk social death in this field, as many dissident Soviet scientists found out.

Bourdieu thus built an escape valve into his otherwise relentless focus on strategies, stakes, and interests in social life by differentiating between economic and symbolic interests, recasting Weber's distinction between material and ideal interests in order to emphasize that symbols are emergent properties of "reality" and thus are "materially" efficacious in their own right.[75] Economic interests concern the need of agents for economic goods and organizational resources in order to get by and get along in particular institutional contexts. Symbolic interests concern the need of agents for a minimal degree of continuity between individual identity and social rules of the game as a requisite of getting by and getting along within given institutional orders.[76] The question of whether a symbolic interest manifests largely as habitual conformity, as strategic positioning in a field, or as an occasional proclivity to risk social death in disregard of immediate strategic considerations remains empirical. A willingness to risk social death, for instance, figured prominently in shaping the reputation of Brezhnev-era Soviet dissidents who survived repression and ended-up willy-nilly as moral authorities in the field of *intelligentsia* politics in the early days of perestroika—figures such as Andrei Sakharov, the dissident physicist and human-rights activist who emerged from internal exile as a virtual saint of pro-democracy activists in the late 1980s.[77]

All of this sets up the mapping of material and symbolic interests onto networks and institutional fields. In doing so, common terms applied to Western market societies, namely, cultural and social capital can be generalized to more status-oriented societies by framing them as subtypes of broader categories of "assets." Conceptualizing social and cultural capital as subtypes of cultural and social assets generalizes this typology by historicizing their range of applicability. The terms cultural and social assets not only aid recognition of sometimes highly misrecognized forms of power in circumstances where markets are either absent or secondary. They also enable the adaptation of concepts formed in a contemporary market context to nonmarket situations like the Soviet order, what Max Weber called status-oriented social worlds.[78] When combined with the above considerations on the explanatory limitations of the identity oriented political process model of social movements, such adaptation leads directly to the trajectory improvisation model of political revolution.

The Trajectory Improvisation Model of Political Revolution

In pursuing economic and organizational resources or engaging in political activities, agents depend on their extant social ties and rely on accumulated skills and embodied mastery of local habits, customs, and traditions in realizing any implicit (habitus generated) or explicit (deliberately formulated) course of action. Strategic agency is thus socially embedded in terms of its "external" (positional) expression in networks and social roles, and its "internal" (bodily) expression in habitus and deliberation. Social and cultural assets situate such agency in strategic relation to negotiated trajectories through social space.

The concepts of cultural and social assets adapt a conventional economic conception of capital, namely, capital as a property asset secured by custom or law, to map assets or advantages that cannot be fully alienated (fully disembodied) through either customary or market exchange.[79] So long as agents are disposed or motivated to play a given social game by its implicit or explicit rules, the concepts of social and cultural assets make intelligible the strategic options available to situated agents at particular points along such trajectories.

A skill embodied as habitus, as disposition, remains inscribed on the body, exemplifying cultural assets. Such assets are either certified in various emblems of professional competence such as tertiary degrees; or affirmed by more arbitrary distinctions eliciting deference to signs of prominence in the arts, letters, or sciences; or both. By contrast, social assets map tangible advantages deriving from degrees of relative access to webs of connections such as "old boy" networks socially closed to outsiders. The insider–outsider boundaries of networks arise from nontransferable shared experiences and the cachet of mutual recognition and identity. A "subspecies" of social assets particularly significant for the analysis of Soviet-type societies—political assets—delineates control of, or access to, positions in a party or state (or party-state) hierarchy as well as the authority wielded by "charismatic" political figures among followers and admirers.[80]

Where social space remains institutionally stable, the typology of assets allows us to conceptualize pursuit of economic and symbolic interests as a strategic disposition to maximize assets by striving to attain, maintain, or enhance institutionally secure positions, with agents striving to convert various assets one to another in pursuit of this end. The typology of assets thus gives rise immediately to the conversion problem, the problem of parlaying economic into cultural resources, cultural into social resources, social into political resources, and so forth as situations change over time and particular assets undergo "devaluation."[81]

As should be clear from the limit case discussed above, the possibility that human beings may diverge from expected patterns of habitus and motivation implicit in the typology of assets by downgrading some strategic considerations or even risking social death at various times should be recognized. Use of the typology of assets to analyze human behavior thus in no way entails acceptance of the proposition that agents' professed beliefs, statements, and identifications can be reduced simply to their strategic utility for deploying some potential asset in a given field at a given point in time. Someone may well profess Christianity or communism for strategic purposes, but absent some fraction of agents who identify with such professions for nonstrategic reasons—reasons rooted in a need for meaning for its own sake—such professions would command little legitimacy among the critical mass necessary to make such identifiers strategically significant in the first place. The erosion of such a critical mass of communist "virtuosi"—dedicated adherents willing to risk social death for the cause—in the Soviet context in the late 1980s, for instance, augmented the demonstration effects of perceived Western success in orienting the political field of late-communist Russia away from Marxism–Leninism and toward neoliberal discourse.[82]

The typology of assets facilitates analysis of how agency is strategically situated in relation to its immediate networks. As agents located in networks negotiate fields, and the latter undergo morphological variation over time, agency appears as an ongoing process of trajectory adjustment of habitus to institutional arrays in fields along paths through time. To the extent that the net effect of trajectory adjustment maintains formal and informal rules of the game, it results in social reproduction of an institutional order.[83] To the extent that it aggravates a decline in institutional salience—a decline in the objective probability of observation of formerly resilient norms—trajectory adjustment may contribute to a secular process of social change at the level of institutions and predominant patterns of cultural representation. Gil Eyal, Ivan Szelényi, and Eleanor Townsley call this "the trajectory correction model of social change," as shown in Figure I.1.[84]

Absent a revolutionary situation, processes of both social reproduction and social change may unfold within the confines of a stable political order. To the extent that trajectory adjustment resolves in favor of institutional reproduction, variations in habitus "correct" in the direction of social change. To the extent that trajectory adjustment resolves in favor of institutional transformation, variations in institutional morphology "correct" in favor of successful high-risk gambits initiated by discrete networks of agents, generating ripple adjustments in other agents' habitus throughout a given field or nest of fields.

The model of trajectory adjustment between habitus and field— strategically modeled on the basis of the typology of assets—thus provides a robust analytic strategy for reconstructing the intersection of event and *longue durée* at the level of social networks and discrete fields of social interaction.[85] We can now refine the identity oriented political process model of social movements in terms of trajectory adjustment by acknowledging the possibility that an "institutional break" may destabilize the trajectory-adjustment process upon arrival at some conjunctural tipping point, triggering a revolutionary situation in the field of state power. Here, the trajectory correction model can be used to reconstruct the recursive dynamics of habitus and field up to the

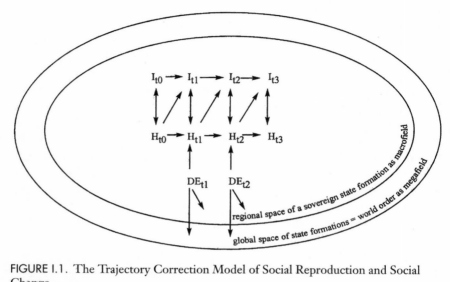

FIGURE I.1. The Trajectory Correction Model of Social Reproduction and Social Change.
Source: Adapted from Eyal et al. (1998: 45).

conjuncture in which institutional patterns of political opportunities disintegrate, for instance, in the struggle occasioned by the crisis of self-legitimacy in the elite field at the top of the Soviet Communist Party in the late 1980s.

Triggered in part by transnational demonstration effects linking geopolitical shifts running against the position of the Soviet Union to elite and professional factions struggling in the party-state to shape the latter's trajectory, this crisis led to perestroika, which in turn changed the structure of political opportunities up and down the status hierarchies of the party-state. We now apply the trajectory correction model of social change to dynamics of institutional breakdown, mapping how agents mobilized and converted various assets in transforming latent organizational capacities into active networks. All that is left is to conceptualize the perceptual shifts that fire the process at the level of agency, although this remains in many ways a formidable task as it requires interpretation of how agents perceived and reacted to conjunctural dynamics with global, regional, and local dimensions on an ongoing basis. The concepts of habitus and field and the typology of assets thus fashion an elegant model for reconstructing the trajectory of social change in revolutionary situations shown in Figure I.2.

H = habitus
I = institutions
DE = demonstation effect
MS = Macrosystem shock = signals unfavorable shift in system environment
TI = truncated institutions
IN = informal network
OS = organizational shells of formerly strongly institutionalized organizations
IO = institutional outcome

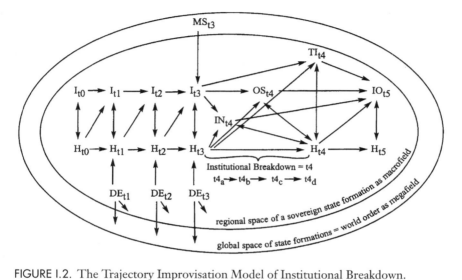

FIGURE I.2. The Trajectory Improvisation Model of Institutional Breakdown.

The initial conditions of the identity oriented political process model here trigger the shift from trajectory adjustment to trajectory improvisation. Trajectory improvisation represents a cumulative shift in behavior reacting to the declining salience of established political institutions. As such, it initially intensifies disorganization of the institutional steering of habitus by rendering the collapse of previous political institutions a figuration, a "story" in which agents suddenly appear as figures in a social drama.

Whether or not political revolution follows depends on the contingent play of factors—the "tipping over" into chaos—engendered by circumstances. Only a reconstructive explanatory narrative fully accounts for such revolutionary outcomes. As Hegel argued long ago, the owl of Minerva flies only at dusk, as the chaotic character of revolutionary breakdowns render prediction of their subsequent dynamics impossible. Here, the ontological character of "predictive impossibility" should be emphasized:

What kind of understanding does chaos theory provide? The object of this understanding is the way in which unpredictable behavior and patterns come to appear. The method of understanding their appearance is by the construction of models, not by breaking systems into their components and then constructing ahistorical deductive schemes, but rather by using ... procedures which concentrate on holistic properties and historical development.[86]

While institutionally stable behavior may someday prove susceptible to some form of scientifically reliable prediction, institutional disintegration will not, for fundamental ontological reasons.[87]

Nevertheless, it remains possible to apply several supplementary generalizations in framing the course of such contingent historical processes, in order to reduce the possible infinity of evidence to some level manageable at the level of an "explanatory narrative" of a historical process of institutional disintegration and subsequent regeneration. The following typology of assets, for instance, organizes evidence in relation to diverse historical situations:

- *markets* map patterns of exchanges of economic goods realized by means of barter or currency exchanges;
- *networks* map patterns of social ties;
- *classes* map patterns of economic interest that form around market exchanges and property rights;
- *status* maps patterns of social inclusion and social closure that form around affinities of lifestyle, consumption, and identity.[88]

Mapping analytic categories like markets, networks, classes, and status groups onto historical reality abstracts from the way social ties combine in actual group life. This presents a clear and present danger of reification, of mistaking the abstract for the concrete, and thus generating false oppositions between class and status or markets and networks that obscure precisely the empirical dynamics we seek to uncover. To preempt this problem, Weber formulated the concept of social class to conceptualize how affinities of lifestyle and identity tend to cluster around class positions in historical contexts where the institutionalization of patterns of market exchanges engender a stable pattern of class differentiation over time.[89] For similar reasons, Peter Evans emphasizes the importance of social embedding in mapping the ways market exchanges, networks and institutions shape one another in empirical contexts over time.[90]

Following such examples, the concepts of cultural and social assets, of status, map the relative strategic weight of upbringing and social ties of particular Russians in particular situations. The typology of assets gives us conceptual tools for drawing a fine-grained picture of how such embedding shapes secular processes at the network level and vice versa, and thus enables a reconstruction of the collapse of Soviet power and subsequent patterns of feudalization. This passage marked a transition from a centralized, status-dominated social order to a more disintegrated situation in which commercial class position began to rival status as a primary vector around which networks formed. The predominance of status rank in Soviet and post-Soviet Russian society cannot be overestimated. Indeed, tensions between often inchoate democratic ideations, on the one hand, and patterns of social closure rooted in status markers of the Soviet past recently destabilized by the logic of political revolution, on the other, plagued the DemRossiia movement. The shifting relation between the horizontal vision of participatory democracy animating DemRossiia activists and political, social, and cultural status hierarchies figured centrally in first inflating and then deflating the relative value of the cultural and social assets embodied in activist networks.[91]

Such considerations raise the question of the relation between the Bourdieuian analysis of social capital outlined to this point and Robert Putnam's conception of social capital as an enabler of civic trust and thus democratic institutions.[92] A persistent problem in Putnam's approach stems from both an insufficiently historicized concept of social capital and a lack of recognition of what here will be called the "value neutrality" of the concept. Attempts to apply Putnam's analytic framework to institutional contexts dense with authoritarian stocks of social assets, such as the Soviet situation in the last years of communism, remain fraught with peril.

In particular, the Soviet social order congealed around interlocking webs of formal and informal networks organized along highly opaque and hierarchical lines. The daily practices in these networks exemplified the logic of the vertical patron–client relation, an authoritarian relation expressed in the Russian word *blat*, literally meaning "influence" or "pull." In the Russian language, blat connotes the use of morally questionable but pragmatically indispensable informal connections to manipulate the redistributive hierarchies of the state for personal advantage.[93] The operations of blat proved central for life chances in Soviet times. That blat operated "behind the scenes" in an opaque fashion meant that pro-democracy activists relying on extant forms of informal cultural and social assets and operating against the authoritarian logic of party-state institutions found it very difficult to extend the "horizontal" ideals of pro-democracy networks, either in their own practices or across a social space crossed by vertical networks of officialdom. As we shall see, this figured centrally in the ability of Moscow-based networks to repeatedly steer regional social movements.

Given this, we see immediately the danger of assuming a priori that extant social assets—measured in terms of the density of social networks and their relative "stickiness," their embeddedness in habitus—always correlates "positively" with a latent potential for democratization or for fashioning a more open and decentralized economy.[94] Kenneth Arrow, for instance, defines social capital as a "dense network of social connections, developed for noneconomic purposes that enhance both political and economic efficiency."[95] This bypasses the problem inherent in the ties embodied in many of Russia's formal and informal networks, namely, the authoritarian institutional patterns that they reproduced, often in altered forms. The institutional dynamics of such networks specifically impeded rather than enhanced democratic practices and economic openness.

For these reasons, "social assets" (and the subtype of social capital) stands as a "value neutral" concept insofar as the mere existence of significant social assets in itself tells us little about the types of collective action such assets may facilitate.[96] When mapping an array of actual social assets, the degree to which it may impede or enhance a particular political or social project must always be assessed empirically, in relation to its fit or lack of fit between a given agent, extant practices, and the fields in which they occur.

Recent refinements of Putnam's concept of social capital point in this direction, insofar as they differentiate what Michael Woolcock calls "bonding," "binding," and "linking" modalities of social capital.[97] Bonding and binding social capital describe horizontal networks. Where bonding social capital typifies networks formed on the basis of kinship and communal identities, binding social capital connects such communal networks on a regional basis. Although largely horizontal in character, particular patterns of bonding and binding may well foster incipient vertical networking and thus be tied to the emergence of patriarchal patterns of power in kinship relations, communities, and various transcommunal associations.

Which brings us to Woolcock's notion of "linking social capital," embodied in networks that tie communal and regional horizontal networks together from above, along verticals of power, authority, and patronage. In a situation like late-communist Russia, the presence in the everyday social realm of vertical networks linked to the party-state apparatus severely impeded the formation of binding, that is horizontal and transcommunal, social assets.

Instead, such contexts encouraged inward and exclusionary forms of bonding social assets at the local level marked by nascent and highly localized pockets of hierarchy. Thus the institutional morphology of the party-state— opaque, authoritarian, and repressive—fostered a markedly closed modality of linking social assets, which in turn generated all kinds of effects at the level of local networks. Among such effects stood the grassroots appeal of an "antipolitical" politics fostering sectarianism, demagoguery, and manipulation from above, as we shall see. When the Gorbachev leadership in the Soviet

Communist Party attempted to appeal to such networks to support reform from above through its perestroika policies in the late 1980s, it lost control of networking processes and instead faced spreading rebellion. Understanding this process presupposes understanding the developmental history of Soviet institutions leading to the Gorbachev reforms.

What Was Soviet Industrial Patrimonialism?

The long skein of "actually existing socialism" in Soviet history exemplifies shifts in both the discursive presentation of the party-state and the broader genres of everyday life. Take the early Soviet infatuation with Fordism—the pattern of industrial organization and management pioneered by Henry Ford and mimicked around the world in the twentieth century.[98] In the late 1920s, the wholesale import of Fordist managerial theory—and specifically Frederick W. Taylor's methods for managing the labor process in assembly line industrial plants—gave rise to an intense struggle between skilled workers and Soviet technocrats on the shop floor.[99] The Stalin leadership subsequently exploited this division to carry out a divide and rule strategy in the form of promoting tensions between "reds" and "experts" in a relentless drive to centralize party-state control over production and eliminate overt political resistance to its command structure. Such drives appealed to party cadre as models of "heroic impersonalism" characteristic of Leninist regimes in their early stages of consolidating centralized domination.[100]

A principal outcome of Stalin's political campaigns in the late 1920s and early 1930s was to render the planning process highly opaque, reinforcing the leadership's tendency to rely on both charismatic appeals to the cadre per se and police state techniques to maintain central command of a more and more improvised industrialization process. Fordist organizational and managerial techniques thus combined in historically distinctive ways with Stalin's growing personal dictatorship to give rise to a novel organizational pattern—"industrial patrimonialism," the fusion of autocratic and Fordist organizational patterns. And this organizational form predominated in the Soviet Union until Gorbachev's ascent.

Industrial patrimonialism can be taken as an ideal-type concept, a conceptual model abstracted from the rich complexity of human institutions for purposes of analytic simplification and comparative classification, and subsequently applied to generate historical models of the Soviet regime over time. Such ideal types are then applied back to history for purposes of classification and for building up empirical descriptions—historical models—of actual institutions.[101]

The ideal type of patrimonialism represents one pole along a continuum of possible forms of extended patriarchal domination seen in history, with the pure type of feudalism lying at the other pole.[102] Weber retrospectively projected patriarchalism back into history to emphasize a common, archaic pattern of domination—the personal domination of a senior male over a household economy (*oikos*), institutionalized on the basis of ritual expressions of fealty and personal loyalty to the patriarch by other males, females, and children.[103] Weber speculated that the origins of traditional kingships—the state—lay in successful attempts to extend this pattern of domination to other extended households, villages, clans, and the like on the basis of the creation of a staff of retainers bound by oaths of personal fealty to the central patriarch.[104] In this way, warrior and priestly castes organized around the staff gained control of economic surpluses extracted in the form of tributes from direct producers, tributes redistributed by the patriarch to his extended retinue.

Such a developmental sequence presupposes a preexisting agrarian economy—a village economy of small farming organized on a kinship basis—from which tributes can be extracted. The sequence implies that the origins of the state were coterminous with the subordination of decentralized agrarian economies to a tribute-extracting status group of warriors and priests themselves mobilized by enterprising patriarchs.[105] Thus, the great tributary economies of ancient civilizations arose out of a patriarchal seizure of power engineered by emerging warrior elites.[106] Weber gave the name patrimonialism to the most autocratic variants of this pattern of extended patriarchal domination, which he argued was exemplified by the Egyptian Pharaohs, the Muslim Caliphates, and the Russian Tsars.[107]

Weber noted less centralized forms of extended patriarchal domination in agrarian societies, the most decentralized of which he called feudalism. Patrimonialism and feudalism thus stand at opposite ends of a continuum derived from extended patriarchal domination.[108] Feudalism historically tends to arise out of a "double" set of tributary relations: on the one hand, between a central territorial ruler and an elite status group of warriors—knights in medieval Europe, samurai in medieval Japan; and on the other, between individual members of the warrior elites and local agrarian producers. Feudal relations between a central king or emperor and individual members of the warrior elite turned on vassalage relations—vows of personal fealty in which central patriarchs promised obligations to vassals and accepted extensive limits on central authority in return for vassals' support.[109]

At the center of vassalage relations lay warriors' pledges to support the central ruler in military campaigns in exchange for being granted the right to appropriate and control the surplus product produced by local agrarian producers or at least gain autonomous access to it, through the obligatory sharing of tributes with warriors on the part of landed notables, as in the case of the Japanese samurai. The empirical question thus becomes when does the elaboration of institutional limits on patrimonialism usher in outright feudal relations.[110]

The concept of patrimonialism powerfully illuminates the historical trajectory of Tsarist absolutism and its development of police state mechanisms in the late-Tsarist period as a counter to various challenges to autocratic rule.[111] The combat-military ethos of the Bolshevik Party—the party as an "impersonal hero organization"—in turn mirrored the patrimonial world from which it emerged, setting the stage for the interregnum of revolutionary oligarchy between the Bolshevik seizure of power and Stalin's consolidation of a personal dictatorship and regeneration of patrimonial mechanisms of rule alongside the more "impersonal-heroic" features of Leninist ideology during the revolution from above.[112]

After Stalin's death, personal dictatorship gave way to the collective domination of senior CPSU figures. The "routinization" of Soviet society, in turn, formed the background from which perestroika arose.[113] Gorbachev's reforms, then, represented an improvised response to the secular decline of a distinctive political order—Soviet industrial patrimonialism—originating from the Bolshevik seizure of power and Stalin's revolution from above between 1928 and 1938, and subsequently "routinized" in the decades following Stalin's death.

The genealogy of Soviet industrial patrimonialism mapped how the Bolshevik Party and subsequently Stalin's dictatorship mediated transnational demonstration effects in those regions under their domination in the 1920s and 1930s, as with the import of Fordist techniques.[114] We read back onto Soviet history the ideal type of patrimonial rulership and combine it with the historical model of Fordist industrial organization to build a genetic portrait, a historical model, of the Soviet party-state as an institutional order that consolidated in the Stalin period, namely, Soviet industrial patrimonialism. While industrial patrimonialism per se is an ideal-type concept, Soviet industrial patrimonialism describes the core of a specific historical complex of institutions.[115]

Over time, the reproduction of industrial-patrimonial authority engendered a novel variant of industrial society stratified into a pyramidal hierarchy of state-engineered social estates and status groups.[116] Moreover, a secular decline in the organizational capacities of Party leaders to mobilize and repress subordinates marked the developmental history of Soviet domination in the post-Stalin period.[117] The developmental logic of this secular decline thus forms the analytic bridge between the genetic model of Soviet industrial patrimonialism and the reconstruction of pro-democracy mobilization in late-communist Russia.

Industrial patrimonialism in the USSR developed through successive phases of revolutionary oligarchy, Stalin's tyrannical absolutism, and a protracted, post-Stalin phase of routinization and dissipation of the party-state's ideological ethos. As the "collective leadership" of the "heroic" Bolshevik period gave way to an informal structure of patronage and personal rulership centered on Stalin and his politburo associates, the transition from revolutionary oligarchy as an impersonal hero organization of ruling revolutionary ideologues to full industrial patrimonialism was gradually effected.[118] Ambiguities in the concept of Stalinism follow directly from the complexities of this transition: official authority in the Stalinist period combined elements of revolutionary oligarchy, despotic personal rulership, and the more routine exercise of authority here called industrial patrimonialism.

What remains distinctive about the Soviet culture of authority stemmed from its fusion of industrial-bureaucratic management and personal rulership by Party plenipotentiaries operating in ways reminiscent of both "movement activists" and officials in previous autocratic regimes.[119] The Soviet party-state collapsed political and economic life into "the administration of things" by fusing the management of all formal organizations with the centralized Party apparatus. Exemplified in Stalin's maxim "cadres decide everything," the party-state's unitary organizing principle—total state administration—gave rise to a hybrid culture of authority combining management principles adapted from the Fordist model of industrial organization, the impersonal-heroic ethos of Leninism, and the domination of officials empowered to intervene in decision-making processes at subordinate levels on an arbitrary, personal basis. Party leaders strove to maintain hypercentralized control of arbitrary authority by institutionalizing a double pattern of appointment, one by the Party, the other by the state, where state officials usually shared power with a Party "double," neither with direct control of the other and thus both dependent on control from above.[120]

In this way, authoritative relations remained both hypercentralized and multiple, underscoring how improvised Stalin's "movement regime" really was. From the perspective of ideational figurations, the Stalinist regime indeed appeared totalitarian. Yet administratively, totalitarianism is an impossible project, underscoring how dystopian, even mundane, the administrative realities of the movement regime under Stalin often appeared. Totalitarianism as project here obscured the multiplicity and contingency of daily life and administrative practices at various levels and sites, and fails as an institutional model.[121] Industrial patrimonialism as ideal type counters this lingering distortion—a distortion in part striven for by the group around Stalin itself.

Instead, industrial patrimonialism distinguishes the figurations of totalitarian propaganda from the institutional realities of the party-state in order to render the latter clearly. Above all, industrial-patrimonial authority revolved around the Party leadership's monopolistic control of appointments to all formal-organizational positions—the *nomenklatura* system, first organized by Stalin as Party Secretary in the early 1920s.[122] Once the nomenklatura system was in place, Stalin relied on both his dictatorial control of the secret police and the mobilization of "the masses" behind top-down "heroic" campaigns to engineer arbitrary turnover from above and prevent officialdom from coalescing into a stratum closed on a hereditary basis. The nomenklatura (literally, "the nomenclature") would thus congeal as a hereditary constellation only in the post-Stalin period, after the passing of the ability of a relative handful of Party leaders around Stalin to terrorize nomenklatura-level appointees from above.

Stalin's ad hoc combination of revolutionary and patrimonial dictatorship was abandoned quickly after the dictator's death. In this period, Nikita Khrushchev's attempts to limit the tenure of senior officials met defeat, and the process of devolution of control over the means of administration from Politburo to the broader stratum of administrative and managerial appointees began.[123] The period of de-Stalinization thus institutionalized a distinctive version of collective leadership in which senior partocratic figures, to protect themselves against Khrushchev-style attempts to limit office tenure, accepted lifetime appointments at the nomenklatura level. Brezhnev's 1964 declaration of the policy of "the stability of cadres" in the wake of Khrushchev's fall signaled de facto partocratic recognition of lifetime tenure for nomenklatura-level officials freed to check the power of the General Secretary from below, on the basis of their own patron–client networks.[124]

The end of Stalin's terrorism from above, followed by the defeat of Khrushchev's attempt to limit the tenure of senior officials, thus cumulatively transformed nomenklatura-level positions into de facto lifetime benefices, initiating the process of devolution of powers that matured as the new estate took hold. Indeed, the first stage of feudalization became entrenched.[125] The reduction of official ideology to a thin rationalization for ubiquitous rent-seeking behavior in formally organized contexts (the pursuit of control over allocative mechanisms, expanded budgetary outlays, perquisites, bribes, and so on) marked the devolution of the party-state into the ossifying industrial patrimonialism of the Brezhnev period in which the power of regional bosses grew at the expense of "absolutist" Politburo domination.[126] Together with totalitarian figurations of "the communist future," the party-state as an impersonal-hero organization withered under such circumstances.

The diffusion of patrimonial authority in the post-Stalin Soviet Union instead facilitated selective appropriation of administrative means by nominal subordinates, engendering the consolidation of quasi-"estates."[127] Unlike the formation of estates under premodern forms of patrimonialism, the creation of corporate forms of autonomous estate power did not accompany the appropriation of administrative means by nominal subordinates under "total state administration" until perestroika. For this reason, the early phases of feudalization unfolded under the nominal absolutism of party-state power.

The language of everyday life under party-state domination reproduced these historical ambiguities. The distinctive Russian word apparat (literally, "the administrative machinery" or "stratum of functionaries") became synonymous in daily speech with rent-seeking officialdom as a whole. Within the apparat writ large, distinctions can be drawn between senior nomenklatura officials, the partocrats (partokraty); the managerial nomenklaturshchiki, the broader estate of rent-seeking managers, administrators, and less-senior Party officials of nomenklatura rank; and plenipotentiaries of the nomenklatura, the apparatchiki.

Beyond the consolidation of the nomenklatura estate, the Brezhnev period witnessed a growing diffusion of power in the direction of a state-engineered status group on which Party leaders remained dependent for technical innovation and economic development, the so-called "specialists" (spetsialisty) of official Soviet parlance, professionals and intellectuals.[128] In this sense, "specialists" collectively referred to the intelligentsia of official Soviet statistics, as opposed to the more restricted, normatively loaded, cultural-ideological notion of the intelligentsia common in everyday Russian usage.[129] Soviet leaders played on the misrecognition entailed in the cultural notion of the intelligentsia by developing a distinct, official identification—the specialists—used interchangeably in official discourse with the intelligentsia.[130] Such misrecognition, however, cut in multiple directions—the social and political assets of official standing did not necessarily translate into the more specifically cultural assets of the older Russian notion of the intelligentsia and vice versa. The Russian intelligentsia in this latter cultural sense thus formed an informal and ill-defined subgroup within the larger specialist matrix.

The administrative categories of the Soviet party-state, in contrast, defined specialists as "mental laborers" and counted them in terms of higher educations and professional occupations. According to the 1989 census, the specialists as a sociological group comprised about 28 percent of the employed Russian population.[131] This diverse stratum included scientists, engineers, teachers, doctors, artists, as well as highly skilled technical workers and department heads within industrial enterprises.

Specialists dominated the middle positions of late-communist Russia. Unlike market-stratified middle classes, Soviet middle positions were, in Victor Zaslavsky's terminology, embedded in a hierarchy of state-engineered status orders vertically monopolized by political and social elites. The middle stratum of Soviet society thus did not form a class in the specific sense of a shared position in an economic market.[132] Moreover, Soviet specialists lacked effective mechanisms of corporate control over professional associations, further distinguishing their collective experience from that of most Western professionals.[133]

Externally ascribed political status and administrative position most often decided the life-chances of particular specialists, giving rise to a thoroughgoing "status fetishism" among holders of elite and middle positions alike.[134] Indeed, Soviet specialists in the late-communist period are more accurately described as having formed a vertically integrated, politically constructed social estate, than a true middle class.[135]

For these reasons, the concept of class must be applied with great caution to Soviet society. Soviet-type socialism recalls Weber's concept of a "status society" more than a market-structured "class society."[136] Simply equating urban professionals per se with the Soviet middle class obscures the importance of two crucial features of Soviet era specialists as a social group. First, unlike in the West, the party-state engineered and controlled status orders of elite professionals in reproducing the specifically Soviet middle stratum. This absence of self-governing corporate associations among specialists rendered the political culture in which their habitus formed and where they operated on a day-to-day business highly authoritarian. And second, elite and middle-level specialists alike remained highly dependent on state-organized economic redistribution and nomenklatura patronage. There was no "market" on which specialists could offer services in return for a fee, rendering the deployment of cultural assets distinct from the market-oriented provision of such assets as a form of cultural capital in Western societies.

The internal, hierarchal differentiation of the specialist estate into a social elite of established professionals, a broader range of middle positions, and a lower layer of "proletarianized" semi-professionals should thus be borne in mind. Such social ranks converted into prestige and influence—including in the sense of blat (influence or pull)—through their use as social and cultural assets, that is, through their relative status. The specifically cultural intelligentsia in the older Russian sense intersected in opaque ways with this estate at all levels.

The principal instrument of party-state ascription of social status—the Soviet system of internal passports—underscores the engineered, state-dependent character of the specialist estate. The Soviet internal passport—more of an internal pass than the external passport familiar to Westerners—functioned as the keystone of a sweeping system of Party control over population movement in some ways reminiscent of the notorious pass system under South African apartheid, giving rise to a distinctively Soviet stratification of places.[137] The Soviet passport engendered both a hierarchy of "closed cities" (*rezhimnye goroda*), in which access to housing and work required a residence permit (*propiska*) issued only after the registration of one's internal passport, and a range of "closed enterprises" (*rezhimnye pred'priiatiia*) virtually segregating the workforce of the military–industrial complex.[138]

The party-state, by means of the internal passport and propiska system, concentrated disproportionately large populations of specialists in a few key cities, a fact of particular importance for the analysis of democratic rebellion in perestroika-era Russia. Moreover, evidence indicates that residents of key closed cities tended to enjoy a considerably higher standard of living than outlying areas. In both these respects, Moscow was archetypal.[139]

Nonmonetized perquisites in the form of assignment to closed cities, priority of assignment of apartments, and so forth—although extraordinarily difficult to measure—translated into the most significant material component of relative specialist privilege in late-communist Russia. Monetary remuneration itself varied widely among specialist subgroups: while members of the prestigious Academy of Sciences of the USSR enjoyed the highest nominal incomes in the Soviet Union, many other professionals (from doctors to journalists to teachers and technical assistants) found themselves with incomes and privileges equal to or even below that of many skilled industrial workers.[140]

Privilege, of course, entails symbolic as well as material advantages, and here the disproportionate prestige enjoyed by specialists stands out. The high prestige of scientists and other accomplished specialists reflected the specialists' position as a *politically* disenfranchised social elite—a social elite perceived as deprived of political power and thus carrying no responsibility for CPSU repression or the economic decline of the late-communist period. Membership in this politically disenfranchised social elite thus gave individual specialists a distinctive combination of social, cultural, and political assets. Such material and symbolic advantages combined with geographic concentration in big cities and the relative dependence of the nomenklaturshchiki on specialist expertise to favor the emergence of specialists as political entrepreneurs, those who create new rules of the political game in revolutionary situations and other periods of social unrest.

A comparative note. The concept of industrial patrimonialism remains an ideal-type description of the institutional culture of authority in routinized party-states modeled along Soviet lines. The extent of its descriptive power depends on three crucial factors. First, was Soviet-style communism imposed by an indigenous movement or an occupying army? Second, to what extent did party-state leaders rely on document-based forms of labor control, such as the internal passport, in reproducing institutional domination? And third, how extensively were prerevolutionary institutions disrupted?

Where party-state control was relatively weak, communism was imposed from abroad, the party-state's use of document-based control over labor and migration remained comparatively moderate, and some autonomous, prerevolutionary social forms—in Poland, the Catholic Church and small peasant farms—survived the communist period. This partly explains why the history of Poland's Solidarity more closely conforms to the image of society mobilizing against the state. In contrast, where party-state control resulted from indigenous movements seizing power and using document-based population control extensively to repress and destroy prerevolutionary institutions—as in the Soviet Union and China—the potential for autonomous action and organizations remained severely restricted to officially privileged groups, such as Beijing students in China and the urban specialists of the late-Soviet period. This highly centralized and restricted context for autonomous agency formed the background of Gorbachev's perestroika reforms.

1

The Specialist Rebellion in Moscow and the Genesis of a Revolutionary Situation

On March 11, 1985, Mikhail Gorbachev gained election as General Secretary of the Communist Party of the Soviet Union. Within weeks, the new General Secretary invoked the slogan of restructuring (*perestroika*) in calling for the renewal (*obnovlenie*) of Soviet socialism.[1] Over Gorbachev's first year, the Party leadership deployed the slogan of perestroika as watchword for a reform designed to overcome the stagnation (*zastoi*) of the previous twenty years, accelerate economic growth, and "revitalize Soviet democracy." The emerging discourse of perestroika thus framed prior rhetoric hailing "mature socialism" and "the transition to full communism" as instead masking a drift away from "the socialist choice of 1917." The new Party leader now suddenly seemed to reject many of the institutional realities and social forms of Soviet society. Indeed, Gorbachev's call to "renew socialism" in part cast doubt on previous Party assertions that socialism "actually existed" under the long reign of former Soviet leader Leonid Brezhnev. The reform program thus reintroduced tensions in official discourse between "the socialist idea" and the nuts and bolts of socialism as practical reality. Coming to grip with these realities and trying to change them would dominate social and political activity throughout the whole period from Gorbachev's ascent to the rise of Vladimir Putin to the Russian presidency fifteen years later.

At the outset of reform, however, the call to renew socialism became entangled with national resurgences across the multinational Soviet Union. Both the Russian leadership of the Soviet state and Boris Yeltsin's successor regime in Russia proper poorly understood such multinational realities. Grasping why perestroika went so quickly awry lies in understanding how reform of the party-state intersected with the multinational character of Soviet society, and the subsequent inability of Russians in central cities like Moscow to grasp the practical consequences of this reality.[2]

In 1985, the distinctive social organization of late-Soviet society intersected with the geographical organization of the party-state to render the fields in which habitus related to institutions highly unique in modern history. Unlike previous sites of political revolution, the Soviet Union was simultaneously a multinational empire and a party-state—a "mono-organizational society"[3]— ruled in the name of a modernist ideology that itself rose to dominance in an earlier revolution. By fostering an ideological emphasis on internationalism and social equality, communist modernism favored both symbolic recognition of the equality of the peoples of the Soviet periphery with those of the Russian metropole and the disproportionate redistribution of resources to key peripheral areas, a pattern highly anomalous in the history of empires.[4] At the same time, economic redistribution in favor of the previously exploited non-Russian regions of the former Tsarist empire precluded neither harsh repression nor aggressive policies of Russification when deemed strategically appropriate by the Soviet leadership.[5] These tensions underlay the *longue durée* of Soviet society, emerging as sources of open political conflict only as the Gorbachev leadership opened the regime to decentralization.

Geographic and Temporal Dimensions of Soviet Disunion in the Early Perestroika Reforms

The constitutional system of the Soviet state combined unitary and federal elements in a vertical hierarchy of elected councils (*sovety*), with the Supreme Soviet of the USSR as the highest legislative body presiding over the whole institutional pyramid. The lower down this pyramidal hierarchy a given soviet, the more limited was its jurisdiction and decision-making authority. In descending order, levels of soviets passed from all-Union, to republican, to "autonomous republics" ("sub-republics") and other "special autonomous regions,"[6] to regions (*kraia* and *oblasti*), to local city, town, rural district, and village (*gorodskie, noselkovye,* and *selskie*) bodies.[7] Although this system indeed formed "a unitary system of the bodies of state power,"[8] this unitary character flowed not from the interlocking hierarchy of soviets itself, but from the constitutionally enshrined "leading and directing force of the Soviet Union," the Communist Party (CPSU).[9]

Indeed, prior to the onset of political reform under perestroika, the Party's leading organ—the politburo, a handful of figures—exercised commanding executive and legislative power in the USSR.[10] The politburo-controlled Party's nomination of all candidates standing for election to soviets rendered meaningless the constitutional stipulation that "all soviets are elective bodies" (Article 3). The leadership's control of nomination in fact constituted a key facet of the *nomenklatura* system of appointments.

On election days, voters received a list of preapproved candidates at polling stations and only assented or dissented to the Party slate. In addition, voting was obligatory, and due to the public nature of balloting—in full view of apparatchiks, not in sequestered booths—voting against the slate was risky indeed.[11] For this reason, from Stalin's time through the late-1980s, Soviet elections routinely resulted in 99 percent of the voters ritually affirming slates selected from above by the Party.[12]

The administrative structure of Soviet government took the form of a Council of Ministers, appointed—again, formally—by the Supreme Soviet. In fact, the politburo of the CPSU selected senior government appointees and passed these selections on to the Supreme Soviet for ritual affirmation, in line with the nomenklatura pattern of stratification. The *apparat* of the Council of Ministers commanded a labyrinthine maze of planning bureaus, allocative and redistributive bodies, employment and social welfare agencies, security organs, cultural organizations, and so on. Virtually all levels of soviets replicated similar administrative structures. The Moscow City Soviet (*Mossovet*), for example, commanded an enormous number of apparat positions, including "eighteen main administrations, twenty-nine independent administrations, nine departments, and a number of commissions, inspectorates, and other services."[13] This train of administrative officialdom served as the real center of political life in the Soviet Union.

Such realities determined the course of Western Soviet studies. Most analysts of Soviet politics only discussed soviets in passing, instead concentrating on drawing charts of administrative offices, mapping "bureaucratic lobbies," tracing regional alignments in *oblast'* administrations, pouring over ideological pronouncements of the Party leadership, analyzing who stood where at which official function, and the like.[14]

The onset of the Gorbachev reforms changed all this, primarily by reviving leading soviets as, more or less, genuine electoral bodies, together with tolerating the emergence of a myriad of autonomous voluntary associations. Here, the initial perestroika policies began to alter deeply institutionalized patterns by forcing the habitus of many officials to adjust to a new reform trajectory. The revival of the salience of rules and regulations ostensibly governing soviets stood as an important trigger forcing such changes in apparat habitus.

At first, however, perestroika largely consisted of administrative measures, largely in the form of "antialcohol" and "acceleration" (*uskorenie*) campaigns. The inability of these early, 1985–1986 steps, to both stimulate the economy and make officialdom more responsive to reform initiatives led Gorbachev and his politburo allies to accelerate instead the policy of "democratization" (*demokratizatsiia*) of the soviets—a policy first announced in abstract terms at the 27th Congress of the CPSU in early 1986.[15] The public confirmation of the deepening of demokratizatsiia followed a special plenary session of the

CPSU Central Committee held on January 27, 1987.[16] This plenum marked the ascendance to full politburo membership of Alexander N. Yakovlev, the "intellectual father" of the political reforms of the late 1980s.[17]

The first stages of unfolding reform—from Gorabchev's appointment as Party General Secretary, to the January 1987 special session of the CPSU Central Committee—thus appeared a highly narrow, top-down affair. At this point, neither the Communist Party leadership nor soon-to-be nationalist activists in the non-Russian Republics of the Soviet Union, yet grasped the thorough-going changes in Soviet institutional life about to be triggered by the deepening of the reform process.

Indeed, prior to the mid-1980s, the highly repressive conditions of Soviet political life in no way mitigated the formation of regional non-Russian political elites as elements of an otherwise highly centralized Soviet federal structure.[18] Ethnic-national elites crystallized even at the level of Autonomous Republics, sub-republican administrative regions designated on the basis of titular non-Russian majorities at the regional level of the Russian Republic itself.[19] As the Chechen conflict exemplifies, non-Russian ethnic elites at the sub-republic level quickly became a major factor in late and post-Soviet Russia.

The emergence of regional ethnic conflicts presupposed secular decline in the incorporative and repressive capacities—the institutional salience—of the Soviet state, a decline with roots deep in the Soviet past. Here, the prior failure of the communist project to fulfill former Soviet leader Nikita Khrushchev's 1960s-era promise "to catch up to and overtake the West" combined with the Soviet legacy of ubiquitous corruption and cynicism in everyday life to reinforce patterns of lamentation over inadequacies of various sorts in all corners of the political field.[20] Perestroika not only brought such lamentation to official prominence, but also exposed to a hitherto unprecedented level of scrutiny deep splits in the Soviet leadership over how to deal with such inadequacies. In the process, the early phase of perestroika created *ex nihilo* a fragile public realm in a political field previously subordinated to sweeping authoritarian controls, opening opportunities for opposition to CPSU power and policies to spread rapidly.[21]

The concentration of various national elites at regional levels in the non-Russian republics proved fateful here, as groups of Armenians and Estonians protected by nationalist "political entrepreneurs" in republican and local power structures became the first Soviet citizens in many decades to successfully organize a sustained rebellion against Soviet power.[22] Estonia led the way in pressing for full independence from the USSR—a drive that initiated "the parade of sovereignties" and triggered a multifold deepening of the process of feudalization. Together, these developments eventually brought an end to the vision of absorbing the periphery of the old Russian empire into an internationalist socialist order centered in Moscow.

All of this points to a striking difference between the non-Russian and Russian opposition movements of the perestroika era. On the one hand, Armenian, Estonian, Georgian, Latvian, and Lithuanian rebels easily adapted extant regional speech and expression surrounding national identity inadvertently augmented by Soviet nationality policies.[23] Such non-Russian figures fashioned a vision of independence by grounding it in a practical program of transforming republic-level soviets into architectures of nascent nation-states.

On the other hand, Russia's nascent democrats lacked a ready-made symbolic linkage between Russian cultural identity and their aspiration to craft an institutional alternative to the Soviet party-state on Russian soil. Instead, Russian oppositional networks under perestroika at first tended to speak in vague Gorbachevian terms of deepening the democratization of the Soviet order, and only later adopted a Russian variant of their peripheral counterparts' strategy of pushing for national independence for the RSFSR. More an improvised gambit to undermine the power of their foes in the CPSU and Soviet federal offices than a political expression of widely shared national aspirations, this strategic shift followed the lead of rebellion on the periphery of the Union.[24]

The virtual absence of Russian nationalism in the early days of perestroika reflected the absence of either a colonial or a nationalist past. Russia stands as one of the few major regions of the world never subject to colonial rule by a western nation, and for this reason the Russian empire developed under markedly different circumstances than the colonial periphery of the western powers. Indeed, Russian independence never expressed itself in nationalist terms, at least in the sense of nationhood perceived independently of empire. At the same time, anxiety over the weaknesses of Russian civilization relative to the global capitalist world—and fears of colonization and subordination to Western powers—runs like a red thread through the political and intellectual history of modern Russia. The Westernizer–Slavophile dispute in Russian society—and its echo in the struggle between *demokraty* and "powerniks" (*derzhavniki*) that emerged in the late 1980s and 1990s—attests to the ambivalence of Russian elites and intellectuals toward the Western-dominated modern world order.[25]

But this is to view Russian–western relations through the narrow lens of the Russian elite and urban Russian intellectuals. Below them, Russia's imperial civilization and autocratic traditions created a social chasm between the imperial center and its own peripheral populations and fostered in both the Tsarist and Soviet periods the reproduction of rigid status distinctions that alienated social ranks one from another and impeded the formation of a national political identity apart from the imperial order.[26] Here the egalitarian eco-nomic image—partially realized at the level of policy—of the Soviet party-state stood in extreme tension with the exclusionary nature of party-state "status fetishism," with the latter dramatically eroding the former.

As the party-state began to breakup in the late 1980s, the unraveling of such institutional contradictions forced individuals to adjust to all manner of novel regional and local arrangements. These novel, preinstitutional arrange-ments themselves resulted from adaption of the hitherto dormant institutional formalities of soviets to the reality of the disintegrating, arbitrary, and in-formal institution of partocratic domination. This "reactivation" of dormant formalisms—or the equivalent reinvention of partocratic rule through various nationalisms—changed the character of Soviet institutions fundamentally, in fact undermining their practical salience. The few partocrats and social move-ments capable of informally combining to devise networks improvising new orders—orders to which disoriented habitus could adjust—thus emerged as trajectory "improvisers," political "entrepreneurs" in an institutional sense.

In this sense, the early perestroika reforms unintentionally begot a process that soon spun out of control from Gorbachev's reformist CPSU leadership. The initial intentions of the latter were much more modest: to overcome the rigid barriers between party-state elite and Soviet society, which had ossified in the Brezhnev years. At the same time, the perestroika leadership had broader ambitions in attempting to reform the Soviet complex of historically existing institutions. How this latter process spiraled out of CPSU control maps the developmental history from reform to revolutionary situation in the last years of Soviet power.

The Radicalization of Perestroika

With the consolidation of a committed reformist leadership at the January 1987 Central Committee plenum, the breadth of reform ambitions began to become clearer. And yet, the consolidation of Gorbachev's position at the very pinnacle of Soviet society in January 1987 failed to translate the call for demokratizatsiia into a clear policy stand. During the course of the protracted internal struggle with more conservative partocrats triggered by the January 1987 plenum, top reformers and their academic allies worked out and fought for concrete measures designed to democratize Soviet elections.[27] It was dur-ing this crucial period that the Armenian nationalist movement appeared and consolidated at the level of the regional party-state in Armenia proper, followed quickly by nationalist mobilization in the Republic of Estonia. Although the Party leadership now faced nationalist radicalization in both the Armenian and

Estonian Republics, such radicalization continued to play a secondary role in top Soviet Party politics in 1988.

Instead, the Party leadership remained preoccupied with internal dissension. Despite significant partocratic resistance, the Gorbachev leadership managed to outflank even senior opposition in calling the Nineteenth All-Union Organizing Conference of the CPSU in Moscow on June 28–30, 1988.[28] The Conference passed several democratizing resolutions, modeling them on several earlier district reforms now held out as political models.[29] Such Conference resolutions eventually became law by decree of the Supreme Soviet of the USSR on December 1, 1988.[30]

The centerpiece of demokratizatsiia as expounded in Conference resolutions created a new union legislative body, the Congress of Peoples Deputies of the USSR (CPD-USSR). The CPD-USSR would be enshrined as the Soviet Union's supreme, sovereign legislative body, meet once or twice a year to debate and act on major policy questions, and consist of 2,250 deputies. In his report to the Supreme Soviet the day before it formally created the new Congress at the federal level—and a Russian variant at the level of the Russian Republic—Gorbachev stressed that creating such bodies aimed at "ruling-out the abuse of power on the upper stories of the edifice of the state."[31]

When the CPD-USSR was not in session, legislative authority passed to a smaller, standing body, a reconstructed (*perestroennyi*) Supreme Soviet of the USSR, to be made up of 542 deputies elected by the Congress from among its own members. The Supreme Soviet, in turn, would appoint the Council of Ministers. Finally, the Congress would appoint the chairman of the Supreme Soviet, who would function as chief executive of the Council of Ministers, a sort of Soviet-style prime minister. Reform leaders at the Nineteenth Conference emphasized that the USSR Congress of Peoples Deputies and the reconstructed Supreme Soviet would make real decisions, not merely ratify those taken in the politburo. In line with these projected institutional reforms, CPSU reformers also stressed the need for a corresponding process of intra-Party democratization.[32]

The curtailment of the Party's leading position and the introduction of a practical division of powers at the top of the regime's pyramidal structure in fact triggered "the war of laws," accelerating the process of feudalization underway since routinization of Party leadership became entrenched after Khrushchev's fall more than two decades earlier in 1964.[33] More immediately, the consequences of the Nineteenth Party Conference shifted "reform from above" to a full revolutionary situation during the first election campaigns to the new USSR Congress of Peoples Deputies in early spring of 1989. Understanding this initial shift from trajectory adjustment to trajectory

improvisation among limited networks of partocrats and their plenipotentiaries presupposes mapping the failure of reform from above, and specifically
the discursive presentation of the regime in the months following the Nineteenth Party Conference.

The reasons for initial uncertainty regarding the situation in mid-1988
stemmed from the Nineteenth Party Conference itself. First of all, Nineteenth Party Conference resolutions left unclarified functional details of the
Soviet Congress of Peoples Deputies and new Supreme Soviet. Absent sweeping reform of electoral procedures, formal restructuring of Soviet political
institutions would mean little, a fact readily grasped in society at large.[34] At
the Nineteenth Conference, the Gorbachev leadership supported reform of
nominating and other electoral procedures, but failed to propose much in the
way of specific steps to be taken. Specification of such detail waited almost
six months as an opaque, nomenklatura-level struggle between supporters of
Gorbachev's political reforms, and the majority either hesitant or hostile
among the partocracy resolved in favor of the reform group's leadership.

Not until their formal publication did the radicalizing character of the
reforms become formalized, in early December 1988.[30] At this time, the USSR
Supreme Soviet announced a tripartite procedure for selecting the new 2,250
Soviet Congress deputies: one-third by direct election in line with existing
federal subdivisions (federal-territorial seats), one-third by direct election from
new districts established by the criterion of 257,000 voters per district (district
seats), and a final third by corporate election within a wide array of officially
designated social organizations, from the Communist Party to trade unions to
professional associations (corporate seats).[35]

Despite the formally open character of the nomination process for two-
thirds of USSR Congress of Peoples Deputies' seats, candidates aligned with
the partocracy continued to benefit from procedural devices favoring local
apparat control. Supporters of outspoken reform candidates organized anti-
partocracy "voter clubs" (*kluby izbiratelei*) as a means of overcoming such
obstacles, marking how splits at the top now encouraged the mobilization
of networks into social movements at the grass roots. Although work place
organizations secured at least the formal right to nominate candidates, potential candidates seeking direct nomination to either a federal territorial
or district seat from below—independent of work place or other organized
channels—required two initial steps: nomination by a precinct-level voter club
and the subsequent securing of a quorum at a district-level "voter assembly"
(*izbiratel'noe sobranie*) of five hundred electors (*vyborshchiki*) whose status required certification by local apparatchiks. Furthermore, district-level "voting
committees" (*izbirkomy*) had to certify the validity of each such assembly and its

results. Regional "voting commissions" (*izbiratel'nye komissii*) often dominated by the partocracy, in turn, appointed and largely controlled these voting committees. To make matters worse, these committees could simply invalidate voter assemblies or candidacies approved by them whenever such "higher" committees deemed it necessary.[36]

Such limitations on electoral participation greatly favored specialists (*spetsialisti*)—those with a tertiary education involved with mental (specialized) labor—over workers, creating a strategic opening for a specifically specialist rebellion at the heart of the 1989–1991 democratic movement. Moreover, these limitations tended to be far more severe in provincial towns and rural regions (strongholds of the conservative partocracy) thus disproportionately empowering specialists in large cities like Moscow and Leningrad, where politburo pressure to reform was more keenly felt. The shift in political opportunities evident in the 1989 campaign thus mirrored the Soviet pattern of state-engineered social and geographic stratification, favoring political entrepreneurship on the part of holders of elite and middle positions in a few key closed cities.[37]

The case of Boris N. Yeltsin, then Moscow Party Secretary, presaged such patterns of network mobilization. In the fall of 1987, the Moscow Party head faced disgrace. At a Central Committee plenum on October 21, 1987, Yeltsin spoke out against the slow pace of perestroika, denounced conservatives in the Party leadership, and criticized the beginnings of a "cult of personality" around Gorbachev. He finished his indictment by asking to be removed from his posts as candidate member of the politburo and First Secretary of the Moscow Party Committee, to which Gorbachev had appointed him in January of 1986. A murky series of events ensued, shrouded in senior party-state practices and official secrecy, from which Yeltsin emerged officially marginalized from the Gorbachev leadership. Yeltsin and Gorbachev became rivals from this point forward.[38]

The politburo formally accepted Yeltsin's resignation as a candidate member in February 1988, after reassigning him to head the State Construction Ministry (*Gosstroi*). Although he remained a member of the CPSU's Central Committee, many observers both in the Soviet Union and abroad assumed that Yeltsin's political career was finished. "The Yeltsin affair," however, proved crucial to cementing the former Moscow Party Secretary as a political folk hero, "a man of the people" (*chelovek naroda*) who had stood up to "the big shots" and paid dearly for it. Yeltsin in fact shrewdly capitalized on combining his networks in the Soviet establishment with populist gestures throughout his tenure as Moscow Party First Secretary—riding buses, standing in lines at food stores, and the like—all the time denouncing the privileges of the partocracy and calling for Party leaders to live modestly and remain "close to the people."

Yeltsin's comeback at the top of high Soviet politics began with his performance at the Nineteenth Party Conference, when he secured a chance to speak over stiff conservative opposition. The spirit of openness (*glasnost'*) being championed at the Conference aided Yeltsin's successful bid to address the Conference—after all, he remained a nominal member of the Central Committee. In his speech, Yeltsin asked that standard Soviet practice be abandoned and that he be "rehabilitated" (*reabilitiroval*) during his lifetime, rather than fifty years hence. In addition, the former Moscow Party Secretary called for a purge of Brezhnev-era holdovers in the Party leadership, reemphasized the need to accelerate democratic reforms, and renewed his populist attacks on "luxurious residences, dachas and sanatoriums" for the Party elite. Although the CPSU leadership dismissed his appeal, Yeltsin had in fact positioned himself to take advantage of the electoral opening the Party would provide in the upcoming elections.[39]

In the summer of 1988, however, the openings promised by the Nineteenth Party Conference paid handsome dividends to the Gorbachev leadership. The mobilization of *intelligentsia* support for reform aided the leadership's drive to remove almost all pre-perestroika regional (*obkom*) Party Secretaries in the Russian Federation between 1986 and 1989.[40] Gorbachev's "bloodless purge" of regional Party Secretaries augured the degree of trajectory adjustment now being pushed on party-state officials from above, and for a short period revived the possibility of a renewal of "impersonal-heroic" campaigns directed by the Party leadership. But the seeming revitalization of politburo power proved short-lived.

First, Armenian activists and the newly organized "Baltic Popular Fronts" took advantage of the opening offered by Gorbachev's policy of openness (glasnost') to radicalize local nationalist sentiment against Soviet domination. Then Yeltsin, Andrei Sakharov, and other Russian political entrepreneurs straddling the boundary between elite membership and political opposition seized the initiative by turning the 1989 elections into an exercise in specialist protest against the Party nomenklatura in general and the slow pace of perestroika in particular. Having paralyzed the partocracy and bypassed the local party apparat—now busily seeking a new base in regional politics in order to survive the purge—Gorbachev found himself deprived of the autocratic staff needed to contain specialist radicalization and soon lost control of the political agenda in Russia proper, just as he had lost the initiative in the Baltics and the Caucuses some months earlier.[41]

Thus purge from above orchestrated without the control mechanism of a centralized and disciplined repressive apparatus unintentionally accelerated feudalization, the very devolution of authority Gorbachev intended to check. At the same time, the intersection of a changing discursive presentation of the regime with shifts in more informal discursive genres in the specialist stratum came into its own. As party-state institutions began to disintegrate at the level of the Union partocracy, individuals in zones protected by more reformist Party networks began to improvise alternative ways of engaging political life. The mobilization of voluntary associations as social movements thus intersected with processes of nascent trajectory improvisation among radicalizing reformers among both specialists and Party figures centered around Yeltsin. In a few big cities protected by reformist officials, this process radicalized activists mobilized by the flowering of informal youth groups—the *neformaly*—underway since 1986.

The Time of the Informals: Voluntary Associations and the Dynamics of Radicalization

From the late 1960s through the early 1980s, the first democratic movement of the post-Stalin era emerged, known variously as the dissident and human rights movement. This movement was small, concentrated among scientists and other professionals, and operated under perpetual siege from the dictatorship. Those few workers active in opposition activity faced particularly terrible repression from the apparat in these days.[42] The extraordinary dictatorial measures aimed at expressions of political opposition from within the working class emerged as a central factor explaining why pro-democratization networking was much easier among established professionals in the mid-1980s. Still, intense repressive measures against even professional groups all but stamped out the dissident movement just a few years earlier, in the early 1980s.[43]

The second period of informal opposition activity began in mid-1986. Difficult to label simply a democratic movement, the rapid mobilization of *tens of thousands* of voluntary associations marked this time. Many associations, however, neither shared common principles, common social networks, nor an overarching commitment to democracy, as did the earlier human rights movement and the later *DemRossiia* coalition.[44]

At first glance, the amended Soviet Constitution of 1988 gave citizens sweeping rights to form autonomous voluntary associations, organize demonstrations, and participate independently in political life.[45] However, these rights—as becomes clear from a careful reading of the constitution—remained subordinate to the *diktat* of the Party, enshrined as "the leading and directing force" not only of society as a whole, but also of all "social organizations" (*obshchestvennia obed"edineniia*).[46] In practice, the degree of toleration afforded voluntary associations remained a bone of contention between apparat reformers and conservatives through the Gorbachev period. Such institutional conditions tied the fate of associations to the political course of perestroika. Indeed, the legal status of voluntary associations on the union level remained unclear until October 9, 1990, when the USSR Supreme Soviet passed a new law on social organizations.[47]

The popular name for voluntary associations in the first years of perestroika, "the informals" (*neformaly*), captured the precarious status of independent social groups. The spread of neformaly began in earnest with the May 1986 adoption of new guidelines on amateur associations and hobby clubs.[48] Such guidelines received a powerful impetus from the January 1987 special plenary session of the Party's Central Committee. This plenum stressed that the success of perestroika depended on increased citizen participation in political life and called for a loosening of laws restricting "anti-Soviet propaganda" that had served for so long as a handy pretext for the ubiquitous repression of autonomous political activity.[49] By the end of the year, tens of thousands of voluntary associations appeared across the Soviet Union.[50]

Voluntary associations, however, remained dependent on official tolerance, which varied widely from locality to locality.[51] The primary reason for this variation was the party-state's control of all physical assets in the country, including meeting rooms, printing presses, and other material means essential for sustained associational activity. In order to gain access to such means, informal groups were required to register with authorities. And the January 1987 central committee plenum left the question of official registration of voluntary associations to local officials. Thus, despite official encouragement from the top to become active in political life, the degree to which ordinary citizens would be allowed to freely associate remained highly dependent on a given informal group's ability to secure meeting places, avoid continual police harassment, and so forth.[52]

Political groups in particular fared very badly outside of a few large cities. Moscow remained the center for the organizational activities of many informal political groupings precisely due to the relative tolerance of the Moscow Party organization under Yeltsin in the first half of 1987, and the physical presence of the all-Union reform leadership in the Soviet capital. Even though the original initiators of the political club Perestroika were from Leningrad, for instance, the hostility of the Leningrad Party forced the club to organize itself through network connections in Moscow, where it came to be dominated by

Muscovites.[53] There were, of course, opposition political activists in smaller towns and rural areas, but they were especially prone to organizational weaknesses due to three factors: their small numbers and relative isolation, their greater vulnerability to apparat co-optation, and the more conservative cast of many provincial apparatchiks, who were inclined to favor repressive measures against oppositional activity.[54]

The Soviet stratification of places, the more lenient attitude of disproportionately Moscow-based party-state reform officials toward voluntary associations, and the centrality of the Soviet capital as spatial mediator of transnational demonstration effects in Russia proper, all favored a city-based and Moscow-centered specialist reform insurgency. For instance, many voluntary associations and *samizdat* (self-published and unofficial) newspapers had to wait until mid-1990 to be registered, when the *Oktiab'rskii* district soviet in Moscow—under the newly elected chairmanship of DemRossiia leader Il'ia Zaslavskii—launched a mass registration drive for social organizations, new political parties, and cooperative enterprises as part of Zaslavskii's revolutionary attempt to build "capitalism in one district." Zaslavskii registered over three thousand five hundred associations and enterprises during this drive.[55] In effect, Moscow as "Union center" maximized conditions favoring emergence of a radicalizing reform movement concentrated among specialists.

The informals of 1987–1988, however, retained a habitus strongly marked by the various youth subcultures of the 1970s and 1980s.[58] A cultural "antipolitics" (*antipolitika*) distinguished many of the most youth-oriented neformaly.[57] This array of urban youth dispositions dominated the informal wave of 1986–1988, called in Russian simply the *"neformalitet."* The subcultural habitus of such groups underscored the degree to which explicitly political grouplets existed in an ill-defined cultural gap between the vast majority of unstable and transient neformaly and more stable networks of reformist cadres and specialists working in official organizations. The distinctive youth subculture of many neformaly, the continuing dependence of voluntary associations on the arbitrary policies of local officials, and the uneasy position of political outsiders between informal activism and official reformism together indicate the political weaknesses of the neformalitet, weaknesses which became particularly apparent with the acceleration of political reform occasioned by the calling of the Nineteenth Party Conference.

Other factors also affected the relationship between the 1986–1988 neformaly wave and the democratic movement of 1989–1991. First, nominally apolitical or single issue groups—or individual members thereof—often found themselves undergoing a process of rapid politicization, for a wide variety of reasons. For instance, Vladimir Bokser, the future DemRossiia electoral strategist, first became active in voluntary associations concerned with the prevention of cruelty toward animals, an experience that led to his rapid politicization:

> In 1985 or eighty six, I don't remember when precisely, I became an activist in societies for the protection of animals. For two years I very actively participated in the work of a number of such associations. There I naturally encountered massive cruelty, which in general reflected our system. Everything that was connected with a barbaric attitude toward animals in fact was a consequence not simply of the cruelty characteristic of people, but of the cruelty characteristic of the totalitarian system. And so there is nothing strange in the fact that I had a definite political experience precisely in such groups.[58]

During Bokser's involvement with animal rights advocacy, the reaction of many apparatchiks on the local level toward *any* form of voluntary sociation—no matter how seemingly innocuous—often proved hostile, increasing the likelihood that participation in voluntary associations would trigger subsequent politicization. This was particularly true with local ecological groups like the *Brateevo* association in the Moscow "microdistrict" (*mikroraion*) of the same name. Initially organized on a neighborhood level in September 1988 by several thousand local residents to combat the exceptionally high levels of district pollution stemming from nearby oil and gas refineries, Brateevo quickly became entangled in a political confrontation with the apparat over future plans for industrial expansion in the district. Eventually, Brateevo affiliated itself with the political opposition by joining DemRossiia.[59] The combined effect of such local dynamics intensified skepticism toward Gorbachev's version of guided democratization and initially favored an emergent neformaly habitus.

The heterogeneous profile of voluntary associations springing up across Russia during perestroika became an additional factor effecting relations between the neformalitet and the democratic movement of 1989–1991. A motley assortment of nationalist informal groups appeared in the RSFSR during the late 1980s, most of which tended to be authoritarian, anti-Semitic, and more favorably disposed to the repressive apparatus of the party-state.[60] Many Russian nationalist sects stood in marked contrast to nationalist movements in non-Russian republics, which took on the mantle of "national liberation," in contrast to Russian "empire savers."[61]

Although Russia's rightist groups proved extraordinarily unsuccessful as vehicles of political entrepreneurship before 1991,[62] they nonetheless underscore the diverse character of voluntary associations. Simple identification of emergent society in the first years of perestroika with nascent democracy per se thus remains misleading.

Dividing voluntary associations into six categories according to orientation clarifies divergent trends of informal activism in 1986–1988. The six categories include (1) apolitical sports, hobbies, and other such associations; (2) youth counter-cultural groups; (3) associations dedicated to environmental or other social issues, such as religious freedom; (4) nationalist groups and movements; (5) human rights defense groups; and (6) pro-reform "political clubs."[63]

Following the passage of the 1987 Law on Enterprises, new economic cooperatives appeared. Although distinct from the neformaly, some *kooperativniki* did develop ad hoc connections with informal political clubs.[64] At the same time, practices of internal democratization spread within formally organized professional associations and other officially established social organizations.

Nevertheless, the 1986–1988 neformaly wave engendered several networks that subsequently developed as grassroots sections of the democratic movement. Indeed, this small but disproportionately influential number of voluntary associations served as forerunners of Moscow's democratic movement.

Networking Across the Hierarchies, 1987–1989

The return of political prisoners and internal exiles after 1986 sparked a resurgence of human rights activism crushed by repression in the early 1980s.[65] The resurgence of human rights groups—from the reconstitution of human rights watch committees to the recreation of samizdat newsletters dedicated to monitoring human rights abuses—pushed informal discourse in a more radical direction and placed the advisability of a socialist orientation among politically oriented neformaly squarely on the agenda.

The appearance of the samizdat newsletter *Ekspress-Khronika* in 1987, founded and edited by former political prisoner Alexander Podrabinek, played a crucial role here. Podrabinek edited the new bulletin in the spirit of the dissident samizdat newsletter of the 1970s and early eighties, *The Chronicle of Current Events* (*Khronika tekushchikh sobytii*), the principle publication of the Helsinki Watch Committee and other human rights groups in the Brezhnev period.[66] Vera Kriger, a later member of Democratic Russia's Coordinating Committee, stated *Ekspress-Khronika*—as opposed to telephone trees or other informal networks—served as the key means by which announcements for demonstrations and other movement-centered information circulated in DemRossiia networks in 1990 and 1991, especially outside of Moscow and Leningrad.[67]

The political revival of the human rights agenda not only served as a vehicle for coordination between local groupings of DemRossiia, it also brought to the fore dissonances between the counter-cultural habitus of more youth-oriented neformaly, the moralist disposition of those who focused on problems of political repression, and the more professional habitus of many pro-perestroika specialists and intellectuals. The reappearance of human rights activism thus arose in complex relation to the neformalitet, and in particular to the internal tensions and splits that plagued informal political clubs.

Some human rights groups in the late 1980s represented a direct resumption of activity by reconstituted networks of Brezhnev-era dissidents, such as the Press Club Glasnost, which attempted to continue the work of the Moscow Helsinki Group disbanded in 1982.[68] Such groups played a marginal role in the political life of Russia in the Gorbachev period, in large part due to the suddenly obsolescent mentality of dissidence in its 1970s incarnation. On the other hand, several groups with a strong human rights orientation who at the same time developed more directly out of the neformalitet of the mid- to late 1980s played a most significant role indeed. Civic Dignity and, especially, Memorial—whose history closely tied to Moscow's political clubs—stood as the most important of such networks.

Civic Dignity formed in late August and early September of 1987, with the goal of reforming legal codes, documenting human rights abuses, helping victims of the Soviet judicial system, and reconstituting a liberal-democratic network along the lines of the Constitutional Democratic Party (*Kadety*) destroyed by the Bolshevik revolution.[69]

> Constitutional democracy—organized popular power—is the basic principle of a social order in which all activity on the part of state bodies is regulated by the law. This law is itself affirmed by the people and secured by the defense—universally applied to all—of the inalienable rights of the person.[70]

Although remaining numerically small, Civic Dignity's pragmatic approach, coalition-building orientation and participation in the Moscow neformalitet helped generalize the discourse of civil society prior to the rise of DemRossiia.

Memorial—an association dedicated to the victims of Stalin's repressions— also originated in the second half of 1987, playing a central role in the transformation of Russian politics during the next two years. More than any other informal association, Memorial brought together younger reformers in the neformalitet and the CPSU itself with middle-aged former dissidents and intellectuals, the "60ers" (*shestidesiatniki*) who formed worldviews during the Khrushchev thaw. Vladimir Lysenko, a CPSU member and early organizer of Memorial, emphasized how reformers

> met Andrei Sakharov ... and many previously repressed persons. Getting to know them, certainly, was the principal turning point in the formation of my worldview. After finding out the truth about what had actually happened, I very seriously changed my attitude to the system and first began speaking out for its radical reform.[71]

Memorial's original Initiative Group (*Initsiativnaia gruppa*) launched a campaign to gather signatures for an appeal to the Supreme Soviet of the USSR in favor of building a memorial "to the victims of illegal repression," which would include a monument and information and research center.[72] Despite the fact that Memorial remained unregistered as an official group until early 1990—due both to internal disagreements over the association's charter, and to hostility and delays on the part of the apparat—this "historical-educational society" (*istoriko-prosvetitel'skoe obshchestvo*) exercised a transformative impact on Russian politics by helping erode the Soviet Communist Party's claim to historical legitimacy.[73]

Memorial's emergence coincided with the reappearance of Stalin as a negative symbol in official Soviet discourse. In his official speech marking the seventieth anniversary of the Bolshevik Revolution on November 7, 1987, Gorbachev raised the "problem of Stalin" in a way not done publicly since Khrushchev's fall.[74] Although fraught with dangers for the reform leadership, "the return of history" stood a precondition of the glasnost' ("publicity") initiative. Yet publicizing information on the scale of repressions committed by the party-state powerfully delegitimated communist rule itself and opened the door for a symbolic challenge to party-state hegemony from below.[75]

Memorial's insistence on historical justice revealed the power of appeals to "universal human values" (*obshchechelovecheskie tsennosti*) among urban specialists and professionals in a social world corroded by the public cynicism of the Brezhnev period.[76] Among urban specialists, the emergence of Memorial exemplified the revival of the human rights agenda personified by the release of Sakharov from internal exile in December 1986. Together with the work of Memorial, Sakharov's reputation transformed the assertion of simple moral conduct into a distinctive political style within Russia's emergent democratic movement at the end of the 1980s, a style shaping speech genres in DemRossiia in 1990–1991. In this sense, Sakharov and Memorial changed the terms of public, political discourse. Indeed, Sakharov and the original members of Memorial's Initiative Group influenced the development of the democratic movement out of all proportion to their number.

Memorial became the first all-Russian [voluntary] organization. And this was certainly no accident, as Russia needed such an organization ... You see, even I was in this small group, the Initiative Group Memorial, which had 15 members, all of whom have since become well-known politicians ... There was Sudko, leader of the most radical of our democratic parties, the Democratic Union ... There were liberal communists, such as Volodia Nasedkin ... there was Father Gleb Yakunin, Afanas'ev, Kariakin, and so forth. The Memorial Association thus united very strong forces.[77]

Contacts made at a neformaly "summit" (*sobeshchanue na vyshem urovne*)—the Conference for Social Initiatives in Perestroika (*Vstrecha-dialog obshchestvennye initsiativy v perestroike*), held in Moscow in August 1987—stimulated the rapid growth of Memorial's influence and of pro-democracy networking generally.[78] A political watershed, the meetings brought together fifty-two fractious groupings in an open opposition conference, the first of its kind seen in Russia since Lenin launched the Red Terror in 1918.[79]

Reform-minded "political clubs" (*politicheskie kluby*) formed earlier in the year provided organizers for this conference. Political clubs distinguished themselves from human rights groups largely by their political declaration of support for perestroika and their hesitancy to openly challenge the institutional preeminence of the CPSU.[80] The political clubs occupied a boundary between grassroots voluntary activism and more established reformist networks, with some clubs more closely tied to younger neformaly—such as the Club for Social Initiatives—and others more representative of established specialists and Party reformers, such as the Club Perestroika.[81] Highly unstable formations, the clubs in fact networked various strands of loyal opposition to the party-state.

The neformalitet thus linked the two distinct idioms of "democratic socialism" and "universal human rights," the first distinguishing political clubs and the second, the reconstituted human rights groups with roots in the Brezhnev period. In Brezhnev's day, active political disaffection in Russia had two divergent manifestations, "revisionism" and "dissidence." Revisionism marked "loyal oppositionists" from "hard-liners," an opposition phrased in the apparat's own political language—Marxism–Leninism—and waged on the apparat's institutional terms, within the confines of Party networks. Especially characteristic of the 60ers, revisionists by and large took a passive stance toward political life during the Brezhnev period.[82]

Dissent, on the other hand, appeared a moral-ethical rejection of many of the party-state's institutional practices, coupled with an insistence that rights officially recognized by Soviet representatives in international agreements and formally granted in the Soviet constitution be respected in practice by Soviet officials. Dissent—literally "different thinking" in Russian (*inakomyslie*)—explicitly challenged the terms of political legitimacy underlying Party doctrine, and in particular the ideological elevation of "party-spiritedness" (*partiinost'*) above legality (*zakonnost'*).

The return of prisoners and exiles—most importantly, Sakharov, in December of 1986—to Russia's major cities signaled the symbolic victory of a movement which had been physically crushed, and set in motion a pattern of inter- and intragenerational tensions between former Party revisionists, younger neformaly, and the "morally pure" legacy of the dissidents and their political heirs. The editor of *Ekspress-Khronika* and human rights activist from the 1970s Podrabinek, for instance, disdained democratic socialists, while Boris Kagarlitsky—a younger, self-proclaimed socialist of the political clubs—treated "liberal democrats" like Podrabinek likewise.[83] Rooted deep in the habitus of both dissent and revisionism as marginal modes of being in official Soviet space, such distrust and disdain bred misrepresentation, misrecognition and open rivalry between groups with divergent generative experiences.

The informal political clubs thus brought together two generations of opposition, an older generation of revisionism and dissent and a younger generation of neformaly and "young socialists," some of whom suffered repression in the early 1980s, such as Kagarlitsky, Pavel Kudiukin and Gleb Pavloskii.[84] Kudiukin—active in Democratic Perestroika and during the 1989 campaign for the USSR Congress of Peoples Deputies—mobilized club members to work for the election of Oleg Bogomolov. A liberal academician and head of the Institute of the World Socialist Economy, Bogomolov had given Kudiukin a job after his release from detention.[85]

Curiously enough, however, *intra*generational tensions often played a more prominent role in the political clubs of the late 1980s than *inter*generational tensions. Among the middle-aged 60ers, distrust marked relations between liberal specialists or Party reformers who earlier compromised with the regime in order to make a career under Brezhnev, on the one hand, and veteran dissenters who suffered great personal misfortune in the 1970s and early 1980s due to their public stance, on the other. Sakharov's pragmatic orientation and ecumenical leanings played a particularly important role in containing these tensions and facilitating pragmatic cooperation among democratically oriented 60ers in the late 1980s.

The younger generation of oppositionists lacked such a unifying figure, remaining prone to splits and factionalization typical of highly marginalized and ephemeral networks. Indeed, as emphasized above, the "politicals" among younger neformaly in no way represented the neformalitet as a whole. The factional modus operandi of neformaly politicals reflected in part abstention from politics among many youth groups, and in part dynamics of tiny grouplets as fertile breeding grounds for sectarian orientations.

From the perspective of the democratic movement of 1989–1991, the Club for Social Initiatives (*Klub sotsial'nykh initsiativov*) and the Club Perestroika (*Klub-perestroika*) stood as the two most important political networks emerging out of the neformalitet. As principal organizers of the August 1987 Conference for Social Initiatives, these two clubs not only facilitated the emergence of associations like Memorial, but also functioned as training grounds for organizers of the political grouplets founded in 1989 that subsequently joined DemRossiia as collective members.[86]

First organized in the winter of 1987 as an "independent club for inter-professional association and contact," Club Perestroika registered as Democratic Perestroika eleven months later, under the auspices of the Central Economic and Mathematical Institute of the Academy of Sciences of the USSR in Moscow.[87] The ties that Club Perestroika/Democratic Perestroika maintained from early on with established professionals gave it many advantages over other neformaly groups, as the club not only gained the sponsorship of a prestigious institute, but also served as meeting ground for a number of midlevel Party reformers.[88] The Club's specialist connections aided the organizers of the August 1987 neformaly conference, underscoring how the cultivation of patrons in official organizations greatly augmented the organizing capacities of voluntary associations in the perestroika period.

Club Perestroika/Democratic Perestroika's strategy of loyal opposition served it well in 1987 and early 1988, insofar as it facilitated the association's ability to network among career-conscious specialists and professionals, to secure regular meeting places, and to publish and distribute a mimeographed journal—"Open Zone" (*Otkrytaia zona*)—diffusing ideas from a diverse array of voluntary associations and neformaly in 1988 and 1989.[89] At the same time, the Club cultivated ties with neformaly outsiders.

The Club for Social Initiatives, on the other hand, formed more an informal group (*neformal'naia gruppa*) in the true sense of the term. Originating out of youth discussion groups in communal apartments on the Arbat in late 1986,[90] the Club evolved as an informal network coordinating activities in the neformalitet. Club participants spanned a range from Viacheslav Igrunov—soon of the Memorial Initiative Group—to "young socialist" oppositionists such as Kagarlitsky and Gleb Pavlovskii. More organizationally fluid and fragile than the Club Perestroika, many participating in the Club for Social Initiatives drifted in and out of the loose networks clustering around both itself and Club Perestroika/Democratic Perestroika.[91] Nevertheless, the Club for Social Initiatives benefited as well from patronage from more established specialists, specifically from the Committee for Social Initiatives of the Soviet Sociological Association.[92]

The Club for Social Initiatives eventually disintegrated in 1988, as many "young socialists" abandoned it in favor of Commune (*Obshchina*) and other socialist and syndicalist groupings. A number of other, less socialist-oriented activists reorganized the remnants of the Club as a nonprofit informational association for voluntary associations tied closely by means of personnel and temperament with Memorial. Thus was born the Moscow Information

Exchange (*Moskovskoe biuro informatsionnogo obmena*, sometimes referred to as the Perspective Information Center in English-language publications), which relocated several times and served as both a meeting place for discussions among politically oriented informals, and an archive of samizdat literature from the Gorbachev period.[93]

Club Perestroika/Democratic Perestroika's connections with CPSU reformers and officials emerged as a continual source of tension between itself and the Club for Social Initiatives. The strategic question of the public stance democratically inclined neformaly ought to take toward senior reformers, and especially Gorbachev, complicated such tensions. These tensions led to the reconstruction of the original Club Perestroika itself in the spring of 1988, whose name change to Democratic Perestroika at the time of the club's registration accompanied the branching off of a number of clubs and groups that crystallized under its auspices, such as Perestroika-88 and the aforediscussed Civic Dignity.[94] Although such tensions did not prevent the two clubs from sponsoring the neformaly summit in August 1987, they nevertheless signaled strategic and philosophical discontinuities that continually undermined the ability of erstwhile democrats to create more stable and effective network alliances prior to the appearance of DemRossiia.

If anything, what loosely linked networks spanning various groups in this period came from outside and above. Most of the political clubs of 1987–1988 accepted the strategic necessity of respecting boundaries of oppositional activity laid down by Gorbachev's "guided democratization," especially the General Secretary's continuing defense of the institutional *sine qua non* of one-party rule. In contrast, informal groups calling for the end of the party-state prior to 1989 constituted the neformalitet's militant fringe. The relative handful of such groups disproportionately impacted the changing terms of political discourse, although never achieving wide organizational influence.

Most prominent among the militant groups stood Democratic Union (*Demokraticheskii soiuz*), which arose out of the informal seminar Democracy and Humanism (*Demokratiia i gumanizm*). Partly in reaction to the Club for Social Initiatives and the Club Perestroika/Democratic Perestroika's relative political moderation, the group formed in the spring and summer of 1987 and remained hostile to compromise with the CPSU under any conditions.[95] The strident anti-Soviet rhetoric and confrontational stance of many seminar participants alienated many both within the political clubs and among the pro-reform intelligentsia. Valeriia Novodvorskaia, who had been confined for a number of years in a psychiatric hospital as a form of political repression, emerged as the Democratic Union's principal spokesperson.[96]

The Democratic Union remained a predominantly *intelligenty* and student phenomenon whose lasting achievement stood as militantly breaking the previous taboo of publicly challenging the legitimacy of one-party rule.[97] Largely by default, the Democratic Union served as diversionary cover for more moderate protest activity in 1988, as Democratic Union members and activities suffered particularly harsh repression at the same time as it internally resisted cooperation with most other neformaly.[98] Such uncompromising radicalism at times provoked harsh retaliation, as in the 1989 death of a former Democratic Union member in Moscow, Igor Antonov, following a police beating that spring.[99]

The rise of street activism in Moscow spearheaded by the Democratic Union signaled the eclipse of the small grouplet phase of the neformalitet, the phase of loyal opposition and its practices of organizing discussions, writing petitions, and drafting declarations.[100] The growth of protest activity presaged the coming of the popular front phase of democratically oriented political activism from below in the summer of 1988. This was the summer of the Nineteenth Party Conference and the formation of popular fronts (*narodnye fronty*) in the Baltics, which sparked the reappearance of spontaneous demonstrations on a wide scale in Russia's major cities for the first time since the Civil War of 1918–1921.[101]

Only one of the voluntary associations engendered during the neformalitet—Memorial—would end up a collective member (*kollektivnyi chlen*) of the Democratic Russia coalition. Instead, three other networks instantiated as groups—two of them appearing for the first time in 1989—emerged at DemRossiia's heart.

The first, the Moscow Tribune (*Moskovskaia tribuna*), crystallized out of self-described "elite" fractions of revisionists and dissidents from the 60ers—the "elite" of the politically marginalized.[102] Second stood the Moscow Association of Voters (*Moskovskoe ob"edinenie izbiratelei*), bringing together voluntary associations and voter clubs (kluby izbiratelei). Finally, a fluid opposition bloc of democratically oriented deputies crystallized in the new Soviet Congress of Peoples Deputies following the spring 1989 elections. Called the Interregional Deputies Group (*Mezhregional'naia deputaskaia gruppa*), this organization formed the third, and key, network bridging movement and counterelite.[103]

The eclipse of the reformist political clubs and youth-oriented neformaly by the spring 1989 mobilization of democratically oriented specialists brought somewhat different dispositional tensions to the surface. While the professionalizing habitus of strategically located specialists generated radicalizing effects paralleling those operative among neformaly, such specialists aligned more closely with the nuances of deepening tensions unfolding high in the party-state, and the nomenklatura in particular. The 1989 mobilization thus presented an opportunity that many in the neformalitet proved incapable of realizing.

Understanding why the 1989 elections in retrospect formed a key missed opportunity for the neformaly requires stepping back a year. In 1988, dispositional tensions ran along three principal fault lines among Moscow's ascendant reformist networks. These dispositional tensions developed between, respectively, the countercultural habitus of younger political activists, the moralist disposition of many specialists and intellectuals influenced by the dissident movement, and the professionalizing habitus of radicalizing reformers emerging out of both specialist groups and the Communist Party itself in the wake of perestroika. The acceleration of political reforms stemming from the Nineteenth Party Conference and the rise of popular-front movements in the Baltics in the spring and summer quickly emerged as primary factors driving radicalization.[104]

The need to prepare for possible participation in the 1989 elections and the powerful intraunion demonstration effect of mass mobilization in the Baltics combined to signal the creation of popular fronts on the Baltic model in the Russian Republic. Yet the neformaly habitus lagged behind the opening of wide fissures in officialdom, as neformaly figures tried to adapt to addressing a much wider public than small groups of intellectuals and radicalized urban youths marginalized by the hitherto stable party-state. These dynamics played out at the regional level in the Moscow Popular Front.

The Moscow Popular Front and the Origins of Revolutionary Mobilization

Local networks organized as the Moscow Popular Front (*Moskovskii narodnyi front*) in stages, from the spring of 1988 through the spring of 1989.[105] The extremely fluid character of participation in, and contact between, political neformaly in the early period of the Moscow Popular Front stands out in the following remark by Vladimir Bokser.

> [In the spring of 1988] I took part in pickets demanding a resolution of the problem of registering the Memorial society . . . And then, in one beautiful moment, I saw pickets next to the movie theater "Russia" demanding that Afanas'ev, Kariakin and Korotich be elected as delegates to the Nineteenth Party Conference—three people who the district-level [*apparat*] . . . tried to block. I joined these pickets, and soon started organizing them . . . This is how . . . I joined

the informal group that turned out to be the backbone of the Moscow Popular Front.[58]

A number of pro-Front street demonstrations, combined with a rally in favor of Memorial's petition drive addressed by Sakharov at Moscow's Dinamo stadium—all held on June 25, 1988, to bring pressure to bear on delegates to the Nineteenth Party Conference to accelerate political reforms[106]– gave popular front organizers new political opportunities. Over the next ten months, the Front led numerous demonstrations and organized other activities openly challenging party-state hegemony, culminating the following spring at Moscow's largest stadium, Luzhniki.

Yet as early as the summer of 1988, Moscow Popular Front protest activities foreshadowed splits between more pragmatic and more ideological activists, splits that came to a head in the spring of 1989.[107] Such demonstrations not only provoked local police repression, but also served as grist for the apparat mill about "counterrevolutionaries" and "anti-Soviet agitation."

The democratization of the Party's attitudes regarding voluntary associations—initiated by the special Plenum of the Central Committee of the CPSU in January 1987 and strengthened by Gorbachev's opening speech at the Nineteenth Party Conference—directly contradicted a decree promulgated by the USSR Supreme Soviet on July 28, 1988. The July 28 decree aimed at curtailing neformaly demonstrations through the erection of a gamut of administrative procedures aimed at strictly regulating street protests.[108] In effect, this decree served as conservative apparatchiks' direct response to the nationalist upsurge in the Baltics and the Democratic Union and Moscow Popular Front protests, revealing the degree of nomenklatura resistance to political reform and the true extent of growing partocratic disunity at the apex of the Soviet order.

Despite this July decree—aimed at radicalizing reformers across the spectrum—shifts in political opportunities favorable to further rebellion appeared more prominent than at any time since the early years of Bolshevik rule. The Moscow Popular Front took advantage of the breach at the top the party-state, first by organizing actions in the summer and early fall of 1988, and then by electing a Coordinating Council (*Koordinatsionnyi sovet*) of nine individuals on November 9, 1988.[109]

Although the Front proved an important vehicle for the mobilization of protests and voters clubs during the electoral campaign for the USSR Congress of Peoples Deputies in early 1989, the ability of "young socialist" factional leaders in the organizing committee to foist a syndicalist economic program on the Front as a whole wound up alienating many erstwhile members and supporters in the late spring and early summer of 1989. By the close of its founding conference on May 20, 1989, the Moscow Popular Front suffered practical stillbirth, due in large part to the syndicalist politics of those who controlled a majority on its Coordinating Council.[110]

Formed among informal groups of educated young Muscovites in the late-Soviet period, the habitus of "young socialists" proved maladaptive to rapid network expansion in the political field it helped open up. Yet, despite the Front's rapid demise, the "popular-front model" of an umbrella of voluntary associations and individual grassroots activists served as a prototype for how to mobilize informal opposition networks into a social movement, first for the Moscow Association of Voters, and then for DemRossiia in 1990.

The rapid marginalization of the Moscow Popular Front in the spring of 1989 signaled, then, not the end of informal political activism, but the eclipse of the neformalitet. The decline of the neformalitet signaled shifts toward agents networking the divide between small circles of relatively marginal youth and intelligentsia activists, and radicalizing specialists practicing professions in the fragmenting party-state.[111] Out of this shift emerged the democratic movement (*dvizhenie*), and then its umbrella organization, Democratic Russia.

Nothing sums up the disappointment and suspicion of many young neformaly toward events in 1989 better than the following quote from Andrei Fadeev, a radical Memorial activist who organized the short-lived split-off from Club Perestroika/Democratic Perestroika, Perestroika-88:

> 1989 arrived, and everyone expected big changes from this year of elections. These expectations were, as usual, unjustified. A large fraction of the people of 1988—those knights of the political circles, discussion clubs, popular fronts and historical-educational societies—were already passing into the darkness of history . . . The time of mass sensations had begun, the swelling tide of the crowd had arrived, thirsting for change and, of course, great leaders [*vozhdi*]. In short, the time of "mass meeting democracy" was upon us, where each listened only to himself, speaking with an eye on the crowd as it chanted first "down with . . . !" and next "hurrah!" The people of 1988 and eighty-nine, of course, closely cooperated and as a consequence intermixed in this or that party or movement. But the difference between them by no means disappeared, as a whole gulf lay between Valeriia Novodvorskaia, the creator of the Democratic Union, and Vladimir Bokser, the inventor of the Moscow Association of Voters. This was precisely the chasm between forerunners and latecomers, and such a chasm cannot be bridged in a single bound.[112]

In hindsight, the ebb of the political resonance of the neformaly and the rise to prominence of more "professionalized" specialist networks could be perceived in the growing mobilization of democratic fractions in the Party itself—especially among educated urban cadres—in the second half of 1988.

Informal intra-Party clubs had been forming among small groups of reform-oriented cadres in a number of Russian cities since at least 1986, a development closely connected to the growing breach in the party-state between Yeltsin's populist calls for deepening reforms, on the one hand, and apparat conservatives represented by the senior politburo member, Yegor Ligachev, on the other.[113]

The character of Gorbachev's improvised "revolution from above" as a center-directed strategy of managed democratization became clear during such struggles at the apex of the party-state in the second half of 1988. The seeds of its eventual failure were sown in the course of the nominating and election campaigns themselves and the inability of the Party leadership to reshape the apparat from a partocratic structure into a functioning instrument of political mobilization under conditions of nascent pluralism, as witnessed with the formation of the neformaly. This failure took concrete form in the first months of 1989, as the conflict over nominating and electoral procedures quickly became the focus of political struggle between what then were called "conservatives," "moderates" and "radicals" in officialdom. The struggle over nominations not only gave impetus to the formation of voters clubs (kluby izbiratelei) and region-wide associations at the grassroots level, it also signaled the open fragmentation of partocratic rule, spearheaded by a revolt among specialists in Moscow.

The Yeltsin and Sakharov Campaigns of 1989

The first phase of specialist rebellion centered in Moscow's high-technology enterprises, technical and scientific institutes, and the Soviet Academy of Sciences. In early 1989, a spontaneous movement to nominate Yeltsin at a number of Moscow enterprises created an opening for the Yeltsin candidacy. Nominated by more than a score of associations, Yeltsin gained nomination as a candidate from Moscow's federal-territorial seat ("National-Territorial District No. 1") at a special citywide voter assembly held in the Hall of Columns on February 21.[114]

Despite Party control of admittance to this meeting, one of the two nominees preselected by the partocracy withdrew his nomination in the face of Yeltsin's evident popularity, ensuring the latter's nomination. In the absence of repressive sanctions directed from the politburo, substantial numbers of midlevel apparatchiks now began to break ranks—replicating Yeltsin's sustained breach of Party discipline—in order to position themselves politically for a post-partocratic future. In short, the 1989 Yeltsin campaign signaled both a rapid acceleration in the secular decline of party-state mobilizational capacities, and the destabilizing emergence of alternative patterns of networking in the partocracy itself. Indeed, Yeltsin's networking sparked a relative handful of senior party-state figures to begin improvising new trajectories outside of institutional channels.

A network joining nineteen pro-Yeltsin enterprises promptly organized itself to promote Yeltsin's campaign, a network soon known as the "Committee of the 19." This committee linked voter clubs to Yeltsin's apparat connections through, among others, his new campaign director, Lev Sukhanov, Yeltsin's former chief of staff at *Gosstroi*, the Soviet Construction Ministry where the erstwhile Moscow First Secretary had been relegated by the Party leadership after his falling out with Gorbachev. Two other apparatchiks who became Yeltsin campaign aides (*doverennye litsa*) at this time—Alexander Muzykantskii, the deputy chairman of the Moscow City Government's Executive Committee (*Mosgorizpolkom*), and Lev Shemaev—both worked with Yeltsin in his days as Moscow Party chief.

Activists in various "intra-Party clubs" of radicalizing CPSU reformers also championed Yeltsin's cause. The director of the Moscow Aviation Institute, Yuri Ryzhov, quickly emerged as an important link between Yeltsin's unofficial campaign team and informal CPSU clubs. Ryzhov knew Yeltsin from the latter's Moscow days, and previously allowed radicalizing CPSU clubs to use Institute facilities. Moreover, Ryzhov himself was running for a seat in the Congress of Peoples Deputies.

> Yeltsin...came to us at the Institute to appear publicly with Ryzhov...[with whom Yeltsin] had very good contacts; this is how we first got to know Yeltsin ...I participated in Yeltsin's campaign when he was still the Chairman of *Gosstroi*. We shot several videos of Yeltsin...and showed them in [Moscow's] Leningrad district and several neighboring districts.[71]

In 1989, only restricted circles of specialists and Party personnel were positioned to appropriate such a rare commodity as a video camera.

Meanwhile, the Moscow Popular Front became involved with the election campaign.

> The [1989] campaign began at precisely the moment that the proposed Election Law for the so-called union parliament was published. This event caused the outburst of our activity, as everyone began to argue and debate the degree to which this proposed Law was actually democratic and to try and work out all of its implications.[58]

The Front soon organized a series of rallies in favor of reformist candidacies. On the day before the election, the Front staged a number of unauthorized pro-Yeltsin rallies around Moscow, thus coordinating grassroots protest with the Yeltsin campaign. Vladimir Bokser and Mikhail Shneider, two Popular Front leaders who headed the "campaign team" (*izbiratel'naia komanda*) of Sergei Stankevich—an "intra-Party club" organizer, Front member, and candidate from Moscow's *Cheremushkinskii* district territorial seat—first linked up with Yeltsin during their work for Stankevich. Bokser, a pediatrician, and Shneider, an electrical engineer and physicist trained in part at the Moscow Aviation Institute, later emerged as top figures in Democratic Russia, coordinating the grassroots side of Yeltsin's 1991 RSFSR-wide presidential campaign. Yeltsin captured 89.4 percent of the vote in 1989, landing an enormous symbolic blow on the partocracy and opening the door to a wider array of trajectory improvisation in apparat circles.[115]

In contrast to the Yeltsin campaign, Sakharov's campaign was a closed affair conducted within one of the most prestigious status group in Soviet society, the membership of the USSR Academy of Sciences. Unlike open seats, election to a corporate seat allotted social organizations required nomination by the organization's membership, registration by its plenary body, and assent of a quorum of members.

Despite Sakharov's nomination by over sixty institutes, however, the Academy's presidium submitted a final list of candidates excluding Sakharov and several other widely supported figures, including the head of the Soviet space program, Roald Sagdeev (nominated by more than thirty institutes), the historian Dmitrii Likhachev (nominated by twenty institutes), and the economists Gavriil Popov and Nikolai Shmelev (together nominated by thirty institutes).[116] On February 2, several thousand scientists and scholars from over thirty institutes demonstrated in Moscow to protest this maneuver in the opening salvo of the specialist rebellion. Although Sakharov could have secured a nomination for an open seat despite the injustice of being excluded by scientific allies of conservative apparatchiks, he declined numerous nominations by voter assemblies in favor of an open challenge to the Academy's presidium.

On the 2nd of February an unprecedented demonstration of Academy colleagues took place, accusing the plenary session of shameful decisions and calling for a boycott of the upcoming [Academy] election—which has been transformed into a farce—and also for the radical democratization of the administration of the Academy in correspondence with the demands of *perestroika* . . . Its seems to me that this demonstration may be the first step in a new stage in the history of the Academy and the nation as a whole. I feel indissolubly connected with the Academy, of which I have been a member for 35 years. I have come to the conclusion that I must be an Academy candidate in the new elections, or I will not be a candidate at all.[117]

In March 1989, disgruntled Academy members formed the Voter Club of the Academy of Sciences of the USSR (*Klub izbiratelei Akademii nauk SSSR*) for the express purpose of electing Sakharov, Sagdeev, and others excluded from the list of nominees for the Academy's corporate seats. The Academy Voter Club nominally represented over 300 scientific institutes and organizations from across the USSR. For the first time, elite specialists created an autonomous vehicle of corporate-estate power near the top of the party-state. Given that the Soviet Constitution specified the automatic administrative subordination of lower bodies to higher bodies in the case of disputes, the creation of such an autonomous body triggered an implicit "dual power" (*dvoevlastie*) situation whose logic entailed the nascent "feudalization" of partocratic authority. The group's ability to circumvent the prerogative of the Presidium of the Academy of Sciences—and thus opening a new path of trajectory improvisation among senior scientific personnel—through the creation of a parallel, ad hoc executive structure would be duplicated repeatedly over the next few years.

The specialist rebellion in the USSR Academy of Sciences was foreshadowed several months earlier by formation of the Moscow Tribune, a self-restricted discussion club that had met monthly since October 1988. This club crystallized an already operative network of leading pro-reform intellectuals capable of facilitating the formation of the Academy of Sciences Voter Club on the eve of the controversy over Sakharov's nomination. The Tribune counted among its members many of the most distinguished intellectual figures in Moscow, including Sakharov, Sagdeev, and two future parliamentary leaders of DemRossiia, the historian Yuri Afanas'ev and the ethnologist Galina Starovoitova. Starovoitova herself contrasted the "elite" Moscow Tribune with "popular" associations such as the Moscow Popular Front. "The Tribune had room for only a few, and it was difficult to get in. In order to get in, you not only had to be considered honorable, but also needed an invitation. In general, its sessions were closed."[118] Starovoitova here signaled how Soviet-era status shaped dispositions in ways that "selected," via habitus, venues through which agents networked.

Indeed, the Tribune formed a network between the USSR Academy of Sciences and groups of nonscientific CPSU reformers. Yuri Ryzhov, the director of the Moscow Aviation Institute, facilitated Moscow Tribune meetings on a number of occasions in the winter of 1988–1989. By the time of the Yeltsin and Sakharov campaigns, the Aviation Institute discreetly connected the Tribune elite and informal groups like the CPSU reform clubs then meeting at the Institute and active in the Moscow Popular Front.[119] In effect, the Aviation Institute served as an ad hoc coordinator of distinct dispositions across networks at the heart of deepening trajectory improvisation.

The formation of the Academy of Sciences Voter Club signaled rebellion at the top of the specialist estate, as well as creating a tacit political alliance of CPSU "radicals," high-status intellectuals from the Moscow Tribune, the Moscow Popular Front, other important voluntary associations such as Memorial, voter clubs, and the Yeltsin-led informal network of pro-reform apparatchiks.[120] Not only had the electoral struggle allied Yeltsin with neformaly actively pushing the boundaries of reform from below. Now, some leading scientists—following Sakharov—found themselves aligned with voluntary associations whom they had previously kept at arm's length. This strategy proved highly effective: under the pressure of an Academy of Sciences Voter Club boycott, only eight of the twenty-three candidates on the presidium's original list received the minimum 50 percent of votes necessary to pass the first round of internal academy voting on March 21. During the second round, held on April 21, many of the excluded "radicals"—including Sakharov—won election on a corporate basis to the Congress of Peoples Deputies from the Academy of Sciences.[121]

The rebellion of specialists driving the Yeltsin and Sakharov campaigns signaled a new stage in the rapid democratization of professional associations underway since 1986, as scores of Moscow's cultural organizations and scientific institutes began openly contesting partocratic hegemony in formal organizations. Suddenly, habitus long adjusted to Soviet routines confronted a new situation as emergent networks of trajectory improvisers took advantage of splits in the partocracy to undermine the party-state's institutional salience. The impact of this rebellion is difficult to overestimate, as it triggered a sustained wave of pro-democracy demonstrations in urban Russia lasting through August 1991, and dramatically shifted public opinion in favor of radical reform.

A series of rallies of upward of 100,000 people at Moscow's Luzhniki stadium endorsed by Yeltsin and Sakharov kicked off the new cycle of mass protest. The largest rally, on May 21, 1989, signaled the breadth of ongoing shifts in Muscovite opinion.[122] For instance, in a December 1988 survey, only 17 percent of Muscovites favored the establishment of a multiparty system (*multipartiinost'*) in the USSR. In a second survey taken in February 1989—with the campaign for the March elections to the CPD-USSR already in full swing—46 percent of Muscovites had come to favor such a system. This shift was particularly pronounced among specialists, with 56 percent responding in favor of multiple parties, as compared to 39 percent of workers. By August 1989, the shift of opinion in favor of political pluralism had spread across much of the Russian Federation.[123]

The rise of the specialists in spring 1989 radicalized perceptual shifts in the life of many professional associations and unions underway for the previous two years.[124] At the same time, the formation of the Voter Club of the Academy of Sciences signaled a working—although fragile—political alliance of radical-reform specialists and younger neformaly active in the Moscow Popular Front and other voter clubs. This informal alliance mobilized previously latent organizational capacities into active networks. "After the formation of the Voters' Club of the Academy of Sciences, contacts between our groups began. People from the Academy of Sciences came to me, for example, to get materials . . . We helped them, and they helped us."[93] Not only had Yeltsin "connected" with the informals by means of the electoral struggle. Now, leading scientists found themselves in practical alliance with "young radicals" whom they had previously kept at arm's length. From this point forward, leading figures of the specialist rebellion who successfully campaigned for election to the new Congress of Peoples Deputies shaped the principal alignments of the nascent democratic opposition. Utilizing their popular, although not fully institutional, prestige, these figures improvised alternative paths to political prominence than those institutionalized in the party-state.

Sakharov's sudden death in December 1989 left Yeltsin as the only democratically oriented opposition leader to command widespread popularity and name-recognition across the Russian Republic. The passing of Sakharov and the rapid ascension of Yeltsin to the center of the opposition political stage deepened tensions between the moralistic habitus of many longtime intelligenty oppositionists, and specialist democrats who began to appear in officialdom. The rise of Yeltsin in turn foreshadowed the emergence of the DemRossiia opposition as "channelers" of trajectory improvisation across the Russian republic. This emergent relation between grass roots and counterelite began to form during the First Congress of Peoples Deputies of the USSR in spring 1989.

The First USSR Congress of Peoples Deputies

The First Congress of Peoples Deputies (CPD) opened on May 25, 1989, in a revolutionary mood, with radicals attacking the Party, military and KGB leaders for the massacre of twenty demonstrators by soldiers armed with shovels and clubs in the Georgian capital of Tbilisi early in the morning of April 9.[125] Whereas Gorbachev and the rest of the Party leadership were intent on pushing through as quickly as possible the election of the five hundred forty-two deputies who would form the new standing USSR Supreme Soviet and then promptly adjourning the Congress, the nascent opposition determined to prevent the Congress from serving as just another rubber stamp of Party leadership.

The publicity surrounding Congress proceedings keyed opposition success in debate. Coverage of the proceedings dominated the official media: for twelve days, Soviet television broadcast Congress sessions live. The televised Congress electrified the peoples of the Soviet Union, as millions of citizens watched heated debates among high officials for the first time in Soviet history.[126]

The legislative results of the First Congress, however, disappointed the opposition and undercut its success in disrupting staid partocratic politics. On the first day, the "left"—at the urging of both Sakharov and Yeltsin—acceded to the election of Gorbachev to the post of Chairman of the new USSR Supreme Soviet. Gorbachev returned the favor by trying to exclude Yeltsin from election to the all-USSR Supreme Soviet, ultimately unsuccessfully, and abruptly treating Sakharov by switching off the latter's microphone, a symbolic watershed that irrevocably alienated many former Gorbachev supporters. Thus began a long decline in the Soviet leader's influence over his primary constituency of specialists and professionals.[127]

Following the flap over the elections to the Supreme Soviet, Yeltsin reaffirmed his determination to press his populist challenge to the partocracy, in line with earlier campaign promises. In a populist speech on May 30, Yeltsin denounced the nomenklatura repeatedly, attacked Gorbachev's failure as an economic reformer, and warned that "in such conditions the danger of a transformation of the Supreme Soviet and its Presidium into an apparat or, as we say, a half-apparat of the Chairman can't be excluded."[128] The broadcast of this speech live to millions of viewers across the Soviet Union secured Yeltsin's place as Russia's most popular politician, while at the same time reinforcing lingering intelligenty uneasiness with Yeltsin as an emerging revolutionary symbol across the Russian Republic.[129]

While events unfolded in Russia, a parallel drama developed in nominally Soviet-dominated Central Europe. There, "round table" negotiations between Polish nomenklatury and Solidarity union and intellectual activists ushered in semifree elections in Poland. Events in both the non-Russian Soviet republics and in Poland thus spurred accelerating shifts in political opportunities, as transnational demonstration effects rippled in the Russian heartland of the Soviet order. Both externally and internally, the *modus operandi* of Soviet officialdom began to disintegrate.

The growing dissension and conflict within the Soviet Communist Party and among USSR Congress deputies over the course of reform created a political opportunity for radical democrats like Sakharov and Yeltsin to found the Inter-regional Deputies Group (*Mezhregial'naia deputatskaia gruppa*) in early July. Although the first preparatory session of the Inter-regional Group took place in Moscow on July 7, 1989, it can be argued that the group "existed practically from the early days of the First Congress of Peoples Deputies of the USSR within the democratic segment of the Moscow delegation, thanks to which this fraction was quickly called 'the Moscow group'."[130] Many members of the new Inter-regional Group developed a working relationship with each other in ongoing meetings held to coordinate developments on the floor of the Congress with the work of activists organizing the ongoing demonstrations at Luzhniki stadium.[131]

Over the course of the next six months, the membership of the Inter-regional Deputies Group totaled two hundred sixty-eight, while an additional 100–140 deputies worked on the periphery of the group in the fall of 1989 and spring of 1990.[132] Between the closing of the First CPD-USSR in June 1989 and the appearance of Democratic Russia in early 1990, the Inter-regional Deputies Group functioned as the most visible center of democratically oriented opposition in the Soviet Union, steering established specialists and Party doubters away from Gorbachev's "socialist choice" and toward rebellion. "An openly declared opposition as such first appeared [in the Soviet Union] from the moment of the creation of the Inter-regional Deputies Group."[133] That the Yeltsin-centered counterelite would take control of several important soviets in the Russian Republic in 1990 can be traced to links between the Inter-regional Group and the multiple networks organized through DemRossiia.

Of the five cochairmen and one secretary elected at the July General Conference of the Inter-regional Group, four would later play early leadership roles in organizing DemRossiia as a voter bloc. The group's five Cochairmen were Yuri Afanas'ev, Victor Pal'm, Gavriil Popov, Andrei Sakharov, and Boris Yeltsin, while the secretary was Arkadii Murashev. Pal'm, a member of the Estonian delegation—and notably the only non-Moscow-based cochairman of the Inter-regional Group—was far more involved with the politics of Baltic secession than that of the Russian Republic. Pal'm's role in the Deputies Group points to a key aspect of Russia's democratic movement—Russian democrats were relative latecomers who early on emulated the Baltic Peoples Fronts (*Narodnye fronty*).

Although the Inter-regional Group originally put forward Yeltsin as Chairman, the group decided instead for five cochairs, an indication of the continuing uneasiness felt toward Yeltsin by many intellectuals: "We wanted to maximize our support, and we did not want to set up a new idol or become identified as the followers of one individual."[134]

As 1989 progressed, the MDG found itself splitting into "moderate" and "radical" tendencies, the radicals being distinguished by their advocacy of the end of the Communist Party's political monopoly. "The Inter-regional Group consisted of two poles, since its members included a majority of the present-day leaders of 'Union' [*Soiuz*, a prominent rightist group in 1990–91].["][55] Il'ia Zaslavskii, who walked on crutches due to a childhood disease,[135] had been elected to one of Moscow's district-territorial seats with the help of the Invalid Society (*Invalidnoe obshchestvo*), and emerged as a leading figure of democratic decentralization in the Inter-regional Group. "Union" (*Soiuz*) emerged in 1990 as the principal bloc of deputies in the Soviet Congress of Peoples Deputies who favored maintaining the territorial integrity of the Soviet Union at all costs. Its leader was the so-called "Black Colonel," the Latvian army officer Victor Alksnis, who favored incremental market reforms implemented by a military regime.[136] But in 1989, the networks that comprised "Union" still wavered as to where they stood on organizational alternatives to the disintegrating party-state, as the disintegration of the Union itself remained, for the time being, a secondary issue in Russian politics.

Such disagreement and confusion drove the moderate-radical split in the Inter-regional Group, weakening its effectiveness and prompting radicals frustrated by the firm lock of the CPSU to begin devising a strategy of establishing an alternative political base in city, regional, and federation-level soviets of the Russian Republic (RSFSR) in the republican elections now scheduled for March 1990. The ability of conservative apparatchiks to control legislative procedures in the Soviet Congress and the USSR Supreme Soviet augmented network radicalization in such directions as summer turned toward fall. The formation of DemRossiia set the stage for the switch of the nascent counterelite's operational base from the Inter-regional Group, to the Moscow and Leningrad city soviets and the yet-to-be convened RSFSR Congress of Peoples Deputies.

The principal contribution of the Inter-regional Group to the genesis of the democratic movement in the end proved to be largely symbolic.

> Seeing the Group from the inside, one couldn't help but be surprised at the extent to which it was disorganized, unstructured, and lacked any base in the localities . . . More than anything, it was a symbol. Chernyshevskii [the nineteenth-century populist writer] was a symbol. The small circle of [Brezhnev-era] dissidents was also a symbol. The Inter-regional Group was perhaps one of the last such great symbols, lacking any firm foundation or even a clear idea of what it wanted and having only a spiritual authority. [55]

Because of their official standing as peoples deputies in the USSR Congress and all-Union Supreme Soviet, radical Inter-regional Group leaders could argue their views in forums whose proceedings were observed widely across the Russian Federation. This meant that local *apparatchiki* hostile to reform had a much harder time preventing the message of the emerging democrats from being heard—at least on national television or in the pages of more liberal newspapers—by the population at large. Less-prominently placed oppositionists had a much more difficult time gaining a wide audience and thus establishing name recognition. Indeed, Russia's democratic movement would be dominated for the next two and a half years by a handful of prominent USSR Congress opposition figures and close associates who established a federation-level presence in the spring and summer of 1989, underscoring how the stratification of places intersected with the reception of the Soviet mass media to presage sweeping change in the *longue durée* of Russian politics.

Following Sakharov's death, Yeltsin, Afanas'ev, Popov, Sergei Stankevich, Galina Starovoitova, Zaslavskii, and a handful of other Muscovites—along with Leningrad deputy and future chairman of the *Lensovet*, Anatolii Sobchak—emerged as the only radical politicians with national stature and popular influence outside of a few urban areas. This fact helps explain why democratic mobilization so consistently revolved around the personalities and strategic moves of this original group of leaders of the radical wing of the Inter-regional Group, in effect centralizing in an ad hoc manner the process of spreading trajectory improvisation. In large part for this reason, the associations that served during the 1989 election campaign as the primary springboards for such leading opposition figures into the USSR Congress—the voter clubs—quickly became the focal point of protest activity in Moscow from mid-1989 forward, overshadowing the activities of various neformaly groups and the Moscow Popular Front.

The Specialist Rebellion

The emergence of a revolutionary situation, dominated by trajectory improvisers around the Yeltsin counterelite, presaged the rise of Democratic Russia. The rise of DemRossiia in turn sprung directly out of the intersection of the disintegrating *longue durée* of Soviet history, and the proximate figurations of radicalizing reformers in Moscow in the wake of the 1989 elections to the Congress of Peoples Deputies of the USSR. Mapping the social contours of this movement organized by trajectory improvisers demonstrates how the global and the local combined in Moscow as splits deepened in the partocracy and social movement mobilization spread.

In this situation, the global manifest locally through rapidly changing perceptions of agents mobilizing in pro-democracy networks. At the center of such changing perceptions stood deepening disenchantment with the Soviet experience and a concomitant "westernizing turn" among nascent networks of Muscovites becoming politically active in favor of deeper democratization. The perception of relative deprivation or inadequacy across global regions often triggers transnational demonstration effects as vectors around which local groups reorganize. Soviet leaders' growing perception of declining Soviet capacities on an international scale and the concomitant shift in favor of reform in the politburo constitutes a classic example of the demonstration effect of western technological and economic dynamism, an effect exacerbated by the failure of Soviet military technology in Afghanistan and the onset of change in Poland.[137] The relative failure of Soviet socialism in its economic competition with the West not only set in motion transnational demonstration effects steering individual partocrats in a reformist direction. This relative failure also steered whole fragments of the specialist stratum in a "westernizing" direction—that is, toward a rhetorical embrace of the liberal model of democratic polity and market economy as political ideals at the expense of socialist ideology.

The Gorbachev leadership's early policies of reconciliation with its Cold War adversaries and its experiments with limited, quasi-market reforms implicitly recognized the superiority of western economies as generators of open-ended economic growth, exacerbating the legitimation crisis of the Soviet order. The maturation of pro-democracy political revolution in Poland and other Central-European party-states only magnified the intensity of such demonstration effects.

How did such dynamics translate between the global level of the Soviet party-state and the regional and local levels of Moscow? Internally, the increasing dominance of specialist positions played an important role in late-Soviet society, although such connections bear careful scrutiny.

By the time of the specialist rebellion of 1989, several patterns of secular change in the relative weights and dispositions of intellectuals and professionals in Soviet society could be observed. First stood the rapid numerical growth in educated professionals between 1960 and the mid-1980s cited in modernization accounts of social change in late-communist Russia. By the early 1980s, the rapid increase in the number of persons with higher educations began to have profound consequences for Soviet society. Between 1959 and 1981 the number of persons with a higher education increased from 8.8 to 19.8 million. By 1984, one out of every four employed persons in the Soviet Union was considered a "mental laborer."[138] By the late 1980s, a number of Soviet social scientists argued that significant numbers of specialists were employed at levels below that of their certified qualification.[139] When combined with a tendency toward a relative fall in average specialist incomes in comparison with that of skilled industrial workers between 1960 and 1980, they reasoned, this overproduction of specialists had caused a decline in the prestige of specialist positions and certificates of higher education.[140]

In short, by 1988 the overproduction of specialists in relation to the number of specialist positions had become acute. Given the high prestige of specialists—scientists, for instance, were ranked as the most prestigious occupation in a number of Soviet surveys conducted in the 1970s[141]—the relative leveling of workers and specialists' nominal incomes and the shortage of prestigious specialist positions emerged in the 1980s as a significant factor aggravating specialist discontent in late-communist Russia.

Such factors played important roles in the formation of the activist base (*aktiv*) of the Democratic Russia movement, which began to network in the wake of the elections to the first USSR Congress of Peoples Deputies in the spring of 1989. DemRossiia Co-Chair Lev Ponomarev rendered the meaning of the distinctive word aktiv as

> those who at any moment are prepared to abandon their work and rush to fulfill a *DemRossiia* task . . . Perhaps twenty such activists can be found in each district [of Moscow] . . . if you multiply 20 by 30 districts, you get 600. Perhaps one thousand such people are really active, as they say, from the inside. But after all, those people who post leaflets number significantly more. The *aktiv* are people who type leaflets, organize telephone trees, and in turn rely on the *aktiv* in their sub-districts.[77]

At the movement's height in spring 1991, DemRossiia leaders claimed to have a Russia-wide membership—encompassing both the aktiv and its broader grassroots networks—of between 200,000 and 300,000.[142] How to assess such claims? As social movements are informal phenomena by definition, the failure of DemRossiia to establish reliable membership records comes as no surprise. Although no basis thus existed for conducting a representative survey of the movement's total population across the RSFSR, it proved possible to conduct a more limited survey of DemRossiia members still active in May 1992, in Moscow.[143]

The correspondence of this survey's findings with interview reports, journalistic accounts, and representative surveys of pro-Democratic Russia voters in the 1990 republican and local elections illustrates a general tendency toward specialist predominance among DemRossiia's Moscow aktiv.[144] Indeed, nearly 80 percent of survey respondents could be classified as specialists in line with Soviet terminological conventions (see Table 1.1). This compares with about 28 percent of the employed populace of the Russian Republic circa

TABLE 1.1. Occupations of Moscow's DemRossiia aktiv circa May 1992.

Occupation[a]	Number of respondents (% of respondent base)
Specialists	142 (79.8)
Service workers	14 (7.7)
Industrial workers	12 (6.9)
Entrepreneurs[b]	6 (3.4)
Self-employed	1 (.6)
Insufficient data	3 (1.7)

[a] The occupational categories on the original survey questionnaire have been combined for presentation here. The original questionnaire was designed to be of maximal clarity to an average Russian, in consultation with Professor Lev Gudkov of Moscow's All-Russian Center for the Study of Public Opinion.

[b] In line with Russian journalistic conventions of 1989–1991, entrepreneur (*predprinimatel'*) indicates primarily directors of semiautonomous cooperatives (*kooperativniki*), many of which served as fronts for businesses controlled by individuals moving primarily from managerial positions in state enterprises. For data on the predominately managerial-*apparat* origins of Russia's new private sector, see Böröcz and Róna-Tas (1995).

1989, as shown in Table 1.2. Table 1.2 further indicates the low participation of industrial workers in the Moscow section of DemRossiia in comparison with the proportion of industrial workers in Moscow's employed populace. Moreover, about 87 percent of respondents had either participated in or completed a postsecondary degree program, in comparison with about 36 percent of Moscow's employed populace.

Technical specialists—largely engineers—comprised 38 percent of respondents with a specialist profile (54 out of 142), confirming interview reports that engineers working in high-tech enterprises of the military-industrial complex

TABLE 1.2. Specialists and Industrial Workers in Moscow's DemRossiia aktiv circa May 1992.

Specialists as percent of employed population of the Russian Republic (1989) and of survey respondents	
Russian Republic	27.9
Survey respondents	79.8
Percentage of industrial workers: employed population of Moscow (1989) and survey respondents	
Moscow	35.5
Survey respondents	6.9[a]

[a] Figures for the Russian Republic have been adapted from Goskomstat SSSR (1990a: 21–35). Moscow's populace in 1989 was roughly nine million. Moscow's large proportion of both workers and specialists underscores the city's distinctive and atypical social profile. Data on Moscow adapted from Ol'sevich (1990: 208–212) and Goskomstat SSSR (1990b: 46–47).

and personnel employed by applied scientific institutes represented the principal source of DemRossiia activists in Moscow. Nearly 66 percent of respondents were over 40 years, indicating the predominance of middle-age urban professionals in DemRossiia's activist core in the capital, a finding that also corresponds strongly with interview reports. In sum, Moscow's urban democratic movement mobilized a largely specialist and middle-aged activist base against conservative CPSU partocrats bent on preserving the Party's political monopoly.

Pro-democracy rebellion among urban specialists widened the growing fissure between conservatives and reformers in the Party leadership at the end of the Gorbachev period by splitting the mass of rank-and-file members. Party membership in postwar Soviet society was a great boon to those seeking a professional career, and by mid-1989, the number of specialists had grown to more than a third of the CPSU's 19 million members.[145] Considerable numbers of these CPSU specialists would participate in the urban democratic movement between 1989 and 1991: 37 percent of delegates to DemRossiia's October 1990 All-Russia Congress, for instance, were Party members, in comparison with about 7 percent of the populace of the Russian Republic.[146]

The considerable overlap between CPSU members and the democratic movement bears emphasis, as the highly misleading impression that the movement and the Party were external to each other persists. In fact, the January 1990 formation of the Democratic Platform of the CPSU (*Demokraticheskaia platforma KPSS*) on the initiative of sixteen informal pro-democracy "intra-Party clubs" subsequently led a mass walkout of the CPSU. The Democratic Platform soon became a "collective member" of the DemRossiia opposition, effectively splitting the Party.[147]

By April of 1990, conservative partocrats were organizing their own CPSU faction, the Russian Communist Party, against pro-democracy activists.[148] Giulietto Chiesa has called the process of fragmentation and factionalization within the CPSU "the emergence of a multi-party communist system," that is, of multiple "parties" within the Party.[149]

Here, relative economic failure—not economic development per se as in modernization theory—figured prominently in driving shifts among specialist attitudes as they absorbed such ideological, social-psychological and geopolitical dynamics. The following statement by a DemRossiia activist and former Party member alludes to these complex dynamics:

> The reasons the democratic movement exists are rooted first and foremost in the economy, the whole of the democratic movement is connected to the economy. If only we could arrange a normal life and proceed down a normal path of development, then perhaps we could stop being preoccupied with politics.[150]

The phrase "normal life" served as a common euphemism among DemRossiia activists both for the economic abundance perceived in the West and for the future prosperity of an imagined post-communist Russia—if only, as several interviewees remarked, the nomenklatura could be removed from power.

A study of subjective measures of relative satisfaction among recent Soviet émigrés carried out in the 1980s confirms this growing discontent, particularly when compared to a similar study conducted by Inkeles and Bauer in the 1950s.

> What is striking is [our] discovery that those who were disproportionately reap-ing the material benefits of Soviet socialist society in the late 1970s were, in general, the least satisfied members of that society. Those who lived in the most desirable cities, had the highest educational attainment, held the most skilled jobs, earned the top-level incomes, occupied the best housing, and dominated consumption in all markets reported themselves the least satisfied. This is in sharp contrast with the findings of the Harvard Project of the early 1950s, in which those who had been the most successful materially expressed the least dissatisfaction with the Soviet society.[151]

As critics of relative deprivation theories of revolution have argued, the mere identification of grievances and oppositional sentiments prior to mobilization cannot in themselves explain the onset of rebellion.[152] Indeed, the identifica-tion of a spreading pattern of grievances and the growing appeal of "western-izing" political rhetoric among perestroika-era specialists only demonstrates the existence of a latent opposition constituency in the late 1980s.

Here the overproduction of specialists combined with an additional, sym-bolic shift in the *longue durée* of Soviet intellectuals and professionals to ex-acerbate specialist discontent in the 1980s. This symbolic factor linked the stagnation of the Soviet economy to the deteriorating geopolitical position of the Soviet regime.[153] Although Soviet ideology rejected liberal political theory, it embraced the capitalist ideal of open-ended economic growth as an end in itself. By simultaneously propagating the value of open-ended eco-nomic growth, promising ever-higher levels of social welfare, and proclaiming the superiority of socialism as a dynamic economic system, the CPSU explic-itly linked the legitimacy of its domination to the realization of consumerist expectations.[154] By the mid-1980s, the dynamic of rising consumerist expec-tations and protracted economic stagnation thus undermined the party-state's legitimacy, generating a political crisis in the heart of the Soviet elite exac-erbated by the relative economic and technological dynamism of Western powers.

In the urban Russia of the late 1980s, then, the institutional problem of the overproduction of specialists combined with the ideological disintegra-tion of Soviet legitimacy, the demonstration effects of western economic and technological dynamism, and political radicalization in Central Europe, the Baltics, and Caucasus, to politicize specialist discontent in a "westernizing" direction. The pro-democracy mobilization of Russia's urban specialists split the pyramidal structure of the Soviet party-state from the top-down, cleaving the Party into competing factions. Together with a second line of top-down cleavage running from all-Union to local soviets, this "pluralization" of Soviet centralism dramatically accelerated the process of devolution of effective authority—of nascent feudalization—from politburo to regional power centers.

The devolution of authority now undermined party-state institutions, disorienting patterns of trajectory adjustment to which habitus was adapted and through which the regime's institutional power reproduced. In this situation, relatively small groups of activists at both the grass roots (the highly local and institutionally marginal level) and among more "official" groups (those intertwined with openly apparat networks closer to the reproduction of power) began improvising trajectories leading to outright collapse of Soviet institutions. Here, the process of reform accelerated in unexpected ways, as the constellation of forces in Moscow's specialist groups began to supplant conservative partocrats in directing habitus across wide fields of Soviet life. The developmental history of Democratic Russia and its drive to seize control of soviet bodies and declare the sovereignty of particular soviets now stood at the center of unfolding events.

2 The Rise of Democratic Russia

The watershed character of the 1989 campaign distinguished the wave of Gorbachev-encouraged social protest that preceded the specialist rebellion, from the revolutionary situation and the democratic movement that followed in its wake. The 1989 election altered the situation precisely by undermining existing institutional practices in favor of realizing previously *faux* institutional principles, principles whose realization in fact de-institutionalized power arrangements. In this way, the elections precipitated a conjuncture in which party-state divisions, elite conflict, and popular uprisings coincided to create preconditions for revolution identified in comparative-historical sociology.[1] As a result, the trajectory along which hundreds of millions of Soviets had previously adjusted their habitus now unraveled, throwing huge populations into confusion. This situation created opportunities for political entrepreneurs to improvise new methods for reorienting habitus in broad social fields suddenly "decapitated" from centralized CPSU supervision. In urban Russia, such improvisation unfolded around realizations of hitherto fictitious laws, as pro-democracy networks struggled to fashion functional representative bodies out of disintegrating Soviet institutions.

The Moscow Association of Voters

While the Inter-regional Deputies Group remained a highly visible but largely symbolic opposition to the partocracy, the Moscow Association of Voters (*Moskovskoe ob"edinenie izbiratelei*) networked a core of "right-hand men" (*doverennye litsa*) of radical-reform candidates during the spring 1989 campaign together with grassroots democratic activists, creating a movement-organization capable of generating a sustained, frontal challenge to *nomenklatura* hegemony. The Moscow Association of Voters thus realized in practice the vision that animated the Moscow Popular Front in late 1988 and early 1989: the formation of a decentralized movement-organization patterned on the Baltic Popular Fronts.

As we have seen, dissatisfaction with organizers of the Moscow Popular Front's central bodies—and in particular, their insistence on a socialist orientation—drove a number of pro-democracy activists seasoned by their experience in the spring elections to organize the Moscow Association of Voters, on the basis of "voter clubs" that emerged in the 1989 campaign.

> A split between socialists and others was under way in the Popular Front, led by the socialists Kagarlitsky and Maliutin. They had a large group, probably the majority . . . It became clear that people simply weren't going to join the Front in the form it had taken, that it was necessary to create something new in order to unify people.[2]

A behind-the-scenes figure who helped shift Moscow's grassroots opposition away from the Front was long-time Memorial-organizer Lev Ponomarev—a physicist and Academy of Sciences member—who helped link an emerging informal network synchronizing grassroots opposition activity with high-status reform groups emboldened by the specialist rebellion, such as the Moscow Tribune.

During the spring campaign, Ponomarev developed working relations with less ideologically inclined Front organizers such as Vladimir Bokser, Mikhail Shneider, and Civic Dignity's Mikhail Astaf'ev. At the same time, Ponomarev remained centrally networked in the Voter Club of the Academy of Sciences, as one of Andrei Sakharov's right-hand men during the internal struggle over the Academy's allotted USSR Congress of Peoples Deputies' nominations in February and March.[3] This emergent network bridged, on the grassroots side, *neformaly* activists from Memorial (the informal association dedicated to commemorating the victims of Stalinism), precinct-level residents mobilized by voter clubs during the 1989 campaign, and Stankevich's election team, informally headed by Shneider. On the side of prominent organizations, the network linked figures in the Inter-regional Group, the Voter Club of the Academy of Sciences, and the Moscow Tribune—such as Sakharov and his ally Galina Starovoitova—forming a bridge between grass roots and counterelite.[4]

> In this first stage, of course, the principal role belonged to the Voter Club of the Academy of Sciences, and to Ponomarev, and Ponomarev most of all. The rest played a much lesser role . . . And as he had a relationship with the Academy Voter Club . . . he was able to see the contradictions [between this club and Memorial] and overcome them.[5]

USSR Congress of Peoples Deputy and opposition figure Il'ia Zaslavskii—a member of both the Inter-regional Deputies Group and the Moscow Popular Front—gravitated quickly toward the effort to organize the Moscow Association of Voters initiated not long after the First Congress of the Moscow

Popular Front, in late May 1989. Following the close of the first Soviet Congress of Peoples Deputies, he had

> suggested that a deputies' group in itself couldn't solve our problems. We needed to rely on a combination of social and deputies' organizations. This suggestion found little support in the Inter-regional Group. On the other hand, it was supported by [voter clubs that joined together in] the Moscow Association of Voters, one of whose first meetings took place in the reception room of my congressional office. I began to regularly participate in the Association, and it was there that I developed the conception of the necessity of seizing power at the local level.[6]

At its founding conference, held on June 27, 1989, the Moscow Association of Voters brought together the core of organizers who subsequently steered the tactical course of the democratic movement in Russia through the summer of 1991: Ponomarev, Zaslavskii, Leonid Bogdanov, Vladimir Bokser, Mikhail Schneider, and Vera Kriger.[3] The only figure of this core group not a founding member of the Association of Voters' leadership body was Father Gleb Yakunin. An Orthodox priest and former political prisoner, Yakunin became a part of the core several months later, with the formation of the *DemRossiia* voters bloc.[3]

The Moscow Association of Voters' core group formed a working network with key opposition figures perceived widely in Soviet society as "radical reform leaders" in the USSR Congress of Peoples Deputies, a perception stemming directly from their prominence in publicly challenging Gorbachev and the partocracy more generally during the first spring convention of the CDP-USSR. This small group of figures included Boris Yeltsin, Andrei Sakharov, Yuri Afanas'ev, and Sergei Stankevich. At the same time, the Moscow Association linked voter clubs, informal groups, and nascent political parties that formed the backbone of the democratic movement over the next two years. The Moscow Association of Voters thus bridged formal organizations and informal networks, mediating the habitus of each as it formed a parallel "field" to fields whose habitus and institutions remained—at least formally—under CPSU hegemony.

Two hundred thirty-one delegates attended the Moscow Association of Voters' first conference, representing thirty-four voters clubs from thirty Moscow districts—including the Voters Club of the Academy of Sciences—as well as the Coordinating Committee of the Moscow Peoples Front, the Voter Club of Memorial, the voter club Orbit from the Moscow Aviation Institute, and "The Committee of the 19," the informal alliance of grassroots activists from nineteen Moscow-area enterprises that had come together to back the Yeltsin nomination in early 1989.[7]

Considerable tension between Yeltsin and Ponomarev's networks persisted in the Association of Voters' first months. Ponomarev was elected Chairman of the Moscow Association of Voters' First Conference only after he acceded—at the insistence of Yeltsin's 1989 campaign organizers Alexander Muzykantskii, Lev Shemaev, and Sergei Trube—to a temporary appointment. At the Moscow Association of Voters' Second Conference, held on September 16–17, 1989, Muzykantskii, the Deputy Chairman of the Moscow City Executive Committee (*Mosgorizpolkom*), became association chairman, although the Association's organizational work continued to be dominated by the Ponomarev group.[2]

Unlike the leadership of the Moscow Popular Front, the Moscow Association of Voters' newly elected leadership body explicitly rejected any programmatic orientation, instead steering the Association toward support of opposition deputies in the Congress of Peoples Deputies of the USSR and preparations for nominating and electing candidates in the republican and local elections scheduled for the spring of 1990.

> The Moscow Association of Voters' charter determined the Association's principal goals: the regular exchange of information between voter clubs, the coordination and conducting of demonstrations and other mass actions, the aiding of deputies in their work on alternative projects and their popularization among the populace, as well as voter clubs in the provinces. The Association has no program, instead orienting its activity to the Inter-regional Deputies Group.[8]

The Association thus combined a minimalist programmatic stance with cover from the Inter-regional Deputies Group in the CDP-USSR to overcome incessant splits over programs and principles that sank previous attempts to unite the Russian opposition. Indeed, for the next six months, the Association simply deferred on programmatic questions to the moral authority of Sakharov and other Inter-regional Group leaders.

Indeed, misrecognition—in the guise of "antipolitical," but still political, symbolism—remained the great strength of the Moscow Association of Voters.[9] Antipolitical activism in late-communist Russia manifest as a minimalist notion of democracy, combined with fierce criticism of everything that smacked of the *apparat* and the partocracy. This minimalist antipolitics allowed the Association to practically connect a wide range of factions and grassroots activists in a way that the socialist politics of the majority in the Coordinating Committee of the Moscow Popular Front could not.

> Why did I join the democratic movement? Precisely because it is a movement, and not a party, and here I can openly express my opinion . . . Moreover, a democratic movement means it is possible to temporarily suspend one's membership.

Well, and so what? No one here will discuss and disgrace me for it. And then I can decide to change my position [on this or that subject], and still remain active in the movement.[10]

The creation of an antipolitical citywide voter association consolidated voter clubs that otherwise may have reverted to incessant factionalism or dissolved altogether. The devolution from late-Soviet discursive presentations, to the more diffuse speech genres of antipolitics, presented a way to mobilize both within and against the party-state, although it generated negative effects several years later.

In the short run, however, the movement segue proved tactically brilliant, as it opened up many highly localized groups to a broader networking process across urban Russia. On August 3, 1989—straight on the heels of the Moscow Association of Voters' founding conference—the voter club in Moscow's *Matveevskii* subdistrict (*mikroraion*) held its own founding conference (*uchreditel'noe sobranie*).[11] The *Matveevskii klub* organized a grassroots network of several hundred volunteers who helped nominate Yuri Chernichenko to stand for election from Moscow's Gagarin district in the spring of 1989. In August, the club established its own twenty-five-member management board (*upravlenie*), complete with cochairmen and working committees on the popular-front model.

> In the city organization . . . could be found Bokser, Popov, Afanas'ev—all of them were there . . . And then there were the district organizations around Moscow, as many organizations as there were districts [*raiony*]. And finally, in each district there were subdistricts [*mikroraiony*]. And we were one of these subdistricts . . . Here in *Matveevskoe* live 40,000 people, which forms the social base of our voter club.[12]

The patchwork of voter clubs around the city eventually networked through the Moscow Association of Voters and determined the latter's loose and amorphous organizational character. Some clubs, such as the *Marksistskii-proletarskii klub* of Moscow's *Taganskii* district, functioned as nerve centers for networks of opposition cells (*iacheiki*) in enterprises and institutes.[13] Six different institutes and enterprises with pro-democracy cells informally connected through the *Marksistsko-proletarskii* club in late 1989 and 1990 included the State Institute for Nitric Industry, the Karpov Institute of Physical Chemistry, the *Sentez-Belok* (synthetic protein) Scientific-Industrial Organization, the Library of Foreign Literature, a music school, and "a small enterprise that produced bacterial specimens for laboratories."[14] Crucial here stands the social profile of such clubs, who were "on the whole, *intelligenty* with a higher education, though among them were a few representatives of the working class."[15]

The internal life of a number of voter clubs centered primarily around networks of activists in apartment buildings united by their support of particular candidates, such as the large voter club Power of the People (*Narodovlastie*) in the *Cheremushkinskii* district. Internal solidarity in this club revolved around the shared experience of people networked through support of then-USSR Congress of Peoples Deputies' nominee Sergei Stankevich that spring.

> Soon after the election, when Stankevich had become a deputy, 98 people gathered to support him not far from my house, on Trade-Union Street. The more active attended this meeting...those prepared to organize the voter club further and unite voters in our district...Then in May [1989] we held the first organizational meeting [of Power of the People].[16]

Ostensibly a member of the Moscow Popular Front, Power of the People illustrates how grassroots and counterelite networks meshed. The link between the Front's "young socialist"-dominated Coordinating Committee and Power of the People functioned largely through informal, "personalistic" networks symbolically enabled by club members' admiration for Stankevich. "In 1989, we had a mostly accidental relationship to the Moscow Popular Front. Our contacts were determined through Stankevich, since he was our candidate and then our Peoples Deputy [in the USSR Congress] and was at the same time an activist in the Front."[17] When Stankevich distanced himself from "young socialist" activists in the Front leadership and began to work closely with Moscow Association of Voters' patrons in the Inter-regional Group, the tie between the Front and Power of the People gradually dissolved, eclipsed by its affiliation with the Association of Voters.

Between July and December of 1989, the Moscow Association of Voters emerged as the dominant opposition organization in the Russian Republic, serving more and more as de facto coordinator of regional democratic groups scattered across the Russian republic. In addition, this association formed as the parent body for the Republic-wide Inter-regional Association of Voters (*Mezhregional'noe ob"edinenie izbiratelei*), organized by the parent Moscow Association and officially proclaimed at a conference of voter clubs and associations from around the RSFSR held on December 2–3, 1989, one of Sakharov's last public appearances.[8] The Association of Voters thus realized the aspiration to create a republic-wide umbrella for grassroots opposition groups in Russia, an aspiration repeatedly frustrated in 1988 and early 1989.[18]

Moscow Association of Voters' activists subsequently emerged as the nucleus of grassroots supporters of DemRossiia in Moscow in 1990–1991. "Prior to the First Congress of Democratic Russia [in October 1990], the main functions of the mass movement in Moscow were in fact carried out by the Moscow

Association of Voters."[19] Not formalized as such until spring 1991, the procla-
mation of Democratic Russia–Moscow as a separate organizational structure
distinct from DemRossiia's republican leadership bodies represented, to a
large degree, simply a formal exercise in renaming the Moscow Association
of Voters. Indeed, before the spring 1991 creation of DemRossiia-Moscow
as a distinct local branch (*otdelenie*), the movement in the city remained synonymous both with the republican bodies of the movement headquartered in
Moscow, and with grassroots activists networked through the Association of
Voters in the capital. "I personally perceive *DemRossiia* as a simple and natural
continuation of the Moscow Association of Voters. And, in my opinion, the
majority [of activists] perceive it this way."[20]

Although the Moscow Association's loose organizational form and minimalist program assuaged the wariness felt toward parties and *apparati* on the
part of many activists mobilized by the 1989 election campaign, it greatly
vexed many of the leaders and members of the political clubs and opposition
groups associated with the *neformalitet*. A figure in the Moscow district ecological association *Brateevo*—which first appeared in 1988—reveals the suspicion
of those who felt themselves suddenly bypassed by the rise of the Moscow
Association:

> People who joined the Moscow Association of Voters were unknown in *neformaly*
> circles, and I was oriented to opinion in the *neformaly*. That is, the voter clubs
> arose out of nowhere and immediately occupied the leading position, and among
> them quickly appeared an *apparat*. They—Bokser, Kriger and so on—began
> playing with the most elementary of slogans, which put me on guard. If these
> people had previously passed through some sort of grouping, such as Democratic
> Perestroika . . . then I could have made inquiries. But there wasn't anybody who
> knew anything about them . . . Nobody knew them, and it turns out that they're all
> of the sudden the leadership! The Moscow Association of Voters quickly created
> a leading center and thus showed its aspiration to lead the whole democratic
> movement in Moscow. This simply repelled me.[21]

Stikhiinskii's mention of an apparat is particularly relevant here, as he clearly
means the core of Moscow Association organizers drawn from the election
teams (*izbiratel'nye kommandy*) that served as the networking bridge between
particular candidates during the spring 1989 elections and individual voter
clubs that nominated them. Being organized on the basis of right-hand men
of individual candidates on a personal basis, the whole dynamic of such teams
repelled the syndicalist leanings of "young socialists" in the neformalitet.[22]
Ill-defined "liberals" would in fact dominate networking in the democratic
movement from this point forward.

Origins of the Democratic Russia Voters' Bloc

In late-spring 1989, revolutionary change in Central Europe augmented shifts from "young socialists" to minimalist "liberalism" as Moscow specialists mobilized in parallel bodies. At the same time, transnational demonstration effects accelerated institutional disintegration at the top of the Soviet party-state as the Polish Solidarity movement won elections based on "round-table" negotiations. Polish developments in turn pushed the situation rapidly ahead across both Central European countries and in regions of the Soviet Union itself, precipitating demonstration effects across the region and reorienting Moscow's nascent democratic movement—forming in the Moscow Association of Voters—in an openly defiant direction.

As summer moved toward fall, the disintegration of regimes in Central Europe accelerated. The mass exodus of East Germans through Hungary deepened changes across the Soviet bloc, culminating in the breach of the Berlin wall on November 9 and revolution in Czechoslovakia two weeks later, events that completely overshadowed the November 7 anniversary of the Bolshevik seizure of power. Indeed, protests against "the Bolshevik regime" observed in several Soviet cities on November 7 heightened the ignominy of a small turnout for the official Revolution Day parade.[23] By the time of the convening of the Second USSR Congress of Peoples Deputies on December 12, 1989, the feeling of revolutionary change was palpable in the Soviet capital, a sense heightened by Sakharov's death on December 15 and the violent overthrow of Nicolae Ceausescu's regime in Romania a fortnight later.

The emergence of a revolutionary situation in the second half of 1989 played into the hands of the organizers of the Moscow Association of Voters and their strategy to "seize power at the local level" in the upcoming spring elections.[6] The Association suddenly needed to put together a united slate of opposition candidates and organize election teams. Overcoming hurdles rightist figures in the party-state began throwing in the path of would-be opposition nominees meant turning the experience garnered in the spring campaigns to new uses. Such were the strategic considerations that drove the formation of the DemRossiia voter bloc.

The radicalization of the Moscow Party Club (*Moskovskii partiinyi klub*)— the midwife of what soon became the Democratic Platform of the Soviet Communist Party—and the expulsion of its Leninist minority in November 1989 gave a strong impetus to the convergence of a coalition capable of challenging the CPSU in the upcoming elections. The Moscow Party Club arose among CPSU specialists networked with the Inter-Club Party Group (*Mezhklubnaia partiinaia gruppa*). Following the election of Inter-Club member

Sergei Stankevich to the CPD-USSR in the spring 1989 elections, the Inter-Club Party Group split in May 1989 into a number of factions, the most radical of which formed the Moscow Party Club, soon known as the Communists for Perestroika.[24] The Moscow Party Club emulated its most prominent member, Stankevich, by joining the Moscow Popular Front in late spring 1989. Over the summer, its membership drifted toward advocacy of a multiparty system (*multipartiinost'*), de-statization of most property (*razgosudarstvlenie*), and loose alignment with the Moscow Association of Voters and the radical wing of the Inter-regional Deputies Group.

In the fall, Sergei Stankevich emerged as a particularly important organizational link between nonparty and party democratic groupings. Stankevich—de facto leader of the *Narodovlastie* voters club, member of the Inter-regional Deputies Group, and a principal figure in the radical wing of the Moscow Party Club—was perfectly positioned to mediate between the counterelite in the USSR Congress, the core of organizers in the Moscow Association of Voters, and the emerging left wing of young pro-democracy reformers in the CPSU. During the organizing of the DemRossiia voters bloc,

> Stankevich played a very important role. The most important person by this time, enjoying a huge popularity [due to his activity in the Congress of Peoples Deputies] . . . Stankevich had mobility. He responded to various inquiries . . . gave interviews on the run, and on the whole tried to make his presence felt everywhere.[5]

The overlapping leadership of the Moscow Party Club and the Inter-regional Deputies Group set the political tone of the DemRossiia voters bloc. Indeed, after Arkadii Murashev replaced Sakharov as the body's fifth co-chairman following the latter's death, the Inter-regional Group's four Russian co-chairmen were *all* Communist Party members. The large number of prominent Party reformers emerging in the leadership of the DemRossiia bloc at this time did not sit well with many former dissidents and more radical veterans of the neformalitet.

> It seems to me, people created *DemRossiia* from that segment of the middle class which preferred a liberal variant of communist politics . . . [T]hese people never faced the brutal alternative of either having to participate in the totalitarian regime or having to resist it . . . In general, many people who had been part of the communist elite in previous years could be found among *DemRossiia* activists.[25]

In the second half of 1989, leaders of various proto-party sects—small party grouplets outside the proliferation of grouplets in the CPSU—began an often mercurial relationship with the consolidating force of the Moscow Association of Voters. For the next two years, proto-parties played at times important roles in the development of DemRossiia. The majority in the most militant of groups, however—the Democratic Union—came out against participating in the 1990 elections. This group soon split into "rejectionist" and "pragmatic" factions. Although Victor Kuzin, leader of the Democratic Union pragmatists, gained election to the *Mossovet* in 1990, the group's salad days as an opposition force were over.[26]

With the growing influence of the Moscow Association of Voters and the concomitant drift of party radicals toward it, intelligenty now faced a choice: either work for the Yeltsin-centered counterelite and its team of organizers in the Association, or remain marginalized in movement networking. A number of such intelligenty chose the second path. This is how the growing withdrawal of Memorial from political activity began, with more political *Memorialtsev* going into Democratic Russia, while the rest concentrated on human rights oriented work in the strict sense of the term.[27]

Preliminary organizing for what would become the DemRossiia voters bloc in January 1990 began with the work of an "electoral committee," Elections-90 (*Vybory-90*), which first met on September 29, 1989, in Moscow at the initiative of the Moscow Association of Voters. The formation of this electoral committee brought together the Association's organizational leadership and a round table (*kruglyi stol*) of neformaly groups, ranging from the Confederation of Anarcho-Syndicalists to Democratic Perestroika. Such groups had been meeting since August to discuss preparations for running opposition candidates in the upcoming elections. Many voluntary associations and opposition networks quickly threw their support behind Elections-90—from Memorial to the Moscow Tribune to the Voters Club of the Academy of Sciences—creating a bridge between reform communists in the Moscow Party Club like Stankevich, and noncommunist democrats grouped around Ponomarev and the nascent core of the Moscow Association of Voters.[28]

Meanwhile, the Inter-regional Group in the USSR Congress of Peoples Deputies tried to set up an election fund to aid opposition candidates in the upcoming spring campaign, but this was forbidden by the Soviet government.[29] Moscow Association of Voters and Elections-90 organizers took up this project by creating the Commonwealth Social Fund (*Obshchestvennyi fund sodruzhestva*) in September. *Sodruzhestvo* quickly printed an informal voters bulletin, Voice of the Voter (*Golos izbiratelia*), and an unregistered newssheet, Position (*Positsiia*). Former "Committee of the 19" organizers and Yeltsin associates edited both of these *samizdat* publications—Voice of the Voter by Lev Shemaev and Position by Sergei Trube.[30] Together, these sheets emerged as important opposition weapons during the 1990 campaign.[31]

The limitations of the Inter-regional Group as a symbolic form of opposition, and the failures of previous attempts to create a united democratic front, guided the work of the organizers of Elections-90. "The insufficiencies [of the Inter-regional Group] sprang from the fact its members were only very weakly connected with each other... Thus we understood that it would be much better if people could become acquainted before hand and fashion a common electoral platform for the next elections."[3] As of November 1989, this "common platform" consisted merely of agreement on the basic slogans for the campaign, "For freedom and democracy!" and "From poverty to well-being!"[32]

In early November, the formation of Elections-90, the disintegration of East Germany, and the continued restlessness of workers—and particularly miners—all combined to disrupt the habitus of conservative partocrats. Wild-cat strikes in the Vorkuta coal mines above the arctic circle in central Siberia proved particularly troublesome, as the Vorkuta City Strike Committee in early November threatened a general miners strike and issued a series of demands closely echoing the thinking of Inter-regional Group radicals and the Elections-90 network, such as the abolition of Article 6 of the Soviet Constitution enshrining "the leading role of the Party," and the direct election of executive posts such as chairmen of Supreme Soviets.[33] Pro-democracy activists among regional workers often faced much higher levels of repression, such as the murder on October 18 of a strike committee organizer in the Donbass region who actively publicized the corruption of local *nomenklaturshchiki*.[34]

Between November and January, the need to work out a broader platform for a united opposition slate and to develop working organizational ties between potential candidates represented the principal tasks of Elections-90.[35] The first task fell to an editorial commission (*redaktsionniia komissiia*) composed of various committee members who hoped to be nominated in the spring, as well as a number of Moscow Association of Voters' organizers. Victor Sheinis, a historian of "the 60ers" (*shestidesiatniki*) generation and member of three predecessor associations of the democratic movement—Democratic Perestroika, the Moscow Tribune, and the Voters Club of the Academy of Science—was chosen to chair the commission and set to work on the text that became the founding statement of DemRossiia.[36]

Moscow Association of Voters' organizers, working closely with Inter-regional Group figures, steered the second task of coordinating opposition candidacies both in Moscow and around the RSFSR.[2] In December, the original Elections-90 committee fell apart, largely due to neformaly fear of an Association of Voters' "takeover." During an interview, Il'ia Zaslavskii of the

Association indirectly confirmed neformaly perceptions of an apparat managing the strategic framework for the upcoming opposition campaign:

> At that time, the Moscow Association of Voters was the only real, organized, effective force resisting the CPSU, while hiding its ideological profile: we were, as they say, mere voters. Nevertheless, when a dubious character would appear, saying "I'm a voter, I want to join you," this character was quickly screened out, and with sufficient strictness.[6]

Such screening processes indicate the extent of movement "quasi-centralization" among trajectory improvisers coordinating network expansion across Russia that fall in Moscow. Indeed, in the following weeks, Moscow Association organizers and Inter-regional Group figures worked intensely to network Elections-90 clones springing up across the RSFSR. On January 4, in Moscow's Science House (*Dom uchenykh*), a fraction of Moscow's original Elections-90 committee allied with the core group formed a new working committee under the same name. The immediate predecessor and direct organizer of the DemRossiia bloc, this network gained momentum at a conference of opposition organizations held in Moscow on January 10–11, when Sheinis' draft received tentative approval.[37]

By this time, the label Democratic Russia supplanted Elections-90 in Moscow:

> Today you hear many differing versions concerning the origin of the name "Democratic Russia". I'll give you my version. On December 10th, the day dedicated [by the United Nations] to the defense of human rights, there was a rally at VDNKh [an exhibition in north Moscow]. And we were writing a statement, which Bokser was supposed to read as a resolution approved by the rally. As things turned out, in the end he called for a vote by the rally as to what the voter bloc ought to be called . . . Bokser stood on the stand and was handed a list with 10 possible names. As he read the resolution to the meeting, he stumbled just as he read "Democratic Russia", and the crowd shouted "Democratic Russia"! I believe *DemRossiia*'s label was born at precisely that moment.[19]

Straight on the heels of the January 2 deadline for filing nomination protocols, opposition slates from around the RSFSR began linking themselves publicly to the nascent DemRossiia bloc in Moscow. Regional opposition slates which allied themselves with DemRossiia in Moscow before the election arose, among other places, in Iuzhno-Sakhalinsk, Leningrad, Nizhnevartovsk, Petropavlovsko-Kamchatskii, Riazan', Sakhalin, Sverdlovsk, and Yaroslavl.[38]

In the meantime, the death of Sakharov unexpectedly strengthened the strategic position of the emerging opposition. Sakharov's death came three days after the opening of the Second USSR Congress of Peoples Deputies, on December 12, 1989. In the days just prior to Sakharov's death, Gorbachev resisted fundamental reforms, then belittled the passing of the Academy of Science's member.[39] In revolutionary situations, defining moments shape the chaotic procession of developments. Sakharov's death created a symbolic center for the democratic movement, while signaling the end of the General Secretary's role as leader of *perestroika*.

In the last week of his life, Sakharov drafted a constitution for a postcommunist federation of former Soviet republics.[40] While the death of the Soviet Union's most renowned champion of human rights created a universal symbol for the opposition, Sakharov's constitution became an instant programmatic focus for the Elections-90 project. Prominent democrats in Moscow quickly rallied around the draft as a framework suitable for a diverse slate of opposition candidates. Gorbachev, in contrast, would scramble for months to rebuild his damaged prestige among radicalizing reformers, maintain a rapidly shrinking center in a polarizing political arena and regain the initiative he had lost to Sakharov's proposed constitution and the direction this proposal had given to a now unifying opposition.

A conference of prospective candidates held in Moscow's Palace of Youth officially proclaimed the Democratic Russia voter bloc (*Izbiratel'nyi blok Demokraticheskoi Rossii*) on January 21 and 22, 1990. Sheinis's text was read aloud at this conference and approved from the floor:

> Our tomorrow to a great extent depends on the form that both the highest organ of state power in Russia and the local soviets will take. In order to ensure that new, courageous, competent and responsible people will enter the soviets, the democratic forces of society need a clear political orientation and a general platform ... The programmatic documents of the Inter-regional Deputies Group, the humanitarian ideas of our great contemporary, ANDREI DIMITRIEVICH SAKHAROV [capitalized in original], and his Decree on Power and proposed draft for a new Soviet constitution will determine the general political orientation of our wide union ... [A]ll candidates, sharing the basic tenets of this program, [are invited] to join the Democratic Russia voters bloc.[41]

DemRossiia's founding statement mirrored the thinking of radicals in the Inter-regional Deputies Group.

> We were tied to the Inter-regional Group and went to their meetings, participating and agonizing over them ... I ended up as chairman of the editorial commission ... and wrote the text on the basis of many, many suggestions.[36]

The founding declarations of three key opposition groups—Inter-regional Group radicals, the organizers of the CPSU's Democratic Platform, and the initial incarnation of Democratic Russia—mirrors the closeness of thinking between all three groups. In one of its initial pronouncements, the Inter-regional Group emphasized that the

> point where unanimity begins is that point where a real parliament ends and fiction starts . . . What is needed are alternative points of views, different ways of thinking. We need organizational forms in order to have a possibility to stand-up for such points of view.[42]

From the moment of its formation, DemRossiia served as the hub of the opposition in Moscow. The opposition showed its new-found political clout on February 4, 1990, when—in the largest demonstration seen in Russia since 1917—a quarter of a million Muscovites turned out to demand the repeal of Article 6, that article enshrining "the leading role of the Party" through constitutional sanctions specifying a one-party regime centered on the CPSU.

Organized by the Moscow Association of Voters, almost the entire spectrum of active pro-democracy associations in the capital city supported the February 4 demonstration.[43] The Moscow Association of Voters-DemRossiia networks further demonstrated their clout in follow-up demonstrations called in cities around the RSFSR for February 25. Protests were held in Khabarovsk, Kharkov, Krasnodar, Leningrad, Orel, Saratov, Stavropol', Sverdlovsk, Yaroslavl, and a number of other Russian cities. Despite an official ban, freezing cold, and a large deployment of police on the streets, 100,000 turned out in Moscow on the 25th. Moreover, allied movements in other Union republics staged simultaneous demonstrations in many non-Russian cities.[44]

Several interviewees stressed the psychological importance of the demonstrations on the 4th and 25th in emboldening opposition activists and supporters alike to take to the streets.

> Critical moments [for the democratic movement] were . . . these two [February] demonstrations, which frightened us very much. We were scared we'd be fired on. But nothing of the sort happened.[45]

The February 25th demonstration

> was forbidden by the authorities. As we marched along the Garden Ring [a broad circle of streets that rings central Moscow], people became frightened and dropped out. But the march was a form of training, which showed that in a dangerous situation we could demonstrate and still be certain that nothing would happen. We were afraid, but no shots were fired![3]

The mass protests of February 1990 were signal events in the developmental history of Russia's most recent political revolution. Particularly significant stood the demonstration on February 4, as it took place on the eve of a crucial plenum of the CPSU's Central Committee of the Soviet Communist Party. Three days later, the Central Committee—reluctantly following a sudden shift to the left on the part of the General Secretary—relented to the opposition's demands and reconciled itself in principle to the idea of a multiparty system. Article 6 of the Soviet Constitution—enshrining the party as "the leading force of Soviet society"—was to be repealed. The abolition of the CPSU's political monopoly finally passed into law on March 13 at the extraordinary (*vneocherednoi*) Third USSR Congress of Peoples Deputies, hastily convened by Gorbachev after his February 5 political about-face.[46] The organizers of the February demonstrations— the Moscow Association of Voters, its grassroots network of voter clubs, and the candidates and counterelite patrons grouped in the DemRossiia bloc—reaped the political fruit of this measure, which profoundly deepened institutional disintegration of the party-state.

The DemRossiia Voters Bloc and the Spring 1990 Elections

Near the end of October 1989, the Russian (RSFSR) Supreme Soviet scheduled elections to republican and local soviets for March 4, 1990. Parallel to Moscow's apportionment of seats for the USSR Congress of Peoples Deputies, the party-state apportioned the capital's seats for the new RSFSR Congress of Peoples Deputies along both federal and district-territorial lines, with one federal seat reserved for Moscow as a whole and thirty-three seats reserved for each district.[47] Citywide seats in the new Mossovet were reduced from the previous 800 to 498. Two sublevels of soviets formally subordinated to the Mossovet would also be elected: 33 district-level soviets (*raiony sovety*) and 157 subdistrict (*mikroraiony*) soviets. The jurisdictions of the subdistrict soviets were pieced together out of chunks of Moscow's 498 precinct-level voting districts (*uchastki*).

The new RSFSR Election Law abolished the practice of reserving seats for social organizations established in the 1989 all-Union elections. Although enterprises and other associations could still nominate candidates, such organizations needed to be certified as voter clubs in their own right for such nominations to stand. As in 1989, nominees were still required to pass through a voter assembly (*izbiratel'noe sobranie*) and then be vetted by appropriate election committees before being certified, although the minimum size of a voter assembly was considerably smaller for subdistrict candidacies than for republic-level and citywide candidacies (150 versus 500).

The emerging patchwork of Soviet election laws allowed sitting deputies in one soviet to simultaneously run for seats in other soviets, although this was forbidden for holders of administrative posts, such as chairmen of executive city committees (*gorizpolkomy*). This caveat would have an enormous impact on the subsequent development of Russia's democratic movement, as many prominent leaders of the Inter-regional Group in the USSR Congress entered the 1990 campaign for local and republican seats. Gavriil Popov and Sergei Stankevich ran for seats in the Mossovet, Il'ia Zaslavskii for a seat in Moscow's *Oktiabr'skii* district soviet, and Galina Starovoitova and Yeltsin for seats in the new CPD-RSFSR. Yeltsin now sought a seat, not in Moscow, but in Sverdlovsk, where he had been a party leader in the 1970s and early 1980s and enjoyed popular support.

The official certification of many opposition nominees by Moscow's city-wide and district-level election committees was secured with considerably less difficulty than in the previous year. Electoral commissions setup by the apparat to screen candidates disqualified only 531 of 3,793—14 percent—of nominees for seats in the Mossovet or city district soviets (*raionye sovety*) registered by the January 2 deadline, a considerably lower percentage than excluded the previous year, during the all-Union elections.[48] In fact, the Moscow Association of Voters managed to place supporters, such as the former Committee of the 19 organizer and then Association of Voters' Chair Alexander Muzykantskii, on both citywide and district-level elections committees.[49]

DemRossiia's inheritance of organization and experience from the 1989 nomination struggle figured here. On the basis of the previous campaign, for instance, the Association of Voters' core discerned how much easier securing nominations at work places than at neighborhood-level voter assemblies proved. Indeed, enterprises and institutes nominated the bulk of Democratic Russia's Moscow candidates in 1990.[2] Such aspects underscored the professionalized habitus characteristic of the city's democratic opposition.

Additionally, the prestige and media access of DemRossiia's de facto leaders in the Inter-regional Deputies Group aided slates of lesser-known nominees.

> Everything was much simpler [than in 1989], because by that time Yeltsin was already a deputy. Everyone knew him very well. People watched television, and they knew everybody, who was our deputy and who wasn't.[50]

In this way, the local and regional stratification of audiences combined with the extraordinary coverage of the spring meetings of the USSR Congress of Peoples Deputies to vault a few to positions of Russia-wide authority in democratic movement networks.[51] Yeltsin thus found himself with the widest name recognition in the Russian Republic among democratic figures, unencumbered by any official organizational ties to the rising DemRossiia movement whose networks so directly centered on his personal prestige. Although Yeltsin soon depended on the movement to mobilize popular support in the big cities, his "official" position above all movements encouraged misrecognition of his interventions within DemRossiia by obscuring them.

As the 1990 campaign got underway, strategists found themselves facing a dilemma: several districts nominated and certified multiple democratic candidates, auguring a split opposition vote and an apparat victory. Indeed, DemRossiia formed too late for the Moscow Association of Voters' core to steer the nomination processes among grassroots assemblies and at work places in a unifying direction.

> In areas where, thanks to confusion and chaos [*nerazberikhi*], several democratic candidates ended-up running against each other, [democratic] candidates began to clash and fight among themselves. And these fights were, God forgive, very sharp. This was the case in the *Oktiabr'skii raion*, where . . . there were seven or eight [such] candidates.[6]

The core group scrambled to remedy the situation, settling on creation of preapproved lists of DemRossiia candidates signed by Yeltsin and a second opposition leader particularly popular in the target district, such as Popov or Stankevich.

> How did we decide on a strategy? We decided to create a bloc of candidates. We then wrote a leaflet, and if a person's name was signed at the bottom, then he almost automatically became a candidate of the *DemRossiia* bloc . . . Thus was formed the bloc of candidates . . . and a sort of general staff [*shtab bloka*]. Yeltsin, Popov and a whole series of other well-known individuals and Voter Association activists made up this staff . . . We met a number of times in Yeltsin's office to review the balance of forces, to discuss which candidates should stand in which districts. Here and there a candidate was removed from one district and shifted to another—this was the sort of work we did.[50]

The extent to which a nominally pro-democracy candidate's fate hinged on the DemRossiia list only became clear in the election's aftermath. If

> you were an official Democratic Russia nominee, it was practically sufficient for being elected a deputy. People voted as they do in India, you know, where a lotus is drawn, and next to it is written "Vote for the lotus!" It was exactly the same here: "Vote for *DemRossiia!*" And everyone did.[15]

Following the vote, the ways the informal core made decisions placing figures on the official campaign list caused considerable friction between the Moscow Association of Voter's organizational leadership, on the one hand, and neformaly activists, volunteers in voter clubs, and candidates officially registered by voting commissions but nevertheless frozen out from above, on the other. Complaints about the "Association of Voters' apparat" or the

"DemRossiia apparat" echoed among oppositionists who felt unfair treatment from campaign organizers.

> Once the campaign itself was over, and several hundred people had been left aside—that is, left off the *DemRossiia* list of candidates—people called every day to tell me what a bastard I was, what a scoundrel, and lots of other things. So many curses hurled my way, I can't remember them all. It was the very worst business, to be in a situation where so many felt intense displeasure with you. You became an enemy of quite a few people.[2]

The final word in selecting who got on the DemRossiia list and who would be excluded fell to Yeltsin and Gavriil Popov, although the Moscow Association of Voters' core took the heat for their—particularly Yeltsin's—decisions. In interviews, several organizers described having to take the fall for counterelite decisions at postelection meetings of local voter clubs, but on this point alone insisted their names remain anonymous.

Such shifting of responsibility from Yeltsin engendered misrecognition among grassroots activists. The semiofficial (*ofitsioznyi*) paper *Panorama* accused Popov and Stankevich of altering candidate lists during the 1990 campaign, leading to strained relations between the paper and the postelection Mossovet and its new Chairman, Popov.[52] But Yeltsin retained, for the time being, a public image of being above the fray.

Although Moscow Association of Voter's semiofficial newssheet Position (*Pozitsiia*) published a complete list of DemRossiia-approved candidates to the Mossovet shortly before the election, leaflets and door-to-door agitation served as DemRossiia's principal means of publicizing its campaign lists because of the continuing difficulty activists faced in getting their announcements published in the print media.[53] Beyond occasional descriptive pieces in more liberal publications, the campaign faced a near blockade when it came to getting candidate lists into established papers. This situation mirrored that of apparat-assigned city administrators, who generally declined to help publicize information on opposition candidates. "In the district soviets, they refused to publish [DemRossiia lists], saying 'This isn't important, go do as you like'."[54]

For such reasons, organizers of the Moscow campaign fell back on their network of volunteers in the citywide alignment of voter clubs as they strove to convey to local voters exactly who received the official nod by DemRossiia's leadership. The DemRossiia campaign concentrated on distributing leaflets with pictures of candidates taking advantage of the wooden style of apparat nominees not accustomed to public debate or political showmanship. Candidates and volunteers distributed such flyers in violation of election regulations, by organizing activist teams to stuff mailboxes, paste flyers in pedestrian walkways under streets (*perekhody*), agitate in front of metro stations, and the like. The material means for such activities flowed in part through aid from figures well placed to use automobiles, xerox machines, and so forth; and in part by the ability of grassroots networks to surreptitiously access mimeographs and copy machines at work places.[55]

> We agreed that pickets were needed at metro stations, at certain pedestrian underpasses [*perekhody*], and in general, where and when it was necessary to appear. The next day I would go there and start the work. And this is how everything was done. Whoever was able stood and agitated, a person with a talent for sketching made big posters, the person who had access at work to copying technology printed leaflets.[56]

The DemRossiia voter bloc elected a substantial number of deputies to the Russian Congress of Peoples Deputies, and won outright majorities in the Moscow and Leningrad city soviets. Although only 116 candidates to the RSFSR Congress of Peoples Deputies adopted the DemRossiia platform in January, after the elections over 200 deputies attended a DemRossiia conference in Moscow on March 31.[57] The overwhelming majority of such deputies were elected from big cities: DemRossiia candidates, for instance, won a remarkable 55 of Moscow's 65 seats in the Russian Congress, and 291 of 486 seats in the Mossovet.[58] In Leningrad, only 20 percent of new *Lensovet* deputies favored the CPSU's official program.[59]

The partocracy found itself again outflanked. Following the election, talk about "illegal provocations" and "widespread violations of Soviet laws" on the part of the opposition during the campaign appeared in the press.[60] Such reactions demonstrated that much of the partocracy remained simply incapable of comprehending competitive politics, let alone adapt their political style to altered circumstances.[61]

The Yeltsin counterelite utilized the partocracy's inability to adjust their habitus to competitive politics in driving wedges between sections of the broader nomenklatura and apparat. The "divide and rule" strategy emerging around Yeltsin began to generate effects in the new RSFSR Congress of Peoples Deputies.

Immediately following the March elections, allied groups of new liberal deputies in the RSFSR Congress who joined local voter blocs as candidates started to refer to themselves collectively, as aligned with Democratic Russia. In a similar fashion, many of the activists that helped nominate candidates in the Leningrad voters bloc—Democratic Change-90—would later form the Leningrad section of DemRossiia.[62]

Two striking factors energized Democratic Russia's 1990 campaign. First, the whole tenor of the campaign reflected the Association of Voters' core-driven meshing of counterelite mobilization from above, and grassroots mobilization from below. At this point, the Yeltsin-centered counterelite in the USSR Congress shifted to the new RSFSR Congress and consolidated de facto steering of the democratic movement.

Second, the prominence of Moscow and the circle of top Moscow Association of Voters' organizers stands out in the formation of a republic-wide opposition umbrella. Yeltsin remained the charismatic center around which opposition mobilization turned for the next eighteen months, stepping into the vacuum created by Sakharov's death and Gorbachev's eclipse as leader of perestroika. And the Association of Voters' core retained its ability to steer the opposition's most important strategic moves during this period, much to the frustration of others to displace it. Reservations or not, the rapid pace of events drove democratic specialists behind the Yeltsin bandwagon.

Dual Power in Russia, 1990

Gorbachev's sudden assent to the abolition of Article 6 on March 13, 1990, raised hopes the Soviet leader would choose a bolder reform course over the preservation of the party-state as an end in itself. Following the sweeping gains made by the DemRossiia bloc in the spring 1990 elections, Gorbachev embarked on a series of erratic and contradictory policy initiatives, seeming to ally the center with parts of the Russian opposition while at the same time taking a harder stance toward the Baltic republics and "extremist so-called democrats." The key to this balancing act was the creation of a new, upgraded Soviet presidency during the extraordinary (*vneocherednoi*) Third Congress of Peoples Deputies of the USSR, hastily convened on March 12, 1990, just eleven days after DemRossiia's success in the first round of the local and republican elections.

Called to formally rescind Article 6 and reform the executive structure of Soviet government, Gorbachev hoped to use the Third CPD-USSR both to retake the reform initiative from the democratic opposition and to keep conservative partocrats on the defensive. This strategy worked for a short while, as discussion of the upgraded presidency dominated the official media for the next several weeks.[63] With the exception of the first president, who would be chosen by the Third CPD-USSR, the Soviet president would be directly elected by secret ballot, serve a five-year term and be limited to two terms in office.[64] The Congress elected Gorbachev to the new post on March 15 by a majority of only 59.2 percent.[65]

The new Soviet presidency weakened the position of the politburo as the chief operational base for high-level partocrats. Gorbachev's positional shift acknowledged the declining prestige of the CPSU, falling steadily since March 1989 and reinforced now by open institutional disintegration of the party-state. Random sample polls conducted by the All-Union Center for the Study of Public Opinion showed that between March 1989 and March 1990, the percentage of respondents trusting the CPSU fell from 38 to 16 percent.[66]

Dismayed by the collapse of Soviet-bloc regimes in Central and South-Eastern Europe and the continuing decline of the CPSU, the pro-Soviet right began to organize its own power structures independent of the polit-buro and Central Committee in late 1989 and early 1990. In October 1989, Ivan Polozkov, lifelong apparatchik, First Secretary of the CPSU in the Krasnodar region, and emerging leader of right-wing Russian communists, openly attacked Gorbachev for "completely shutting down the Central Committee apparatus."[67] So was born the apparat-led initiative to create a Russian Communist Party as a distinct organization within the CPSU, ostensibly to redress the fact that only the RSFSR lacked its own republican section.[68]

From the moment he assumed the powers of the enhanced Soviet presidency through the early fall of 1990, Gorbachev proved incapable of breaking out of the pattern of inconsistently tacking between openings to the democratic opposition and comprises with the pro-Soviet right.[69] At the heart of this process stood accelerating feudalization. The nascent tendencies toward feudalization in the Brezhnev period now accelerated relentlessly, a process triggered by the institutional disintegration of partocratic power at the apex of the party-state's "virtual federalism" and symbolized by Gorbachev's assumption of new presidential powers to compensate for the deterioration of authority in the party General Secretary's apparatus. Spreading rapidly along national and ethnic lines, feudalization as a process remained opaque to rightist, Gorbachevian and many opposition-democratic networks alike, marking their habitus as disposed to the geographic and ethnic center of the multinational Soviet imperium.[70] Indeed, this process would not even be partially comprehended within many Russian elite and specialist circles until much later in the 1990s.

In 1990, however, federal and ethnic mobilization across the Union remained subordinate in the Soviet capital to immediate political tactics consuming the various splinters of erstwhile Russian leadership. Here, the General Secretary's wavering between March and September derailed the opposition from carrying-through the process of unification begun earlier with the formation of Democratic Russia. During this period, various levels and associations of the democratic movement often found themselves operating independently of one another as different political entrepreneurs and fractions groped for a strategy and argued over tactics in an unstable political environment further complicated by Gorbachev's policy zigzags. But the opposition had gained a name: DemRossiia.

The formal announcement of the creation of a DemRossiia faction in the new Russian Congress of Peoples Deputies—scheduled to open on May 16, 1990—came at a conference of radical-reform deputies held in Moscow on April 14.[71] A series of preliminary meetings organized by Moscow-based deputies-elect laid the groundwork for this founding conference soon after the first-round of the March elections, on the basis of campaign networks.[36] Following the second-round of voting on March 18, participation in such meetings expanded to include deputies-elect from other regions.

A handful of double deputies (*dvazhdy deputaty*) elected to seats in more than one soviet shaped the developmental course of the democratic movement between March 1990 and August 1991. Five such deputies seated in both the USSR and the RSFSR Congresses of Peoples Deputies—Boris Yeltsin, Yuri Afanas'ev, Galina Starovoitova, Nikolai Travkin, and Nikolai Vorontsov—emerged as key organizers of meetings that prepared the ground for the DemRossiia legislative bloc. Together with an RSFSR deputy-elect from Leningrad, Victor Dmitriev, and former Moscow Association of Voters Chairman and now RSFSR deputy-elect Lev Ponomarev, these five shaped the initial political profile of the DemRossiia legislative fraction.[72]

By the April 14, 1990, gathering of pro-democracy RSFSR Congress deputies-elect, the strategy of the future Democratic Russia legislative bloc had emerged.

> We began by developing our general program for the First Congress...
> Then...we created several commissions on different topics: strategy and tactics, economics, and so on. In all, we had only a month to get ready, from April until the middle of May, but in the end we outflanked the communists.[3]

The election of Boris Yeltsin as Chairman of the reconstructed Russian Supreme Soviet emerged as the most immediate goal set by DemRossiia parliamentary leaders in April.[73] Thus even before the Russian Congress opened, "the democrats" hoped to gain control over the apex of RSFSR governance. Even though Gorbachev held no seat in the Russian Congress, the General Secretary, and the newly formed Russian Communist Party (RCP) quickly formed an alliance to stop Yeltsin's bid for the highest executive post in the Russian Federation.[74]

Not that the Russian Communist Party leadership and Gorbachev were on good terms, however. Ivan Polozkov, the provisional leader of the RCP and a persistent Gorbachev critic, emerged as the standard-bearer of the conservative partocracy in early 1990. Polozkov and the Russian Communist Party's future Ideology Secretary, Gennadii Zhiuganov, showed few qualms about allying themselves with noncommunist, chauvinist grouplets on the margins of Russian political life. The election of Polozkov as head of the RCP undercut those Democratic Platform members who, as late as April, still hoped that the new Russian-section of the CPSU could accommodate those trying to pull the party in a democratizing direction.[75]

Polozkov ran against both Yeltsin and Gorbachev's hand-picked candidate, Alexander Vlasov, for the chairmanship of the Russian Supreme Soviet during the First CPD-RSFSR. Neither Vlasov nor Yeltsin mustered enough support to gain the chairmanship of the Supreme Soviet on the first ballot, although Vlasov strove to coopt the nationalist mood gaining ground in the Congress.[76] Polozkov supplanted Vlasov as Yeltsin's opponent on the second ballot, but again neither candidate secured a majority. Finally, on the third ballot, the DemRossiia bloc managed to patch together a coalition with moderate communists and independents sufficiently strong to elect Yeltsin over second-time candidate Vlasov as Chairman of the RSFSR Supreme Soviet, by a vote of 535 to 467.[77]

Yeltsin wasted little time in moving on to the question of sovereignty for the Russian Federation. On June 12, by an overwhelming majority—907 in favor, 13 against, and 9 abstaining—the Russian Republic declared itself a sovereign republic, and asserted "the superiority of the laws of the RSFSR" over those of the USSR on Russian territory.[78] The new Supreme Soviet— split almost down the middle between pro-DemRossiia deputies and various communist fractions—convened the following day to begin legislating for a now sovereign RSFSR.[79] Just what sovereignty meant in practice, however, remained unclear, although such declarations quickly became known as "the parade of sovereignties" in the world press.[80]

Six days prior to Yeltsin's ascent as Chair of the Russian Supreme Soviet, the Leningrad City Soviet (*Lensovet*) elected Anatolii Sobchak Chairman by a lopsided margin. Sobchak immediately announced a "revolutionary restructuring" of city governance, emphasizing that a pro-democracy majority now controlled the city and that "there will be no dual power."[81] Such confidence proved groundless.

The rise of Yeltsin to the second most prestigious post in the Soviet Union together with the election of DemRossiia majorities to the Moscow and Leningrad city soviets in fact created a dual power situation (*dvoevlastie*) in the heart of the Soviet regime's power base, the Russian Federation government and the RSFSR's two principal cities. In so doing, the democrats triggered "the war of the laws" (*voina zakonov*)—a chaotic clash of jurisdictions engendered by lower-echelon soviets declaring sovereignty, whatever this meant practically, over higher-echelon soviets.

In retrospect, the "parade of sovereignties" and "war of the laws" signaled creeping feudalization, as the always arbitrary application of Soviet legal codes intersected with the practical devolution of sovereign power. For the next fourteen months, apparat plenipotentiaries from the center would repeatedly tangle with republican, regional and local deputies flexing their new-found political muscles.[82]

On June 15, the RSFSR Supreme Soviet elected Ivan Silaev Chairman of the Council of Ministers.[83] Silaev functioned as the Republic's head of government, while Yeltsin—as Chair of the Supreme Soviet—controlled the RS-FSR's legislative agenda. An economic apparatchik, Silaev previously held posts in the Ministries of Aviation and Machine-Building, and became acquainted with Yeltsin in Sverdlovsk, during the 1970s.[84] In assembling a governing team over the next month, Yeltsin and Silaev drew almost exclusively from two sources: reformers with an apparat background; and academic economists who became enamored of monetarist economic theory. Remarkably, only one figure—Galina Starovoitova—would ever be simultaneously active in both the leadership of the DemRossiia movement and Yeltsin's Russian government, starkly demonstrating just how narrow was the network linking DemRossiia and the Yeltsin counterelite.[85]

Silaev's team included four pro-market economists: Boris Fedorov, the Minister of Finance; Gennadii Fil'shin, a Deputy Chair of the RSFSR Council of Ministers; Victor Yaroshenko, the Minister of Foreign Economic Relations; and Grigorii Yavlinskii, a second Deputy Chair of the Council of Ministers. Although more moderate than fiery DemRossiia leaders like Yuri Afanas'ev and Il'ia Zaslavskii, the Yeltsin-Silaev team was far more radical than the Union government. Mikhail Poltoranin, for instance, the new minister for the press and mass media who had been fired as editor of *Moskovskaia Pravda* in 1987 for publishing one too many stories exposing nomenklatura privileges,[86] now favored an official investigation of the CPSU during its long rule.[87]

The strategy of the Yeltsin-led Russian government evolved over the summer of 1990 into an effort to force Gorbachev to enter into a ruling coalition with the left and form a government of national salvation, a strategy that culminated in the August drafting of "the 500 Day Plan" for a swift transition to a market economy.[88] Although in April, Gorbachev decided against taking such a radical course, the RSFSR's appointment of Boris Fedorov and Grigorii Yavlinskii gave legislative weight to devising sweeping economic change. And when Mikhail Bocharov—a pro-marketization industrial manager, member of the Inter-regional Deputies Group in the USSR Congress, and a pro-DemRossiia deputy in the RSFSR Congress—proposed implementing a 500-day transition to a market economy in the Russian Republic from the floor of the Russian Supreme Soviet, the idea quickly intrigued Yeltsin and his economic ministers. On July 6, the Supreme Soviet named Yavlinskii Chairman of the Commission on Economic Reform.[89] In the weeks that followed, the commission drafted the 500-Day Program of the RSFSR Government.

In the meantime, the Yeltsin-Silaev government proposed a "Decree on Power" forbidding the joint holding of leadership positions in political parties and top administrative positions in government ministries or state-run enterprises.[90] The right bitterly opposed this measure, as it aimed squarely at disenfranchising nomenklaturshchiki across the RSFSR. Ivan Polozkov—confirmed as head of the Russian Communist Party at the latter's Founding Congress the very day the Decree gained approval[91]—spoke out vehemently against it.

Il'ia Zaslavskii later identified the decree as a major blunder, as it prevented Yeltsin from assuming the leadership of the Democratic Russia movement or creating his own political party, a central factor as developments unfolded.[6] Whether or not this is what Yeltsin wanted at the time is another matter. For the moment, the decree furthered the misrecognition of actual relations between Yeltsin and DemRossiia.

Soon, the new Russian government openly courted the political support of coal miners once again striking across the Soviet Union. The strikes proved particularly worrisome to both Gorbachev and the right, as the miners' demands now closely echoed those of the democratic opposition in calling for the resignation of both Gorbachev and Ryzhkov. Moreover, strikers called for depoliticization along the lines of the Decree on Power and the revocation of CPSU privileges.[92]

On the eve of the 28th Congress of the CPSU—scheduled to open on July 2—Gorbachev thus faced resurgent miners' strikes demanding his ouster, a new antireform Russian Communist Party hostile to his conception of perestroika, declarations of independence in the Baltics and sovereignty in Russia, and the collapse of Soviet domination in Central Europe. To make matters worse, in late June the CPSU's Democratic Platform threatened to quit the party altogether unless Gorbachev accepted its program of social democracy and marketization.[93] The General Secretary now faced a series of irrevocable decisions. Split the CPSU and unite with Yeltsin and the left? Or embrace the authoritarian and Brezhnevite positions of the Russian Communist Party and everything he had fought against as initiator of perestroika?

During the first days of the 28th Party Congress, tens of thousands of opposition protesters appealed for "the Bolsheviks to give-up power." At the same time, several hundred rightists from the neo-Stalinist United Workers Front rallied in favor of a call to transform the CPSU Congress into a "Congress of communist resistance."[94] On July 12, Yeltsin announced his resignation from the Soviet Communist Party.[95] Two days later, on July 15, approximately 100,000 pro-democracy demonstrators rallied in Manezh Square—right off Red Square in downtown Moscow—demanding accelerated reforms and denouncing the nomenklatura and the Russian Communist Party.[96]

During the Congress, Gorbachev faced a barrage of rightist criticism from apparatchiks dismayed by the revolutions in Central and South-Eastern Europe, the Baltic independence movements, and the relentless decline of the power and prestige of the Party. Pro-reform speakers found themselves upstaged in the right-wing uproar.[97] Gorbachev managed, however, both re-election as General Secretary, and approval of his reform course, to be given a vote of confidence in the closing days of the Congress.[98] The reform program ratified by the 28th Congress, however, merely reprised slogans about perestroika and "the socialist choice," dismaying the party's left. On July 17, Popov and Sobchak followed Yeltsin and resigned from the party, and much of the rest of the Democratic Platform followed the next day.[99] Several weeks later, the Moscow Party Chief Yuri Prokofev admitted that some nineteen thousand CPSU city members quit in July alone.[100] The 28th—and as it turned out—final Congress of the Communist Party of the Soviet Union thus closed without resolving basic questions, while splits in the apparat widened and institutional disintegration of the party-state progressed relentlessly.

Soon after the close of the 28th Congress, Gorbachev again tacked left. In late July, Yeltsin and Gorbachev began negotiations over both implementing a Union-wide 500-Day Program modeled on the RSFSR plan, and drafting a new Union treaty to eventually replace the old Soviet Constitution.[101] A working group of economists and policy advisors headed by Stanislav Shatalin and including RSFSR Deputy Chairman Grigorii Yavlinskii eventually put together the blueprint for the rapid transition to a market economy in the Soviet Union proper. On August 15, Yavlinskii introduced the details of the Russian government's 500-Day Program.[102] Two weeks later, Shatalin's group announced the draft for the Union-wide 500-Day Plan.[103]

Dual power had forced a fundamental realignment of political forces at the very apex of the fragmenting Soviet power structure. But the significance and extent of dual power was by no means limited to the republican level. While political entrepreneurs and apparatchiks struggled to set the agenda at the apex of the Soviet order over the course of 1990 and somehow capture the widening process of trajectory improvisation, dual power situations developed in many regions and localities of the USSR. The Soviet capital itself emerged as among the most significant cases of regional dual power, where the new pro-democracy majority of the Moscow city soviet launched a city-level "revolution" under the leadership of Gavriil Popov.

Democrats Come to the Mossovet

A long-time CPSU member, Gavriil Popov had been dean of the economics faculty at Moscow State University in the 1980s and then editor of the prestigious academic journal, Questions of Economics (*Voprosy ekonomiki*), before coming to prominence as a prolific commentator in pro-reform periodicals such as Moscow News (*Moskovskie novosti*) and Little Fire (*Ogonek*) in the late 1980s. Popov gained election to the USSR Congress of Peoples Deputies on a corporate basis, as a member of the Union of Scientific and Technical Societies. He rode to prominence during the specialist rebellion of spring of 1989, after the refusal of the Presidium of the USSR Academy of Sciences to grant Sakharov one of the All-Union seats allotted the Academy.[104]

Popov's outspokenness as a figure in the Inter-regional Deputies Group during the First Congress of Peoples Deputies in June 1989 made him a nationally known figure—a position he used to sweep into office in the Moscow City Soviet (Mossovet) at the head of DemRossiia's city ticket in March 1990. Late on the evening of April 20, Popov was elected chairman, and Sergei Stankevich—a second prominent "double deputy" from the CPD-USSR— was elected deputy chair.[105]

The new Mossovet Chair quickly set about trying to implement broad economic change in the Soviet capital. The openness of the DemRossiia majority to Popov's plans triggered the differentiation of factions in the new Mossovet, as well as sounding alarm bells in local apparat circles. The initial formation of political fractions among Mossovet deputies-elect mirrored the alignment of given deputies with particular voter lists. Thus, out of 489 seats, the DemRossiia bloc claimed 281 members, the apparat bloc "Moscow" 94 deputies, and a Russian authoritarian bloc, Fatherland (*Otechestvo*), 10 deputies. Remaining deputies positioned themselves as independents.[106]

Even before his election as chair, Popov declared himself ready to work with the holdover city administration in order to placate apparat fears and clear the way for effective governance. To demonstrate his sincerity, Popov recommended retaining a moderate apparat figure, Yuri Luzhkov, as head of the city's executive committee (*gorizpolkom*).[107] Despite winning the election and Popov's conciliatory gestures, however, relations with party rightists deteriorated.

Such deterioration stemmed from developments prior to the election. In January of 1990, the CPSU-dominated city administration—sensing impending defeat in the March elections—switched the ownership of thirty-four buildings from the city to the Soviet Communist Party. Partocrats quickly realized that loss of control over the city executive committee threatened the nomenklatura's local property monopoly, and—by extension—abilities to run a gamut of routines, from the ability to control appointments, to extracting private consumption from nominally official assets. In one of its first legislative acts, the Mossovet annulled this decision, setting off a protracted struggle over the status of many buildings around the city.[108]

To make matters worse, a number of opposition deputies elected to both the Mossovet and district (*raiony*) soviets were beaten up by police in connection with disputes over election irregularities.[109] Then, on April 20, Gorbachev further exacerbated tensions by using his new presidential powers to issue a decree transferring the right to issue permits for public demonstrations from the Mossovet to himself.[110] The Mossovet refused to recognize this decree, which remained a source of friction between the city administration and the Soviet leader for months.

Popov tried to smooth over tensions with Gorbachev on the protest issue by negotiating with the General Secretary over anti-Soviet demonstrations planned for May 1. After reaching agreement that antiregime protestors could march past the reviewing stand, Popov reciprocated Gorbachev by standing next to him on top of Lenin's tomb during the official parade. During the opposition phase of the march, Gorbachev stood impassively as motley groups of demonstrators shouted "Down with Leninism!" and "Down with partocracy!" Gorbachev and the rest of the politburo left before the opposition demonstration ended.[111] A Moscow Association of Voters' core member, Vladimir Bokser, singled out the strident character of the May 1 demonstration as an "ultra-leftist blunder" that undermined a possible working arrangement between Gorbachev and the opposition.[2]

Before the closing of its first session on July 7, the Mossovet passed a large number of reform measures, the majority of which concerned either the capital's supply of consumer goods or the management and ownership of state-controlled retail outlets and housing. For instance, Popov's government attempted to change Muscovites into local owners of their own apartments.[112]

In addition, the Mossovet tried to counter local food shortages through a mix of policies, ranging from requests to the center that the city be allowed to retain 12.5 percent of industrial production for barter from surrounding areas; to the imposition of rationing through the issuing of ration coupons (*talony*) for certain goods such as sugar and tobacco; to the creation of the preliminary legal framework for wholesale "barter exchanges" and autonomy for retail outlets; to the restriction of the ability of noncity residents to buy goods in city shops. For most of 1990, shoppers were required to present either a passport or a "buyer's card" (*visitka*) issued by the Mossovet when purchasing items in city-operated stores. This last measure proved particularly ill conceived, as it caused widespread resentment among residents of surrounding counties (*oblasti*) accustomed to coming to Moscow in search of goods that could not be found in provincial stores. Sensing a political opening, apparat-controlled soviets in such border counties (*oblastnye sovety*) retaliated by withholding deliveries to the city scheduled by the central planning ministries, thus intensifying Moscow's chronic shortages.[113]

In the meantime, the Mossovet's decrees legalizing managerial autonomy in retail outlets and the turning over of apartments from city to tenant ownership foundered on the city government's lack of support from the center. The apparat treated such decrees as without legal validity and thus null and void. Completely lacking a broader legal framework within which private property could be registered—let alone bought and sold—the apartment turnover and the transformation of retail trade foundered. To make matters worse, the Mossovet not only failed to reassert city ownership over the thirty-four buildings the Moscow Party Committee had seized in January, it found that 80 percent of property in the city belonged officially to various departments of the party-state.[114] As fall approached, the failure of Popov's strategy of "democracy in one city" became clear.

At the same time, Moscow's elected democrats found themselves pulled into discord by Popov's growing reputation as a dealer ready to compromise with corrupt officials and "gray" marketeers in order to achieve privatization as quickly as possible.[115] Intellectuals suddenly facing the collapse of state-supported incomes found Popov's emphasis particularly troublesome, and many began to speak up for the defense of "the cultural intelligentsia" being pushed aside by a rush of "businessmen" (*biznesmeny*) and "shady operators" (*teneviki*).[116] Rumors of unofficial deals between the city Chairman and the local apparat generated misgivings among DemRossiia activists, misgivings compounded by Popov's informal negative remarks on the grassroots democratic movement. Although officially a leader of DemRossiia, Popov

> recognized a mutual relationship between Democratic Russia and himself only from the perspective of the "father-mentor." . . . He would help individual people, but the movement as a whole, no. That's how he treated us, considering us a lumpenized organization.[19]

In a long article on democratic strategy and tactics published in Little Flame (*Ogonek*) in December 1990, Popov warned of the dangers of a quick victory by "the negative coalition" of "amorphous social forces" represented by "the democratic movement."[117] Moreover, Popov found himself more and more at odds with both nominal allies in the Mossovet, and pro-democratic majorities in a number of the city's district soviets, over questions of policy and the long-term place of the soviets per se in Moscow's future.

In the wake of the March elections, nominal democrats held majorities in twenty-one of Moscow's thirty-three district-level soviets (*raisovety*).[118] By September, only seven raisovety were still controlled by self-proclaimed DemRossiia majorities, nine had no controlling faction, and seventeen had fallen back under the control of the old CPSU district apparat. Two raisovety even declared themselves sovereign in relation to the Mossovet following disagreements over policy and jurisdiction, extending "the declaration of sovereignties" to the lowest possible level in the Soviet system.[119] Feudalization now spread relentlessly.

The spectacle of democrats in open conflict over the role of soviets and the over-all direction of reform began to undermine the confidence of the city electorate. And the Mossovet's preoccupation with economic and housing reforms that came to naught in the face of a rapidly deteriorating supply situation inflicted further damage on Moscow democrats. Rumors of corruption spreading with Popov's policies only magnified such problems. A number of activists expressed criticism about Popov's alleged deal-making. "Frankly speaking, I believe that where there's smoke, there's fire . . . they [Popov and his subordinates] abused their offices gravely."[15]

Such fragmentation formed the background for the more radical majority of one of the city's district-level soviets, the October raisovet now chaired by yet another double deputy, the USSR Congress' prominent Inter-regional Group figure, Il'ia Zaslavskii.

The Archipelago of Democracy

Unusual for a well-known political figure, Zaslavskii's decision to run for a seat in Moscow's October district soviet in the 1990 elections stands out. The capital's raisovety were small, highly constrained bodies located far down the vertical hierarchy of soviets.

Zaslavskii gave as a rationale for his move a "desire to illustrate with practical deeds what . . . [I have] worked for in the Congress of Peoples Deputies of the USSR."[120] If elected chair of the October raisovet, he promised "to build capitalism in one district."[121] Zaslavskii's name recognition as an influential leader of both the Inter-regional Group and the Moscow Association of Voters, his association with the DemRossiia voter bloc, and his direct participation in

Bokser and Shneider's campaign organization gave him and the DemRossiia district slate an easy victory. The October district soviet's DemRossiia majority promptly elected Zaslavskii Chairman.[122]

Zaslavskii set in motion changes that quickly became known as "the October revolution." Directly rebuffing Gorbachev's July call during the 28th CPSU Congress for "progressive forces" to unite behind perestroika, Zaslavskii rejected the notion of reforming the party-state all together, instead calling for "new structures" without vanguards.[123] The "new structures" Zaslavskii had in mind included not only voluntary associations and parties, but also opposition-controlled soviets at various levels, which he dubbed "the archipelago of democracy" (*arkhipelag demokratii*). The 1990 elections brought

> not simply a change of authority in several regions of the country. In defiance of official ideology, it's now clearly possible to take power ... A new archipelago has formed. Not the GULAG, but an anti-GULAG, an archipelago of democracy.[124]

According to Moscow's city administration, 231,600 persons lived in the October district. Although fifty-two thousand of these "worked in organizations or enterprises connected with science or scientific equipment" and eleven thousand were doctors, the district also housed fifty-seven thousand pensioners and twenty-eight thousand construction workers.[125] Yet not a single union worker or activist was elected to the district soviet. Indeed, the archipelago of democracy exemplified the specialist profile of DemRossiia. Out of 145 deputies elected in 1990, fully 91 percent had a degree of higher education, with 141 listing the occupations given in Table 2.1:

TABLE 2.1. Occupations of Deputies Elected to October *Raisovet*, 1990.

Occupations	Number of respondents
Technical engineers	75
Teachers	16
Legal system employee (*iuridicheskoe*)	10
Cultural and artistic employees	5
Economists	4
Enterprise directors	2
Komsomol organizers	2
Party functionaries (*apparatchiki*)	1
Military personnel	3
Students in higher education	2
Pensioners	2
Clergy assistant	1
Enterprise worker	11

Source: "Kto est' kto," *Piatnitsa* (No. 1, 1990: 2).

Use of the official status of the October soviet to register an enormous number of independent associations—from samizdat newspapers to economic cooperatives to opposition political parties—emerged as the most significant change implemented during Zaslavskii's tenure. Over the course of 1990, the raisovet would register over four thousand such entities.

> What positive results did we achieve? . . . [T]he Helsinki Watch Committee, the independent journal *Glasnost'* and the journal *Referendum* were registered. Many well-established journals who hadn't managed to liberate themselves from the tutelage of the editorial board of *Pravda* were registered as well, journals such as Flame (*Znamia*) and October (*Oktiabr'*) . . . [Our second achievement] was the registration of 3,500 enterprises, including private enterprises, a colossal break-through in favor of business. After we were finally overthrown [in February 1991] . . . it simply became impossible [for independent formations] to register in Moscow: as everyone knows, corrupt officials demanded enormous bribes in exchange for registration. The whole process came to a halt.[6]

"The October revolution" came to a close when the district soviet effectively blocked Zaslavskii's ability to convene a working majority the night of February 13–14, 1991.[126] The gradual breakdown of support for Zaslavskii among the soviet's DemRossiia majority arose in part out of rumors of scandal surrounding the explosion of business activity that flourished in the district in the second half of 1990 as the city plunged into a winter of generalized shortages.

In an open letter to the local newspaper Currents (*Kuranty*), Zaslavskii's opponents cited his "apparat of consultants, helpers, and executives" and the "autonomous associations, firms, investment centers, and other commercial enterprises" created in their hands. "All other enterprises in the district (co-operatives, small private enterprises, the self-employed, and so on) can get access to channels of supply and sale only through the monopolistic structures headed by them."[127] Several letters published alongside the above in the same issue of Currents, however, strongly supported Zaslavskii, his work for ordinary residents, his aid to entrepreneurs, and his mass registration campaign on behalf of political parties, voluntary associations and businesses.

In fact, the splintering of the DemRossiia majority in the October district soviet arose less out of corruption and more from disputes over how to achieve de-statization (*razgosudarstvlenie*) of state property. Such disputes reflected deeper disagreements as to how soviets should function as organs of democratization. Zaslavskii's growing conflict with his erstwhile DemRossiia colleagues in fact mirrored a widening split in the movement as a whole. On the one hand, some favored representative-style democracy, with professional politicians elected to run streamlined governmental agencies in an executive fashion. On the other hand stood those who advocated maintaining the soviets either as organs of direct democracy, or as full-time, fully staffed parliamentary bodies. The conflict over the role of soviets in Russia's political future triggered both Popov and Zaslavskii's development of a program of "de-sovietization" (*desovetizatsiia*)—literally, the abolition of the soviets and their replacement by an American-style division between legislative and executive arms of governance—in the fall of 1990 and the winter of 1991.[128]

The rationale behind de-sovietization emerges clearly in Zaslavskii's account of his fall from power in the October raisovet.

> Given their complete underdevelopment, the [district's] political institutions … determined the economic possibilities and the limits within which a managerial team could be created … [We] proved unable to appoint people with a clearly defined program to the district's government, to the district executive committee. In other words, people were selected according to the "antiprinciple"—"he's not a *nomenklaturshchik*, thus he's good." But this was by no means true. Thus many people were chosen randomly, some of which weren't bad as leaders, but a good half of whom had no intention of working for my program ["capitalism in one district"] … What kind of people were these? First of all there was a group of "procedural democrats," that is, people who saw the observance of procedures and not the final policy result as the top priority. What is more, these people themselves couldn't see that they were observing the procedures of a political body that in and of itself was absolutely illegitimate, and thus they couldn't see the transitional character of the Supreme Soviet [and other soviets] … Seizing power in the soviets only made sense as a strategy to liquidate these very soviets and to create in their place a normal state [*normal'noe gosudarstvo*], perhaps of a western-European sort … A second group … were the populists, often very right-wing types, supporters of social justice, who understood by this that everything should be divided equally and gobbled up as each saw fit. These people began their work in the district by organizing pogroms [*pogromy*] at residences where the *nomenklatura* lived. It's important to keep in mind here that they mostly beat up and assailed doormen … It then became necessary to call both of these groups to order due to the fact that the procedural democrats were simply incapable of doing any work, and the populists were behaving in an impermissible and, at times, despicable manner. I decided to send a notice to the [local] prosecutor, in order to call those responsible for the pogroms at residences to account … Then both of these groups immediately united with the communists. Suddenly, the correlation of forces [in the *raisovet*] had shifted against us: it turned out that less than a third of the deputies were convinced marketeers [*rynochniki*] … We managed to hold on to several executive positions and thanks to this were able to implement further reforms. But both our positions and our reforms were being gouged out, criticized and subjected to constant attacks from below. We hung on for about a year.[6]

Two paths of differentiation in the democratic movement over the course of 1990 emerge from Zaslavskii's account of events in the October soviet. The first crystallized at the level of the counterelite and among those political entrepreneurs among the grassroots *aktiv* who aspired to join it, as articulated by Zaslavskii and Popov. Such figures now defined the democratic movement's end in a much more explicit way, in terms both of "capitalism" and dynamic, results-oriented "executive leadership," here called "executive liberals."

The second path emphasized the DemRossiia 1990 campaign slogan, "all power to the soviets." This slogan united the political neformaly, many older generation dissidents epitomized by Sakharov, and the first phase of the democratic movement between the 1989 and 1990 election campaigns. Calling this second tendency "proceduralists" stresses the importance of popular access to the democratic process, seen as a counter weight to nomenklatura privatization. Between these two stances appeared various populists, mixing liberal, social-democratic, and nationalist rhetoric and avoiding more technical disputes between executive liberals and proceduralists.

Conflict between executive liberal emphasis on de-sovietization and the proceduralist stress on the transformation of the soviets into true democratic bodies generated a great deal of distrust between pro-democracy deputies sitting in various bodies right through Yeltsin's disbanding of the Russian Supreme Soviet in October 1993. Given Popov and Zaslavskii's emphasis on the need for professionalism among democratic leaders, it is easy to loose sight of the fact that many proceduralists also were deeply concerned about the lack of professional attitudes among nominal DemRossiia deputies.

Populism and a lack of realism among the activists of his district concerned Aleksei Kashirin, for instance, a member of the Peoples Power (*Narodovlastie*) voter club and a deputy in Moscow's *Cheremushkinskii* district soviet after the March 1990 election. Following this election, many in the club expected that "since a new group is coming to power, the manna of heaven will sprinkle down on us ... we will be fed, clothed, supplied with vodka. Thus there was a clear lumpen tendency."[15]

Kashirin clarifies the professionalizing orientation of many proceduralists in his account of the inability of the Democratic Russia majority in the district soviet to achieve much in 1990. During the 1990 elections,

101 or 102 out of 142 *raisovet* deputies won due to their being on the *DemRossiia* list. In principle, we could set policy in the district. But the split into factions began immediately. During the election of the [soviet's] Chair the first difference appeared. Some took a position that amounted to turning representative organs of power into some kind of amateur, unprofessional bodies. That is, they argued that sessions should be held, votes taken and questions decided when deputies could find time after work, and in the meantime the Chair and the Deputy Chair could handle the majority of the work. They thus proposed that deputies shouldn't work in the soviets on a professional, regular basis. But this group was in a minority. The majority ... wanted the district soviet to function as a

representative body in the normal sense of the word, on a professional basis, with people working regular hours to develop programs and so on...But as things turned out, the posts of Chair and the chairs of standing committees were freed [from other employment], but the mass of deputies, of course, were not: they weren't able to cut themselves off from their previous jobs. And there really was no possibility of this, as the *Mossovet* did not support the concept 100 percent. They encouraged it to a certain extent, but in the end failed to support it.[15]

In contrast, proponents of de-sovietization argued that to transform the entire interlocking hierarchy of soviets into full-time legislative bodies staffed by dozens, hundreds, of full-time representatives was a recipe for legislative paralysis and inefficiency. Arguments for de-sovietization were often greeted, however, with hostility at the grass roots.

As the contrast between Zaslavskii and Kashirin's visions of professional politics demonstrates, one DemRossiia deputy's professionalism was another's dilettantism. The conflict between executive liberals and proceduralists thus developed as a conflict both of style and substance, and cut across the differentiation of positions among movement political entrepreneurs. For instance, an emphasis on disciplined political organization, "full power to the soviets," and opposition to de-sovietization as Popov and Zaslavskii conceived it came to distinguish Nikolai Travkin's Democratic Party of Russia in the second half of 1990.[129]

The rise of a professionalizing counterelite of political entrepreneurs in the soviets generated both centripetal and centrifugal pressures at the grassroots level. The professionalizing orientation of many pro-democracy deputies and proto-party leaders both created a centripetal force in mobilizing democratic protest, and deepened tensions between the emerging counterelite and the activist base of the democratic movement. Indeed, a moralist habitus continued to flourish at the grassroots level and among many pro-democracy specialists, reflecting the movement's origins in the neformalitet and the heyday of the voter clubs during the 1989 and 1990 election campaigns.

A moralist disposition generated contradictory effects among individual specialists, impelling some to either withdraw into inactivity or to embrace the rejectionist politics of various radical, syndicalist, and human-rights-oriented informal groups that continued to be active. The perception either of infighting among pro-democracy political entrepreneurs, or of counterelite distaste for street politics, thus functioned as a powerful centrifugal counter-weight to the centripetal force of charismatic leadership, a counter-weight reinforcing sectarian differentiation and disillusion at the grass roots. The democratic networks formed in 1989 and early 1990 thus continually fractured and reorganized.

The differentiation of habitus, political style, and articulated position among both political entrepreneurs and grassroots activists in the democratic movement became more pronounced as 1990 unfolded. The emergence of a dual power situation in soviet bodies enhanced such differentiation. As the perceived need to protect Yeltsin's sovereign government—and thus an institutional shield for autonomous political activity—became a primary unifying factor among oppositionists, the dynamic of dual power in the soviets began to directly shape the developmental course of mobilization and differentiation in the democratic movement as a whole. In this situation, the fortuitous adaptation of received institutional arrangements to purposes not previously associated with them fused the strategic development of the democratic movement irreversibly to the decaying institutional world democrats found themselves in upon election to soviet bodies.

Gorbachev's strategy, with its emphasis on the need to revive the soviets as genuine representative bodies as a political counterweight to the nomenklatura estate, breathed life into the dead letter of the codes and regulations that nominally governed procedures in the soviets. Between 1988 and 1990, such procedures began to have consequential effects in the world of late communism. Indeed, proceduralism—an insistence on the importance of laws, codes and so forth in the soviets—was an essential weapon in the opposition's struggle against the arbitrary rule (*proizvol*) of shadowy party committees over the life of the soviets. Proceduralism, however, formed a double-edged sword, as the apparat itself also fell back on a proceduralist strategy to block reform in a considerable number of instances.

> When they [conservative apparatchiks] find themselves within the archipelago of democracy, they try to play a game with democratic principles...Their goal is to render the democrats ineffective. Thus an insignificant number of conservative deputies in our district soviet, employing the extensive rights granted the minority, are trying to sabotage the decisions of the executive committee. At the same time, conservatives outside the archipelago continue to operate according to the usual authoritarian methods.[124]

The realization of the limits of localized soviet power by two Moscow leaders of the opposition thus inspired the strategy of de-sovietization. However, the centrality of Yeltsin's new Russian government and the RSFSR's declaration of sovereignty under which the democratic movement could be partially protected from direct repression by reactionary groups in the apparat emerged as a major flaw of the de-sovietization strategy. Indeed, the RSFSR Congress and the Russian Supreme Soviet stood as the most important loci of dual power in Russia.

Moreover, the formal legitimacy and institutional access gained by elected democrats through positions in the soviets helped carve out a larger and larger autonomous space in which established pro-democracy papers, the Soviet television and radio network, and semiofficial (*ofitsioznyi*) and underground (samizdat) bulletins and newssheets could operate. The Moscow City Soviet's Popov administration arranged start-up funding for a number of independent mass circulation papers such as Independent Gazette (*Nezavisimaia gazeta*) and Currents (*Kuranty*) and played a central role in launching an independent radio station in the capital, Echo Moscow (*Ekho Moskvy*). The mass registration of samizdat bulletins, newssheets and journals by the October district soviet further widened ordinary Muscovites' access to a great variety of opinion rooted in the dissident movement, the neformalitet, the specialist rebellion of 1989, the new democratic movement, and sources abroad. Indeed, transnational demonstration effects refracted through regional circumstances generated a variety of outcomes.

For such reasons, neither Yeltsin's government nor the democratic movement as a whole could afford to deemphasize the importance of the sovereign laws promulgated by the Russian Supreme Soviet. After all, the adaptation of soviets by the opposition under conditions opened up by Gorbachev's guided democratization led to a protracted standoff between divided powers reminiscent of 1917. The logic of this standoff in turn steered the internal fragmentation of the democrats according to various opposition stances toward soviets as an institutional form. And as Popov's pact with the local Moscow apparat soured, Zaslavskii's October revolution stalled, and then the Yeltsin-Gorbachev 500-Day Plan began to unravel in the fall, the motley opposition faced a dilemma: where to go from here?

3 Democrats on the Offensive

Preoccupied with the struggle to establish dual power, many pro-democracy leaders in the soviets by mid-1990 had ceased to interact with the voluntary associations and informal networks that functioned as grassroots vehicles for their spring campaigns. A small number of peoples deputies, however, argued that the ultimate success of democratic transformation depended on the existence of a dynamic, unified, and organizationally effective democratic movement at the grassroots level. These deputies and their allies in voter associations would network the organizational unification of Russia's democratic opposition in the fall of 1990. But in so doing, an emergent *DemRossiia* movement "core" in Moscow would centralize Russian democrats behind, paradoxically, a Moscow group itself using dual power to split the Soviet party-state. While on the surface appearing to centralize political power in the Yeltsin counterelite, this complex process in fact intensified feudalization across the Russian Republic.

Party or Movement?

In the wake of Yeltsin's ascension to leadership of the Russian Republic, the organizers who directed DemRossiia's March election campaign announced a plan to create a Russia-wide, opposition umbrella organization (*obshchaia organizatsiia*) provisionally called "the Democratic Russia movement" (*Demokraticheskaia Rossiia-dvizhenie*). As a first step toward realizing this project, the Democratic Russia Organizing Committee (*DemRossiia orgkomitet*) was created in Moscow at a June 24 conference of Russian voter clubs called at the initiative of the Moscow Association of Voters.[1] The Democratic Russia orgkomitet envisioned DemRossiia dvizhenie as uniting disparate informal groups, voluntary associations and grassroots activists into a social movement (*obshchestvennoe dvizhenie*) working for the democratic transformation of Russian society from below.

The creation of DemRossiia dvizhenie originated out of an aborted experiment in forming a party out of the voter clubs and other participants in the elections of March 1990, itself a departure for organizers of the Moscow Association of Voters. What had happened since the summer of 1989 to alter Association of Voters' organizers regarding the desirability of creating a party structure as the basis of advancing the goals of the democratic movement? First, in the spring of 1990, such organizers no longer had an upcoming election around which to network the grass roots. "In the spring of 1990 there was a definite lull, people were simply exhausted."[2] Second, the large number of opposition deputies in various soviets and the abolition of Article 6 fundamentally altered the political situation. And finally, experience with the Moscow Association of Voters had shown the downside of a loose, amorphous movement organization for opposition political entrepreneurship.

> During the winter we decided it was necessary to create a party. The Moscow Association of Voters was not the best [organizational form]... We had a basic sense of the need for finances, we needed means with which to function. But the Association of Voters and the voter clubs didn't give us the possibility of collecting dues, it was such an amorphous structure... On the other hand, a party is already a much stricter structure.[3]

The move to create a new party combining the strength of radical-reform deputies in soviets of various levels and the organizers of the democratic campaigns in Moscow and Leningrad quickly gathered steam, paralleling the formation of the DemRossiia faction among deputies-elect to the CPD-RSFSR.

> Lev Ponomarev wrote an appeal and I wrote a charter for the future party... And completely by accident... Lev wrote this appeal in the presence of Il'ia Konstantinov [of the Leningrad Popular Front]. This was just after the elections, they had both just become peoples deputies. Konstantinov signed and in the corridor grabbed Travkin, saying "Kolia [the familiar for Nikolai], sign this appeal." And Kolia said "OK, I'll sign!" He simply signed quickly and that was it: thus Travkin became head of the Democratic Party of Russia.[3]

Prospects looked bright for the new party. When world chess champion Gary Kasparov joined the party-building effort, these prospects looked even brighter, as Kasparov brought both his transnational prestige and his considerable financial resources from chess winnings—much of it located in foreign bank accounts—to the project.[4]

The founding conference of what was eventually called the Democratic Party of Russia, however, got off to a rocky start. At the conference—held on May 26–27, 1990, in Moscow—disagreements over whether the new party should have a unitary or a federal structure, and should elect a single chair or a trio of cochairs, led to a split between Nikolai Travkin, on the one hand, and significant sections of the Moscow and the entire Leningrad delegations, on the other. Travkin became widely known in 1989 due to the effectiveness of his televised speeches as a member of the Inter-regional Deputies Group.[5] When on the second day the majority of the conference sided with Travkin's unitary conception and elected him sole chair of the nascent Democratic Party, Marina Sal'e led a walkout by the Leningrad delegation, followed by Ponomarev and Kriger.

Sal'e, Ponomarev, and others opposed to Travkin's unitary conception soon announced the creation of the Free Democratic Party of Russia (*Svobodnaia demokraticheskaia partiia Rossii*), a rump of the leadership cores of the Leningrad Popular Front and the Moscow Association of Voters that never developed beyond a tiny grouplet, in large part due to its founders' subsequent preoccupation with the Democratic Russia movement.[6] At the same time, Yeltsin—now chairman of the RSFSR Supreme Soviet and having just overseen passage of the Decree on Power—declined involvement with efforts to fashion a party out of the social movement that he still depended on. "The Chairman of the Supreme Soviet or the President of the Russian Federation during the time of his chairmanship or presidency should suspend his membership in any party or social organization, in order that he can be the defender of the whole people."[7]

In the meantime, organizers of the Democratic Party of Russia (DPR) argued that the 494 delegates at the Founding Conference represented ninety-nine cities and eighty-five regions (*oblasti*) of the RSFSR, adopting a "Declaration of Principles" with a program close to that announced by the DemRossiia voters bloc in January 1990.[8] Although Travkin and other DPR organizers' ability to create party sections so quickly in many Russian cities clearly impressed figures in the Moscow Association of Voters and the Leningrad Popular Front, they remained unalterably opposed to Travkin's leadership style. During the Democratic Party of Russia's Founding Conference, "from the very beginning Travkin conducted the sessions . . . as if they were production conferences, that is to say, he was the boss and everyone else were subordinates."[3] In the fall of 1990, Marina Sal'e accused Travkin and the DPR of "neo-Bolshevism," a charge that—fairly or unfairly—stuck to "the party of Travkin" among many grassroots activists.[9]

The relationship between the Democratic Party of Russia and DemRossiia developed in a complex manner over the next fourteen months. On the one hand, Travkin and prominent figures in the Moscow Association of Voters and Leningrad Popular Front who predominated in the DemRossiia orgkomitet now openly distrusted one another. On the other hand, local sections of the DPR around the RSFSR and even district-level groups of the new party in Moscow led a push among DPR activists to join DemRossiia dvizhenie when the latter was formally created in the fall of 1990.

During the First Congress of *DemRossiia dvizhenie*...Travkin stated that there was no need for any kind of movement, what was needed was a party. But when it suddenly became clear that all of the regional sections of the DPR in the provinces were actively joining *DemRossiia* and intended to work together so as not to split the democratic forces, then Travkin joined the movement. As it turned out, DPR activists in many places worked on their own and, surprisingly, even many DPR organizations worked on their own.[2]

In fact, the frequent public clashes between Travkin and the Moscow and Leningrad voter leaders often were of little practical concern to many DPR and DemRossiia activists. A member of the *Brateevo* district section of Dem-Rossiia in Moscow, in which DPR members were active in 1990–1991, noted that the heated conflict over organizational and policy questions that developed between Afanas'ev and Travkin in the summer and fall of 1991 met with "indifference in our organization...No split occurred in our association between members of the Democratic Party of Russia and others."[10] That local DPR sections in the end functioned as de facto DemRossiia sections rather than party organizations seriously undermined Travkin's goal of creating a distinctive party identity, which is a prime reason he was opposed to participating in the Democratic Russia coalition in the fist place. But Travkin had little choice in the end. Not only the DPR grass roots, but most of his deputy chairs, favored the DemRossiia project from early on.[11]

The Rise of DemRossiia dvizhenie

At a June 24 Moscow Association of Voters conference attended by delegates from over fifty Russian cities, the Democratic Russia Organizing Committee (DR orgkomitet) announced its aim as the convention of "a congress of democratic forces" from across the RSFSR in order to create the Democratic Russia Movement (DemRossiia dvizhenie).[12] At a meeting held in Moscow on July 14, the DR orgkomitet expanded to twenty-seven members and elected Arkadii Murashev Chair, Lev Ponomarev Deputy Chair and Mikhail Shneider Secretary.[13] The committee set October 20 and 21 as the dates for DemRossiia dvizhenie's Founding Congress in Moscow.[12]

Murashev had by this time been elected chair of the Inter-regional Deputies Group in the USSR Congress of Peoples Deputies, while Shneider had been appointed an aid to Popov with an office in the *Mossovet*.[14] The three top executive position in the Democratic Russia orgkomitet thus were occupied by leaders of the parliamentary opposition in the USSR and RSFSR CPDs, and by an aid to the pro-democracy chair of the Mossovet, formalizing a network structure linking grassroots activists at the base with an emerging counterelite at the vertices of the Russian Federation.

And yet, the Russian Federation now controlled by the Yeltsin counterelite was simultaneously agitating to *decentralize* Soviet power from the Union to the Republics, and thus aligning itself tactically with centrifugal networks outside the Russian Republic. The symbolic embrace of decentralization thus masked highly centralist tendencies in Russia's democratic networks, which only emerged on the level of the Moscow *aktiv* itself.

> The movement we are creating demands a professional, paid apparat [*profes-sional'nyi oplachivaemyi apparat*], without which the movement will be helpless. Let this apparat be small and strictly controlled by the movement's elected organs; but there must be an apparat.[15]

The DemRossiia orgkomitet's moves to create an "apparat structure" to coordinate the new movement generated controversy within the Moscow Association of Voters, proving particularly contentious among the Association's grassroots aktiv. Indeed, hard feelings aroused by the exclusion of various pro-democracy candidates from the DemRossiia list during the spring election campaign deepened suspicion of the emergent centralizing tendency around the Yeltsin group at the grass roots. In June and early July, bitterness over the handling of the candidate lists threatened a split in the Moscow Association of Voters Coordinating Committee (*Koordinatsionnyi sovet*), and at a stormy session of this coordinating committee on June 23, several accused Bokser, Kriger, and Shneider of manipulating the election campaign.[16] After securing reelection as leaders of the Association, the emergent, Moscow-based "movement core" retaliated by suspending several such activists from the coordinating committee.[17]

The DemRossiia orgkomitet not only faced "splitters" at the grass roots of the Moscow Association of Voters during the summer of 1990, but also encountered difficulty getting prominent opposition leaders in the soviets to participate in their work or even publicly support the idea of creating an umbrella organization capable of bringing voluntary associations, nascent political parties, grassroots activists, and pro-democracy politicians in soviets together under one banner. While Mossovet Chairman Popov made his office available to the orgkomitet for the founding June 24 meeting, for the most part Yeltsin, Stankevich, Afanas'ev and others remained preoccupied with power struggles in the soviets.

> At that time, you understand, our appeal to political leaders . . . to help create *DemRossiia dvizhenie* met with a guarded response. And these reservations largely consisted of doubts about how things would turn out. They all said things like "How many people will actually show up at the Congress? Will anybody come at all? . . . Yes, yes, we will see, we'll try to do something. But we need to think

about." But after a large number of delegates—real delegates—showed up at the First Congress and the big hall we rented was filled, well, this produced a certain effect.[3]

Opposition deputies whose initial involvement in the DemRossiia orgkomitet proved the exception to this pattern played a crucial role in helping the new movement get its feet on the ground. USSR Peoples Deputy Arkadii Murashev and RSFSR Peoples Deputies Victor Dmitriev and Lev Ponomarev were founding members of the committee. Il'ia Zaslavskii arranged an office for the Moscow Association of Voters—and emergent DemRossiia—core in the October district, and former "Committee of the 19" member and now Mossovet deputy and Popov aid Alexander Muzykantskii helped secure an office for the orgkomitet at No. 8 Crimean Embankment.[3]

While Murashev and some other prominent Democratic Party of Russia members concentrated on their work with the DemRossiia orgkomitet, Travkin and his associates in the DPR leadership focused their coalition-building efforts on informal negotiations with the newly created Social-Democratic Party of the Russian Federation (SDP) and figures in the CPSU's *DemPlatforma* that formed the Republican Party of the Russian Federation in October 1990. The Social-Democrats associated themselves with postwar western parliamentary democracies, while the Republican Party emerged from disgruntled members of the CPSU.[18] Following the collective resignation of the majority of *DemPlatforma* members from the Communist Party during the latter's 28th Congress on July 18, 1990, such negotiations aimed at creating a "democratic alliance" of opposition parties.[19]

On August 2, representatives of the Democratic Party of Russia, the Moscow Association of Voters, the *Babushiinskii* district voter club, and several other associations attended a meeting held in Moscow on the topic of creating a pro-democracy alliance.[20] One month later, on September 4, a conference of the same Democratic Party of Russia together with the Social-Democratic Party and the "Party of the Democratic Platform of the Russian Federation"— soon to be the Republican Party of Russia—announced their intention to form a new pro-democracy bloc.[21] The announcement of this tripartite coalition appeared to bring the efforts of the three proto-parties and the DemRossiia orgkomitet together.[22]

Relations between Travkin and the emergent DemRossiia core continued to be difficult, however, and this strain would in turn drive some highly placed Democratic Party of Russia figures toward a primary affiliation with the Democratic Russia orgkomitet. World chess champion Gary Kasparov, for example—the financial force behind the DPR's new semiofficial (*ofitsioznaia*) newspaper, *Demokraticheskaia Rossiia*—abruptly made the paper independent of the Democratic Party of Russia with the publication of the third issue.[23]

By late August, the DemRossiia orgkomitet was gaining support from the grass roots of its three affiliated proto-parties, a process aided by the presence of future Republican Party leader Vladimir Lysenko on this orgkomitet.[24] By September, the orgkomitet was issuing communiqués, circulating *samizdat* first drafts for a DemRossiia charter, and aiding efforts to create local Democratic Russia sections in many of the Republic's cities and towns. By early October, local founding congresses of DemRossiia dvizhenie took place in Orel, Tomsk, and Yaroslavl, before the First All-Russian DR Congress.[25] By late November, over seventy local sections of Democratic Russia were created in the RSFSR.[26]

The DemRossiia orgkomitet rendered a central organizational influence on the republic-wide movement, enabling "Moscow central" to steer the movement on a federation-wide basis. Near the end of September, Victor Dmitriev circulated a samizdat draft outlining the structure of the new movement as he envisioned it (see Figure 3.1). As indicated in this chart and the draft Movement Charter (*ustav*) circulated with it, the standing executive body and tactical coordinator of the movement on a day-to-day basis would be the coordinating committee (*Koordinatsionnyi sovet*). The coordinating committee would in turn design and staff its own executive bodies, centralizing in practice a movement symbolically championing decentralization of the Soviet regime.

A Council of Representatives (*Sovet predstavitilei*) envisioned as an enlarged policy-making body of representatives drawn from the movement's diverse constituent associations, parties and grassroots activists would, in turn, elect the coordinating committee. The Council of Representatives would meet as needed to set the overall strategic direction of the movement, compose DemRossiia declarations and announcements, and decide on joint actions such as demonstrations. Dmitriev's draft Charter proposed to apportion seats on the Council of Representatives in the following manner. First, a certain number of Council seats, left unspecified, would be set aside for DemRossiia's most important collective members, such as parties, influential voter clubs, and important social organizations like Memorial. Second, a series of working commissions (*rabochie komissii*) would be created by the Founding Congress and their chairs elected from the Congress floor; these chairs (*predsedateli*) would then automatically be included in the Council of Representatives. Third, a number of Council seats open to individual members were to be filled by nominations and elections from the floor of the Founding Congress. Finally, Dmitriev envisioned the creation of a financial body—the Democratic Russia Fund (*Fond Demokraticheskoi Rossii*)—that would accumulate funds on the basis of donations, rent conference rooms, print literature, pay a small movement staff, buy

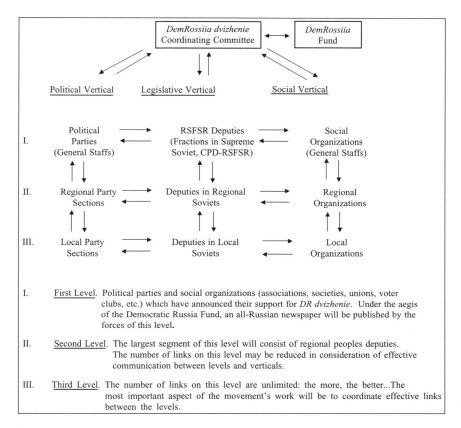

FIGURE 3.1. Proposed Organizational Framework of DemRossiia dvizhenie.
Source: Samizdat mimeograph of chart drawn by Victor Dmitriev of the DemRossiia
Organizing Committee, Sept. 28, 1990.

materials for leaflets and posters, publish a Russia-wide newspaper, and aid
local sections suffering partocratic repression at the local level.[27]
    The creation of such a fund had been a top priority of the DemRossiia
Organizing Committee since the latter's creation in June, and the fund first
met and opened a bank account in early August, 1990. Yurii Afanas'ev originally headed the fund, but a series of disagreements between Afanas'ev and
other fund organizers led to his resignation and to Leonid Bogdanov's elevation to the fund's top administrative position, executive director (*ispolni-
tel'nyi direktor*).[3] The Democratic Russia Fund later organized and financed
a "Sociological Service," *DR Sotsio*, which conducted surveys of DemRossiia
Congresses and so forth during the next year.[28]

The organization of the Founding Conference itself revealed the emergent pattern of counterelite formation in DemRossiia dvizhenie proper. First, the orgkomitet—the core group who organized the Moscow Association of Voters networks on a daily basis—designated recently formed local sections to send delegations according to regional quotas set by the orgkomitet itself. Second, the orgkomitet invited DemRossiia-aligned peoples deputies from the USSR and RSFSR CPDs and Supreme Soviets to attend the Founding Conference. And third, the orgkomitet apportioned a number of delegates on a quota basis from the leadership bodies of the movement's collective members, along the way reserving seats for the orgkomitet itself.[29]

DemRossiia dvizhenie's Founding Congress took place in Moscow's Russia Hotel on October 20 and 21, 1990, attended by 1,429 delegates, including 1,181 delegates affiliated in one way or another with 71 local sections, as well as 32 USSR peoples deputies, 104 RSFSR peoples deputies, and 121 delegates selected by the Moscow core, now instantiated as the movement's orgkomitet.[30] A survey of delegates reported that about 67 percent of delegates belonged to one of several proto-party groups. While only 3 percent of delegates were current CPSU members, over 37 percent of such delegates formerly belonged to the CPSU.[31] By the time of the Second Congress of DemRossiia dvizhenie, held on October 9–10, 1991, in Moscow, however, over 61 percent of delegates identified themselves as being nonparty (*bespartiinyi*) in a similar survey.[32] Many delegates who aligned themselves with proto-parties at Dem-Rossiia's Founding Congress would, over the course of the next year, come to see their primary affiliation as lying with the movement and not a given party leadership, a perception which consolidated networks around the Moscow Association of Voters core, now working as the dominant grouping in the new DemRossiia Coordinating Committee.[33]

After some rancorous debate, the Congress approved the Organizing Committee's proposal to allow both collective and individual membership by incorporating this proposal into the movement's Charter. The Charter declared the movement

> a mass social-political organization of voluntary associated parties, social organizations, movements and individual citizens . . . Any citizen can join the movement if they are at least sixteen years of age and recognize the Movement's Charter . . . The certification [*oformlenie*] of individual and collective membership in the movement in each region will be determined independently at the grassroots level.[34]

Seven proto-parties joined DemRossiia dvizhenie as collective members at the Founding Congress, although the Travkin leadership of the Democratic Party of Russia (DPR) decided against formally joining the new movement. But due to the caveat in DemRossiia's Charter that allowed members of parties and organizations to join the movement on an individual basis, many DPR delegates proclaimed themselves individual members of DemRossiia dvizhenie anyway. And many local sections of the DPR across the Russian Federation joined DemRossiia dvizhenie on a regional basis. In the end, Travkin was forced to relent, and agreed that the national DPR would become a collective member of the movement on January 13, 1991. Although Murashev and Kasparov remained in the DPR for some months, Travkin's initial refusal to join Democratic Russia widened the rift between him and those DPR figures aligned with Murashev and Kasparov.[35]

Despite discord on various issues, the Founding Congress approved the programmatic emphasis developed in the DemRossiia orgkomitet's draft documents with little dissent. The official DemRossiia dvizhenie Charter adopted at the Congress closely matched Dmitriev's draft. In a Declaration adopted at the close of the Congress, DemRossiia dvizhenie recognized "the idea of an independent, free, democratic and prosperous Russia" as its principal inspiration, and called for

> a free market, free enterprise, free competition of various forms of property...political, ideological and cultural pluralism...the liquidation of the Communist Party's monopoly in all spheres of social life...the dismantling of the totalitarian system and the creation of a state of law...the democratization and de-party-zation [*departizatsiia*] of the organs of justice, law enforcement, security, and the military, and the establishment of control over their activities on the part of elected bodies...the replacement of the military draft by an alternative service option or the establishment of an all-voluntary military...the consistent realization of the right of national self-determination...[and] the social defense of the weakest and most oppressed groups in society

The Declaration concluded with a call to

> create on all levels social committees of *DemRossiia dvizhenie*, uniting peoples deputies, activists of democratic parties, organizations, movements, and all citizens prepared to take up the concrete tasks of political and economic reform...to widely publicize the goals of the movement...[and] to conduct a variety of non-violent protest actions against the reactionary activities of the totalitarian regime, including political strikes and—in the extraordinary circumstance of a direct threat to democracy and the sovereignty of Russia—to launch a campaign of mass civil disobedience.[36]

Various other resolutions and declarations of the Founding Congress made clear the new movement's strategic subordination to Yeltsin's RSFSR government and the 500-Day Plan.[37] And as in Dmitriev's draft, the Charter adopted by DemRossiia dvizhenie's Founding Congress allowed the Council of Representatives both to set its own agenda, and to create a coordinating committee independently of the Congress. In this way, the Moscow core gained practical control of day-to-day coordination of DemRossiia dvizhenie networking and Federation-wide symbolic gestures.

Ponomarev made clear that this had been the intention of the DemRossiia orgkomitet all along.

> At the Founding Congress, we consciously wished to avoid having anyone elected [to Democratic Russia *dvizhenie*'s leadership bodies], nobody in the *orgkomitet* wanted anything to be decided at the Congress. We simply hoped that a few general positions and declarations would be worked out and the Charter approved ... and then later we could decide [organizational matters] in the so-called Council of Representatives ... There was no need to elect a Council of Representatives at the Congress, as this Council would be composed of representatives of organizations that had already joined the movement, as well as of regions, counties and so on which had already held local Founding Congresses. The Council of Representatives was thus created by structures from all across Russia that sent representatives to sit on this Russia-wide body ... And we trusted, frankly, the regions in this matter.[38]

Delegates to the First Congress who gave such administrative power to the Moscow Association of Voters and Leningrad Popular Front failed to recognize how such administrative influence translated into political power. This lack of recognition flowed from a literal reading of how the Charter structured the movement in a fairly decentralized fashion, with local and regional bodies retaining authority to regulate membership. As Sergei Stikhiinskii, a syndicalist in the Moscow district association *Brateevo*, argued,

> In general, the structure of *DemRossiia* around the country was like a puff pastry [*sloenyi pirog*]. On the all-Russian level, it is one thing, on the regional level something else, and on the city and district level something yet again. Many different levels exist, in fact. And in reality, *DemRossiia dvizhenie* lacks any strict mechanism of organizational control.[10]

Stikhiinskii goes on to counterpose charisma and status to organizational control. The influence of the Democratic Russia core "is an influence that stems from the image [*vliianie imidzha*] of a number of leaders."[10] This judgment coincided with the DemRossiia core's. Leonid Bogdanov, for instance, attributed the core's influence among grassroots activists in Moscow to the practical confirmation of the core's recommendations by experience.[3]

Such assessments underestimate the organizational side of the question, as hinted at by a local Moscow activist.

I am certain that 80 percent of the activists in the Moscow Association of Voters and *DemRossiia dvizhenie* never once glanced at either the Association or Democratic Russia's Charter. The only people who read such documents were those involved with writing them.[2]

The influence of "Moscow central" over the development of the movement as a whole thus developed along network lines that remained somewhat organizationally obscure. As we have seen, the DemRossiia orgkomitet was entrusted at the close of the Founding Congress with selecting the members of the movement's Council of Representatives in line with Dmitriev's outline, preserving the de facto emergence of core centralization in the networks comprising DemRossiia dvizhenie as a whole.

The Democratic Russia orgkomitet convened the First Plenum of the Council of Representatives on December 8–9, 1990, in Moscow, including representatives of fifty-three regional DemRossiia sections, several dozen RSFSR and USSR peoples deputies, and the Organizing Committee itself.[39] The Council Plenum proved incapable of fully resolving all organizational questions concerning the election of the coordinating committee in two days, however, and reconvened to finish its work on January 12–13, 1991.

In the meantime, the Moscow core used a closing decision of this plenum on December 9 to proceed with forming the leadership bodies of the coordinating committee. On December 12, six cochairmen of the coordinating committee—all of them USSR or RSFSR peoples deputies—were elected at the coordinating committee's first session: Popov, Afanas'ev, Murashev, Father Gleb Yakunin, Ponomarev, and Victor Dmitriev.[40] The election of Popov and Afanas'ev—who, along with Yeltsin and *Lensovet* Chair Anatolii Sobchak, were among the most well-known opposition leaders in Russia—consolidated a high public profile for the new movement, many of whose top leaders were still relative unknowns outside of democratic circles in Moscow and Leningrad.[41]

Although in the summer of 1990, Yeltsin declined to become officially involved with partisan organizations, he was in fact the de facto leader of DemRossiia dvizhenie, given the movement's open declaration of its strategic subordination to the Yeltsin-led RSFSR government. The informal coordination between the formally separate leaderships of DemRossiia dvizhenie and Yeltsin's RSFSR governments became a little clearer near the end of the year. In December, 1990, Yeltsin appointed Gennadii Burbulis—a Yeltsin ally from Sverdlovsk who became a member of the Democratic Russia movement's Council of Representatives—to an advisory body, the Presidential Council, created by Yeltsin in December of 1990, the only direct representative of the movement in Yeltsin's RSFSR government until July, 1991.[42]

The territorially stratified character of Soviet society aided the DemRossiia orgkomitet, and by extension Yeltsin's Russian government, in engineering this outcome. Many regional and local activists in DemRossiia found it difficult to arrange travel and accommodations outside of their base cities and towns: after all, internal passports, residence permits and so on gave great leverage to the regional *nomenklatura* in these matters. The geography of the Russian Federation, with its distances and poorly developed transportation and communication infrastructures, magnified such institutional obstacles to free exchange of information and travel between Moscow and what Muscovites call "the outlying districts" (*periferiia*). In this way, continuing partocratic domination of regional institutional devices left standing as the party-state disintegrated in the center exaggerated the Moscow core's control of the movement's "virtual" decentralization.

Moreover, recurrent splits at the movement's regional and local levels generated rival pretenders to seats on the Council of Representatives, which met roughly once a month and had no fixed membership. This created an opening for the Democratic Russia core to assert a definite organizational control over the movement's "puff pastry" structure through the selection of those pretenders most likely to support the core's position in the Council.

> Each provincial cell [*iacheiko*] gathers on the local level and elects its leaders, who are then sent to Congresses and the Council of Representatives in Moscow...And in many *oblasti*—in Tambov and in other areas—there were splits, as you know, splits of *DemRossiia* into two parts, with each considering itself legitimate. Ponomarev then chose precisely the ones who supported him to invite to Moscow for a meeting, to ensure that they would vote the way he needed them to.[43]

Stacking the Council with Muscovite acquaintances represented a second method the emergent DemRossiia core used to secure sympathetic Council of Representative majorities.

> By using an apparat selection process, Bokser and Zaslavskii succeeded in placing Muscovites into more than half the positions on the Council of Representatives, and then to a certain extent guided [these representatives]. That is to say, they domesticated the Council by means of the predominance of the Moscow group in the Council.[44]

Access of coordinating committee cochairs to the official press, secured both by contacts with reformist journalists and positions in the all-Union and RSFRS soviets, further aided the predominance of the Moscow group over DemRossiia dvizhenie's Federation-wide leadership. Popov's articles appeared regularly in *Moskovskie novosti* and *Ogonek*. Zaslavskii emphasized how a journalist friend who wrote an essay about him in *Moskovskie novosti* proved critical in getting his otherwise "dilettantish" 1989 election campaign going.[45] Oppositionists lacking access to the pro-reform press in Moscow or to the national television network via the soviets remained confined to samizdat and the semiofficial press (*ofitsioznyi*) and many provincial democrats were frozen out completely by the conservative local media.

All of this needs to be placed in the context of struggles in the wider democratic movement, some of it remaining outside DemRossiia's orbit altogether. These groups tended to be highly sectarian and concentrated in the capital. Indeed, in 1990, two variants of pro-democracy protest developed in Moscow: the democratic movement that culminated in DemRossiia dvizhenie and which received fairly wide coverage in the official press; and the rejectionist activity of more radical groups still regularly subject to repression and a virtual press blockade. Rejectionist activism in fact increased in 1990. The pages of the samizdat bulletins *Ekspress-Khronika* and *Panorama* from 1990 are filled with reports of demonstrations. Almost daily, human rights activists, Democratic Union radicals, refugee groups, and so forth protested on the streets of Moscow. But rarely were these activities given much attention in the wider press. The burning down of the apartments of two *Panorama* correspondents, for instance—one in May, the other in September—attracted practically no attention.[46] Even when repressive activity directly touched the DemRossiia movement, it was not fully reported in the official press.[47]

The media spotlight on dual power and the *dramatis personae* of the counterelite rebellion at the top of the party-state reflected a "stratification of audiences"[48] in the Soviet polity. Pro-democracy journalists depended on more reformist *nomenklaturshchiki* for access to the press, and wrote for opinion and interest in the specialist urban circles that defined their social orbits. In contrast, police harassment, the inability to distribute publications widely, and a general shortage of newsprint and other material means severely limited the semiofficial and samizdat press. This stratification of audiences closely intertwined with the estate-like character of the Soviet social order. Indeed, the hierarchical ordering of status orders in everyday life limited access to the reception of certain messages, as well as access to channels of publicity. In this way, a nominally decentralized, Republic-wide democratic movement symbolically reinforced misrecognition of the obscure manner in which the Moscow core operated centralizing influence over the movement's tactical and strategic development.

Again, we see hypercentralization at the same time as the party-state was disintegrating, shifting power to regional networks—but with the caveat of their dependence on local and regional patrons operating more and more "beheaded" wings of the Union-level party-state. At the center of this stood the Yeltsin counterelite, decentralizing and disorganizing Union institutions as much as possible, while simultaneously striving for a de facto centralization of the Russian democratic movement behind the figure of decentralization. Thus the circumstances that fostered rapid feudalization—the decentering of sovereignty to many regional "sovereignties," rather than its outright collapse—become clearer.

All of this exaggerated the de facto influence of DemRossiia's Moscow core in the Russian movement as a Federation-wide whole, a phenomenon intensified by the practices of the Yeltsin-led counterelite in the Russian Congress of Peoples Deputies and the Moscow and Leningrad soviets. The Moscow center of DemRossiia dvizhenie now steered the democratic movement's networks of voluntary associations and informal groups in a direction strategically harmonized with Yeltsin's strategy of using a sovereign Russian Federation government to create a dual power to Gorbachev's all-Union center and thereby cripple the Soviet regime. The DemRossiia organizational core and the Yeltsin-allied counterelite thus oversaw the strategic development of the democratic movement at the grassroots level in Russia through the movement's Second Congress, held two months after the August Revolution in October 1991.

The Collapse of the 500-Day Plan and the "Baltic Events"

The rise of DemRossiia dvizhenie and the consolidation of its organizational leadership in the hands of the Moscow Association of Voters and Leningrad Popular Front cores in the second half of 1990 occurred in a context of deepening regime crisis in the Soviet party-state. What brought the various pro-democracy grassroots networks together on discrete occasions during the fall of 1990 was not so much Yeltsin's leadership or DemRossiia's program, as apparat "reactionaries" (*okhraniteli*) who from mid-1990 forward began to mobilize a counterrevolution against "the democrats."[49] This counterrevolution mobilized against Gorbachev's acceptance of the 500-Day Plan at the USSR-level.

Almost from the minute of the Plan's announcement, the hitherto pliant Union government headed by Nikolai Ryzhkov rebelled against it. At the end of August, Ryzhkov repeatedly warned that, as Prime Minister, he would refuse to implement the Plan because of the hardships it would cause workers. And yet the polarization deepening throughout Soviet power structures rendered Ryzhkov's "centralized social-democratic" strategy—and the habitus of figures like the Soviet Prime Minister in general—irrelevant. Indeed, Yeltsin countered Ryzhkov's "centrist" moves immediately, by pressing the Plan as hard as possible. On the opening day of the Second Russian Congress of Peoples Deputies, he emphasized the urgency of launching Shatalin's program as quickly as possible.[50] On September 17, 1990, Gorbachev seemed to close the door on foot-dragging regarding the Plan, asking the USSR Supreme Soviet for "special powers" to implement it. The Supreme Soviet readily complied, strengthening the Soviet president's ability to rule by decree.[51]

But instead of moving quickly on the Plan's measures, Gorbachev again stalled for time. In mid-October, Yeltsin lost patience and blasted the General Secretary's wavering, voicing his suspicion that the Russian government was being set-up.[52] Gorbachev countered by objecting to Yeltsin's "confrontational ardor" (*zapal*) and "dictates."[53]

Another month slipped by as Gorbachev continued to hesitate. Meanwhile, the polarization between radicals and reactionaries grew apace. Rumors swirled in the capital around the significance of the appearance of four airborne army divisions outside Moscow in late September.[54] The city's food shortages grew worse and the right attacked Popov's Mossovet administration for letting the potato harvest in the capital's adjacent agricultural districts rot.[55]

The mix of Gorbachev's back-tracking on 500 Days, the army maneuvers, and the bitter accusations between radicals and reactionaries over the food situation poisoned the political atmosphere and erased the optimism generated by the Yeltsin–Gorbachev rapprochement in August. On October 12, Gorbachev issued a decree "protecting state property in Moscow" aimed at Popov's administration, signaling the hardening of the General Secretary's position toward his supposed allies in the 500-Day Plan.[56] Three days later, Yeltsin launched a salvo at Gorbachev in the RSFSR Supreme Soviet: the Yeltsin–Gorbachev feud had resumed its familiar course. On October 17, reform economist Grigorii Yavlinskii resigned his post as deputy chair of the RSFSR Supreme Soviet, saying Gorbachev's unwillingness to implement the Shatalin Plan doomed the republican effort as well.[57] On October 31, Shatalin himself openly attacked Gorbachev for delaying the 500-Day program.[58]

On October 20, the Founding Congress of DemRossiia dvizhenie opened in Moscow, calling for Ryzhkov and Gorbachev's resignations. Popov, his attempt to turn Moscow into a "free-market showcase" in shambles, began to openly rethink the strategy of "seizing power at the local level." In an open letter to the delegates of the DemRossiia Congress, Popov laid out two scenarios for the following months: either Yeltsin and DemRossiia would force Gorbachev to accept a coalition government, or, failing this, democrats would be forced to go into complete opposition. If this second scenario materialized, Popov warned, "Russia must secede from the USSR," and—in those soviets where the left did not have full control—"we must resign our posts."[59] Popov set to work laying out his strategy of de-sovietization, blaming the institutional structure of the soviets themselves for hamstringing the opposition and saddling democrats with partial responsibility for the relentless economic decline.[60]

Less than three week after the close of DemRossiia dvizhenie's Founding Congress, scattered groups of Stalinists and democrats alike rallied against Gorbachev's "vacillations" on the 73rd anniversary of the Bolshevik seizure of power. The left's call to turn Revolution Day parades into a protest against "communist terror" was overshadowed by the attempt of a lone gunman to assassinate Gorbachev—who was standing hundreds of yards away on Lenin's tomb—with a shotgun.[61] On November 15, the right-wing "Union" (*Soiuz*) faction in the USSR Supreme Soviet demanded that Gorbachev take stern actions to halt "anarchy" and save the Soviet Union. "Union" leader Victor Alksnis, the so-called "Black Colonel", warned "unless needed steps are taken, people will take to the street with arms. This won't be a military coup, the army will simply be defending its own human rights."[62]

In the now tense political climate, Gorbachev abandoned the 500-Day Plan on November 16. The Soviet president then immediately decreed himself even more emergency powers, disbanded the advisory presidential council (the last high body on which Alexander Yakovlev—the "father of *perestroika*"—still sat), and created a new Security Council staffed by senior officials of the KGB, army and Ministry of Internal Affairs.[63] Gorbachev, however, left the door open to compromise by continuing negotiations with Yeltsin on a new Union Treaty. A draft of this treaty granting considerable powers to the Republics in a new "Union of Sovereign Republics" was released in late November.[64] Alksnis and other rightist remained dismayed with ongoing treaty negotiations and continued to criticize Gorbachev for weakness and vacillation.[65]

After the abandonment of the 500-Day Plan, Gorbachev found himself under the pressure of a growing right wing mobilization in the Party, military and security apparatuses. Near the end of the month, the minority pro-Soviet faction in the Lithuanian Communist Party appealed to the USSR Supreme Soviet to "take all necessary measures" to guarantee "the constitutional rights" of pro-Soviet Russian residents of the Baltic Republic.[66] On December 1, Gorbachev issued a decree removing the relatively reformist interior minister, Vadim Bakatin, from his post, replacing him with an open reactionary, Boris Pugo.[67] Ten days later, KGB head Vladimir Kriuchkov went on national television to warn that "anti-communists are trying to seize power" and to state the case for a "law and order" crackdown.[68]

The opposition, meanwhile, continued to press ahead. On November 27, Yeltsin hastily convened the extraordinary (*vneocherednoi*) Third Congress of Peoples Deputies of the RSFSR,[69] which approved the republican phase of the 500-Day Plan. On December 2, DemRossiia leader Galina Starovoitova warned that Gorbachev was preparing to use his extraordinary powers to launch a coup d'etat (*gosudarstvennyi perevorot*).[70] The situation on the eve of the opening of the Fourth USSR Congress of Peoples Deputies, set for December 17, could not have been more tense.

On December 20, three days into the Fourth CPD-USSR, Eduard Shevardnadze—along with Gorbachev and Yakovlev one of the three original architects of perestroika—resigned his post as Foreign Minister on live national television. Shevardnadze, without advance warning to Gorbachev, warned of the danger of an "approaching dictatorship" and lamented the "scattering of the democrats."[71] On December 25, USSR Prime Minister Ryzhkov suffered a heart attack, soon after resigning his post. Having been granted even more additional powers to rule by decree, Gorbachev at the end of the Congress forced through the appointment—in the face of strenuous criticism from the floor—of long-time *apparat* figure Genadii Yanaev to the new post of vice president. Shortly after the close of the Fourth CPD-USSR, Gorbachev appointed another long-time *apparatchik*, Valentin Pavlov, as the new Prime Minister.[72] The General Secretary now found himself surrounded by the gray eminences who would lead the failed coup attempt against him in August 1991: Yanaev, Pavlov, KGB chief Kriuchkov, Interior Minister Pugo, Defense Minister Yazov, and Speaker of the Supreme Soviet Anatolii Lukianov. In the closing days of 1990, Gorbachev also created an all-powerful executive presidency invested with a long list of emergency powers.

In the first days of 1991, the General Secretary turned his attention to the upstart Baltic Republics. The pro-independence governments of Lithuania and Latvia found themselves at the receiving end of a particularly harsh flurry of presidential denunciations. Gorbachev's uncharacteristic belligerence shook many leaders of Russia's democratic movement. While a small handful such as Sergei Stankevich continued to hold out hope that Gorbachev would remain committed to a reform course, the majority of the counterelite prepared for an imminent crackdown.[73]

On January 11, 1991—one day after Gorbachev had issued a demand that the Lithuanian government "immediately restore the USSR Constitution"[74]—a shadowy "Committee of National Salvation" declared itself the instrument of "presidential rule" in Lithuania and appealed for aid from the Soviet armed forces. The appeal was largely for show, as tanks and infantry from local Soviet bases had already seized the Press House in Vilnius and were on the move throughout the Republic.[75] In Lithuania, the republic's deputies and government were taken virtual hostage by troops ringing the parliament—the former Lithuanian Supreme Soviet—on January 13. Later that same night, fourteen civilians protesting the introduction of martial law were killed at the Vilnius television tower, some of them gunned down by automatic weapons and others crushed by tanks. Seven days later, four protesters were shot in Riga resisting a military takeover in Latvia launched under the aegis of yet another Committee of National Salvation. What became known as "the Baltic events" were underway.[76]

Despite the global media's focus on the upcoming arrival of the United Nation's January 15 deadline for Iraq to withdraw its forces from Kuwait, many governments, particularly in the West, condemned the situation in the Baltics. At the same time, Yeltsin flew to Lithuania, returning to Moscow the day after the killings in Vilnius, and hinted at the need to create a "Russian army" independent of Soviet control, a remark quickly denounced as "unconstitutional" by Gorbachev.[77]

The harsh criticism of the Baltic events in pro-democracy sections of the mass media prompted the Soviet leadership to try and constrain the growing press autonomy established under *glasnost'*. On January 11, *Gostelradio*—the USSR mass media conglomerate—suspended the independent news agency *Interfax* and the television program *Vzgliad* (Opinion). *Vremia*, the main news program of central television, failed to report the violence in Lithuania on January 14, although central television reported the deaths in Vilnius the next day.[78] Newly independent newspapers like *Nezavisimaia gazeta*, however, covered the Baltic events in detail, while samizdat circulars, semiofficial bulletins, and voluntary associations distributed news from Lithuania and Latvia among opposition networks.[79] And in a number of clubs affiliated with the Moscow Association of Voters, videos of events the night of January 13 and 14 were shown to hastily gathered groups of supporters. "In the voter clubs we got hold of video tapes of the outrage [in Vilnius] filmed on the spot."[80]

On January 13, over a thousand pro-democracy activists protested the Baltic events by marching to the Lithuanian consulate in downtown Moscow, protected from police interference by several Mossovet deputies.

> I personally marched alongside Stankevich . . . 1,500 people marched in the column . . . The police accompanied us, but didn't block our way . . . [Stankevich] was, after all, Deputy Chair of the *Mossovet*, and therefore we didn't run into any trouble.[80]

Mass Mobilization Against the Party-State

The coordinating committee of DemRossiia dvizhenie moved quickly in response to the new situation. In a bulletin released on the thirteenth, the Committee warned "Today Lithuania, tomorrow Russia" and called a mass protest in Moscow for the upcoming Sunday, January 20.[81] Yeltsin met openly with the DR dvizhenie Coordinating Committee on January 18 to discuss both the upcoming demonstration and the overall strategy of the democratic movement.[82]

On that Sunday, approximately 200,000 people massed in central Moscow shouting DemRossiia slogans and calling for Gorbachev's resignation, the largest anti-government rally since the February 4, 1990, demonstration, and among the largest in Russian history. This would be the largest outpouring of street protest in 1991, exceeding those that took place in August during the failed hard-line coup attempt.[83] In a communiqué read at the January 20 demonstration, Yeltsin excoriated Gorbachev.[84] Three days later, *Pravda* accused Yeltsin of plotting to seize power.[85]

In an address to the USSR Supreme Soviet on January 22, Gorbachev veered again and distanced himself from the Baltic events by denying any prior knowledge of the military's actions in the capitals of Lithuania and Latvia. "Under no circumstances do the events which occurred in Vilnius and Riga reflect the policy of the presidential authority...I categorically deny any speculation, suspicion or slander in this regard." After expressing sympathy to the families of the victims, he criticized the opposition for its take on events, and called for discipline, order, democratization, and perestroika.[86]

Gorbachev's statement brought the Baltic events to a close, with the pro-independence governments in Lithuania and Latvia resuming operations as the military occupying Vilnius and Riga withdrew to its bases. But the General Secretary's equivocal statements further eroded his position. To make matters worse, the very day of his statement to the Supreme Soviet denying responsibility for the Baltic crackdown, the Soviet president decreed into law a poorly conceived and unpopular currency reform devised by the new Soviet prime minister, Valentin Pavlov.[87] The ground under the political center had all but vanished.

Over the next several weeks, counterelite figures attacked Gorbachev in the harshest terms yet, initiating a period of maximal tension between heads of the Soviet and Russian governments that would last through the end of March. On January 28, Yeltsin denounced the General Secretary for planning joint army and Interior Ministry patrols in many Soviet cities, including Moscow. The Russian leader stressed that such patrols violated human rights and the Soviet constitution.[88] Then the RSFSR government attacked Gorbachev and Pavlov's sudden announcement of price rises of as much as 200 percent.[89] On February 19, Yeltsin spoke on national television, setting a new precedent by demanding Gorbachev's resignation, reiterating his earlier call for the creation of an independent Russian military, and hinting at a possible withdrawal of the RSFSR from the Soviet Union. On February 20, chairman of the USSR

Supreme Soviet Lukianov termed Yeltsin's speech "illegal," "a call to violate the Soviet Constitution," and an incitement "to create an emergency situation in the country."[90]

Some centrist Russian deputies were taken aback by Yeltsin's pronouncements, creating an opportunity for conservative deputies to try and slow the momentum of the RSFSR government.[91] On February 22, several hundred thousand demonstrators mobilized by DemRossiia rallied in central Moscow in support of the Russian government, while the Russian Supreme Soviet voted to convene a special session of the Congress of Peoples Deputies of the RSFSR to review the situation on March 28.[92] The Soviet oligarchy was undergoing rapid fragmentation and polarization, with open party-state disintegration accelerating on all levels.

For the first time, Yeltsin as head of the Russian Republic had reiterated what had long been said at the grass roots of DemRossiia dvizhenie, that Gorbachev must resign. Lev Ponomarev viewed Yeltsin's call for Gorbachev's resignation as the culmination of the movement's development to that point.

> In general, we had the possibility to meet Yeltsin and his immediate staff and thus influence him . . . Yeltsin's statement that "The President must resign!" was, indisputably, a result of our influence.[38]

During this period, DemRossiia dvizhenie experienced its largest growth and activity. By March 1991, more than three hundred branches (*otdeleniia*) of the movement existed, including in all the administrative capitals of the Republic's regional districts (*oblasti*).

> After Vilnius, so many people became active, there was simply a mass influx . . . We took a number of steps to create movement organizations in industrial enterprises. During the January 20 demonstration on Manezh Square, we made an appeal [to join the movement], an appeal which was heeded. We then sent telegrams to our provincial sections calling for the creation of enterprise cells.[93]

Alongside the DemRossiia movement, the first months of 1991 revived many of the Moscow Association of Voters' district and subdistrict clubs.

> I remember the great weariness in the Moscow Association of Voters' Council of Representatives . . . [But] the spring of 1991 brought a kind of second wind, caused by the seizing of the Press House in Riga, the army in Vilnius . . . and then Yeltsin's trip to Tallinn and Riga.[2]

Images of tanks in Vilnius "greatly agitated everyone and caused an upsurge of political activism . . . We then took the decision to create our own [local district-level] association of voters."[80]

The revitalization of Moscow voter clubs created a powerful local network of Democratic Russia sections in Moscow. The city's movement organizers claimed that over 100 DemRossiia dvizhenie networks formed at enterprises and institutes in the first two weeks of February alone.[94]

> We formed our district *DemRossiia* organization at the end of January and the beginning of February 1991 . . . The organization was founded on a coalition basis . . . [and included] our voter club, several [voter] cells in enterprises and institutes . . . perhaps two dozen members of the Democratic Party of Russia, and a symbolic handful of members of the Republican Party.[2]

The revival of Moscow's movement organizations coincided with the formation of the all-Union movement coalition. On January 26, representatives of popular fronts and voluntary associations from across the Soviet Union met in Khar'kov, Ukraine, to create an all-Union opposition umbrella, the Democratic Congress (*Demokraticheskii kongress*). Attended by the Lithuanian popular front *Sajudas* and DemRossiia dvizhenie, whose delegation was headed by Yurii Afanas'ev, such organizations stood among the principal initiators of this congress.[95] The new Union-wide united front elected a Consultative Council (*Konsul'tativnyi sovet*) and appealed for "the consolidation of the efforts of all democratic forces to peacefully liquidate the totalitarian regime, to dismantle in a civilized manner the imperial-unitary structure, and to create sovereign democratic states."[96] The Democratic Congress formalized the de facto working alliance between the Baltic independence movements and Dem-Rossiia already in place, and, together with calls for Gorbachev's resignation and the creation of an independent Russian army, signaled the maturation of revolutionary deadlock between radicals and reactionaries on the scale of the Soviet Union as a whole.

The Referendum on the Fate of the Soviet Union and the 1991 Presidential Campaign

At the height of the Baltic crisis, the USSR Supreme Soviet approved Gorbachev's proposal to conduct a Union-wide referendum on the fate of the Soviet Union. The Supreme Soviet's resolution envisioned a simple yes–no vote either affirming or rejecting the amended Soviet Constitution, together with its toughened strictures governing secession, phrased in wording sufficiently vague to assuage both nationalist and democratic sentiments.[97]

In the aftermath of the Baltic debacle, however, the rightist countermobilization underway since September 1990 stalled, giving the democrats an opportunity to expand their strategic position. The separatist Lithuanian government quickly moved to preempt the referendum by holding a yes–no referendum of their own on Lithuanian independence. On February 8, 91 percent of the Baltic Republic's eligible voters affirmed the declaration of independence.[98]

Russia's opposition took advantage of changed circumstances to add measures to the referendum ballot favorable to the democrats in relevant republican and local jurisdictions. Yeltsin's RSFSR government, for instance, managed to introduce a measure calling for a new Russian presidency and direct presidential elections onto the referendum ballot.[99] On March 6, the Mossovet voted to place a measure on the referendum ballot asking voters to approve or decline the introduction of a directly elected mayor in Moscow.[100] Several weeks earlier, the *Lensovet* placed its own question on the introduction of a mayorship in Leningrad on the ballot.[101]

On February 22, however, Yeltsin denied favoring the secession of the Russian Federation from the USSR and essentially equivocated on his stand toward the Union question itself.[102] The Russian leader then changed course by "declaring war" against the Union government and calling for the creation of a powerful democratic party to displace the CPSU in a speech delivered in an open meeting with the leaders of DemRossiia dvizhenie.[103] The next day, March 10, tens of thousands of demonstrators turned-out at Democratic Russia-called demonstrations in Moscow and Leningrad to support Yeltsin.[104]

Given Yeltsin's mixed signals on the referendum, the organizational core in DemRossiia dvizhenie's Coordinating Committee treaded delicately in campaigning for a "no" vote. The added question on a Russian presidency gave DR dvizhenie an opening to prevent Gorbachev from using a "yes" vote on the Soviet Union as a mandate for reasserting central control over republican, regional and local soviets.

> During the campaign against the referendum, we knew very well that we were going to lose, and never counted on a victory . . . We knew that we would lose, due to the way the referendum question was formulated: it was simply difficult for people to answer such a formulation "no" . . . Our tactics consisted of trying to explain to people why it was impossible to vote "yes," that the question had been put specially, in a way that favored the preservation of the Union in its current form. We also were for a Union, we explained, but not the Union of the communists.[93]

Despite certain loss on the Union question,

> the referendum campaign proved useful, because it allowed us to strengthen our organization and consolidate our forces. For all practical purposes, the referendum campaign rehearsed the 1991 presidential campaign . . . In the spring of 1990, we still were unable to conduct a truly RSFSR-wide campaign, reaching

only about 25–30 percent of the RSFSR's districts. During the referendum campaign, however, we had a presence across Russia, practically everywhere, perhaps with the exception of one or two regions. Moreover, we managed to send our posters to the remaining 70 regions in a centralized fashion, as we already had established regular communications with local sections and could more or less conduct the campaign in a coordinated fashion. This was a very important general rehearsal [for the June presidential campaign].[105]

By the time of the vote on March 17, 1991, the "no" campaign of the democratic opposition in urban Russia and the nationalist oppositions in many non-Russian republics began to form a counterweight to the government's main strength, rural areas of Russia and Central Asia dominated by the reactionary wings of the partocracy. The referendum passed by 71.3 percent in the RSFSR, but in Moscow and Leningrad, the victory was much narrower, with 46 percent of Muscovites and 43 percent of Leningraders voting no. Any advantage that either Gorbachev or the right hoped to gain from winning the first question disappeared when 69.7 percent of RSFSR voters approved the creation of a Russian presidency.[106]

When, in the two weeks leading up to the referendum, miners went on strike in the Kuzbass demanding Gorbachev's resignation, the elimination of press censorship, and the transfer of the coal industry from Soviet to RSFSR control, the center's hope of gaining breathing-room from winning the first question faded altogether.[107] That large pluralities in Moscow and Leningrad voted in favor of establishing directly elected mayorships further tarnished the center's victory. By the time of the vote, the Russian opposition had managed to turn the vote from a simple referendum on the Union into a supplementary vote of confidence in Yeltsin, who announced his candidacy for Russia's president as soon as an election could be scheduled. "For the first time in decades the head of the Soviet state and Communist Party found himself in fact dependent on the outcome of a popular vote."[108]

DemRossiia dvizhenie regarded the referendum results as a map of Russia's political geography circa March 1991.

One could model [political attitudes] in our society on the basis of the referendum. There were two questions: the question on Russia and the question on the Union. As it turned out, almost 70 percent voted favorably on the Russian question, while on the question of the Union about a third voted no...Approximately a third of Russia's citizens stood for consistently democratic positions: that is, those who voted yes for the introduction of a Russian presidency and no on the question of the Union. These were our firm supporters, about 30–35 percent of the voters who had made a clear choice for democracy and the market. The next bloc of voters was volatile, and could shift here or there...two circumstances pushed [the approximately 30 percent of] such voters to approve the Russian presidency: either out of simple faith in Yeltsin's personality, without thinking about civil society; or simply due to a preference for order...And finally, approximately a third of the citizenry represented a bastion of reactionary and conservative forces.[105]

Bolstered by the opposition's neutralization of the Union referendum and by the continuation of the pro-RSFSR political strikes in the Kuzbass and their spread to Vorkuta in the far north and to the Donbass in southern Russia and the eastern Ukraine, the democrats now turned their attention to the upcoming Third RSFSR Congress of Peoples Deputies, set to open March 28. The referendum campaign and the miners strikes had turned the upcoming Third CPD-RSFSR from the threat of a possible conservative overthrow of Yeltsin into an opportunity to pass constitutional changes needed to establish the legal framework for the new presidency and schedule a Russian presidential election.[109] And DemRossiia dvizhenie's call for a mass, pro-Yeltsin rally transformed the opening day of the Congress into an opportunity to consolidate the counterelite hold on Russia's government.

Gorbachev now moved to directly confront Russia's democratic movement on the streets of Moscow. First, on March 21, the USSR Supreme Soviet banned the March 28 rally, and extended the ban until April 15.[110] The Soviet president also decreed that the Soviet Interior Ministry would temporarily take-over police functions from the Mossovet, and ordered the army to aid the Interior Ministry in preventing demonstrators from taking to the streets on March 28.[111] In the wake of Gorbachev's actions, the Mossovet refused to recognize his decrees, issuing a permit for the March 28 demonstration and seconding Yeltsin's call for the creation of a united opposition party.[112]

By the morning of March 28, the Soviet government had mobilized thousands of police and soldiers, who fanned out across central Moscow and blocked off Manezh Square, the announced end point of the protest procession, with trucks and armored vehicles.[113] Despite the show of force, hundreds of thousands gathered in Pushkin Square, and the Soviet leadership decided against ordering the police and army to forcibly breakup the rally. At the same time, organizers managed to restrain protesters from storming police barriers.

> Forming a human chain, we stood in an uncomfortable position on Pushkin Square between the police and enraged people who, from time to time, tried to break through us and storm the police lines. We had to stand there a long time and try and convince protesters not to do this.[114]

The pro-democracy demonstrations on March 28 turned into a show of force by Moscow's democratic movement. That day stood out as a very powerful demonstration . . . but I was not especially alarmed. To a great extent, a sense of alarm had been pumped-up by the authorities . . . I considered the situation to be just another normal demonstration, and I had a fairly calm attitude about the whole affair.[10]

Moreover, the inability of the center to deter mass protest made a powerful impression on delegates arriving for the opening session of the Third CPD-RSFSR. "Gorbachev ordered troops onto the street to confront us . . . This very strongly influenced the Congress."[38] While the protest continued in the streets, the Congress passed resolutions demanding the removal of troops and abolishing Gorbachev's decrees banning rallies in Moscow and taking control over the city's police functions. The next day, Gorbachev relented and ordered the troops to withdraw.[115]

As a result, the Russian Congress of Peoples Deputies swung back in Yeltsin's favor. During an acrimonious eight-day session, the Third CPD-RSFSR ended up giving the chairman of the Supreme Soviet additional powers, as well as agreeing to introduce a Russian presidency and calling a special presidential election for June 12.[116] The DemRossiia leadership interpreted Yeltsin's successes at the Congress as a direct result of March 28. "We managed to convince the CPD to give Yeltsin additional powers, under the pressure we exerted on it from below."[38]

In the wake of the Third CPD-RSFSR Congress, DemRossiia dvizhenie tried to strengthen its links with the pro-Yeltsin strike leaders in the Kuzbass and Vorkuta, who had managed to continue their political strike for over three weeks.

We actively began to work with the miners unions, meeting together in Moscow for several conferences. A number of the miners strike committees met in Moscow . . . [and] drove the influx [into DR *dvizhenie*] at this time.[93]

The miners presented the center with a politicized, anti-regime workers movement, newly recovered from the broken promises and partocratic disruption of independent workers organizations that followed the strike wave of 1989. In hopes of persuading the strikers to relent, a hunger-striking miner was invited to address the USSR Supreme Soviet by its chair, Anatolii Lukianov. The miner Malykhin, however, renewed the call for Gorbachev's resignation, and demanded the dissolution of the USSR Congress of Peoples Deputies and the transfer of power to the republics.[117] The Russian government backed the miners' demands for Gorbachev's resignation prior to the Third CPD-RSFSR, and during the Congress reaffirmed its support.[118]

The formation of working links between the miners and DemRossiia dvizhenie represented a new stage in the democratic movement, outlining a strategy for toppling the Soviet political order and completing a political revolution in Russia. Constitutional reforms introduced in connection with the formation of an RSFSR presidency would create a legitimate alternative government capable of ruling Russia proper, while ongoing negotiations for a new Union treaty would serve as a forum for negotiating a peaceful dissolution of the Soviet empire. At the same time, the coordination of the urban democratic movement and miners strike committees through strategic moves of the Democratic Russia Coordinating Committee created a united front strategically allied with Yeltsin and the DemRossiia faction in the RSFSR Supreme Soviet capable of pressuring the center from below and preventing a counterrevolutionary coup. The combination of a general political strike of urban democrats and miners would force wavering apparat forces to agree to roundtable negotiations (*kruglyi stol*) proposed during the Third CPD-RSFSR, at which a peaceful transfer of power from the center to the Yeltsin government could be realized.[119] On April 16, the Moscow newspaper *Kuranty* published a series of DemRossiia declarations outlining the above strategy and appealed for popular support.[120]

The militancy of the miners and the spread of strikes across Byelorussia pushed a number of prominent figures in the democratic movement to question the need for any negotiations with the center.[121] The rejectionist position in DemRossiia felt a Czech-style general strike would in itself trigger the collapse of the regime. The majority in the DemRossiia core, believing this scenario too optimistic, hoped to turn Yeltsin's presidential campaign into a vehicle capable of mobilizing a political revolution loosely modeled on the Czechoslovak and Hungarian patterns but taking into consideration the circumstances faced by the democratic movement in the Soviet Union. Of radical figures like Bonner, Vladimir Bokser commented that "they simply didn't understand that Russia wasn't Czechoslovakia, but a completely different country."[105]

The Russian Supreme Soviet enacted regulations for presidential nominations and campaign laws on April 24, although the May 18 deadline for filing nominations passed only on May 8. The body approved two methods for nominations—the collection of 100,000 signatures, and nomination by work collectives—and passed draft constitutional amendments outlining the Russian presidency on April 24. The new president would serve for five years, and would share the responsibility of appointing a Council of Ministers with the RSFSR Supreme Soviet. The amendment preserved most of the institutional arrangements inherited from the Soviet period, including the double parliament consisting of the biannual Congress of Peoples Deputies and the standing Supreme Soviet.[122] Enjoying the support of DemRossiia dvizhenie, Yeltsin's candidacy appeared a *fait accompli* by the time the RSFSR Supreme Soviet enacted such laws.

But just as the campaign began in earnest, the candidate himself reached an agreement with Gorbachev and leaders of eight Soviet republics on a new Union treaty during secret negotiations, an agreement quickly dubbed by the press "Nine plus One" (nine republican leaders plus Gorbachev). Nine plus One abandoned a Yeltsin-led campaign of civil disobedience in favor of a reform pact between moderate fragments of the nomenklatura and the Russian counterelite. The pact left Gorbachev's position as Soviet president intact. The Russian presidential candidate failed to advise DemRossiia's coordinating committee of his negotiations with Gorbachev and other republican leaders, undercutting a general political strike (*vseobshchaia politicheskaia stachka*) for April 26 called for in Moscow by both the leaders of DemRossiia dvizhenie and striking miners.[123]

The Gorbachev–Yeltsin joint text branded "intolerable" attempts "to incite civil disobedience and strikes" and "to call for the overthrow of existing, legitimately elected bodies of power," terms that struck miners as onerous.[124] The strike went ahead, and over thirty-four million workers at 160,000 different enterprises reportedly walked out on April 26, albeit mostly under economic— not political—demands.[125] The momentum for a sustained campaign to remove the Union government, however, faltered, and a rift opened between Yeltsin, on the hand, and militant strike leaders and radicals in DemRossiia, on the other. And yet, the Democratic Russia core had completely subordinated both its strategy and tactics to the group immediately around Yeltsin.

The many negative consequences of de facto movement centralization behind a figure who remained officially "above" the movement while he simultaneously pursued devolution of sovereignty from institutions nominally "above" him now began to manifest. In the absence of any organization commitment from its nominal leader, Yeltsin's abrupt shift to compromise with the Union leadership left the DemRossiia core suddenly adrift. Indeed, Yeltsin's opaque maneuvers deeply confused the movement core that had made his stand as a candidate in Russia's upcoming, initial presidential election possible at all. Here, the retention of highly centralized local and regional elements in the DemRossiia strategy undercut the habitus of core figures unexpectedly, from above, restraining trajectory improvisation to Yeltsin's immediate circle in Moscow among the DemRossiia core while deepening trajectory improvisation in regions all across the Republic. The seemingly paradoxical course of feudalization was, in fact, deepening.

Yeltsin moved to limit the damage from all of this at a meeting with the DemRossiia core, assuring them that Nine plus One created opportunities for realizing the movement's basic goal of reorganizing Union bodies of power, as well as guaranteeing elections for a new USSR Congress of Peoples Deputies and the Soviet presidency no later than six months after the signing of a new Union treaty. Over the objection of radicals and despite unhappiness with Yeltsin's *modus operandi*, the DemRossiia Council of Representatives called for support of the agreement in the first week of May and reaffirmed the movement's backing of Yeltsin's presidential candidacy.[126]

Yeltsin then flew to Kuzbass to try and end the strike without demoralizing his supporters. The Russian figure emphasized how Nine plus One transferred jurisdiction over the mines from the USSR to the RSFSR governments, and that support for his presidency would make Russian sovereignty—and miners control over the shafts—a political reality. Yeltsin's trip to Siberia succeeded, as miners not only agreed to suspend their strike "until the full implementation" of the Gorbachev–Yeltsin "anti-crisis program"—announced the same day as Nine plus One—but also promised to nominate Yeltsin as their presidential candidate as members of certified workers collectives.[127]

In the meantime, Gorbachev faced threats from rightist networks. In the CPSU, the General Secretary held onto his post despite increasing calls for his ouster.[128] Although Gorbachev parried such reactionary threats, Alexander Yakovlev, the former Politburo member known as the intellectual father of perestroika, interpreted the latest apparat rebellion in the CPSU against the General Secretary as signaling the exhaustion of the Party's capability of reforming itself and resigned his Party membership.[129] At the same time, Gorbachev confronted growing impatience among rightist deputies from the "Union" (*Soiuz*) bloc in the Congress of Peoples Deputies of the USSR. "Union" head Victor Alksnis even began threatening to convene a special session of the USSR Congress of Peoples Deputies in order to remove Gorbachev and declare martial law.[130]

The General Secretary, however, resisted Union's push for emergency rule. Gorbachev underscored his latest tack by announcing on May 7 a provisional agreement between himself and various republican leaders on the shape of the new Union treaty. This agreement implicitly recognized the Baltic right to secession and Russia's declaration of sovereignty, while at the same time elevating the legal status of Russia's own regional republics to a status equal with that of Union republics proper.[131] In hindsight, the radically feudalizing character of this agreement stands out.

The General Secretary now again stalemated the rightist challenge from both "Union" and the CPSU, going so far as to accuse Alksnis of fomenting a coup d'etat.[132] For the time being, the hardliners again found themselves off-balance, their hopes for an imminent declaration of emergency rule through the Soviet presidency frustrated.

If Gorbachev hoped to salvage his perestroika program by relenting to the weakening of the Union, Yeltsin's decision to join Nine plus One signaled the Russian figure's strategic independence from his supporters in the democratic movement. Just as among CPSU and "Union" reactionaries, DemRossiia radicals were caught off-guard, and scrambled to adjust to the changed strategic environment. Within the ranks of DemRossiia dvizhenie, latent fissures and disagreements in both the aktiv, and the coordinating committee and Council of Representatives, came into the open.

The de facto centralization of the movement now began to backfire, as the rationale driving Yeltsin's pursuit of a compromise to consolidate a shift of sovereignty to his own circle, above the heads of the DemRossiia core, remained unfathomable to a movement core who, in fact, had been cut out of the very process of steering the movement from above that they themselves had engineered for the head of the Russian Supreme Soviet. The Yeltsin entourage's pursuit of Russian sovereignty now centered on a strategy of decentralization of the Union, while maintaining hypercentralized political power in the Russian Republic proper. The unintended consequence of feudalization would spread wildly as a result, although this outcome remained inconceivable to the immediate Yeltsin counterelite, the DemRossiia core, or the movement aktiv alike. From this point forward, the movement would drift from its late-March zenith, into deepening factional discord, and eventually—between the fall of 1991 and the winter of 1993–1994—complete dissolution.

Nine plus One and the Split Between Movement and Counterelite

Between mid-January and mid-April, the logic of the dual-power confrontation between Gorbachev's center and Yeltsin's RSFSR government at the apex of the fractured Soviet oligarchy drove mobilization at the grass roots in a unifying direction. Beneath the surface appearance of unity projected by DemRossiia dvizhenie during these months, however, patterns of fragmentation rooted in both the *neformalitet* and the democratic movement of 1989–1990 continued to manifest. But such disagreement would only expose the DemRossiia core's machinations to the aktiv once Yeltsin abandoned this very core. The hypercentralist strategy of Yeltsin in the Russian Republic proper was, in fact, prefigured in the preceding months by moves emanating from Mossovet Chair Gavriil Popov.

In early 1991, prior to Yeltsin's sudden attempt to compromise with Gorbachev from above, Popov—the elected, DemRossiia chair of the Mossovet—emerged as the most controversial figure in Moscow's democratic movement. Dogged by rumors and press reports of corruption since mid-1990, Popov's early 1991 pamphlet, *What Is to Be Done?*, and its proposal to create an executive-style mayor during the referendum campaign, developed the theme of de-sovietization (*desovetizatsiia*) in unexpected directions. Calling for the replacement of soviets by streamlined legislative bodies and powerful executive administrators, the pamphlet urged:

- a strong center and the limitation of the sovereignty of the republics during the transition period,
- tough [*zhestkii*] executive power at all levels during the transition period, and
- the resolution of the fate of the USSR after two or three years of reforms.[133]

Popov's positions seemed to undercut the main weapon of Russia's democratic movement—the sovereign RSFSR—and to dismiss the relevance of pro-democracy deputies already seated in the soviets. In light of the call for "tough administrative power at all levels," the proposal to create a mayor generated little enthusiasm among the aktiv. The Mossovet's vote to amend the March 17 referendum by attaching a "yes–no" question on the creation of the post of mayor in Moscow

> forced us to think long and hard. For what reason did we need a mayor? It seemed senseless! Nevertheless, they [in the *Mossovet*] had come up with the proposal . . . [After thinking about it] we said, "All right, maybe its a good thing: a mayor is something new, perhaps it can help us break with the old and try something different." [Then *DemRossiia* decided] . . . Popov was our candidate. Popov's candidacy didn't generate any real enthusiasm. By that time, we had many question concerning Gavriil Kharitonovich.[80]

In opposition to many in the movement who advocated revitalized legislative bodies, Popov

> argued for a strong, in essence authoritarian, power as a necessity for implementing democracy. He tried to prove that the predominance of executive over legislative bodies would secure a more effective administration in the transition period . . . In contrast to Popov, I believe the *Mossovet* should be made into a strong and effective body, that legislative organs must balance executive organs. But Popov uses [the shortcomings of the *Mossovet*] to show that it's simply a bad institution.[44]

Whereas Afanas'ev expressed the dissatisfaction with Popov felt by many activists in DemRossiia's local organizations, Popov also became a symbol of the unhappiness felt by a number of proto-parties toward the DemRossiia core. A figure in the Social-Democratic Party explained his party's displeasure with Popov.

His conception in essence envisions an uncontrolled and authoritarian executive power, which under our present conditions simply opens the door to corruption. I think that no capital in the world is as corrupt as Moscow is now...We also opposed the economic policy of Popov's team...[whose] rationale we define as *nomenklatura* privatization, that is, aiding the transfer of property into the hands of both representatives of the old *nomenklatura* and new businessmen connected to them.[114]

Other tensions grew as well between proto-parties in DemRossiia dvizhenie and its Moscow core. For instance, the unqualified support of DemRossiia for the separatist policies of the Baltic peoples fronts at the January founding of the all-Union Democratic Congress signaled deepening problems "the national question" now caused in the democratic movement. The Democratic Party of Russia declined to join the Congress due to the refusal of the Baltic independence movements to recognize human rights as a higher priority than national self-determination.[134] The hardening anti-Union position of many DemRossiia dvizhenie activists and leaders during the referendum campaign, however, emerged as the principal factor engendering misgivings among several proto-parties toward DemRossiia's stand on nationalism.

We have always been against the collapse of the Union, always. We have always said that the communist regime and the state are different things. Of course it is necessary to remove the communist regime, but the state?...[O]ur history is...closer to that of the United States than the British Empire...Therefore we should not encourage nationalist movements.[134]

[DemRossiia] stood for some kind of "pure abstract liberalism" or "pure abstract democracy" as the only positive ideal. Which meant that, under the circumstances we had, they stood for dismantling the Soviet empire into as many pieces as possible...I felt that if you dismantled the country into 50 new democratic states, you would have a terrible mess from which we would never get out alive.[135]

In mid-April, a leaflet surfaced criticizing the April 13 decision of DemRossiia's Coordinating Committee to remain in the all-Union Democratic Congress.

The defense of the rights of the individual is an unshakable law for us, and it makes no difference whether a Union or a republican authority threatens these rights. Unfortunately we are forced to point out that a series of organizations that have joined the Democratic Congress have openly proclaimed the priority of national rights over the rights of individuals...*DemRossiia dvizhenie*, as has been repeatedly stated, is a coalition of various political forces...The coalition must as a minimum respect the interests and wishes of its partners. We are forced to state that the April 13 vote [to reaffirm *DemRossiia*'s membership in the Democratic Congress], passed by a technical majority, ignored the basic principles of a coalition.[136]

Such concerns led the Democratic Party of Russia, the Constitutional-Democratic Party of Peoples Freedom, and the Russian Christian-Democratic Movement—all DemRossiia dvizhenie members—to organize a bloc within the movement opposed to the rapid disintegration of the Union, Civic Accord (*Narodnoe soglasie*).

> The battle with the communist regime that has laid waste to our motherland [*rodina*] must not lead to a battle with the state as such, for only a strong democratic state can guarantee the rights and freedoms of the individual. We wish to change a political regime, not to destroy the state, since both the right and the left would perish under its ruins ... [T]wo political tendencies have formed in the country's democratic movement: the left-radical tendency, the actions of which are leading to the destruction of the Union as a state and to the dismemberment of the Russian Federation; and the constructive-democratic tendency, which strives to preserve the unity of the Russian Federation and to create a new Union state. Both tendencies must have an equal right to self-expression within the framework of *DemRossiia*.[137]

The announcement of Nine plus One temporarily assuaged some of the fears of Civic Accord. Where tensions between leaders of the proto-parties and the DemRossiia core—centered on the latter's modus operandi—remained in the background before April, they spilled out into the open in the aftermath of the new Union treaty negotiations. At a difficult meeting on April 25, the DemRossiia Coordinating Committee divided between those who advocated a "mild response" to Nine plus One, and those who demanded "an angry rebuke" to the agreement.[138] At the April 25 session of the Committee, two figures who enjoyed great popularity among the rank and file—Yuri Afanas'ev and Leonid Batkin—reacted with particular dismay to the Gorbachev–Yeltsin announcement of Nine plus One.

> Afanas'ev ... took the position that, in light of the agreement, we must immediately go into opposition to Yeltsin, accusing him of treachery [*predatel'stvo*] ... [T]he main idea and tactic of the radical pole around Afanas'ev was a sharp confrontation with the central government [in hopes that] the Union would collapse ... We [the *DemRossiia* core] understood that, in any direct confrontation with the Union government, we would undoubtedly suffer a defeat, not to mention the fact that a civil war would follow. Given that the Soviet Union was a nuclear power and the fact that the center had absolutely all coercive structures at its disposal, it was simply impossible to go down this road. It would have been naive to think that we could have gone toe-to-toe [*stenka na stenku*] with the center ... This was naive, but it was the essence of the position taken by

Baktin [and Afanas'ev]...In fact, they did not understand the specific character of Russia, something typical of a part of the humanistic elite in Moscow. They thought that the development of political processes in Russia must take the exact same course as in eastern Europe.[105]

Afanas'ev and Baktin's position clearly enjoyed significant support among DemRossiia activists and striking miners in the days immediately following the announcement of the Gorbachev–Yeltsin accord. But the radicals found themselves in a minority at the plenum of the Council of Representatives that met on April 27, when a majority voted to back Nine plus One.[139] Such disagreements over Nine plus One broke the momentum of radicalization at the grass roots which had gathered steam ever since the Baltic events. Indeed, the series of squabbles between various movement fragments over the strategic direction of DR dvizhenie during the period running from Nine plus One onward augured a growing split between the soviet-based counterelite and the grassroots aktiv.

At the city's district level, DemRossiia's Coordinating Committee expelled a rejectionist head of the Zelenograd voter club from the movement.[140] At the citywide level, Afanas'ev and Baktin's sharp criticisms of "apparat maneuvers" in the first days after Nine plus One garnered sympathy among the aktiv, many of whom knew of irregularities connected with top DemRossiia organizers stretching back to selection of candidates placed on the official DR voters bloc list just prior to the 1990 election. Although Afanas'ev soon reigned in his criticism to go along with Nine plus One, Baktin remained publicly opposed for several weeks, even threatening to resign from the movement.[105] The Council of Representatives subsequently backed Afanas'ev as a DemRossiia candidate in a special run-off election for Moscow's district-territorial seat forty-one in the CPD-RSFSR.[141]

Although Afanas'ev and Baktin remained in DemRossiia—thus consolidating the movement's de facto subordination to Yeltsin—both men began criticizing a "new DemRossiia apparat" and Popov and Il'ia Zaslavskii's combining of chairs of city soviets with "commercial activities." Afanas'ev identified the source of the tension

as fundamentally different attitudes to political power and to the "apparatization" [*apparatizatsiia*] of *DemRossiia dvizhenie*...[Zaslavskii] got mired in over his head in commercial deals...in the October district soviet, a political structure which became entangled in hundreds and hundreds of various commercial enterprises...And Popov, after all, didn't oppose this position.[44]

The failure of proto-parties who joined DemRossiia dvizhenie to grow after 1990 seemed to confirm concerns that the movement would eclipse and stunt the development of democratic political parties. Tensions between the pro-Yeltsin majority in the DemRossiia core and the Afanas'ev radicals in the Coordinating Committee created an opening for proto-party leaders to criticize the core for its organizational practices.

> We continued to work in *DemRossiia* . . . but there were constant conflicts between the representatives of the parties . . . and the [old] Moscow Association of Voters leadership. This group . . . strived to appropriate all *DemRossiia* leadership posts. There was simply a difference of approaches as to the nature of Democratic Russia, especially in Moscow. Was *DemRossiia* a coalition of various party and non-party organizations, or some sort of homogeneous organization with individual membership?[114]

The Coordinating Committee's endorsement of Popov as DemRossiia's mayoral candidate in Moscow amplified discord among the city's grassroots activists in the wake of Nine plus One. In early May, a controversy broke out in the Mossovet over both the chairman's proposal for nominating mayoral candidates, and his plan to concentrate "extraordinary powers" (*chrezvychainye polnomochii*) in the new office of mayor.[142] Talk of a powerful executive mayor set off alarms among proceduralist democrats seated in the city's various soviets. As the campaign progressed, Popov also underscored his intention to create stock exchanges (*birzhi*) and other experiments that alarmed *intelligenty* fearful of nomenklatura privatization.[143] Opinion polls taken in the spring indicated Popov remained more popular among the pro-democracy electorate at large than among the DemRossiia aktiv itself, a factor that encouraged Popov to ignore grassroots activists.[144]

Prior to the Yeltsin and Popov campaigns, voter clubs and associations functioned as de facto DemRossiia district organizations in Moscow, and many of these district associations considered themselves collective members of DR dvizhenie. But the campaigns prompted the Moscow core to create an organizationally distinct Moscow section (*otdelenie*) of DemRossiia dvizhenie. Three aspects of the democratic movement in Moscow, however, presented the DemRossiia core with a unique set of difficulties in organizing a citywide section.

First, Moscow was the operational base for senior figures in the movement's member parties, some of whom undermined the DemRossiia core's modus operandi. Vladimir Kutukov, a member of the Taganskii district voter club, spoke with resentment of the Democratic Party of Russia's attempt to steer new recruits into the DPR, and complained that Republican Party leaders had surreptitiously used DemRossiia telephone lists for recruiting purposes.[2] On the other hand, a member of Brateevo, a neighborhood association affiliated with DemRossiia, dismissed the relevance of "squabbles" in the coordinating committee to relations between party and nonparty activists at the grassroots level.[10]

Second, the proximity of the city's array of Democratic Russia district organizations to the movement's RSFSR-wide leadership meant that grassroots members sometimes circulated rumors about "the DemRossiia apparat" and tensions in the Coordinating Committee. Finally, the pro-Yeltsin majority in this Committee—the DemRossiia core—contended with the revolutionary aspirations of the city's aktiv. Moscow, after all, had been the site of almost weekly mass demonstrations from mid-January through the end of March and grassroots militancy reached an apex in the capital.

With the announcement of Nine plus One, the Coordinating Committee's abandonment of a campaign of civil disobedience in favor of the Gorbachev–Yeltsin compromise sowed confusion among the aktiv.

> Our radicals never understood that *DemRossiia dvizhenie* had a centrist line. More precisely, if from the very beginning we had taken a centrist position, this would have been unpopular and thus undermined the mass character of our movement.[105]

Here, a key DemRossiia core member virtually confessed the highly manipulative politics that the core more and more resorted to in order both to sustain viability in grassroots networks, and to remain an adjunct of Yeltsin's counterelite.

To prevent such factors from interfering with the presidential campaign, DemRossiia's Council of Representatives continued to allow the DemRossiia core to make policy decisions for the local chapter by setting up the Moscow City Organization of Democratic Russia (*Moskovskaia gorodskaia organizatsiia Demokraticheskii Rossii*). This was done by engineering both the election of Vladimir Bokser as chair of the Moscow section, and other members of the Yeltsinite DemRossiia core itself to the Moscow City Organization's Coordinating Committee, a move that triggered immediate opposition from most of the proto-party leaders. "The Coordinating Committee of Democratic Russia's Moscow section was for all practical purposes the Coordinating Committee of the movement as a whole."[24] In the wake of challenges by party leaders to the new DemRossiia Moscow section, the core issued a leaflet certifying "the legitimacy of the election of the Coordinating Committee of the Moscow City Organization of *DemRossiia*."[145]

Beyond the discord surrounding the founding of Democratic Russia's Moscow City Organization, the Yeltsin campaign presented the DemRossiia core with difficulties relating the concerns of a now radicalized aktiv to Yeltsin's much broader and more diffuse electoral base.

> [Yeltsin] reflected a very diverse balance of forces, among which *DemRossiia* occupied only one place, though a very influential place... On the one hand, Yeltsin could not have become President, he could not have become Chairman of the RSFSR Supreme Soviet in 1990, if *DemRossiia* had not exerted an enormous effort on his behalf to secure these outcomes. On the other hand, Yeltsin's personal charisma also played a significant role... Thus relations between Yeltsin and *DemRossiia* were extraordinarily complex.[146]

Indeed, Yeltsin remained only partially dependent on the DemRossiia core to run his campaign. Gennadii Burbulis, the former USSR Inter-regional Deputies Group and Democratic Party of Russia figure, emerged as the real head of the Russian Supreme Soviet Chair's campaign organization. During the first months of 1991, Burbulis moved from a member of Yeltsin's advisory Presidential Council to the position of the RSFSR Chair's personal spokesman and trusted confidant.[147] Although Burbulis remained a member of DemRossiia's Council of Representatives, he had for all practical purposes ceased to participate in the movement's organizational work by the spring of 1991.[43] On the contrary, Burbulis and his campaign staff formed an intermediary body between the Democratic Russia core and Yeltsin himself, to the frustration of core figures.

> Burbulis was the nominal head of the whole business. Yet Burbulis... came in like a big boss, gathered us together and gave out his directives: "You need to do this, you need to do that—so do it!" And then he left us to fend for ourselves in the localities and regions, to figure out who to call, who to distribute material to, and so forth.[3]

Yeltsin demonstrated his distance from DemRossiia dvizhenie during the campaign, especially when he announced Alexander Rutskoi as his vice presidential running mate. Rutskoi, a former Afghan war hero who had sided with Yeltsin in late March during the Third CPD-RSFSR, founded the Communists for Democracy faction in the RSFSR Supreme Soviet.[148] Yeltsin's move paid considerable dividends, as several days after Rutskoi's selection, a group of army officers named Servicemen for Democracy signed a letter calling on rank-and-file soldiers to vote for the chair of the Russian Supreme Soviet as RSFSR president.[149] Thus began Yeltsin's courting of Soviet military leaders, a strategy rewarded during the August coup.

The campaign benefited from the official positions of counterelite figures, which gave it access to material means and a degree of protection from repressive measures.[150] Such aid helped the campaign overcome an explosion wrecking DemRossiia's main office in Moscow early in the morning of May 16 that destroyed many of the files and telephone lists then at the DemRossiia core's disposal.[151] Alexander Muzykantskii, for instance, in his capacity both as a Mossovet deputy and member of the city executive government, quickly secured a new headquarters for the movement.[152] And Burbulis' position in the Russian government and Ponomarev's status as a Russian peoples deputy helped them arrange the speedy shipment of campaign posters, photocopied leaflets and so forth to local DemRossiia sections around the RSFSR.

> One night, I was sitting in a car loaded with posters…We got to the Bykovo airport about 2:30 in the morning. A sleepy eyed fellow walked up and said "What's up guys?" We replied, "We're from Yeltsin, we need to ship some posters to the regions. Where are the planes that fly-out tonight?" "Well, maybe five planes are heading-out to different regions." "How can we get this stuff to the pilots, where can we meet them?" "Well, what the hell, let's go to the dispatcher's office."[3]

The rightist partocracy finally realized how self-destructive any appearance of apparat obstruction of the Yeltsin campaign might be. The anticlimatic Fourth RSFSR Congress of Peoples Deputies convened between May 21 and 25, and with little controversy approved the draft constitutional amendments establishing a Russian presidency prepared in previous weeks by the Russian Supreme Soviet.[153] "In essence, the cause had already been won before the election, since it was absolutely certain that Yeltsin would be victorious."[93]

On June 12, 1991, Yeltsin won a plurality of 57 percent in the first direct election of a national leader in Russian history. Popov emerged from the election with an impressive 65 percent, while Anatolii Sobchak, the pro-Yeltsin chairman of the *Lensovet*, was elected mayor of Leningrad by 66 percent of that city's voters. In addition to electing Sobchak, Leningrad delivered a symbolic blow to the nomenklatura by voting to restore the city's pre–World War I name, St. Petersburg.[154]

While Gorbachev remained preoccupied with fending off partocratic attempts to remove him, Yeltsin prepared to assume the Russian presidency. The leadership of DemRossiia dvizhenie had argued during the Yeltsin campaign that the election of a new, pro-democracy president would create "a legitimate authority" on Russian soil to counterbalance the partocracy.[155] When, at a press conference sponsored by Democratic Russia the day after the election, Popov spoke out in favor of creating a "powerful alternative party," the DemRossiia core could only have been heartened.[156]

Popov, however, had something else in mind. In the month following the election, Moscow's new mayor resigned his post as cochair of DemRossiia and initiated a sweeping program of "de-sovietization" in the city, a program that strained relations between DemRossiia dvizhenie and the mayor. On July 1, Popov abolished by decree the inter-locking hierarchy of district and precinct-level soviets and replaced them with ten prefectures. When combined with decrees issued the previous week giving himself emergency powers, Popov's moves caused a rebellion in the district soviets (*raisovety*) and in the Mossovet itself, a rebellion that pushed many proceduralist pro-democracy deputies into alliance with CPSU deputies against Popov's executive liberalism. Popov responded by suggesting that raisovety deputies "look for work elsewhere." In mid-July, the Moscow prosecutor's office declared the Moscow mayor's actions in violation of the Soviet constitution. Popov responded by appealing to Yeltsin, who issued a decree in late July giving Popov a *carte blanche* to restructure until the next RSFSR Congress of Peoples Deputies in the fall. Popov, in effect, had managed to "de-sovietize" the capital.[157]

In the summer, Popov also joined together with Eduard Shevardnadze, Alexander Yakovlev and Leningrad mayor-elect Sobchak to create a new organization, the Movement for Democratic Reforms (*Dvizhenie demokraticheskykh reform*), on the basis of a network of ex-CPSU and CPSU reformers, an organization reflecting Popov's preference for creating a "united democratic party" on the territory of the whole Union.[158] Besides Popov, Republican Party figure Vladimir Lysenko, a trio of former Committee of the 19 organizers with personal ties to Yeltsin—Alexander Muzykantskii, Lev Shemaev, and Sergei Trube—and Alexander Rutskoi, Yeltsin's new vice president, joined the Movement for Democratic Reforms in June and July.[159] Although privately dismayed by Popov's virtual abandonment of DemRossiia dvizhenie, erstwhile colleagues in the movement's Coordinating Committee maintained a cordial public attitude toward the new mayor in hopes of cooperating with the Movement for Democratic Reforms on particular issues.[160]

The reaction of many grassroots activists toward Popov's moves were of an all together different character. Indeed, more than a few activists considered the mayor to have betrayed his campaign staff and volunteers, especially following Popov's appointment of several highly unpopular apparatchiks to posts in the mayor's office. "Today people are simply embarrassed and ashamed to show their registration cards certifying them as members of the Initiative Group that collected signatures for Popov's nomination."[2] Not all district-level activists opposed Popov, however, attesting to deepening splits in the networks that constituted the city's grass roots. Yakov Gorbadei, a DemRossiia activist and member of the Zelenograd district soviet, sympathized with Popov and his attempt to confront "the lack of the ability to work effectively [*nerabotosposobnost'*] of the soviets and the democrats in them."[140]

Yeltsin himself continued to distance himself from DemRossiia dvizhenie. First, he snubbed the movement by reserving most of the seats at a June 29 meeting with "the democratic public" for Russian government officials.[156]

Then, following his presidential inauguration on July 10, Yeltsin emulated Moscow's new mayor in by-passing prominent DemRossiia figures and appointing a new RSFSR government dominated by reformers with a centrist apparat background. The only exception to this pattern were the appointments of Galina Starovoitova as an advisor on nationalities and Pavel Kudiukin to the Labor Ministry, although by this time Kudiukin was in de facto opposition to the DemRossiia core.[158] Thus Yeltsin's most steadfast supporters outside of apparat circles found themselves shut-out of the new governing team.

On July 20, the Russian president issued the "de-party-zation" decree (*ukaz o departizatsii*) over strong protests by the partocracy. The DemRossiia core privately came to regard the decree as a mistake, as it forced the movement to disband its network of enterprise cells created during the previous five months.[161] The inability of the core to confront Yeltsin over his order to essentially disband its own movement in enterprises starkly attests to the core's collapse as an effective vehicle of pro-democracy networking.

At the same time, the "de-party-zation" decree only further incensed conservatives frustrated by their exclusion from negotiations with republican leaders over a new Union treaty. Three days after Yeltsin signed the "de-party-zation" decree, twelve hard-line writers, generals and prominent CPSU officials signed a belligerent letter, "A Word to the People" (*Slovo k narody*).[162] Among the letter's signatories stood Interior Minister Boris Pugo, agriculturalist figure Vasilii Starodubtsev, and Alexander Tiziakov, a leader of rightist apparatchiks in the military-industrial complex, all of whom sat on the eight-member State Committee for the State of Emergency (*Gosudarstvennyi komitet po chrezvychainomy polozheniiu*) declared the morning of August 19.

By late July 1991, wide splits had opened between Gorbachev's nominal political center—busy negotiating a murky, decentralized vision of a new Union with the Russian government—and the right, now openly mobilizing in the USSR Congress of Peoples Deputies, the Russian Communist Party and the military. And around the left pole of Russia's political spectrum, July brought not only a growing distance between DemRossiia dvizhenie and its erstwhile electoral champions, Yeltsin and Popov, but also witnessed the advent of fragmentation within the DemRossiia parliamentary bloc in the Supreme Soviet, and the end of close working relations between most nominal Democratic Russia deputies and the movement's Coordinating Committee.

The Fifth RSFSR Congress of Peoples Deputies opened on July 10, and quickly dispatched with its first order of business, inaugurating Yeltsin Russian president. After bickering for seven days, the Congress on July 17 selected Ruslan Khasbulatov as provisional chair of the Russian Supreme Soviet and adjourned until the fall, without accomplishing much of anything else.[163] The

Fifth CPD-RSFSR signaled the end of a functional DemRossiia bloc in the Supreme Soviet, plunging Democratic Russia deputies into a pattern of internal fragmentation that had been presaged among pro-democracy factions in Moscow's city and district soviets.

> [Before the Fifth CPD-RSFSR] . . . a number of well-known disagreements occurred, but as a rule, the *DemRossiia* bloc nevertheless managed to vote in a consistently solidary manner in the Congress of Peoples Deputies and the Supreme Soviet . . . But then *DemRossiia* split. A prominent group of deputies refused to support Khasbulatov, and I was among them.[146]

Together with the drift in DemRossiia dvizhenie noticeable since the June presidential election, the factiousness among Democratic Russia's parliamentary bloc brought disintegration of networks linking the democratic movement's aktiv and the RSFSR peoples deputies they helped elect.

> From the very beginning, relations between DemRossiia dvizhenie and Democratic Russia in parliament were not particularly close, even though several deputies, such as Sheinis, were members of DR *dvizhenie*'s Coordinating Committee. But such deputies rarely appeared at Committee meetings, as they became more and more absorbed in parliamentary work. In this way arose a certain lack of understanding of each other's goals . . . Simultaneously, parliamentary deputies began to feel themselves demeaned by participation in the movement: after all, people in the Coordinating Committee remained virtual unknowns, whereas members of parliament were becoming very well known . . . And thus I felt the origins of a psychological parting of the ways.[38]

The condition in which the DemRossiia core found itself in July reflected its unstable position between movement and counterelite, its conflicted organizational mission, and its total inability to face the disastrous errors it had committed as de facto movement centralizers. Although DemRossiia dvizhenie presented itself as a movement of society against the partocracy, the core in fact now played the role of a de facto political machine for Yeltsin and other counterelite figures.[164] The contradictions of this position now starkly presented themselves. The core's dependence on a charismatic figure who had reached out in a populist fashion to Russia's disenfranchised specialists and workers but who in fact remained based in the radical-reform wing of the fragmented Soviet nomenklatura reduced the core to a combination of social-movement type anti-politics and tactical work on behalf of a figure, Yeltsin, who declined all organizational commitments.

Seemingly abandoned by Yeltsin and riven by discord, the Coordinating Committee found itself mired in internal conflicts. For his part, Afanas'ev pushed the Coordinating Committee toward a more critical evaluation of Yeltsin's compromise with Gorbachev and began to adhere to strict monetarist economic principles, sounding more like former British Prime Minister Margaret Thatcher every day. The embrace of economic austerity by the erstwhile champion of the grass roots did little to stem the flagging enthusiasm of the aktiv, as the Coordinating Committee's preoccupation with economic policies oriented to cooperatives and businesses over the previous, more balanced emphasis on both privatization and social defense caused a significant number of DemRossiia activists to lose enthusiasm for the movement.[2] At the same time, many principal figures of DemRossiia's proto-parties ceased to participate altogether in the movement's citywide bodies.[165]

For the most part, district-level activists remained indifferent to the move of CPSU "formers" toward Popov's Movement for Democratic Reforms, and sat on the sidelines as the Afanas'ev radicals, the DemRossiia core and proto-party leaders squabbled over the national question and the organizational details of Democratic Russia's stillborn city section. One activist, admitting his "complacency" after Yeltsin's election, took a long vacation during the summer.[80] The televised announcement of a Union-wide state of emergency on August 19 interrupted such internal bickering and withdrawal.

4

August 1991 and the Decline of Russia's Democratic Movement

E arly on the morning of August 19, 1991, Russians awoke to television and radio announcements of the resignation of President Gorbachev "due to ill health" and the declaration of a "state of emergency." The latter entailed the "disbanding of all structures and administrations . . . acting in violation of the USSR Constitution," the "suspension of the activities of political parties, organizations and movements that hamper the normalization of the situation," the banning of "rallies, protests and strikes," and the introduction of martial law in Moscow, Leningrad, and a number of other key locations in the Soviet Union, including the Baltic republics. The announcements asserted that official power now resided in the hands of an eight-member State Committee for the State of Emergency (*Gosudarstvennyi komitet po chrezvychainomy polozheniiu*, or GKChP), led by Vice President Gennadii Yanaev.[1]

A different reality lay behind the GKChP announcement of Gorbachev's "resignation." On the afternoon of August 18, Gorbachev's Chief of Staff, Valerii Boldin, and the head of the KGB's Security Directorate, Yurii Plekhanov, arrived at the Soviet president's vacation residence at Foros in the Crimea, where all communication lines had gone dead. Boldin and Plekhanov demanded that Gorbachev sign a communiqué handing power over to the State Committee or resign. When Gorbachev refused to do either, he and his family were placed under house arrest and held until the night of August 21.[2] The falsification of circumstances surrounding the State Committee's assumption of power subsequently served as the basis of official indictments against members of the GKChP.

Before Gorbachev's release on the evening of August 21, the circumstances surrounding the formation of the GKChP remained unclear. Yet opponents of the State Committee immediately branded its assumption of power a coup d'etat. From the post-Stalin, partocratic perspective of "collective leadership," however, the removal of one figure from senior authority certainly did not constitute a coup d'etat.

Prior to the week of August 19–24, the party-state could conceivably have been revived—at least in the short term—as an instrument of partocratic domination, if the right could have succeeded in reimposing *apparat* dictatorship and then reinstated Article 6 of the Soviet Constitution. But the dissolution of the CPSU liquidated the institutional bearer of party-state domination that had shaped political life in Russia for more than seven decades—an event whose permanence was etched in subsequent years. Destroying the CPSU as a political form of rule and the territorial entity it constructed, the Soviet Union, turned these events into a political revolution, a language that ties the representation of events to their *longue durée*.

Yet such observational language can obscure the motive and habitus of principals immediately at stake. Above all, prevention of the signing of the new Union Treaty on August 20, 1991, represented the paramount objective of the State Committee for the State of Emergency. Rebroadcast of an earlier statement by USSR Supreme Soviet Chair Anatolii Lukianov on the morning of August 19 confirmed that disrupting the signing of the new Union treaty stood as the primary goal of the GKChP.[3] Lukianov claimed that Nine plus One, the Novo-Ogarevo treaty, violated "the will of the people" as expressed in the March 17 referendum and represented a "dangerous" step that would only exacerbate "the war of the laws." The opposition's designation of the declaration of a state of emergency as a coup d'etat (*perevorot*) became an integral element in the counterelite's improvised strategy of resistance to the GKChP, and the widespread diffusion of this sobriquet on August 19 played a central role in the rapid collapse of the State Committee's authority.

August 1991

The State Committee for the State of Emergency presented its assumption of power as preventing "fratricidal civil war," securing "the restoration of law and order," and stopping "the war of the laws." The GKChP framed its "Appeal to the Soviet People" using themes presented in the rightist lament of July, "A Word to the People" (*Slovo narody*).

> Taking advantage of liberties granted and crushing the shoots of newly emergent democracy, extremist forces have developed whose aim is the liquidation of the Soviet Union, the dismemberment of the state and the seizure of power at any cost. The results of the nationwide referendum on the unity of the fatherland have been trampled underfoot . . . Before our very eyes, all the democratic institutions,

created by the will of the people, are losing their authority and effectiveness. All this is a consequence of the deliberate activity of those who, in blatant violation of the Basic Law of the USSR, are in fact carrying out an unconstitutional coup d'etat. The goal of such people is unlimited personal dictatorship. Prefectures, mayoralties, and other unlawful structures have been increasingly usurping the power of soviets elected by the people.[4]

The State Committee thus justified its activities in legalisms predominate in official discourse since Gorbachev prioritized the creation of a state of law in the early years of *perestroika*, so long as the fiction that Gorbachev remained incapacitated and Yanaev had assumed the powers of the presidency in accordance with the constitution could be maintained. To reinforce the image of the GKChP's legality, Chairman of the USSR Supreme Soviet Anatolii Lukianov called a special session of the USSR Supreme Soviet on August 26 to ratify the State Committee's activities.[5]

Claims to GKChP legality immediately emerged as the prime target of the State Committee's opponents, becoming the principal symbolic weapon of the anti-GKChP resistance. First, an "Appeal to the Citizens of Russia" asserted that Gorbachev's removal had been "the result of a rightist, reactionary, and anti-constitutional coup d'etat" and called for a return "to normal constitutional development." Released at nine the morning of August 19 and signed by Yeltsin, RSFSR Prime Minister Silaev, and RSFSR Supreme Soviet Chair Ruslan Khasbulatov, the appeal finished by calling on soldiers to disobey GKChP leaders.

Second, a Yeltsin decree issued in the early afternoon codified the Russian leadership's evaluation of events as official policy of the RSFSR government.

I decree:

1. That the announcements of the committee [GKChP] are considered illegal and the actions of its organizers constitute an anti-constitutional coup d'etat and thus are nothing other than a crime against the state.
2. All decisions taken in the name of the so-called committee for the state of emergency are illegal and have no force on the territory of the RSFSR. The territory of the Russian Federation is governed by the laws of the legally elected government, represented by the President of the Supreme Soviet and the Chairman of the Council of Ministers and all state and local administrative organs of the government of the RSFSR.
3. The actions of government officials who implement the orders of the above committee are subject to the Legal Code of the RSFSR and shall be prosecuted under the law.

This decree has legal validity from the moment of its signing.

Late in the afternoon, Yeltsin issued the third key document, appealing to soldiers and officers of the USSR to disobey the orders of the GKChP.

> The country faces the threat of terror . . . Do not let yourselves be caught in a web of lies, promises and demagogic arguments about military duty! Do not allow yourselves to become a blind weapon serving the criminal will of a group of adventurers who have violated the Constitution of the USSR . . . You can build a throne of bayonets, but you will not long be able to sit on such a throne. A return to the past is impossible and will not come to pass. The days of the conspirators are numbered.[6]

By Monday evening, the Russian opposition controlled the symbolism of legality, turning the charge of illegality back on the GKChP. On Tuesday, the anticoup resistance successfully split the armed forces, disrupted the oligarchic chain of command, and forced the committee to either accept defeat or risk a bloody civil war with greatly diminished chances of success. On Wednesday, the GKChP collapsed, initiating a process culminating five months later in the dismemberment of the Soviet Union. Why?

Several immediate reasons help clarify the State Committee's rapid collapse. Instigators of the GKChP, fearing leaks, informed an extremely narrow circle of confidants of their intentions and prepared an initial list of less than a hundred opposition politicians and organizers to be arrested early on the morning of the nineteenth.

> Only about twenty people knew anything was going on, which explains the putsch's semi-comic character. And these twenty-odd persons were mostly senior officers, people who didn't understand the real situation in the country.[7]

Not that the State Committee did not intend to arrest a much larger number of people. Indeed, the GKChP ordered 250,000 pairs of handcuffs to be sent to the capital a few days prior to declaring an emergency.[8] Delays in conveying orders, foot-dragging, and insubordination by a handful of KGB, military, and police officials allowed many of the designated detainees to elude capture. Yeltsin's evasion of arrest proved the most damaging of all. KGB Major General Victor Karpukhin, disobeying orders to detain the Russian president at his dacha outside the capital early on the morning of the nineteenth, instead allowed Yeltsin to leave for Moscow.[9]

Indeed, disobedience and confusion were widespread. Nearly all leading *DemRossiia* figures, with the exception of populist Tel'man Gdlian, also escaped detention.

> I found out about [the coup] at six in the morning, give or take a few minutes, and within a quarter of an hour I left home. I supposed at first that things would go as they had in Poland, but for some reason I was not immediately arrested.

It turned out that the order for my arrest was not conveyed until 7:20 AM. I was on the list of seventy-three persons to be arrested, and even listed among the nineteen persons to be detained as quickly as possible. They [the instigators] made a whole series of blunders. The explanation for these blunders lies in the fact it was not just society that was divided: by that time, the KGB and the army were split, and this was, after all, not just a coup against Yeltsin, but also against Gorbachev...Naturally, if [the GKChP] had brought a wider circle of people into its preparations, it could have prepared reliable lists of persons to carry out the arrests and seize us in the middle of the night...But to do this, they would have needed to draw one or perhaps two thousand people into the plan, which, of course would lead to a leak of information and the failure of the scheme.[7]

Bokser's invocation of the Polish precedent and his description of the extraordinarily narrow circle of plotters indicates both the GKChP's strategy and habitus. The State Committee in fact patterned its actions on party-state models for reimposing order, as executed in Hungary in 1956, Czechoslovakia in 1968, and Poland in 1981.[10] The success of such a scenario, however, presupposes a highly obedient administrative apparat and military and security forces loyal to the existing chain of command. Although rightist individuals and groups may well have been encouraged by the counterrevolutionary mobilization of the past ten months, the State Committee failed to enlist the most active rightist leaders in their plan, catching its most important constituency off-guard. Some of these rightists even speculated that Gorbachev masterminded "the farce" in the wake of its failure.[11]

Thus the GKChP's conduct indicates its members regarded themselves in terms of routine norms of *partiinost'* (party-spiritedness), rather than as rightist political entrepreneurs. The scenario enacted beginning the night of August 18 assumed the swift arrest of prominent counterelite figures, and combined with the declaration of martial law in a few key cities, would be sufficient to restore the authority of the Soviet center and thus reestablish the apparat chain of command. Interrogations of surviving leaders of the State Committee conducted in the aftermath of its collapse reveal how seriously the instigators overestimated the loyalty of their subordinates and lacked internal consensus over the degree of force to employ.[12]

A quick review of events brings this home.[13] Within hours of announcing the state of emergency, high-ranking KGB officers allowed key opponents to escape arrest. Then a special police detachment and a tank brigade from the Taman division broke ranks and pledged their loyalty to the RSFSR government late Monday evening. On Tuesday, two senior generals, Pavel Grachev and Yevgenii Shaposhnikov, refused to storm the Russian "White House," the building where sessions of the Russian Supreme Soviet took place and Yeltsin had holed up on the morning of the nineteenth. Also on Tuesday, Mayor

Anatolii Sobchak persuaded General Victor Samsonov to disregard GKChP orders to occupy Leningrad with tanks and armored personnel carriers.

Having escaped detention, Yeltsin and other pro-democracy figures regrouped at the White House and decreed the members of the GKChP "renegade leaders of a coup d'etat." Few would learn until years later of rumors that Yeltsin became drunk overnight.[14] What mattered that evening occurred outside the White House.

Although the numbers of "defenders of the White House" (*zashchitniki belogo doma*) assembled by Monday night measured in the low tens and not the hundreds of thousands, their presence, combined with that of defecting police and army troops, rendered any assault a costly proposition. Suddenly faced with the prospect of committing a massacre on the scale of Tiananmen Square, senior commanders and GKChP leaders alike hesitated for another twenty-four hours. Unsure of the loyalty of senior officers and dismayed at having to order the army to fire on demonstrators on the streets of Moscow, Defense Minister Dmitrii Yazov finally acted on his own and ordered his troops to withdraw on the morning of the twenty-first. Unable to establish effective lines of command and facing widespread disobedience across the Soviet Union, the State Committee disintegrated within a few hours.

On August 20, 21, and 22, large numbers of republican and regional soviets released statements declaring their opposition to the State Committee.[15] And in a telling account, a DemRossiia activist recalls an encounter with a municipal police officer at a subway station on August 20.

> [Anticoup] leaflets were plastered everywhere outside the metro exit. Inside the station stood a policeman, next to a single leaflet, the only leaflet inside the entrance. I wanted to take it down and carry it home with me [to protect it], but suddenly he said "Cousin, I've been guarding that leaflet all day."[16]

Indeed, the symbolic rendition of events changed as rapidly as events in real time. The rapid dissemination of counterelite figures' edicts and appeals linked opposition networks to symbolic advantages of anti-GKChP resistance between Monday morning and Wednesday evening. Although the State Committee suspended the publication of all but nine national and Moscow-area newspapers and magazines,[17] anti-GKChP journalists in Moscow produced mimeographed "special issues" (*ekstrennyie vypuski*) of many banned papers.[18] By special decree, the RSFSR Ministry for the Press and Information registered the new paper, Joint Gazette 11 (*Obshchaia gazeta 11*), on August 20. Joint Gazette 11 provided an *ofititsioznyi* outlet for journalists attached to eleven suspended periodicals to collaborate in providing independent information and resist the State Committee.[19]

Television amplified the symbolic effects the GKChP unwittingly generated. Television journalist Vadim Medvedev, for instance, prepared and edited a report on the introduction of martial law in Moscow in the hour before the evening broadcast that showed Yeltsin standing on a tank outside the White House, appealing for citizens to come to the defense of Russian democracy. In the rushed minutes before the broadcast, Medvedev's supervisor allowed the report to be broadcast without fully screening its contents. Thus began what Victoria Bonnell and Gregory Freidin have called a "televorot"—a play on the Russian word *perevorot* (coup d'etat) loosely interpreted as "TV uprising"—at Soviet television during the crucial days of August 19–21.[20]

In an attempt to turn a deteriorating situation in their favor, the State Committee held a joint press conference late on Monday afternoon. The live television broadcast of this event proved disastrous to the eight gray-suited GKChP members, and especially to State Committee chief Gennadii Yanaev, whose hands began shaking in response to reporters' inquiries regarding the state of Gorbachev's health. Yanaev at one point suggested that "when Gorbachev recovered, he could return to carry out his duties," sowing confusion among supporters and opponents alike. Not only did journalists laugh at some of his answers, several reporters asked incredulous GKChP members if they believed they had committed a coup d'etat. An Italian correspondent went so far as to ask the Committee if it had "asked General Pinochet for advice."[21]

By the time Gorbachev walked out of his plane onto the tarmac in Moscow early in the morning of the twenty-second, the symbolic defeat of the State Committee was complete. The GKChP failed to grasp the political dynamics engendered by dual power, and in particular the legitimacy the sovereign RSFSR enjoyed among a number of military and security personnel. State Committee figures overlooked signs that some senior military personnel viewed the Russian government positively, such as the June 1991 letter signed by nine officers supporting Yeltsin's presidential candidacy.[22] The State Committee thus proved incapable of the spontaneous political entrepreneurship on which the counterelite thrived.

The State Committee's partocratic habitus, restorationist in character, impelled it to shore up a sagging regime, not overthrow a political order. Moreover, the narrowness of this habitus showed in the GKChP's inability to anticipate or control its symbolic projection. From a strategic point of view, the State Committee poorly interpreted the political state of affairs in the USSR in August 1991, and particularly the degree of unity in the military, security services, and administrative apparat of the Soviet regime. But had coup leaders secured several loyal divisions and ordered the killing of unarmed demonstrators, the White House could have been quickly stormed although such a step may have triggered a period of civil strife across the Soviet Union. The incompetence of the GKChP thus emerges as the proximate cause of its rapid failure, with dual power between the Russian and Soviet regimes serving as the ultimate cause of the collapse of the State Committee. DemRossiia dvizhenie in the streets served a "minor" role here, as acknowledged by a Moscow core figure.[23]

The ill-fated GKChP attempt to declare a state of emergency opened up an unexpected opportunity for the counterelite to radicalize the revolutionary process by discarding the pacted transition with Gorbachev and dismantling the CPSU. The counterelite's use of street-level resistance to the State Committee thus framed the symbolic reception of the second phase of events, between August 22 and 24, most tellingly in the projection of the death of three young demonstrators killed by an armored personnel carrier trapped in an underpass between a crowd of protestors and some barricades near the White House early on the night of August 21. The spontaneous character of street protest and popular resistance in Moscow during the three days of State Committee existence lent itself well to the counterelite's revolutionary emplotment of events in the days immediately following the GKChP's collapse.

The mobilization of activists through DemRossiia dvizhenie's local phone tree and the production and distribution of flyers with Yeltsin's August 19 decrees and appeals contributed to defense of the White House. Leonid Bogdanov and Vera Kriger arrived at DR dvizhenie's tiny new office on Petrovka Street early Monday morning and began phoning district-level activists and instructing them to rush to Manezh Square as quickly as possible.

> The network we had created and developed—a network of district coordinators and voter clubs—allowed us to rapidly initiate a chain reaction of telephone calls around Moscow ... Of course, people came on their own, but our work helped orient and coordinate the protest. This information traveled very quickly around Moscow.[24]

By mid-morning, Bogdanov and Kriger began redirecting demonstrators from a sealed off Manezh Square to the *Mossovet* and the White House. Many demonstrators, however, simply showed up on their own.

> People went spontaneously ... From the metro people walked silently in one direction, toward the White House, without saying a word to anybody. The situation was such that if a person left and something happened, that person would never forgive him or herself. Next to me stood a woman who came and joined the chain of women [surrounding the White House the night of the twentieth] only in order to find her daughter, a student at the Moscow Aviation Institute. She couldn't find her, in such a crowd it was impossible to find anybody. She told me "If anything happened to my daughter, if I remained at home and she died, I don't know how I could live after that."[25]

An activist observing a spontaneous flurry of barricade-building around the perimeter of the RSFSR Supreme Soviet building the afternoon of August 20 noted that many White House defenders obviously had experience in the art of "protest democracy" (*mintingovaia demokratiia*). As a crowd built a barricade, somebody

> ran quickly to Luzhkov [an official in the *Mossovet*], slipped him a piece of paper and got his signature allowing picketing on the streets and the blocking-off of traffic leading to the White House. Many people who stood on the barricades knew nothing about this, as the press for some reason let it slip-past, but in fact the barricades were certified [by the *Mossovet*]. That's our habit: you can't allow illegal actions.[16]

The motley assortment of people who threw themselves into tearing up streets and side-rails to build barricades struck another activist.

> I'll never forget how in a single row, standing shoulder to shoulder, worked a *liuber* [a "cultural rightist" youth known principally for body-building and provoking street-clashes with "hippies"] in checkered pants and his irreconcilable enemy, a punk in a Mohawk...A policeman in his uniform stood alongside a homeless person [*BOMZh*, an acronym for "person without a defined place of residence"]. Now normally, if a policeman saw a homeless man on the road, he would grab him and haul him off to the slammer first thing.[26]

Such accounts reflect how street protest from the nineteenth through the twenty-first created a shared referent in memory linking identity to a common experience of popular resistance—a referent capable of generalization through mediums of symbolic representation and political ritual.

By Monday afternoon, leaflets reproducing Yeltsin's various appeals and decrees appeared on walls all over the city's central district. Organizers working with photocopies and mimeographs available in the *Mossovet* coordinated a significant portion of the production and distribution of these leaflets.[27] The tattered flyers left hanging on walls served as an everyday reminder of anti-State Committee resistance in the Russian capital for months.

Having organized the hiding of the archival materials of the Moscow Information Exchange (the *neformaly samizdat* research center MBIO) on Monday, longtime Memorial activist Viacheslav Igrunov spent Tuesday and Wednesday in the Mossovet putting together an RSFSR-wide list of oppositionists on the basis of fragmentary DemRossiia files.[28] Although a number of other DemRossiia dvizhenie and neformaly activists discussed preparations for a protracted resistance campaign, the rapid collapse of the GKChP rendered such efforts superfluous.

On Tuesday, between 75,000 and 150,000 rallied in front of the White House to hear Yeltsin speak and to cheer on the Russian president, while protesters ringed the building with barricades. A group of enterprising activists then produced a tens-of-meters-long Russian tricolor flag, carrying it up and down the streets of central Moscow and creating a spectacular symbolic effect in the media.[29] Meanwhile, the largest single anti-State Committee demonstration of August 19–21 took place in Leningrad's Revolution Square, where approximately 200,000 rallied against the GKChP. On the night of August 20–21, roughly seventeen thousand maintained a vigil outside the White House. Early in the morning, the three young protestors met their death.[30]

The penultimate demonstration during the Moscow upheaval occurred on the first day of the revolution's second phase, Thursday, August 22. A crowd of more than 100,000 gathered in a victory celebration at the White House, where Yeltsin announced that the activities of the GKChP had been officially "terminated."[31] The Russian government moved to capitalize on the turn of events by renaming a plaza adjoining the White House Freedom Square and setting off a fireworks display over the city after sunset. That evening, a crowd of several thousand protesters tore down the symbol of the secret police, a giant statue of Cheka-founder Felix Dzerzhinsky in front of the Lubianka prison, KGB headquarters.[32]

Gorbachev chose not to appear at any of these events. Instead, the Soviet leader gave a press conference to journalists in which he refused to blame the CPSU for the State Committee or break with the Party, tying this decision to "the socialist choice."[33] The habitus of the Soviet president thus not only steered him away from identifying his person with the symbolic recasting of that week's events. The history inscribed on Gorbachev's body also inadvertently helped identify the party-state with socialism per se, shifting effective authority toward the Russian government.

The next day, August 23, Yeltsin consolidated this authority by inviting Gorbachev to speak at the Russian Supreme Soviet where, on national television, the CPSU General Secretary, in front of a Russian tricolor flag that had displaced the hammer and sickle, unexpectedly faced ritual humiliation by Russia's now dominant politician. The Russian president commanded Gorbachev to read a USSR Council of Ministers meeting from August 19 showing overwhelming support of the GKChP among its Gorbachev appointees, and then compelled the Soviet leader to ascent to suspension of the Russian Communist Party.[34]

Yeltsin thus forced Gorbachev to enact a ritual of subordination of the sudden "vassal" to the new leader, reversing authority relations and bringing rites of feudalization to the center of Russian political symbolism. The Russian president secured his personal ascent that same day with the appointment of Air Force Commander Yevgenni Shaposhnikov—who had ignored orders from the GKChP—over State Committee figure Dmitrii Yazov to the top of the Soviet defense establishment.[35]

On August 24, the Russian government transformed a funeral march for the three young protesters killed on the night of August 20–21 into a public ritual of nation building. Framed by Russian tricolor flags, the symbolic invocation of Russia's national rebirth dominated the proceedings. In a eulogy to the slain protestors, Yeltsin went so far as to ask the victims' families to forgive him for failing to protect their sons. In abeyance of Soviet symbolism, Gorbachev spoke, thanking Russians for saving democracy. Later that day, Yeltsin announced Russia's formal recognition of Estonian and Latvian independence.[36] Gorbachev also resigned as General Secretary of the Communist Party, signing a decree extending the Russian president's suspension of the Party to the whole Union.[37]

The emplotment of events from August 19 to 24 as a struggle between "coup" and "revolution," between "plotters" and "democrats," decisively shaped their representation. The rapid ability of the Russian counterelite to undermine the GKChP reoriented dispositions aligned momentarily into a confluence with lasting institutional consequences, thus reshaping the discursive parameters of Russian politics. In so doing, the now generically identified democrats discredited Bolshevik language and redefined Russian official discourse in terms of the defense of democracy and of Yeltsin's political ascent. The rapid abeyance of the phrase "August Revolution" and the return of deep ambiguities surrounding use of the term "democrat" stand as principal consequences of the Yeltsin government in the 1990s. But in August 1991, the symbolic effects of such shifts in official language were enormous.

Origins of "Revolution from Above"

August 1991 left the Russian government facing four immediate tasks: resolving the problem of the Union, easing the Gorbachev-led remnant of the Union center from power, liquidating the command economy, and transforming the administration of the Russian Republic by resolving "the war of the laws" between republican, regional, and local soviets. This final task required the passing of a new Russian Constitution, already being drafted in the Russian Supreme Soviet prior to August 19, as well as the calling of a founding election and the consolidation of a pro-Yeltsin political organization independent of the RSFSR administrative structure capable of mobilizing support for such measures among the populace. How the goal of liquidating the command economy overwhelmed the final task emerges as the central story of early post-revolution Russia.

In the days immediately following the August events, the Russian government consolidated its hegemonic position over Gorbachev's now greatly weakened Union center. On August 24, the day Gorbachev suspended the CPSU, the RSFSR Council of Ministers issued a decree transferring administration of all USSR economic and communications ministries, and control over CPSU and KGB archives, to the Russian government. In no position to object, Gorbachev in effect acknowledged the shift of power to the RSFSR by issuing a final decree on the twenty-fourth transferring day-to-day administration of the Soviet economy to a new committee chaired by RSFSR Prime Minister Ivan Silaev, the Committee of the Four.[38] Although leavened by economist Grigorii Yavlinskii—the architect of Russia's original 500-Day Plan—this Committee included longtime Gorbachev ally Arkadii Vol'skii and Yury Luzhkov, apparatchik turned Gavriil Popov aid and head of the Moscow city executive committee (*Mosizgorkom*). Although the operational life of the Committee of the Four would be brief, its profile prefigured that of the Yeltsin-appointed team (*komanda*) that would implement "shock therapy" (*shokovaia terapiia*) in the winter of 1991–1992.

The disintegration of the Union now rapidly accelerated. By the time the Chairman of the Supreme Soviet of Kazakhstan, Nursultan Nazarbaev, announced his intention to move his republic toward independence on August 27, Ukraine, Byelorus (formerly Byelorussia), and Moldova (formerly Moldovia) had already declared independence from the USSR. In his announcement, Nazarbaev laid out the new reality: Nine plus One remained "part of the past," a federation was "no longer possible," and bilateral negotiations between republican leaders would shape a new, loose "confederation" of former republics with a "minimal center" to replace the Soviet Union.[39] Soviet President Gorbachev found himself head of a disappearing realm, reduced to signing decrees transferring many of the Union's former operations to the Russian government.

Convened on September second, the Fifth "extraordinary" (*vneocherednoi*) USSR Congress of Peoples Deputies discussed elaborate plans for restructuring a new Union government, although such structures in the end would prove mere timeserving arrangements. For instance, the newly created "upper house of the USSR Supreme Soviet,"—the State Council (*Gosudarstvennyi sovet*)—signaled its subordination to the new order on its first day of business by recognizing the independence of the Baltic republics.[40] Representatives from only four republics deigned to show up for this first session.[41]

In the meantime, three post-August moves by the Russian president aroused immediate controversy. First, Yeltsin's August 26 statement reserving Russia "the right to reconsider the question of boundaries" set off alarms in non-Russian republics, especially in the newly independent Ukraine.[42] After a week of terse back-and-forths in the media between Ukrainian and Russian leaders, Russian Vice President Rutskoi flew to Kiev to negotiate a "mutual understanding" on various questions.[43] Thus began the process of bilateral, often secret, negotiations that would eventuate the liquidation of the USSR by agreement between the leaders of Byelorus, Ukraine, and Russia later that fall—and unwittingly entrench feudalization. Indeed, the habitus of those now improvising trajectories across Soviet space powerfully reinforced the feudalizing tendencies running rampant.

Second, the Russian president's decree appointing representatives, de facto governors, in Russian regional jurisdictions (*krai* and *oblasti*) further stirred controversy. The stated purpose of this action, "to coordinate the activity of the executive bodies of the RSFSR and the regions," signaled Yeltsin's intent to curtail local soviets, presaging a Popov-style move toward de-sovietization.[44] The outcome of such arbitrary moves deepened feudalization as well.

Finally, the influence of Popov's strategy in Moscow since early 1991 on the Russian president's strategy became clear when, on August 28th, Yeltsin decreed Popov wide-ranging new powers to administer Moscow by executive fiat. This move incited opposition from many of Moscow's new entrepreneurs, who feared such a concentration of power would create conditions for a refurbished apparat-style monopoly in the city.[45] In actuality, Yeltsin was now improvising center-regional pacts between personalistic networks ceding sovereignty from center to region in return for regional "strongmen" pledging support to the Russian president no matter what RSFSR—and subsequently, Russian Federation—laws said. Again, the feudalizing consequences of such an organization of Republic-wide political power are, in retrospect, striking.

Yeltsin made a final gesture of deference toward Gorbachev's position by holding a joint interview with the Soviet president on American television.[46] From this point forward, Russia's president virtually ignored the Soviet leader, quickly becoming embroiled in a set of maneuvers designed to prepare the ground for the introduction of a sweeping economic reform without first having clarified the ultimate relation of the Russian government to the erstwhile Union, the non-Russian republics, or to any legal principles of regulating such relations.

The week prior to the reconvening of the Russian Supreme Soviet on September 19 issued in a period of turmoil at the top of the Russian government, in part triggered by Yeltsin's September 11 decree subordinating the office of Russian prime minister together with his cabinet, the Council of Ministers, directly to presidential control. The Russian president specified that the government implement "the policy developed by the President and the highest organs of power in the RSFSR, in order to secure the realization . . . of a dynamic economic reform model and the execution of radical economic reforms."[47]

On September 16, Ruslan Khasbulatov, the acting Chair of the Russian Supreme Soviet, called a special plenum that approved a law introducing executive-style governorships in Russia's regions, but under the proviso they be directly elected.[48] Yeltsin, on the other hand, insisted on the power to appoint and fire governors at his discretion, and further complained to Oleg Rumiantsev, Chairman of the RSFSR Constitutional Committee, that the draft constitution taking shape did not give the president the powers required to implement economic reforms.[49] The next day, under fire for his economic policy from various quarters, RSFSR Prime Minister Ivan Silaev resigned, leaving the Russian president also the country's prime minister, given Yeltsin's September 11 decree subordinating the Council of Ministers directly to himself.[50]

Silaev's disavowal of a tentative agreement signed by a Yeltsin representative and several officials from non-Russian republics served as the immediate pretext for the prime minister, indicating disarray in the Russian government over Yeltsin's growing hints of implementing a Russian variation of Polish "shock therapy."[51] Although Yeltsin quickly reappointed Silaev as head of the delegation conducting negotiations with republics over their future relations,[52] the damage was done. Thus the full Russian Supreme Soviet convened amid signs of tension between Russia's president and the Republic's standing legislative body, tension that grew explosively in the next two years.

Yeltsin himself failed to attend the opening of the Russian Supreme Soviet. This session quickly bogged down in the controversy over the new law on local governors, deputies' unhappiness with the government's progress in economic reform, and the questions of finalizing who would be the permanent Chairman of the RSFSR Supreme Soviet and how to reorganize the post-Silaev Russian government. As these controversies dragged on, Yeltsin flew with Kazakh leader Nazarbaev and Ukrainian leader Leonid Kravchuk to Nagorno-Karabakh on a highly publicized but ultimately unsuccessful "peace mission" to try and negotiate an end to the long Armenian–Azerbaijani war. Russian Supreme Soviet deputies, not knowing how to react to the evident confusion and beginning to fear Yeltsin's relentless concentration of powers in his own hands, continued to bicker without resolving most of the pressing questions on the legislative agenda.[53]

In an interview, Sergei Stankevich expressed his concern over the growing discord and lack of coherent policy on the part of both Russia's president and government, noting that the need to launch economic reforms seemed to be at loggerheads with the desire of Russian officials to consolidate power over the Union.[54] On the one hand, Yeltsin virtually disappeared from the political stage for the next month, biding his time until the reconvention of the Fifth RSFSR Congress of Peoples Deputies in late October. On the other, when Russia's Fifth Congress of Peoples Deputies did reconvene, it eventually decided to appoint Ruslan Khasbulatov full, not acting, Chair of the Supreme Soviet on October 29.[55] Although unsuspecting at the time, the Congress had created a new focus of dual power. And at one pole of this dual power, the Russian president conceived change in time-honored apparat manner—revolution from above.

The Decline of DemRossiia dvizhenie in Moscow

While Yeltsin moved to consolidate his position as chief power broker in the post-August Soviet Union, DemRossiia dvizhenie resumed its mid-summer course of internal disintegration in Moscow. As in the summer, disagreements over the national question, the relative weight of executive and soviet bodies during the transition, the *modus operandi* of the DemRossiia core, and the movement's relationship with Yeltsin and Popov drove fragmentation within movement networks.

In the weeks prior to the August events, negotiations over a new Union treaty showed the fragility of nominal movement unity. While the counter-revolutionary right feared the treaty would destroy the political power of the partocracy and liquidate the Soviet Union, by mid-August, an entirely different distrust of Novo-Ogarevo—the "Nine Plus One" agreement between Yeltsin and Gorbachev—congealed in DemRossiia dvizhenie. An assortment of pro-Afanas'ev "radicals," self-styled "liberals" such as Arkadii Murashev, and several members of the old Moscow Association of Voters' organizational core such as Gleb Yakunin, objected to the "secret" character of treaty negotiations and openly worried that the document would gut Russian sovereignty, preserve a unitary Soviet state, and thus the hegemonic position of the *nomenklatura*.

> The coming of the Novo-Ogarevo treaty represents the second round of the re-structuring of the communist *nomenklatura*, a *perestroika* of *perestroika*. In essence, the signing of the Novo-Ogarevo treaty, supported by the communist center, preserves in the center's hands all the principal levers of power while delegating certain elements of executive authority to republican political elites, the majority of which remain communist. The treaty thus creates political conditions favorable to the communist variant of economic reform, that is, a reform that liberates small entrepreneurs and some medium-level enterprises serving the consumer market from the tutelage of the state but leaves the key positions in heavy industry—"the commanding heights"—in the hands of Union and republican authorities.[56]

On the eve of the August upheaval, the DemRossiia core thus found itself divided. Riven by objections from Afanas'ev and others, the pro-Yeltsin core subgroup proved unable to gain DemRossiia's endorsement of the proposed Union treaty.[57] Moreover, chess champion Gary Kasparov's funding of the movement's key newspaper allowed him to align its editorial position with Afanas'ev, thus depriving the pro-Yeltsin core subgroup of control over the nominally official movement publication. On the other hand, the pro-Union bloc of proto-parties affiliated with the movement welcomed the treaty.[58]

In the wake of the August Revolution, the Moscow core in DemRossiia dvizhenie's national leadership swept the movement's pre-August anxiety regarding Novo-Ogarevo under the rug and once again embraced Yeltsin, thus restoring the working majority that controlled the Coordinating Committee for the past nine months. Held in Moscow on September 15, the first post-August plenum of the movement's Council of Representatives outlined a comprehensive program for consolidating "revolutionary gains." The program's main elements included the consolidation of DemRossiia dvizhenie as a force for further transformation, the rapid adoption by the RSFSR Congress of Peoples Deputies of the new constitution being drafted under the aegis of a committee in the Russian Supreme Soviet, the calling of new elections for Russia's highest legislative bodies "no later" than the winter of 1991–1992, and the rapid acceleration of the process of privatization and "de-statization" (*raz-gosudarstvlenie*). At the same time, the Council of Representatives stressed the need to delegate Yeltsin temporary powers to institute economic reforms and backed the Russian president's appointment of *de facto* governors in Russian regions.[59]

The DemRossiia core now pushed again for unconditional tactical subordination of the movement to the Russian president. Early signs of the potential discord such subordination raised between movement, Russian peoples deputies, and the Yeltsin-led "team" (*komanda*) in the presidential apparatus appeared in September as a conflict between Popov's Moscow administration and much of the city's grassroots *aktiv*.[60] Although Popov and the *Mossovet* had been locked for almost nine months in a fruitless struggle with the USSR Ministry of Internal Affairs over the latter's obstruction of the appointment of pro-reform General Viacheslav Komissarov as police chief in the capital city, Popov in early September issued a decree appointing Arkadii Murashev to the post instead. This measure incensed many democrats among both Mossovet deputies and DemRossiia activists already suspicious of the Mayor's emphasis on centralized executive leadership, some of whom interpreted Popov's move as an attempt to cover-up corruption associated with the mayor's privatization drive.

Twelve Mossovet deputies, including Democratic Union leader and long-time Popov critic Victor Kuzin, went on a hunger strike to protest Popov's appointment of Murashev on September 4. Popov explained his action by claiming that, in the wake of the August events, a civilian would be better suited to the job of police chief. On September 6, an officer of the RSFSR Service for the Security and Protection of State Property barred hunger-striking deputies from entering the Mossovet building. On September 7, Komissarov led a demonstration attended by many district-level DemRossiia activists from KGB headquarters to the city soviet building, demanding Popov reverse his decision. The next day, the new Chairman of the city soviet appealed to Yeltsin and the Presidium of the Russian Supreme Soviet to protect the rights of Mossovet deputies from "illegal interference from the mayor." Popov remained unmoved, even after several hunger strikers had been hospitalized, and at a September 18 meeting with DemRossiia leaders, ruled out a compromise with the hunger strikers. Murashev remained in his new post for the time being.

The Komissarov incident generated anxiety in mid-September among RSFSR Supreme Soviet deputies troubled by Popov's violation of Mossovet procedural norms and the *carte blanche* given the Mayor by Yeltsin decrees. On September 20, the Russian Supreme Soviet passed a resolution supporting the Mossovet and Komissarov's appointment and sent a delegation to "save the hospitalized hunger strikers."[61]

At the same time, the incident triggered a wave of disillusionment in Moscow among the DemRossiia aktiv and sympathetic *intelligenty* in many of the city's district organizations. Returning from a two-week rest following the August coup, *Zelenograd*-district activist and district-soviet (*raisovet*) member Yakov Gorbadei found himself

> extremely surprised to find that in just two weeks, a large number of *raisovet* deputies had begun cursing the new authorities, moreover, with practically the same phrases used earlier to denounce the previous authorities … In short, the fact that the deputies now cursed Popov and Yeltsin made a powerful impression on me.[62]

The Zelenograd district spawned Moscow's first leftist split-off from Dem-Rossiia dvizhenie in December 1990 to January 1991, as a protest against the movement core's *modus operandi*. Now additional DemRossiia activists from Zelenograd and other districts joined this earlier split-off, called Freedom (*Svoboda*), in the September 7 pro-Komissarov demonstration in downtown Moscow. Besides radical DemRossiia activists, the Democratic Union and several anarchist groups also participated in this demonstration. Thus Moscow witnessed a unique event: a former Soviet General leading a motley rally of radicals, anarchists, and sections of the DemRossiia aktiv in protest outside KGB headquarters.[63]

A second demonstration of pro-democracy activists opposed to Popov took place on Sunday, September 15. Significantly, contingents from two proto-parties closely aligned with the DemRossiia core and emergent Russian "neoliberalism"—the Party of Free Labor and the Party of Constitutional Democrats—joined populist and radical groups like Freedom and the Democratic Union to support the Mossovet hunger strikers.[64] Other DemRossiia-aligned proto-parties also seized on the Komissarov incident to press their case against Popov and "the DemRossiia apparat." On September 16, Travkin's Democratic Party of Russia complained that the capital had turned into "a zone hostile to political activism," pointing to the mayor's aid to "Moscow's rulers, [the core of] *DemRossiia dvizhenie.*"[65]

Much to the chagrin of the DemRossiia core, during the Democratic Russia Council of Representatives meeting held on September 15, the Council came out in support of the Mossovet and Komissarov, in part due to the combined weight of the pro-Afanas'ev and proto-party delegates. Trying to limit the influence of such dissent in the movement, the core-dominated Coordinating Committee maneuvered to have the Moscow City Organization of Democratic Russia officially adopt a pro-Popov policy by means of the de facto control exercised over this body by the core group. October raisovet Chair Il'ia Zaslavskii, who strongly supported Popov's attempt to "de-sovietize" the capital city, played a particularly active role here, stating to reporters that DemRossiia dvizhenie supported Popov and even calling a "mass demonstration" for September 25 to support the mayor.[64] On the eve of this rally, Popov attended an early conference of a new political party, the Movement for Democratic Reforms (*Dvizhenie demokraticheskikh reform*), at which he called on DemRossiia dvizhenie to form its own party, distinct from the mayor's.[66] In the wake of the small rally the next day, Popov consented to a negotiated settlement with the hunger strikers.[67]

Given Popov's lack of interest in participating in DemRossiia, the Democratic Russia core's maneuvers to support the mayor in an intrademocratic faction fight in defiance of majority opinion in the movement's Council of Representatives only antagonized large sections of the movement's grassroots aktiv. At first glance, the DemRossiia core's strong support for Popov in the face of the latter's virtual abandonment of DemRossiia dvizhenie in favor of his own party-building effort may appear odd. However, Popov continued to grant office-space in the Mossovet to core members Mikhail Shneider and Vladimir Bokser, who functioned for a time in the spring of 1991 as Popov aides in the city soviet.[68] More importantly, Popov and the core reached an informal understanding that in return for DemRossiia support, Popov would appoint an unspecified number of DemRossiia activists to positions in his new mayoral administration, again demonstrating feudalizing tendencies. "We had an agreement with Mayor Popov allowing us to nominate persons to serve in his government... but [he] managed to outmaneuver us and avoid taking-on our people."[23] In fact, by the spring of 1992, Popov had only made one such appointment.[69]

The Popov controversy distracted attention from DemRossiia's program for the rapid transformation of Russian political institutions put forward by the Council of Representatives on September 15. A *Nezavisimaia gazeta* article on the September 15 Council of Representatives plenum said little about the program adopted at this meeting, instead concentrating on the hardening of three squabbling "tendencies" in the movement.[70] The piece identified the "Yeltsinites" (the DemRossiia core subgroup and their supporters), Afanas'ev-style "radicals" worried by the concentration of executive power, and *derzhavniki*, "power-niks," advocates of Russian geopolitical power and the maintenance of the Union in as strong a form as possible. These last appeared in the Civic Accord bloc, composed of Travkin's Democratic Party of Russia and two small proto-parties. The lack of interest evinced in the Council of Representative's programmatic statements and its focus on the projected disintegration of DemRossiia pained the core group, which released a flyer to the press on September 18 expressing "deep regret" that the media "had publicized misleading information on the results of the plenum of DemRossiia's Council of Representatives."[71]

The Komissarov incident, the anti-Popov demonstrations on the seventh and fifteenth, and the DemRossiia core's maneuvers to secure an outwardly pro-Popov policy in the Moscow City Organization of Democratic Russia helped breath life into yet another attempt to create an alternative, citywide DemRossiia umbrella. Calling itself the Moscow Association of Democratic Russia (*Moskovskaia assotsiatsiia Demokraticheskoi Rossii*), this umbrella pushed six of DemRossiia-Moscow's largest and most effective grassroots association into de facto opposition to the movement's Coordinating Committee majority.[72] Among such district-level associations stood *Narodovlastie*, the voter club that served as Sergei Stankevich's base of support in the 1989 election.

> We became very dissatisfied with the authorities in Moscow, and especially with the personnel policy of the Mayor... who knew the word *perestroika* and other terms connected with democracy only from newspapers. In fact, Popov had the very same approach to personnel, he retained the same executive staff. And in general, the approach was also more of the same: the same old bribes, the

same old red tape [*volokita*]. In dismay, we told ourselves "How could this have happened?" Then came the time of the so-called democratic schizophrenics [*demshiza*] in the *Mossovet*, a term employed at that time by our gentlemen, our leaders, in *DemRossiia*. The *Mossovet* had long planned to appoint General Komissarov [and others]... and then Popov drags in Murashev... A series of *Mossovet* deputies announced a hunger strike in response. I found myself sympathizing with these deputies, for Popov's policies had aroused many questions. In the opinion of these deputies, [Murashev had been appointed] in order to cover-up future abuses of power connected with privatization... In light of these events, the Moscow Association of Democratic Russia, an association of district-level *DemRossiia* representatives and individual members came to a decision... We decided we had found a cause, that Komissarov must be appointed police chief by decision of the Russian Supreme Soviet... After this, I begin to critically evaluate the situation developing within *DemRossiia*.[26]

According to DemRossiia's Charter, Kashirin enjoyed the right to attend Coordinating Committee meetings as a district-level representative of *Narodovlastie*. The Komissarov incident inspired him to begin exercising this right, where he familiarized himself with the core's methods of controlling the all-Russian Coordinating Committee sessions, the all-Russian Council of Representative meetings, and the Coordinating Committee of the Moscow City Organization of DemRossiia. Kashirin discovered that the open Coordinating Committee sessions of the latter

were open in a nominal sense only. Getting into Pushkin Street 22 was a sufficiently complicated proposition for a mere mortal, often an impossible one... Not to mention the Russian Coordinating Committee, which met in the *Mossovet*. As is well known, almost no one gets into the *Mossovet*. Very few know how permission is actually granted. But I got in simply by using my right of entry as an aide to [*Mossovet* deputy and *Narodovlastie* ally] Pykhtin... Getting into the RSFSR Coordinating Committee proved a constant problem, but I had this piece of paper, a [permanent] entry pass [*propusk*], and I was able to get into Committee meetings independently of [core members'] wishes. I wouldn't go so far to say that they openly opposed my presence, but the atmosphere and the look they gave me proved their unhappiness.[26]

Under the Soviet Communist Party, the requirement of an "entry permit" (*propusk*) to enter most government buildings proved an effective way of deterring contact between citizens and apparatchiks. In order to see an official, one needed a propusk to make an appointment. In order to get a propusk, one needed to have already established a personal relation with the official one desired to see. Squaring this circle proved a most effective means for preventing access to nominally open leadership meetings.[73] By circumventing this institutional device, the creation of the Moscow Association of Democratic Russia undermined this core's ability to steer still-active grassroots supporters in Moscow to the degree possible earlier.

As an alternative to the DemRossiia core-organized Moscow City Organization, the rise of the Moscow Association of Democratic Russia during the Komissarov controversy thus threatened the core's dominance of Russia's democratic politics as a whole. This alternative city association now joined Tel'man Gdlian's People's Party of Russia and five other proto-parties united by their opposition to the Moscow City Organization of DemRossiia to call a citywide conference of activists and member associations opposed to Popov and to the DemRossiia core's continued support for the mayor. Held on October 10, this conference called itself the Coalition of Democratic Forces of Moscow (*Koalitsiia demokraticheskikh sil Moskvy*).[74] The anti-Popov wings in DemRossiia's Moscow branch used this conference to map out the reconstruction of soviets as an institutional form, on the basis of new legislative, not centralized executive, structures.

Together, such developments pointed to increasing distance between long-time political outsiders turned pro-democracy activists and former communists around Yeltsin and Popov. Indeed, behind the alphabet soup of citywide associations lay a growing split between key figures of the Russian counterelite turned ascendant political rulership, and the aktiv as it formed and developed between the spring 1989 elections and the August events. Such widening splits signaled the unraveling of the very networks that had brought Yeltsin and Popov to power.

Speaking for blocs of grassroots aktiv in a situation highly opaque to pro-democracy voters in the city, the Coalition of Democratic Forces of Moscow conference issued an appeal to the Russian Supreme Soviet in early October 1991 to intervene in Popov's administration in the wake of the Komissarov incident.

> Recognizing the necessity of reform of city government in Moscow, we are categorically opposed to the forms and methods currently being used by the Mayor's office to implement change. The absence of a legal foundation for self-created administrative bodies...represents an extreme danger for the birth of democracy...Taking into consideration the fact that the city's district-level soviets as currently constituted no longer represent the political or economic wishes of residents, we call on the Supreme Soviet to disperse on the basis of a carefully thought-out procedure the district soviets in Moscow, to schedule new elections on the basis of [current] legislation or form new municipal soviets on the basis of the deputies of the *Mossovet*.[75]

The Second Conference of the core-steered Moscow City Organization of Democratic Russia took place in the Mossovet two days after the close of the Coalition of Democratic Forces of Moscow's meetings. Bokser decided to select out the latter's supporters by means of the propusk, a move designed to insure a pro-core turnout and thus counter any impression that the just-concluded meetings of Coalition of Democratic Forces spoke for the majority of DemRossiia's Moscow grass roots. DemRossiia's central political organizer did not anticipate, however, that such maneuvers might be difficult to conceal from broader scrutiny by this time. When Pavel Kudiukin, the Social-Democratic leader nominally still a member of Democratic Russia's Council of Representatives, found himself excluded from the hall, the new local pro-democracy radio station Echo Moscow (*Ekho Moskvi*) circulated the story, thus leading to a new round of rumors about "the DemRossiia apparat" in Moscow's democratic circles.[76]

Although the Coalition of Democratic Forces of Moscow soon collapsed, its brief existence inflicted considerable damage on DemRossiia as a whole. The shift of public attention to the now ruling Russian government, and the lack of interest of the latter in the movement which helped bring it to power, played central roles in the drift of popular attention and the decline and fragmentation of pro-democracy networks. While internal maneuvers in the movement might draw less scrutiny over all in such a situation, their effects were magnified for the body of activists still remaining. And absent formal relations between movement and the new Russian government, such maneuvers only increased fragmentation in DemRossiia overall.

The immediate reason for the collapse of the Coalition of Democratic Forces of Moscow arose out of splits over the national question at DemRossiia's Second RSFSR-wide Congress, held on November 10–11 in Moscow. Such disagreements drove the liberal-nationalist grouping, Civic Accord, out of DemRossiia altogether. The proto-parties entered the Coalition of Democratic Forces of Moscow with a somewhat different agenda than the voter clubs and DR district organizations of the Moscow Association of Democratic Russia opposed to the core-controlled city organization. While the Moscow Association of Democratic Russia objected principally to the DemRossiia core's embrace of Popov's strategy of de-sovietization and the mayor's perceived penchant for "nomenklatura privatization," the proto-parties hoped to use the new coalition to force the DemRossiia core in the Coordinating Committee to agree to a broad public discussion of the future and character of the movement as a whole.

Democratic Russia formed as a coalition of various platforms, orientations and parties dedicated to the goal of fighting the monopoly of the CPSU. Today this goal stands achieved . . . [and] the question of a radical reorganization of the movement demands attention. [We see four possible paths ahead]: 1) The disbanding of the organization . . . 2) The creation of a "super-party" [*superpartiia*] on the basis of the movement. Such a tendency characterizes a section of the

Moscow leadership, and as a result of this, the Coordinating Committee very often attempts to make decisions that fall outside the boundaries of the movement as defined by its Charter. A paradoxical situation has thus developed, in which decisions taken by a part of the leadership of *DemRossiia* stand in direct contradiction to the policies of the movement's member parties . . . We thus suggest 3) transforming *DemRossiia* into a coalition of parties, movements and groups [thus eliminating membership on an individual basis] . . . Finally, it would be possible 4) to abolish *DemRossiia*'s Moscow center, preserving only its regional organizations, which would decide their own fate and take their own decisions on an individual basis.[77]

In a samizdat mimeograph circulated in October, the Democratic Party of Russia stated that although it supported the creation of effective executive administration in principle, Popov's policies in fact represented a victory for a section of the apparat over the movement. This, in turn, created

a complex situation in *DemRossiia dvizhenie*. On the one hand, [Popov's] Movement for Democratic Reforms (DDR) is apparently relying on *DemRossiia* [for popular support] . . . On the other hand, people such as Afanas'ev refuse to even associate with members of the DDR. Thus, the DDR is in fact undermining *DemRossiia*.[78]

During the early fall contention among DemRossiia's Moscow activists, the core's strategy consisted of holding on to tactical hegemony over the movement and limiting the spillover from the Komissarov incident without alienating Popov until new Russian elections could be called. Thus the core counted on their erstwhile patron, Yeltsin, to call such elections as soon as possible, in anticipation that Russia's president would turn to the core to organize a pro-Yeltsin party, exactly the "super-party" the now-stagnant proto-parties feared. Given this scenario, the revolutionary program adopted by DemRossiia's Council of Representatives could finally take center stage. The combination of the Popov-centered turmoil among the capital's democrats and Yeltsin's virtual withdrawal from the political stage at the end of September, however, undermined the viability of this scenario.

The core's hopes now hinged on the outcome of the Fifth RSFSR Congress of Peoples Deputies, scheduled to reconvene at the end of October, 1991. Midway through October, yet another ominous storm cloud appeared on the core's political horizon. In order for elections to be called, either by the Fifth RSFSR-CPD or by Yeltsin himself, the upcoming Russian Congress would need to adopt a new Russian Constitution to replace the Soviet-era document still in force. Oleg Rumiantsev, a leading Social-Democrat, member of DemRossiia dvizhenie's Council of Representatives and Chair of the RSFSR Supreme Soviet's Constitutional Commission, presented a draft constitution to Russia's

standing parliament on October 10—a draft whose provisions entailed restructuring Russian political institutions and thus created a rationale for holding a
"founding election."[79] Much to the consternation of some democrats in the
parliament and the whole of DemRossiia dvizhenie's leadership, the Supreme
Soviet rejected the draft and charged the Constitutional Commission to draft
yet another constitution, which Yeltsin would present to the Fifth RSFSR
Congress of Peoples Deputies "for discussion only." Thus parliamentary opponents of Rumiantsev's draft united to remove the question of voting on a
new constitution from the Congress' agenda.[80]

Yeltsin's absence from the debate over the draft constitution vexed
DemRossiia's core leadership. The Russian president

> simply disappeared, he went on vacation. And great confusion and vacillation
> reigned [in Moscow], everything remained unclear. For all practical purposes,
> the government ceased to function, that is, nothing new had been put in place
> after Yanaev [the GKChP]. The problems accumulated relentlessly, and we [Lev
> Ponomarev and Gleb Yakunin] decided to travel [to the Russian President's dacha
> in the Black Sea resort of Sochi] to give Yeltsin an ultimatum. The *DemRossiia*
> Coordinating Committee composed a letter stating that if Yeltsin in the very
> near future failed to announce decisive measures, create a government of na-
> tional salvation excluding figures such as Lobov [a *nomenklatura* figure]... and
> embark on radical economic reforms, then *DemRossiia* would go into opposi-
> tion. This was put in writing: we would go into opposition... Thus we flew to
> Sochi unannounced, fearing Yeltsin might not receive us... We waited, and the
> next morning he met with us. He read the document very slowly, I remember,
> very slowly, paying attention to each phrase, and finally said: "I agree with what
> you've written here. In the very near future I'll make an announcement at the
> Russian Congress. I'm prepared to act..." I must admit that it appeared to me
> that Yeltsin had already decided to take radical steps, though, as it turned out,
> not the steps we recommended.[81]

The Fifth Extraordinary Congress of Peoples Deputies of the RSFSR reconvened in Moscow on October 28 with anxiety over economic decline in
the face of the coming winter and confusion among deputies over Russia's
political direction and place in the Union. In his keynote address, Yeltsin
made a proposal for "the period of radical economic reform." During this
time, the Congress would allow the president to both function as head of
Russia's government and assume sweeping powers normally delegated to
the Supreme Soviet. Yeltsin would further appoint a troika of deputy chairs
(*zamestiteli predsedateli*) of the Supreme Soviet. One of this troika of deputy
chairs would serve as first deputy chair, a sort of assistant prime minister; a
second would head economic reform; and the third would oversee the remaining ministerial portfolios. The Russian president would also be granted full

authority to conduct negotiations on the federation with the Union and other republican governments. Yeltsin argued that by taking full responsibility for economic reform, he would be able to implement an extensive and coordinated economic program, while at the same time taking on full personal responsibility for unpopular measures such as price reform that legislators would otherwise find difficult to enact.[82] On November 1, the Congress agreed to the Russian president's blueprint.[83]

The day before assenting to Yeltsin's proposal to transfer many legislative functions to the president, the Congress voted to postpone consideration of a new constitution and of constitutional amendments not touching on the Russian president's proposal or matters concerning the seating of deputies until the Sixth Russian CPD.[84] Although several days later Yeltsin made an impassioned plea for the Congress to resolve "as soon as possible" the intractable question of the new constitution,[85] having gained extraordinary powers he now in fact assented to the postponement of the constitutional question until the convention of the Sixth CPD-RSFSR in the spring of 1992. Moreover, the president asked the Congress to postpone for one year elections for regional administrators that had been scheduled for December by the Russian Supreme Soviet, in return for agreeing to allow regional soviets to be included in a consultative capacity in the process of installing and removing the regional plenipotentiaries Yeltsin had begun appointing in the immediate aftermath of the coup.[85]

The Fifth Russian Congress of Peoples Deputies thus closed with Yeltsin, like Gorbachev before him, concentrating an enormous number of powers in an executive office, the Russian presidency, he himself created. But the Russian president's failure to call a founding election meant that he had at most a few months, until the Sixth Russian Congress of Peoples Deputies, to engineer an economic breakthrough. Failing this, the CPD-RSFSR retained the power to strip Yeltsin of his extraordinary powers.

On November 6, Yeltsin appointed the troika of deputy chairs to his new government. The position of first-deputy chair—dubbed "Assistant Prime Minister" in the press—went to Yeltsin's closest advisor, Gennadii Burbulis, the former DemRossiia figure who had gravitated away from the movement to Yeltsin aid over the last year. A young, monetarist economist, Yegor Gaidar, became vice chair in charge of economic reform.[86]

The DemRossiia core thus proved unable to draw the Russian president into the revolutionary program adopted by the movement's Council of Representatives on September 15. Although the concentration of emergency powers in Yeltsin's hands and the president's promise to implement sweeping economic reform pleased the core, Yeltsin's failure to push through a new constitution, call a founding election, or appoint a DemRossiia dvizhenie figure to his new government left the core on the sidelines of what was shaping up as a new revolution from above. Indeed, the DemRossiia core now found itself facing the movement's Second Russia-wide Congress, scheduled to open on November 9 in Moscow, in the awkward position of defending the still unrevealed program of a de facto leader who refused to make any commitment to the movement and who now appeared ready to stake the fate of the political revolution on his own political charisma and a relative handful of economic advisors.

On the day DemRossiia dvizhenie's Second Congress opened, events in Checheno-Ingusetiia—a region of the Caucasus Mountains in southern Russia bordering Georgia—further weakened the core's fragile position by thrusting the national question unexpectedly to the top of the agenda. On October 27, this small Autonomous Republic of the Russian Federation held a presidential election, won by a Soviet Air Force General turned Chechen nationalist, Dhzokhar Dudaev. Besides being subdivided into district-territorial regions (*krai* and *oblasti*), many Soviet republics also contained nominally autonomous territorial subunits known as ASSRs (Autonomous Socialist Soviet Republics) and Autonomous Areas. These quasi-republics and regions had been created where concentrations of "national minorities" lived.[87]

Dudaev promptly declared Chechnya independent of Russia and separate from the Ingusetian zone to the west. On November 2, the CPD-RSFSR decreed the Chechen election invalid. Yeltsin followed with a decree of his own, declaring "a state of emergency" in Checheno-Ingusetiia on November 9 and ordering Dudaev removed from power. Yeltsin soon backed down when he realized force would be necessary to remove the Chechen president. The consequences of feudalization now began to undermine Yeltsin himself. Indeed, from this point forward, Chechnya would undermine the Russian president's legitimacy and practical abilities in office.[88]

At the same time as the Checheno-Ingusetiia situation deteriorated, a small war broke out in October in Georgia. On one side stood Georgian guerrillas loyal to new, ultra-nationalist Georgian President Zviad Gamsukhurdia. On the other, separatists in the Georgian Autonomous Republic of South Osetiia wishing to secede from Georgia and unite with the Russian Autonomous Republic of North Osetiia took up arms.[89] The situation all along the Russian-Georgian border appeared to be spiraling toward what the Russian press called "a new Nagorno-Karabakh" after the Armenian region of Azerbaijan that had fallen into intermittent warfare with the Azeri government in 1988. At this time, the Russian press began to lament darkly about the "*levanizatsiia*" (Lebanonization) of Russia, signaling that the process of feudalization had risen to new levels.

Yeltsin's declaration of a state of emergency in the North Caucasus and its implications for the future of Russian statehood (*gosudarstvennost'*) triggered a counterchallenge from the left to the core group's adherence to Yeltsin at DemRossiia dvizhenie's Second Congress. Led by Yuri Afanas'ev, this challenge, in turn, initiated the exit of nationalists in the proto-party bloc Civic Accord from the movement. Early on the first day, conference delegates overwhelmingly gave a vote of confidence to the coordinating committee's pro-Yeltsin position. Indeed, fewer than 100 of 1,298 delegates voted against this motion.[90]

Afanas'ev, however, argued for a policy of "conditional support" for the Russian president, while avoiding a direct challenge to the conference's pro-Yeltsin position.

> Our support must not be thoughtless and automatic. We must be hypercritical [*pridirchivy*] and treat with considerable attention the content of economic reform. We must be partners in the development of reform policy, and avoid passively approving them.[91]

Afanas'ev, alarmed by the declaration of a state of emergency in Checheno-Ingusetiia, indicated his disagreement with the president's policies on the territorial integrity of Russia by contrasting Yeltsin's phrase "Russia is united and indivisible" (*edinaia i nedelimaia*) with his own formulation, "Russia is united but divisible" (*edinaia no delimaia*).[92] Afanas'ev's position represented the anti-Union thinking characteristic of many older "60ers" (*shestidesiatniki*) influenced by the human rights movements of the Brezhnev era, such as Andrei Sakharov's widow Yelena Bonner.[93]

Representatives from the Civic Accord bloc of proto-parties took a dim view of such suggestions, objecting to members of the Coordinating Committee who pushed decisions offensive to their bloc through this Committee. A figure in the Democratic Party of Russia, Il'ia Roitman, and Mikhail Astaf'ev, head of the Constitutional-Democratic Party of Peoples Freedom, had leveled strong criticism at the Coordinating Committee's spring 1991 decision to align DemRossiia dvizhenie officially with the all-Union Democratic Congress, whose member organizations included many separatist movements in the non-Russian republics. Now in the fall of 1991, Roitman minced no words in stating his party's support of the Union and a united Russia, and both he and Astaf'ev argued again for the strengthening of the role of collective members over individual members in the movement's internal life.[94]

On the final day of the Congress, the core joined with those aligned with Afanas'ev in proposing and successfully passing through the Congress an amendment to DemRossiia dvizhenie's Charter expanding the number of members elected to the coordinating committee by the Congress, as well as allowing the Congress to determine directly the size of the Coordinating Committee. These alterations symbolically strengthened the weight of individual members over collective members. The parties of Civic Accord abruptly left the movement, citing their earlier objections to the movement's organizational structure and singling out in particular Afanas'ev's phrase "Russia is united but divisible" in trying to convince their own members of the necessity of leaving DemRossiia.[95] In fact, delegates at the Second Congress ignored Afanas'ev's suggestion of tolerating regional secession from the RSFSR, instead affirming the core's position that for the time being a moratorium on the question of border changes should be observed by all republics of the Soviet Union.[96]

Afanas'ev's argument for "critical support" for the Russian president on the course of economic reforms fared considerably better. After hearing Yeltsin's new Deputy Chair Yegor Gaidar give a technical speech focused on fiscal and monetary details of the upcoming economic reform, the Second Congress resolved to support Yeltsin conditionally.

> The movement's membership recognizes that the failure of reform would spell defeat not only for Yeltsin and the members of his government, but also for all of the democratic forces of the peoples of Russia. Such a defeat would increase the danger of the rise of fascism and engender chaotic uprisings and anarchy. The seriousness of the situation demands, however, not unconditional support for the reform course, but considered, carefully thought-through support that leaves room for criticism and the presentation of alternative means for resolving fundamental problems. The Congress thus considers it advisable to create a Reform Committee as an organizational component of the movement.[97]

Within five weeks, the Coordinating Committee organized the Social Committee for Russian Reforms (*Obshchestvennyi komitet rossiiskikh reform*), envisioned as duplicating the federative organization of DemRossiia dvizhenie and thus creating regional forums through which movement activists and supporters could convey criticisms and suggestions up through the Coordinating Committee and thus to members of the Yeltsin government itself. Yeltsin critics Afanas'ev, Leonid Baktin, and Marina Sal'e played active roles in organizing this committee.[98]

Both the core's majority position in the Coordinating Committee, and, for the most part, its pro-Yeltsin policies gained solid approval from the delegates of DemRossiia's Second Congress. In accordance with the new Charter, the Congress directly elected five Co-Chairs of the Council of Representatives and twelve members of the Coordinating Committee, for a total of seventeen leading positions elected from the floor. Ten of the seventeen persons elected to steer the movement on a day-to-day basis were members of the 1990–1991 core or closely aligned with them. The Afanas'ev group represented a small minority of this leadership, although two gained election as Co-Chairs, Afanas'ev himself and Marina Sal'e.[99] Although the number of representatives on the Coordinating Committee delegated by collective members remained uncertain in the wake of Civic Accord's departure, the experience of the last year demonstrated that such representatives rarely attended Committee meetings, thus allowing the core to dominate the proceedings.[100]

The press, however, played up the split with Civic Accord and discord between the core group and the positions of Afanas'ev and his allies, creating the impression of a wide split in DemRossiia dvizhenie.[101] In contrast to this perception, the majority of grassroots members still active outside Moscow and Leningrad/St. Petersburg remained inclined to support Yeltsin and the core group. Lev Ponomarev suggested that Civic Accord jumped on Afanas'ev's phrase "united but divisible" as a means of driving a wedge between their own grassroots members and DemRossiia.[81] Il'ia Zaslavskii insisted that no real split had occurred at the Second Congress.

> There wasn't any split at the Second Congress, only a few parties left. These parties totaled perhaps 15 percent of the membership of *DemRossiia*. Moreover, the other parties remained. Judge for yourself: would you really call the departure of 9 or 10 percent of the members a split? I would describe this "split" more in terms of a little pile sliding off the mound on your plate.[23]

Press reports of splits throughout the movement posed a more serious problem for the DemRossiia core than the departure of Civic Accord itself. Lacking a move by Russia's president to transform DemRossiia dvizhenie into a political party, the restlessness of much of Moscow's grassroots aktiv only grew. The bad press stemming from the splits and factional maneuvers surrounding the Komissarov incident portended more trouble ahead if Yeltsin failed to actively recruit a wider, more diverse base into the organization. Without the president's voice, any attempt to create a core-centered "super-party" would founder on the sectarian proclivities of the narrower and narrower circles of those still active in DR dvizhenie. To make matters worse, *Nezavisimaia gazeta*, the only major Moscow-based newspaper that consistently covered DemRossiia's internal life, appeared by November 1991 to have consigned the movement to history. Indeed, DemRossiia in Moscow now appeared to most outside observers as a faction-riven swamp. Absent active intervention on the part of Yeltsin, the core group remained helpless in the face of such trends.

No such help would be forthcoming. Although the core group stuck publicly to Yeltsin, several came to resent members of his new government. By the spring of 1992, Il'ia Zaslavskii referred collectively to Yeltsin appointees as "the technocrats." Zaslavskii admitted that DemRossiia's influence on the formation of Yeltsin's government had been very minor. And the reason for this was the coming to power of the technocrats, for whom *DemRossiia* cleared the way, and who repaid us by trying to isolate us from power, as we, following the collapse of the CPSU, were the only unified, organized and effective political structure left in the country. Closely connected to the attempt to isolate *DemRossiia* was an unprecedented campaign of slander against us in the mass media.[23]

In this comment, Zaslavskii reproduces commentary more typical of Soviet times than the actual circumstances in which he operated. Coordinated media campaigns to disparage opponents in fact ebbed in the early 1990s. Zaslavskii's commentary attests to the frustration felt by the core of DemRossiia dvizhenie with the now unpropitious circumstances and the core's own blunders and machinations, as well as to the residual effects of a Soviet-formed habitus.

As the DemRossiia core began to digest the reality of its disempowerment, the Russian president moved ahead. By the first week of December, Yeltsin secured the necessary room to launch an economic revolution from above by announcing the freeing of most prices on the first of January. Gorbachev had been reduced to a near figure-head, the RSFSR Congress of Peoples deputies had granted Yeltsin extraordinary powers, and a much-altered version of the August 20 Union treaty—now called a Treaty on Economic Community—had been tentatively agreed upon by most Soviet republics in early October at a summit in Alma-Ata, Kazakhstan.[102] This treaty created a common economic zone between the republics, while delegating the center only token responsibilities and allowing republics full political autonomy. True power would reside in a new State Council, composed of representatives of the republican governments.

Shortly before winning election on November 1, Ukrainian leader Leonid Kravchuk announced he would never sign a new Union treaty and that the Ukraine would become a fully independent state. By the last week of October, only seven republics still intended to participate in the new all-Union State Council.[103] Any hope of preserving even the outward shell of the Union dimmed still further.

Yeltsin thus began his revolution from above, not with economic reform, but by suddenly and unexpectedly reaching agreement with Kravchuk and the leader of newly independent Byelorus (formerly the Byelorussian Republic), Stanislav Shushkevich, to form a three-way confederation between the three slavic republics, thus liquidating without warning the Soviet Union.[104] The agreement caught Gorbachev and other Union republics completely off-guard. But the now irrelevant Soviet president could only protest from the sideline as the new Commonwealth of Independent States (*Sodruzhestvo nezavisimikh gosudarstv*) took shape over the ensuing weeks.[105] On December 25, Gorbachev spoke on television, announcing his resignation as Soviet president and the end of the Soviet Union as such. That same night, the Russian tricolor replaced the Soviet flag over the Kremlin, as Gorbachev left office for retirement. The last Soviet leader had been the first to leave office voluntarily.

The Miscarriage of "Revolution from Above"

When the Russian, Ukrainian, and Byelorussian presidents suddenly announced a "pacted dissolution" of the Soviet Union in December, they created an instant issue for hitherto reeling Unionists in the now fully independent Russian Republic. Indeed, the intrusion of the national question into the debate at DemRossiia's Second Congress represented the tip of the iceberg for democrats both inside and outside DemRossiia dvizhenie. December brought the revival of all the thorny issues stemming from the entanglement of the Russian idea of nationhood with a long imperial past stretching back through the Soviet era into old Imperial Russia.

The immediate prospect of Russia losing its hegemony over the former Union suddenly galvanized right-nationalist groups undergoing extensive demoralization since the August revolution, and sent a number of Yeltsin allies, including former DemRossiia parliamentary leader Il'ia Konstantinov and Vice President Alexander Rutskoi, scurrying away from the president and toward an uneasy alignment with communist and ultra-nationalist remnants.[106] *Pravda*, *Sovetskaia Rossiia*, and other rightists papers suspended in the wake of the August coup for "collaboration" managed to regroup and have themselves unbanned over the course of the fall. Together with the new ultra-nationalist daily *Den'* (Day), the imperial right thus again controlled a wide-circulation press available to publicize its ideas and distribute information. So began the post-August phase of the reformation of the new Russian right,[107] a development which caught Russia's urban democratic activists unprepared. So also began a long struggle among the Russian president, pro-democracy politicians and fractions, and a motley assortment of rightist groupings to redefine the terms of Russian national identity, a struggle whose far-right dimension attained prominence until the decline of rightist figure Vladimir Zhironovsky in the second half of the 1990s.

Within six weeks of the freeing of most prices on January 1,[108] opposition to Yeltsin's policies grew steadily in the Supreme Soviet. The opposition now gained two new targets: First Deputy Chair Yegor Gaidar and Vice Minister Gennadii Burbulis, targeted by the right as the architect of the dismantling of the Union. A campaign in the Supreme Soviet aimed at denying Yeltsin his extraordinary powers and reestablishing parliamentary control over legislation during the upcoming spring Sixth Russian Congress of Peoples Deputies soon got underway.

In the wake of Yeltsin's January "big bang," yet another split emerged in DemRossiia dvizhenie, a split that signaled the end of the democratic movement of 1990–1991. This break arose from the minority of Afanas'ev and Marina Sal'e in DemRossiia's leadership. In January, this minority began to object vehemently to the sequencing of economic reforms and especially to the perceived predominance of the nomenklatura over the privatization process, but found themselves overruled by the DemRossiia core, which insisted that the movement had no choice but to support Yeltsin in the strongest possible terms. Afanas'ev expressed the rationale behind the minority shift into open opposition to Yeltsin in the spring of 1992.

> Russia has no real entrepreneurs. Rather, there exist groups of people who rely principally on the spheres of [currency] exchange, trade and finance. Such are Russia's entrepreneurs—sharp operators [*del'tsy*], I wouldn't even know what to call them ... In Russian society the main problem consists in the fact that property owners are nowhere to be found. There is one owner, and that is the state. The lack of property owners means that no economically independent persons exist. No kind of middle class in such conditions can develop ... Currently a monopolistic state-capitalism, so to speak, is emerging as our path of development. If we continue down this road, then we may acquire the worst of all possible alternatives to socialism. That is, a society just as repressive, lacking democracy, with the very same arbitrary rulership, perhaps even worse than during the time of communist domination.[109]

After having their calls for a strongly worded criticism of the reforms rebuffed at a mid-January Council of Representatives meeting, the three principal minority leaders—Afanas'ev, Sal'e, and Leonid Baktin—decided to suspend their membership in DemRossiia at the end of January and launch a campaign among the aktiv to convene an "extraordinary" movement Congress, in hopes of deposing the core's majority position in the Coordinating Committee.[110] Indeed, Afanas'ev and his allies interpreted approval of the resolution expressing "conditional support" for Yeltsin's reforms during DemRossiia dvizhenie's Second Congress as a sign that a majority of the aktiv would support them in the event of a split with the DemRossiia core.

But much had changed since April 1991, when Afanas'ev's opposition to the Nine plus One treaty negotiations found wide support at the grassroots level. Already, the Komissarov incident had driven some of Moscow's grassroots aktiv out of DemRossiia. Exhausted by revolution and economic hardship, the movement's dwindling activists showed little inclination to distance themselves from the Russian president. Caught off guard by their inability to rally the grass roots behind them, the Afanas'ev group agitated unsuccessfully for the next six months in hopes of convening an extraordinary (unscheduled) movement Congress. After a poorly attended "alternative" Democratic Russia Congress in July 1992 failed to attract much attention, the three principal organizers of this faction—Afanas'ev, Sal'e, and Baktin—resigned from the movement. Nevertheless, they remained popular among the aktiv, and their decision to lead a failed challenge against the Coordinating Council in the first half of 1992 drove the final nail in the coffin of DemRossiia as it had existed in 1990–1991.

Afanas'ev himself characterized the remnant of the movement as a vehicle for "young careerists." A more measured assessment follows.[109]

> When Afanas'ev left . . . the loss of the leaders of "the 60ers" [*shestidesiatniki*] became obvious, leaders such as Afanas'ev, Baktin and a whole series of representatives of the Moscow intelligentsia. This development proved a strong blow to *DemRossiia* . . . [M]iddle-aged people, in my opinion, had played the most important role in the movement. Their numbers were not great, but their influence in society was relatively large. The Union deputies of 1989 still remain legendary figures in our society: Stankevich, Zaslavskii, Afanas'ev . . . In my opinion, the departure of such people greatly weakens the movement and portends its further crisis and decline.[111]

DemRossiia's now splintered tangle of pro-democracy parties, voluntary associations and grassroots networks soon found themselves thrown on the political defensive in the face of a wave of small but sensational pro-Soviet demonstrations that rocked Moscow in February 1992. The outbreak of at times violent antireform protest coincided with the emergence of the public split between Yeltsin and the Supreme Soviet, a split rooted in parliamentary dismay both with the course of "shock therapy" and the perceived collapse of Russia as a "great power" (*velikoderzhava*) in the aftermath of the disbanding of the USSR. Russia's upstart right found its legs with the convening of the Congress of Civic and Patriotic Forces (*Kongress grazhdanskikh i patrioticheskikh sil*) in early February. At this meeting, erstwhile Yeltsin ally and sitting Vice President Alexander Rutskoi lashed out at economic reform and called for "a state of emergency in the economy."[112]

The emergence of *velikoderzhava* in Russian discourse at this time foreshadowed the subsequent emergence of the derzhavniki, the "power-niks," of subsequent years. At the same time, the internal articulation of pro-democracy networks in a few large cities such as Moscow with Yeltsin's immediate entourage remained largely obscure to those not directly involved at the grassroots level in such cities. For these reasons, "the democrats" became identified with Yeltsin's government per se, while the grassroots movement of DemRossiia failed to gain a lasting presence in public symbolism. The subsequent conflict between "democrats" and derzhavniki was widely perceived as an interelite power struggle, with the notion of democracy over-identified with the Yeltsin entourage.

The last significant pro-reform demonstration of 1992 took place in Moscow on February 9, when roughly fifty thousand presidential loyalists staged a counterprotest to a communist-led demonstration in another part of the capital.[113] Two weeks later, a bloody riot on the streets of Moscow staged by "red-browns" (*krasno-korichnevye*)—the pro-reform epithet for those following the Congress of Civic and Patriotic Forces—shook political observers and citizens alike. A confrontation between Mayor Popov and red-brown leaders' right to protest sparked the riot and raised the specter of renewed civil strife in a society exhausted by relentless economic decline and political chaos.[114]

The spectacle of confrontation between the executive and legislative wings of the nation's government, when combined with the tenor of press coverage of the February 1992 demonstrations and riots, gave the impression of widespread resistance to the reform course. The red-brown riot signaled the deterioration of already unsettled Russian politics. In the month before the convening of the Sixth Congress of Peoples Deputies, more and more deputies in the Supreme Soviet began to criticize Yeltsin and his course, unsettling Russia nascent political order, an order institutionalized in only the most preliminary sense.

The Sixth Russian Congress opened on April 6 with former Yeltsin allies Vice President Rutskoi and Supreme Soviet Chairman Ruslan Khasbulatov now leading the call to strip the president of his special powers, remove Gaidar and Burbulis from the government, and install a parliament-controlled prime minister and government.[115] Debate on a new Russian Constitution went nowhere, and hours slipped by in debates over whether the former RSFSR should be called the Russian Republic or merely Russia. On April 19, several thousand frustrated pro-Yeltsin demonstrators brawled with red-browns in downtown Moscow. After storming out of the hall on several occasions during particularly vitriolic anti-Yeltsin speeches, the president eventually agreed to sack Burbulis and resign as prime minister in return for the Parliament's appointment of Gaidar as prime minister and the president's retention of reduced powers of decree. In all, the Sixth Congress of Peoples Deputies dragged on for fifteen days, damaging the political standing of most of the major players and intensifying the process of feudalization.

Meanwhile, Popov's reform of Moscow again bogged down, and the Mayor now complained that little could be achieved at the local level. During the Sixth Russian Congress, Popov commented publicly that bribery was inevitable and perhaps ought to be officially codified at standard rates. Although the mayor offered such comments to a hypothetical question during a press interview, they caused an uproar and forced him to resign within two months.[116]

Yeltsin's partial defeat at the Sixth Congress triggered a now quixotic attempt at party-building on the part of the more and more isolated DemRossiia core. On May 26, 1992, the core called and organized an Assembly for a Referendum (*Sobranie za referendum*) in Moscow, attended by about 350 people.[117] Called in part to prod Yeltsin into acting on his threat to call a constitutional referendum, the calling of the Assembly led the DemRossiia core to push forward its drive to turn the remnants of the movement into a new political party "unconditionally supporting" the Russian president. Three days later, Yeltsin announced that a national-scale referendum would be held "no later than the fall."[118]

The DemRossiia core's launching of a referendum campaign in such circumstances signaled a "core habitus" caught between an elite without commitments to its activist base, and an activist base itself demobilizing and adrift. Over the next ten months, Yeltsin erratically changed course on several occasions, all the while keeping a now rump DemRossiia at arm's length. The departure of popular figures like Yuri Afanas'ev, the core's now naked dependence on Yeltsin's erratic moves, and the Russian president's aversion to involvement in or even promotion of the movement, all alienated larger and larger numbers of former activists and supporters. The dizzying rearrangement of alliances of this or that figure formerly associated with DemRossiia further undermined any possibility of movement revival. When, a few days prior to the core's Assembly for a Referendum, the former DemRossiia Coordinating Committee member and Chairman of the Democratic Party of Russia, Nikolai Travkin, joined Vice President Rutskoi and industrial lobbyist Arkadii Vol'skii to form a "centrist" opposition to Yeltsin's "radical" reforms, the heyday of DemRossiia appeared over.[119]

By the spring of 1992, DemRossiia had changed from a powerful social movement into a much narrower organization operating as an adjunct to the Russian president's growing struggle with the Russian Congress of Peoples Deputies. In hindsight, the Yeltsin government's neglect of DemRossiia and its failure to push for a "founding election" in the fall of 1991 rapidly curtailed the Russian president's room for maneuver once economic decline weakened his charismatic authority. The very logic of decentralization and "dual powers" that served Yeltsin so well in his drive to undercut Gorbachev now turned against the Russian president. As Yeltsin's vision of attempting a "market revolution" from above stalled with the defection of erstwhile supporters during the April 1992 Sixth Congress of Peoples Deputies, the new government found it lacked the authority to call elections. The ineffective Russian Congress and Supreme Soviet, with their large contingents of holdover apparatchiks and webs of contradictory rules and procedures inherited from the Soviet era, now paralyzed effective governance. The process of feudalization spread relentlessly across the new Russian Republic.

Chances Missed, September 1991 to April 1992

Behind the rightist failure to seize power in August 1991 lay the achievement of the democratic opposition in establishing dual power in the soviets, transforming the Russian government into an alternative to the Soviet center, and disrupting lines of apparat command and control. From the elections in 1989 to mid-1991, Yeltsin grew from a prominent oppositionist to elected head of an insurgent dual power in the Russian Federation. The rapid August collapse of a reactionary segment of the partocracy, however, failed to clarify the course of three factors leading to the collapse of Soviet power. First stood the fragmentation of the partocratic elite, breaking lines of authority within the apparat. Interdependent with this first factor was a second, the rise of sustained democratic mobilization at the grass roots, especially among intelligenty in a few big cities. Together, these two factors facilitated a third, the growth of a pro-democracy counterelite brought to power in the wake of August 1991.

Reemergent society, although, remained weak, fragmented, concentrated in a few big cities, and rooted in personalistic networks of specialists. The image of heroic resistance in the streets beating back the grasp of reactionary partocrats obscured the role of insubordination and divided loyalties in the apparat, military, and security services. Even a member of the DemRossiia core noted in an interview the "minor" role of the movement in defeating the State Committee for the State of Emergency during its brief existence.[23] Image here, though, was paramount. The linkage of the defeat of the State Committee to resistance from below in the political rituals of nation-building staged in the days between the State Committee's collapse and Gorbachev's decree suspending the Soviet Communist Party represented the zenith of Yeltsin's achievements as a revolutionary entrepreneur.

The institutional realities behind the symbolic consecration of events, however, meant that democratic consolidation remained far from assured. As the consequences of political revolution deepened following August 1991, the weaknesses of a political movement linking a charismatic elite informally and subordinately to an urban, specialist-based patchwork of social movements became evident. Having helped prepare the ground for a political revolution that came suddenly and unexpectedly, DemRossiia found itself with the daunting tasks of extending its social base, uniting its various wings, and developing a positive program of institutional transformation.

The change of social-political conjuncture effected by the political revolution in August thus created conditions that undermined the continuing viability of the democratic movement as it had existed prior to the coup. As DemRossiia's core organizational leaders realized almost immediately, the key to survival lay in the transformation of the movement into a pro-Yeltsin political party under the aegis of Russia's president. As the movement character of DemRossiia and the suspiciousness of the aktiv toward party-building and other "apparat-like" activity constrained the core's maneuvering room, only an initiative coming from Yeltsin himself could guarantee the creation of such a "super party."

The DemRossiia core's September 15 formulation of a revolutionary program calling for a founding election in the winter of 1991–1992 aimed openly to push the Russian president toward party-building. Yeltsin, however, hesitated throughout the fall in committing to a post-August strategy. When he decided to move, following a protracted absence from the political stage in October, he chose to appeal to the Supreme Soviet for emergency powers rather than pushing for new elections. Then, while preparing for the implementation of "shock therapy"—essentially a revolution from above designed to dismantle the command economy and create a market economy from scratch—the Russian president and his counterparts from Byelorus and Ukraine suddenly and secretly engineered a pacted dissolution of the Soviet Union and eliminated the shell of Gorbachev's Soviet presidency.

Believing they had a majority in the Russian Congress of Peoples Deputies, the Yeltsin group's decision to delay pushing for new elections thus deferred carrying through the revolutionary transformation of the soviets and the creation of a new institutional basis for Russia's fragile political society. This decision would, in hindsight, prove disastrous, as the failure of Yeltsin to complete the political revolution by prioritizing new elections in the fall of 1991 condemned DemRossiia to relentless decline and internal fragmentation and thus deprived the president of his only base of organized support outside reformist-apparat circles.

Perhaps Yeltsin would have found it as difficult to call a founding election in the fall of 1991 as he eventually did following the rebellion of the Sixth Russian Congress of Peoples Deputies against "shock therapy" in April 1992. After all, the continuing free-fall of the economy, the question of empire, and regional rebellion in Russia itself—embodied in the Chechen declaration of independence on October 27, 1991—created overwhelming priorities for Russia's president in the wake of the August coup. Still, the magnitude of the factors constraining Yeltsin in the fall of 1991 should not obscure his tendency to lapse into an apparat style of rule or to favor a technocratic revolution from above. Once achieving undisputed authority as sole head of the Russian government, the president abandoned the push for founding elections to se-cure popular legitimacy for reform and remove the most pressing institutional legacy of the Soviet era, dysfunctional soviets dominated by former officials.

The weakness of much of Russian society relative to fragmented but still powerful segments of military, industrial and security apparat strata revealed itself in Yeltsin's post-August shift to a strategy of neoliberal revolution from above. This social-economic revolution was directed by the core of yet another elite configuration, this time drawn largely from reformist ex-communists and a small number of economists and policy experts from academic institutes.[120]

Over the next months, the conflation of defense of reform with defense of Gaidar's "shock therapy" narrowed the scope of policies designed to consoli-date a civil society to the implementation of price reform and the achievement of macroeconomic stabilization in a way that paralleled the symbolic reduction of representative democracy to defense of the person of the president. The vision of civil society inherited from Central Europe in the late 1980s—the vision of a complex array of self-organizing voluntary associations, political parties, civic institutions and markets—shifted to a much narrower concep-tion of civil society as the creation of "the market" in and for itself. The whole question of how to politically and socially enfranchise the vast majority of Russians thus slipped from the political agenda.

5 Interregnum

The Russian president's opting for a "revolution from above" in early 1992—with its disregard of political movements and grassroots activism—shifted politics back toward groups clustered around the still ill-defined realms of Russia's executive and legislative wings of federal administration. Yeltsin and his various advisors assumed the decree of policies would translate into coherent actions steered and monitored by themselves. But the operations of federal governance proved incapable of either steerage from above or administrative coherence, instead splintering into strife between the presidency and the Congress of Peoples Deputies. As governing paralysis unfolded, the *DemRossiia* grass roots—lacking support from above or an electoral *raison d'être*—shrank and fractured in the wake of the anti-Yeltsin riots of February 1992.

At the same time, deepening economic decline made explicit the spread of poverty among urban Russians. In the winter and spring of 1992, the rapid appearance of economic goods in city shops reversed decades-old Soviet patterns of an economy of permanent shortage—"too much money chasing too few goods"—with intermittent market devices. The effect of seeing goods that could not be purchased—"too little money chasing too many goods"—further disoriented and splintered the urban specialist base of the democratic movement. Yeltsin's amalgamation of all manner of special powers thus triggered opposition from the legislative wings of Russia's new national government just as pro-democracy activists experienced profound economic disorientation.

As growing paralysis between plebiscitarian and parliamentary governance unfolded in the summer of 1992, a Russian *intelligent* observed "the economic breakthrough here outdistances the consolidation of new power, which in essence has not even begun."[1] The negative facets of this economic "breakthrough" (*proryv*) reinforced paralysis from above and—absent a social movement linking factions in the center to significant sectors of the grass roots—devolution of political power to regional networks and sectoral alignments. The Yeltsin group in turn relied more and more on mass media organs in Moscow to try and steer political perceptions.

Absent a coherent political party with roots in localities, the populace identified "the democrats" more and more with the practical consequences of presidential power. By default, democracy in the abstract thus came to mean in practice plebiscitarian rule, the "extraordinary" power proclaimed by the Yeltsin team and the power symbolically transferred it by Russia's Fifth Congress of Peoples Deputies. Yet the *raison d'être* of such extraordinary powers appeared precisely as the "de-statization" (*razgosudarstvlenie*) of society.

All of this underscores why decentralization nominally overseen by plebiscitarian rule does not necessarily entail "governmentality," a prerequisite for the applicability of effective governance.[2] Feudalization—the segmentation of a plebiscitarian regime where regional powers appropriate localities as private domains whose interrelations depend on personal bargains among regions and between regional powers and a nominal central power as such—may also result. From April 1992, Russian society experienced the latter.

Into the Vortex

The resurgence of the legislative wing during and after the Sixth Congress of Peoples Deputies in April 1992 launched a debilitating struggle over governmental power. The president's new prime minister, thirty-five-year-old economist Yegor Gaidar—appointed during the Congress as a means of displacing moves in the parliament against Yeltsin's collection of emergency powers—now emerged as the most prominent figure in the executive's quasi-plebiscitarian leadership. Alongside the president himself, Gaidar quickly became a magnet for critics of "shock therapy," as legislators and various social groups insisted on a change of economic policies.

Meanwhile, the decline of Moscow's DemRossiia activist base continued apace. The departure of Afanas'ev and Baktin's grouping in mid-July—after the failure of their "alternative" DemRossiia conference—accelerated disintegration of the *aktiv*. Executive indifference only reinforced the marginality of a shrunken, "unconditionally" (*bezogovorochnyi*) pro-Yeltsin core. Indeed, the rump Moscow core would grope for months to revitalize urban democratic activism without symbolically contradicting self-subordination to presidential rule.

The future of DemRossiia was now the least of Yeltsin's concerns. As summer turned toward fall, practically all symbolic attention shifted to growing splits within and between the presidential apparatus and parliamentary groupings as Gaidar's "shock therapy" triggered resistance throughout society, including elements of the democratic movement of 1990–1991.[3] With the coming of autumn, the heretofore provisional speaker of the Sixth

Russian Congress of Peoples Deputies, Ruslan Khasbulatov—having consolidated regular control of the speaker's position and built himself into a national figure through outspokenness against Yeltsin in the summer and early fall—now turned to repealing the Fifth Congress' grant of special powers to the Russian president, going into outright opposition to Yeltsin in early October.[4]

By the end of the month, Russian newspapers warned of a political situation deteriorating day by day between parliament and executive.[5] Some began to mention the need for a new constitution.[6] Then, in late November, the Chair of the new Constitutional Court, Valerii Zorkin, ruled that Yeltsin's ban against the CPSU had gone too far and that regional and local bodies of the Communist Party must be permitted to reorganize.[7]

On December 1, 1992, the Seventh Congress of Peoples Deputies convened under Khasbulatov's tutelage. At this Congress, more and more deputies turned against the Russian president's attempt at plebiscitarian governance as paralysis spread on the federal level. Yeltsin stayed away from proceedings for days trying to arrange a compromise with various groupings. Then on December 9, the president unexpectedly announced his intent to defy further Congress measures and organize a referendum abolishing the soviets, to be replaced with an ill-defined parliament. The president thus threatened the Congress with federalizing Gavriil Popov and Il'ia Zaslavskii's 1990–1991 strategy of "de-sovietization"—in effect, consolidating a plebiscitarian form of rulership without a plebiscite. Yeltsin called for a walkout by those who supported him, but found less than two hundred deputies out of over a thousand followed.[8]

Forced to retreat, the president now aimed at a minimal compromise with a working majority of the Congress. Deputies rejected the reappointment of Gaidar as prime minister, ultimately settling on apparat candidate Viktor Chernomyrdin instead.[9] In the wake of this fiasco, Yeltsin fell back from problems of reform policy, abdicating such tasks to the Chernomyrdin government as the president pursued confrontation with the Congress of Peoples Deputies on a more fundamental level, via a referendum "on the foundations of the constitutional system" approved in principle at the Seventh Congress for April 11, 1993.[10]

In the meantime, the consolidation of Chernomyrdin as prime minister brought an end to the attempt at revolution from above launched in early 1992. The new government, built on reorganized networks of officials—some drawn from the economic sectors of the apparat, others from scattered groups of democratic politicians and academics—represented an improvised compromise. Relations between Yeltsin's appointed government and his quasi-plebiscitarian staff now receded into the shadows. At this point, "democracy" became entwined with personalistic rule as law itself was subsumed in the protracted struggle between executive and legislative wings of governance. It thus remains difficult to speak of the rule of law in early postcommunist Russia in any meaningful sense.

The president's withdrawal from policy and shift in strategy toward open confrontation with the Congress of Peoples Deputies, however, seemed to offer renewed hope to DemRossiia's remaining Moscow core. In the wake of Yeltsin's now confrontational posture toward the Congress, core figures finally found a way to coordinate their search for a viable grassroots issue with "unconditional" support for the president: a drive for a constitutional referendum handing Yeltsin full plebiscitarian powers through abolition of the Congress and the Supreme Soviet.[11] In effect an adjunct to the paralyzing struggle between executive and parliament, this issue nevertheless proved a way to temporarily revive the movement as a petition drive.[12]

The Russian president's new determination to dissolve the Congress of Peoples Deputies and the Supreme Soviet now threatened a range of interests and groups associated with these bodies, while Chernomyrdin's government sided more and more with Yeltsin. Over the next several months, the Supreme Soviet and the Russian presidency engaged in a Byzantine struggle for position, often passing laws or issuing decrees that directly contradicted one another. On March 10, the "extraordinary" (*chrezvychainyi*) Eighth Congress of Peoples Deputies convened as the legislative branch tried to reassert dominion in Russia's federal government and halt Yeltsin's push for a referendum.[13]

Conflict, instead, deepened. The Eighth Congress ended in impasse between presidential and parliamentary powers, with the Congress refusing to authorize a referendum despite pleas and threats from the presidential administration.[14] At this point, Yeltsin bypassed the Congress altogether by unilaterally decreeing the terms and date of the referendum, rescheduled now for April 25. In the meantime, the Congress and Supreme Soviet would be allowed to continue to function, but with the provision that any congressional actions at variance with presidential announcements regarding the referendum would be automatically null and void.[15]

Together with DemRossiia's referendum petition campaign, Yeltsin's open confrontation with the Eighth Congress of Peoples Deputies revived elements of the grassroots campaign of 1990–1991 among specialists and youth groups in Moscow.

When a now embattled Russian president appealed for popular support in his struggle to dismantle the Congress and the Supreme Soviet, Moscow witnessed a large pro-democracy rally openly supporting Yeltsin. Tens of thousands of demonstrators marched in Moscow on March 28, 1993, as the Ninth Congress of Peoples Deputies prepared to convene just a few weeks after the Eighth had closed.[16]

In such an atmosphere, hopes that the March 28 demonstration might revive the democratic movement dissipated as the Russian president turned away again from grassroots mobilization in favor of shifting negotiations with various apparat fragments and groups of economists, punctuated by erratic appeals to "the people." Here the inability of DemRossiia's core to organize grassroots politics independently of the presidential apparatus proved fatal. Combined with growing impoverishment among urban *intelligentsia*, the rump core's inability to steer between "unconditional" support of the president and grassroots mobilization brought a final dissipation of DemRossiia's urban networks. The late March rally thus served more as a reunion of the old DemRossiia coalition, than a portent of things to come. Indeed, by the time of the rally, political paralysis at the height of governmental bodies showed signs of incipient "routinization" as an element of Russian political life.[17]

Although Yeltsin openly defied Ninth Congress proceedings, the president found it difficult to assert authority over lower legislative and administrative bodies. The Ninth Congress of Peoples Deputies led to still further polarization, diminishing prospects that some "center" between the executive and legislative branches of governance might be found.[18] The waning search for a pacted settlement now centered on behind-the-scenes maneuvering between elite fragments.[19]

As spring moved toward summer, conflict between Russia's president and his parliamentary opposition centered on Yeltsin's push for a new constitution—and, by extension, a plebiscitarian pattern of Russian governance—via referendum. In early June 1993, the president by-passed the legislative system altogether in convening a Constitutional Conference (*Konstitutsionnoe soveshchanie*).[20] Lacking effective means to assert itself over either soviets or nominally subordinate levels of administration, the Yeltsin group pressed ahead with the Constitutional Conference through most of June.[21]

At the same time, some of Russia's federal legislators tried to obstruct the executive wing of Russian government. But such figures suffered from a dearth of effective power, partly as a result of their transfer of extraordinary authority to the Russian Presidency in the fall of 1991 and their ascent to a referendum on governance at the Seventh Congress of Peoples Deputies. Moreover, federal legislators suffered from an inability to agree on any coherent policy alternatives to Yeltsin, let alone stabilize mechanisms of governance in the new Russian Federation outside presidential authority. Although now partially backed by Russia's Constitutional Court—albeit with little in the way of legal reasoning—the legislative wing found itself discounted by Yeltsin's administration.[22] All the Court could do was block the implementation of any constitutional changes and to serve as a sounding board for a plethora of spokespeople, some of them tangential, some of them reactionary. The more and more internecine struggle between the executive and legislative wings of Russia's government unfolded as economic circumstances continued deteriorating. The realities of the faltering economy undercut the popularity of both the Russian president and the Supreme Soviet. By spring 1993, the average specialist income had fallen below that of the average pension, that is, below the nominal poverty line. Indeed, by June 1993, only 10 percent of the former specialist estate in Russia could be considered "middle-class" specialists, that is, specialists with incomes above the nominal poverty line working in the new market sectors of the economy.[23]

The disintegration of the social base of the 1990–1991 democratic movement in the postcommunist period flowed directly from the very policies championed by the political leadership of the specialist rebellion. Specialists employed in the state-financed enterprises of the military industrial complex and in educational and public health organizations found themselves especially hard-hit, with doctors, teachers, and engineers experiencing sharp and pronounced downward mobility. The state-engineered character of the specialist stratum under communism and its dependence on state-organized economic redistribution rendered it particularly vulnerable to the erosion of status and income under conditions of "shock therapy," a far cry from the expectations of many specialists to transform their state-engineered status into a viable market, i.e., class position. Many would-be entrepreneurs with a professional profile outside the managerial apparat only survived by using their computer and other technical skills to devise an ad hoc infrastructure to service demands for foreign outlets for mercantile capital, currency speculation, money laundering, tax dodging and other more mundane accounting, marketing, and information-processing needs of new interest alignments, as well as the needs of foreign businesses in Russia.[24]

Such realities quickly dispelled hopes of DemRossiia activists for transition to the "normal life" perceived in the West, as a large majority of specialists found themselves impoverished under the economic shifts of 1992–1993. The economic consequences of change thus intersected with the deterioration of the political situation, placing the habitus of many specialists at odds with their dwindling hopes.

> If only we could arrange a normal life and proceed down a normal path of development, then perhaps we could stop being preoccupied with politics, we could take a vacation. And I so much want a vacation: just to sit quietly in front of the television, not think about anything, and watch a detective show like your "Santa Barbara."[25]

If an oppositional habitus dedicated to unconditional support for a nominally all-powerful president incapable of grasping the importance of grassroots activism now turned against remnants of DemRossiia's aktiv, where did active support for the executive come from? The answer lies in part with the primary beneficiaries of economic reform in the first years of postcommunist Russia.

The importance of tracking the postrevolutionary fate of various apparat segments cannot be overemphasized in this regard. For instance, David Lane and Cameron Ross stress discontinuities between the Soviet elite and the post-August Yeltsin government by showing that few former high Party leaders found their way into the latter.[26] However, discontinuity looks more like continuity when one shifts attention from the partocracy per se to the broader managerial *nomenklatura* and apparat. The Institute of Sociology of the Russian Academy of Sciences reported in 1994 that 74 percent of Yeltsin governmental appointees were former *nomenklaturshchiki*—ironically enough, the economic-managerial wing of the nomenklatura and its immediate apparat subordinates.[27] Managers and economic administrators both retained control of remaining state enterprises and dominated the still nascent privatization process, reengineering themselves as the dominant fragment of emergent Russian capital.[28]

Identifying the size of the nomenklatura remains in part a definitional problem, related to how one cuts off the nomenklatura proper from apparat subordinates and managerial personnel. This definitional problem cuts to the heart of political organizing in the Soviet and postcommunist contexts, for how one defines such categories relates to how one conceives the communist order. For instance, gray areas stand in marking cut-off lines between senior party-state nomenklaturshchiki and senior managers of large and important enterprises.[29] The latter—wavering in their loyalties throughout the late-Soviet and early post-Soviet periods—began to assert themselves as members of Moscow-oriented blocs and to engage in privatization schemes of their own as Yeltsin's rule weakened.

Things Fall Apart

Such conditions formed the context in which events now unfolded. As summer drew to a close on September 21, 1993, the Russian president went on national television to announce the disbanding by decree of the Supreme Soviet and Congress of Peoples Deputies. In this way, Yeltsin would force adoption of a new constitution abolishing the Congress and Supreme Soviets altogether. In the meantime, the Russian president arrogated to himself the functioning of Russian governance between constitutional orders.[30]

Rightist and some centrist deputies in the Congress and Supreme Soviet framed Yeltsin's move as a "seizure of power" and tried to cast the debilitating struggle between presidential and parliamentary wings of Russian government as between a legitimate legislative body and a usurping power, much as Yeltsin himself had done during the August 1991 events. The defection of some pro-democracy supporters in Russia's parliamentary bodies to at least tactical alignment with such deputies sowed confusion. The irony of some legislators who had welcomed the State Committee for the State of Emergency now standing up to Yeltsin receded in the chaotic circumstances.

A stalemate quickly developed between the two wings of government, as some deputies from the Congress and Supreme Soviet refused Yeltsin's commands and began a siege of the Russian White House, the very building from which Yeltsin had personalized resistance to the State Committee in August 1991. Yeltsin responded by encircling the White House with Moscow police and Russian military personnel and eventually cutting off electricity and water supplies to the building. Among the early "defenders of the White House" stood Oleg Rumiantsev, a staunch defender of parliamentary procedures whose 1991 draft constitution, if adopted, may have served to consolidate new representative institutions in the Russian Federation of late 1991 and early 1992.[31]

As the siege wore on, the number of deputies dwindled toward a hard core of anti-Yeltsin figures, who continued to speak for "the people" while organizing paramilitary grouplets on the extreme right "in defense of the White House." Scattered objections by democratic groups against the president during the siege signaled the confusion sowed in the populace by the turn of events.[32] The continuing presence of Ruslan Khasbulatov, Congress speaker, and Alexander Rutskoi, Russia's vice president, propped up the claims of those remaining in the White House to represent the populace as a whole, although as the siege wore on the number of deputies remaining dwindled to a band of hard rightist opponents of Yeltsin.[33]

On the evening of October 3, 1993, a confused situation descended into chaos as "storm troopers" purportedly defending the now minority of Congress deputies appeared in trucks on the streets of Moscow, announcing their intentions to take *Ostankino*, the main Russian television tower and broadcast center in Moscow. In the late evening and early morning of early October 3–4, a barricaded staff at Ostankino came under fire from elements supporting the siege. A few hours later in the Kremlin, Yeltsin secured the support of Army commanders through their chief, General Pavel Grachev. In the early morning of October 4, the world viewed the spectacle of the Yeltsin government shelling the White House, a process that lasted for hours, until Khasbulatov and Rutskoi gave themselves up for arrest that afternoon.

After the destruction of the Russian Congress of Peoples Deputies and the Supreme Soviet, the Russian president opted for institutionalizing his regime with a greatly weakened parliamentary profile and the extension of regional personal appointments directly through the presidency. At the core of the new order lay direct presidential appointment of the prime minister of the lower house of Russia's new parliament, the Duma. To remove this figure through the legislature required three separate votes of the Duma as a whole, after which the president could instead dissolve the Duma and call new elections, leaving governance in his appointees' hands.[34] At the same time, the upper house of parliament—the Federation Council—consisted of representatives of Russia's eighty-nine regions (*okrugi*), appointed directly by the president except in cases where such figures gained office prior to the beginning of such appointments.[35] The shadow of patrimonial rule lay long over Russia's new institutions.

And yet, patrimonial rulership presupposes both the fealty of lower bodies to the centralized *diktat* of the person of the ruler and the ability of such a figure to maintain preeminence over appointments and decisions in all political spheres. In modern conditions—with formal organizations, bodies of law, universal education, mass communications, and the rise of human rights as both a secular ideal and a progenitor of social movements—patrimonialism appears either as an outright centralized dictatorship, or at least a centralized web of entrenched officialdom covered by a patina of *faux* democracy, very far from conditions obtaining in Russia in late 1993.[36]

Earlier in Soviet times, the Stalin dictatorship came much closer to classical patrimonialism, and the rise of "collective leadership" in the post-Stalin period in turn gave rise to a variant of partocratic patrimonialism—the impersonal dictatorship of an ideal, the party-state, realized as the arbitrary rule of the nomenklatura.[37] Yeltsin's government may have been arbitrary, but it strove for disbanding central control in many areas, and it at least tried to project the notion of representational democracy, both to sections of the Russian populace and western governments. The habitus and worldview of Yeltsin's entourage and his broader administrative supporters all reflected this, as well as the Soviet past in which they came of age.

The field in which Russia's presidential regime found itself following the disbanding of the Supreme Soviet in early October 1993 suffered from the consequences of political revolution against an imperial order, the rapid disintegration of the Soviet economy, and its own inchoate abandonment of grassroots political association. On the one hand, the accrual of vast powers in the hands of the presidency emerged from the destruction of the Soviet regime in circumstances where the central pro-democracy association, DemRossiia, remained subordinate to the Yeltsin counterelite emerging out of the Soviet apparat. Upon gaining power, the president's entourage abruptly changed course and abandoned the movement.

On the other hand, the very rise to power of this faction predicated the decentralization of power to lower rungs. Called "the war of the laws" (*voina zakonov*), this strategy presupposed alternative means of institutional consolidation at lower levels. But such means were either marginalized politically—DemRossiia—or simply did not exist, encompassing everything from organs of local law to active civic participation to stable currency markets to viable economic units oriented to market exchange.

Following the bloody disbanding of the Supreme Soviet in early October, 1993, however, more immediate tasks occupied the Yeltsin administration. The regime now tried both to consolidate presidential rule, and revive the democratic movement as a political organ of this rule—two years and almost two months following the August revolution of 1991. The effort of Yeltsin's government to patch together a pro-reform political party from remnant networks of the old DemRossiia coalition, however, proved difficult.

The December 1993 elections saw fragments of the 1990–1991 DemRossiia coalition scattered among five factious and hastily organized blocs of candidates. These included Russia's Choice, led by Yeltsin's first prime minister, Yegor Gaidar; the Yavlinskii–Boldyrev–Lukin bloc, soon known as "the Apple" (*Yabloko*); the Democratic Party of Russia, Travkin's party; the Russian Movement for Democratic Reforms, Gavriil Popov's group; and the Party of Russian Unity and Accord. The last two of these failed to cross the minimum 5 percent threshold established for seating in the new Duma, while Russia's Choice garnered only 40 of 225 seats allocated by party lists. At the same time, over the previous two years, leading members of Russia's Choice had alienated themselves and the Yeltsin government from "the Apple" and Travkin's party, which received only 8 and 5 percent of the national vote, respectively.[38]

The inability of Russia's democratic factions to reunite in new circumstances underscores how earlier opportunities to build a pro-reform party had been squandered. Having long since neglected building a stable, pro-reform party, the Russian president instead faced humiliation in the wake of impressive showings by Vladimir Zhironovsky's ultranationalist group, and revived pro-Soviet sentiment in the new Communist Party of the Russian Federation (CPRF) in the December 1993 elections.[39] Denied once more the parliamentary majority he had come to covet, Yeltsin bowed to political reality in January 1994 and appointed a government dominated by Soviet-era industrial managers under Chernomyrdin's prime ministry.

In the face of such humiliation, and under pressure from some remaining DemRossiia regional figures to resist any idea of working with Russia's Choice, remnants of the DemRossiia core now tried to form a party independent of either *Yabloko* or Gaidar's faction. Organized by longtime Dem-Rossiia figures Lev Ponomarev and Lev Yakunin in early 1994, this attempt to fashion a political party out of the remnants of DemRossiia—under the name the Federal Party of Democratic Russia (*Federal'naia partiia Demokratich-eskii Rossii*)—gained little attention or membership. Although nominally headed by Duma figure Galina Starovoitova, the effort soon collapsed.[40] Outside of a handful of Duma deputies, the DemRossiia movement now stood as more remnants of a shattered voluntary association, than an active presence.

The confusion of many former DemRossiia activists and elected figures at lower levels reflected the opacity and chaos of Yeltsin's attempt to refashion Federal governance in the wake of the fall 1993 disbanding of the White House.

> I supported Yeltsin's decision to dissolve the regional soviet [*raisovet*] in Moscow after the uprising [*rospusk*] at the White House . . . But it is necessary to say, that after the uprising, the apparat gained full control of the situation in localities. Earlier, before [the 1990] elections to the regional soviet, Party organs functioned as a sort of arbitrary restriction [*ogranichenie proizvola*] over local officials [*chinovniki*]. And after elections, deputies operated as a restriction over these same officials. But after the uprising, instead of hopes for "presidential control" over such local officials, it turned out that the President became a plaything in the hands of such officials, who acted now both free of the state, and of their own uncoordinated [*razrosnnyi*] situation.[41]

The 1993 shelling of the White House thus turned out to be the final debacle for the 1990–1991 democratic movement. At the same time, Yeltsin's new presidential rule—a plebiscitarian form of governance—found itself with little in the form of actual administrative powers in the regions. Such circumstances formed the context in which economic reform unfolded.

Emergent Economic Powers in Russia, 1992–1994

Shock therapy in early 1992 simultaneously freed most price controls and decapitated the Soviet planning system in Russia. Nevertheless, many of the ministerial and industrial subsidiaries of the Soviet system—and their officials and managers—remained in place. As prices skyrocketed, those connected with the now "headless" commodities segments of the Soviet command economy—either by dent of official position or through various "gray market" ties[42]—stood to take advantage of the situation by selling natural resources abroad for dollars and deutsche marks, and unloading foodstuffs and other goods in the consumption-starved big cities at rapidly escalating prices.

A relatively small number of networks of private traders, state managers, and government officials thus quickly amassed huge stocks of liquid capital. Such liquid capital stocks in turn enabled these same informal commercial networks to engage in extensive currency speculation on internal gray markets for "hard"—that is, non-ruble—currencies (*valiutnye den'gi*), as well as to import consumer goods to sell to Russian consumers at inflated prices. Few DemRossiia activists engaged in such activity.[43] Instead, younger *kooperativniki* or "cooperators"—heads of semiautonomous cooperatives established under Gorbachev's *perestroika* and often hailing from the *Komsomol*, the Communist Youth League—and pragmatic Soviet-era industrial and financial mangers began forming informal networks from which later financial–industrial groupings developed.[44] Formation of habitus and positions in fields here outflanked symbolic commitments.

Hyperinflation, however, threatened the value of wealth amassed in this manner almost as soon as it accumulated, so those involved scrambled to find ways to shelter stocks of rubles in "hard" (*valiutnye*) currencies.[45] The government provided an avenue by licensing "commodity brokerage houses" (*valiutnye birzhi*), in which a relatively small group of new "entrepreneurs" could convert rubles into hard currency—something not yet legal for the rest of the population—and buy and sale raw materials in both rubles and hard currency.[46] The birzhi created havens shielding export and import profits from hyperinflation, and provided an ideal mechanism for sheltering capital from an infant and barely functioning tax collection system. The Yeltsin government arranged political cover by tolerating the commodity brokers' tax dodging and transfer of assets into foreign currencies, and looking the other way as a handful of brokers parlayed their connections into financial networks built on export and import revenues.

The government also tolerated commercial networks' use of the birzhi to launder profits gained from the nominally illegal practice of trading rubles at highly advantageous rates on the internal black market for hard currency, and then recycling the ruble profits back into hard currencies through the commodity brokerages.[47] In 1992 and 1993, currency speculation served as a primary source of wealth for the kooperativniki and "gray marketeers," who formed one leg of the triad of traders, commercially active state-enterprise managers, and government officials on which the financial networks of this early period rested.

In this way, a classic pattern of "mercantile capital accumulation" emerged.[48] Embedded in complex networks of money laundering operations and currency speculation executed under the cover of brokerage houses—many of which subsequently evolved into private banks—such patterns remained opaque. Mercantile capitalism represents the amassing of monetary wealth on the basis of commodity trading, as opposed to the sale of goods by manufacturers or services by direct providers.[49] Mercantile patterns of accumulation helped consolidate networks linking three institutional arenas, namely, government offices, state-enterprises, and commodity brokerages and banks in the infant private sector.

Ties between bankers, currency speculators, commodity brokers, public officials, and enterprise managers who controlled access to Russia's mineral wealth thus became the center of the economic order. Highly placed politicians in the Yeltsin government facilitated the whole process, and many began to extract their "cut" of the wheeling and dealing. Indeed, the number of elected officials who became wealthy over the next few years is truly sobering. Moscow's Mayor Yuri Luzhkov and the financial network he controlled through the Moscow city government exemplified this trend. Indeed, after 1992, Luzhkov acquired a reputation as a principal liaison between *biznes* and city officialdom.[50]

Nothing better illustrates the depth of penetration of racketeering schemes to the very heart of the Yeltsin administration than the case of then Defense Minister Pavel Grachev. In 1993 and 1994, Grachev almost certainly oversaw the use of the Russian military to import stolen consumer goods such as cars and appliances for sale on gray markets, using troop withdrawals from eastern Germany as a cover for the operation. Dmitrii Kholodov—a Russian journalist working for the daily Moscow Youth Leaguer (*Moskovskii komsomolets*) who began to expose Grachev's corruption—was assassinated by a briefcase bomb in October, 1994.[51] Crucially, Grachev secured obedience among key military units to Yeltsin's order to shell the Russian Supreme Soviet in October 1993. Informal, personal relations here trumped both legality, and loyalty to the state as such—"charismatic impersonalism" in earlier days of the party-state—exemplifying the feudalization of party-state relations.

Shadow World

In a speech televised to the Federation and the world in January 1994, Yeltsin stressed the need for civil peace and a bloodless resolution of disagreements in the wake of the events of late 1993.[52] Moves toward civil peace continued with the amnesties of the 1991 State Committee for the State of Emergency and leaders of the September and early October 1993 parliamentary rebellion against Yeltsin, including Ruslan Khasbulatov and Alexander Rutskoi.[53] And yet, the Yeltsin government launched its first war against Chechnya just a few months later, in December 1994.

Ultimately, reasons for the Chechen invasion can be traced to the need to reestablish federal authority and revive Russian oil interests in the North Caucasus, where Chechnya's location played a central role. Proximately, the cause lay at the doorstep of then Russian Defense Minister Pavel Grachev, architect of both the war, and a purge of senior military personnel who disagreed with it.[54] On the eve of the invasion, Yeltsin's need to revive some viable popularity in the wake of its rapid decline rendered him susceptible to Grachev's advice.

The first Chechen intervention, however, unfolded as a disaster for the Russian presidency, both in the immediate failure of Russian military forces, and the political consequences of a drawn-out civil war on the Federation's southern periphery. Moreover, the intervention tarnished Yeltsin's image among those pockets of supporters left from the early 1990s. On December 28, new Russian Vice Premier Nikolaii Yegorev, and head of the Federal Counterintelligence Service, Sergei Stepashin, assured citizens that "armed conflict in Chechnya will be settled in ten days."[55] But the war stumbled on despite repeated assurances from presidential figures. By the time the conflict drug on into a hostage crisis in the southern Russian town of Budyonnovsk in June 1995, the popularity of Russia's president collapsed into single digits.[56]

1995 also witnessed the launching of the Federation's first sustained program of privatization of state-controlled enterprises, consolidating "voucherization" (*vaucherizatsiia*) begun earlier. Distribution of shares (*aktsii*) of the large state monopoly Gazprom without receipts, however, served to open the new campaign of sustained privatization.[57] The new shares program distributed fractions of ownership to employees of enterprises and vaguely described "others" for trade or sale on ill-defined "markets."

Due to the absence of enforcement bodies on the local level, the lack of receipts, the jerry-rigging of details, and the naiveté of the populace—regarding both the particulars of "share-ification" and the whole idea of private enterprise—the program favored all sorts of opaque dealings. Among the numerous ways devised for using shares to horde assets stood everything from discounting the value of enterprises, through the location of assets in dummy enterprises, to the exchange of shares for a few rubles. The M-M-M pyramid scheme stood as an archetype of such maneuvers.[58]

Given the confounding array of deals suddenly available to the bewildered populace, some institutions—such as the Russian Orthodox Church—found it necessary to reassure prospective purchasers:

> Up to now, the voucher form of privatization has aroused censure. But beyond all the insufficiencies of such vouchers stands the absence of real securities [*tsennaia bumaga*]. The investment fund "Radonezh" is attempting to maximally use this complex situation for the benefit of Orthodox Christians and the Russian Orthodox Church as a whole. Today, we can assert which attempts by enterprises have given positive results. Readers now have the opportunity to find out details of investment funds and markets in state short-term funds [GKOs, or *Gosudarstvennye kratkosrochye obiazatel'stva*].[59]

The rapid decline of economic indicators of all sorts only compounded the mystifying character of such appeals to a population with practically no experience with financial devices. Indeed, by 1994, Russia had experienced its own version of the Great Depression (see Figure 5.1).

As the Chechen war, privatization, and economic depression continued, Russia's second election in two years loomed ahead. Fractiousness at the democratic pole of Russian politics increased as elections approached in

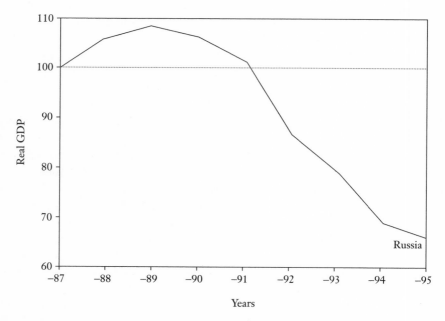

FIGURE 5.1. Changes in Real GDP in the Russian Federation, 1987–1995. *Source:* Milanovic (1998: 26).

December 1995. A new, nominally pro-democracy party—organized entirely independent of DemRossiia networks—appeared around *apparatchiki* centered on Prime Minister Chernomyrdin. This party—Our Home is Russia (*Nash dom Rossii*)—expected voter support in a solid enough position to function as a bridge of sorts between Yeltsin and various factions of the Duma, eclipsing Russia's Choice in this role.[60]

The election, though, went badly for Our Home is Russia, which gathered only about 10 percent of the vote. The remnants of DemRossiia fared worse. Although a rump of Russia's Choice salvaged independence from its opposition to Yeltsin's Chechen morass, it failed to transfer it much beyond former DemRossiia supporters who remained loyal to Yeltsin from 1992 up to the Chechen invasion.[61] *Yabloko* ("the Apple") already served as the principal vehicle for those grassroots *intelligenty* who remained politically committed to democratic politics while evincing disillusion with Yeltsin, picking up 45 seats—close to 7 percent—in the vote. The Democratic Party of Russia— the last major organizational link to the 1990–1991 DemRossiia movement— failed to win any seats through proportional representation, dropping below the minimum 5 percent for representation in the Duma set under the new constitution.[62]

Only in the wake of electoral catastrophe did remnants of the Democratic Russia core finally realize their marginality, though significant activism had subsided long ago, soon after the March 28, 1993, rally. Some drifted toward nominal independence from the president, others migrated to various minor political jobs working for him, and still others withdrew from politics. "Beheaded" regional networks of the old DemRossiia coalition had since made various provisional arrangements with local groups, or simply disintegrated altogether.

The Russian president now faced the first months of 1996 in a precarious situation. As the presidential election loomed and voucherization and low-level warfare in Chechnya dueled for public opinion, Yeltsin searched for options. Facing the choice of whether to cancel the elections outright—ruling by decree on an openly arbitrary basis—or proceeding with a high-risk vote in the face of manifest unpopularity, Yeltsin wavered for months before opting to proceed.[63]

Spring 1996 brought a small revival of Yeltsin's image in the populace. This revival of some popularity was largely "negative," however, as Russia's nascent "oligarchs" (*oligarkhi*)—seven figures emerging out of privatization in dominant positions in Russia's mercantile economy—poured funds into the media to blanket airwaves with photographs and footage of Stalin's terrorist regime and other Soviet miseries.[64] The pro-Soviet positions and general ineptness of Yeltsin's principal challenger—the Communist Party of the Russian

Federation leader, Gennadii Zyuganov—failed to expand his share much beyond the entrenched 25 percent of the vote available from pensioners and workers still aligned with the Soviet past.[65]

Three days before the runoff with Zyuganov, the president suffered a heart attack. The Yeltsin campaign both hid the president's infirmity from the populace,[66] and won the runoff anyway, in part due to widespread unwillingness in the population to electing the Communist candidate in his stead. In this way, Yeltsin fractured the vote, surviving to defeat Zyuganov.

The 1996 presidential election kept Yeltsin in office, and destroyed any hopes of reforming the Soviet Union, no mean achievement. In this sense, the 1996 presidential election proved historically decisive. What becomes decisive in the *longue durée*, however, means little to those directly experiencing crushing economic depression. For this reason, the Russian president's popularity never really recovered, it simply increased momentarily in comparison with one of its most reactionary opponents.

Indeed, in the aftermath of the past three years, the disintegration of the remnants of DemRossiia and deepening impoverishment steered groups around Yeltsin into practical alignment with the winners of the privatization process, who in turn had consolidated their positions by "loaning" the Yeltsin campaign funds in return for access to selected shares in enterprises and state natural-resource monopolies. In the wake of the election, the moniker "loans for shares" (*zaimy za aktsii*) emerged as the byword for renewed privatization in 1995–1996.

"Loans for shares" created avenues for the formation of political economy arrangements linking the cities and the countryside through networking among sectoral figures, in disregard of the hopes of the early 1990s. Thus arose the power of the oligarchs, who dominated Russia politically from Yeltsin's reelection until the economic collapse of August 1998. And the rise of the oligarchs stands as a primary vector of feudalization. Understanding this process requires a more careful look at privatization.

The Rise of the Oligarchs

Privatization occurred in two phases, implementing the ideas of Anatoly Chubais, a key architect of Yeltsin's post shock therapy reforms. Appointed Chairman of the State Property Committee (*predsedatel' Goskomiteta po upravleniiu gosydarstvennym imushchestvom*) in November 1991, Chubais became first vice minister in charge of economy and finance (*Pervyi zamestitel' Prem'er ministra po voprosam ekonomicheskoi i finansovoi politiki*) in November, 1994. Chubais designed the contours of voucherization, and then conversion of vouchers into shares (*aktsiia*) in 1995–1996. Despite being sacked as first vice minister in February 1996,[67] Chubais resumed working for Yeltsin's reelection just a few weeks later, before being appointed chief of staff (*rukovoditel' Administratsii Presidenta*) following the presidential election, in July 1996.[68] Privatization retained Chubais' imprimatur throughout.

Now recall that voucher privatization ran from 1993 through mid-1994. The centerpiece of the program distributed voucher shares in Russia's state-owned assets to the Russian populace for a nominal fee. Financial-commodity networks rising out of the hard-currency commodity brokerages (birzhi) soon began offering various "get rich quick" offers to Russian citizens unfamiliar with concepts like a stock market for their voucher-shares, as in the M-M-M pyramid scheme. Unsurprisingly—through arrangements such as insider deals in which enterprise managers controlled workers' shares, and, most importantly, the mundane consequences of a few relatively savvy figures operating in circumstances poorly understood by the populace as a whole— the majority of shares ended up in the hands of commodity brokers, bankers, enterprise managers and officials from the shock therapy period.[69]

Thus arose a pattern of "political capitalism."[70] Political capitalism signals the utilization of elected or appointed positions and political connections to monopolize trade opportunities, amass newly privatized property, and create cartels, syndicates, and financials empires, in a context where work itself is at least partially commodified. Note that commodification can occur where wages are "fixed" and work falls partially outside the market as a whole. In this last since, political capitalism may supersede mercantile arrangements, yet grow out of them.

In mid-1990s Russia, political capitalism originated from the fusion of mercantile networks with control over enterprises through political networks, as workers began to face reorganization of some enterprises along "market" lines, albeit in an environment lacking market setting of many wages or even of a range of commodity prices. Indeed, Russian political capitalism emerged as a highly opaque and rigged process, distinct from the "containment" of such tendencies by both functioning civic law, and "enterprise" and "shareholder" capital in the West.[71]

The new phase of privatization between 1995–1996 consolidated political capitalism in the concrete form of commercial oligarchies, the financial–industrial groups (*finansovo-industrial'nye gruppy*) or FIGs. In effect, renewed privatization transferred state assets *en masse* to narrow financial–industrial networks that gained control of banks, brokerage firms, enterprises, and so on. The process remained opaque—though formally registered in July 1996, the first "official" FIG actually followed the formation of several dozen "nonofficial" FIGs starting the previous year.[72] The rise of the FIGs, in turn, tied closely to Yeltsin's plebiscitarian politics, although the nuts and bolts of collusion between emerging oligarchies and Yeltsin's reelection team would not gain wide press airing until the fall of 1996.

In retrospect, the origins of such collusion are clear enough. With a presidential election scheduled for spring 1996, both the Duma and Yeltsin began showering subsidies down on various regions of Russia in order to shore up support. Yeltsin's credibility had been badly damaged by his decision to follow Grachev's advice and invade Chechnya at the end of 1994. The war combined with high levels of deficit spending in other sectors to exacerbate the government's budget shortfalls, which were becoming chronic. Gaping budget deficits in turn magnified the government's growing inability to pay salaries and pensions in a timely fashion.[73]

As we have seen, by late 1995 deep distrust again characterized relations between the president and the legislature. Under the system of presidential rule created by the constitution adopted in the wake of the shelling of the Supreme Soviet, the Duma itself remained a weak body whose real power lay in its ability to assert some voice in domestic economic affairs and obstruct the government by blocking the administration's legislative initiatives. By denying the Duma much of a role in forming government policy, Yeltsin failed to give deputies an incentive to take responsibility for the government's reform measures.[74] Moreover, the war in Chechnya and the strained relations between Yeltsin and the Communists meant that in 1995 and early 1996, the majority in the Duma remained inclined to oppose the president at every turn.

Alarmed by the degree of Yeltsin's unpopularity, the opposition power in the Duma, and the possible threat to their positions implicit in a Yeltsin loss in the coming presidential elections, emergent oligarchs scrambled to find a way to bail the Yeltsin government out of the growing financial impasse it faced in late 1995, while still avoiding paying taxes on assets. The oligarchs Boris Berezovsky, chair of the LogoVaz FIG, and Mikhail Khodorovskii, founder of the Menatep FIG, joined forces with Yeltsin appointees to ease the budget crisis and transfer additional state assets to the oligarchies in one fell swoop.[75]

As a result, the second phase of privatization became known retrospectively as "loans for shares" (*zaimy za aktsii*), where oligarchies loaned the government money in return for shares in state-owned industries. Loans for shares transferred large chunks of Russia's oil and mineral wealth at bargain prices to the oligarchies in a series of opaque arrangements. LogoVaz FIG head Berezovsky actually bragged that he had been offered over one billion dollars for the newly created Siberian oil firm Sibneft, which he reportedly acquired during loans for shares for only 100 million dollars.[76] The 1996 formation of the FIGs, then, merely "legalized" what had already occurred.

Then-Prime Minister Chernomyrdin presided over the whole process. The former head of GazProm, the Soviet natural gas monopoly listed as one of the Russian Federation's largest private companies in 1998, Chernomyrdin's tenure as prime minister during "loans for shares" politically embodied "nomenklatura privatization," the transfer of state assets to personal ownership by former Soviet economic officials and younger Communist Youth League (*Komsomol*) administrators and specialists. Indeed, though Chernomyrdin denied it, Russian and Western press reports numbered the former prime minister among Russia's wealthiest men.[77] Growing public knowledge of the Yeltsin campaign's financial support from the FIGs in the second half of 1996 reinforced the perception of extensive corruption at the top of the regime.[78] Indeed, financing of Yeltsin's 1996 campaign far exceeded laws passed in the Duma regarding regulations of elections.[79]

As a consequence, little investment flowed to retool factories or create service-oriented enterprises to meet the needs of the Russian populace. Indeed, much of Russia's economy had not even been fully monetized.[80] During Yeltsin's second term, a growing minority of the population failed to receive regularly paid salaries or pensions, while the salaries and pensions of those who got such payments often proved too meager to live off. According to a study of wages in seventy-eight of Russia's eighty-nine regions made by Yeltsin's own presidential apparatus in 1995, only fourteen had average per capita incomes exceeding the minimum subsistence level established by the government itself.[81] Moscow stands out with a per capita income at 316 percent above this same level, far greater than any other region in Russia, reflecting the "mercantilist" character of the Moscow-centered Russian cash economy and the political character of capitalist relations.[82] For those such as the impoverished outside of mercantilist flows, the situation changed little in the late 1990s.[83]

Simply put, many Russians experienced some degree of "cash starvation" during the reform process, meaning that day-to-day economic survival depended on the handout of goods on factory floors, barter arrangements, and the tried-and-true Russian tradition of growing potatoes and cabbage on small private plots allotted citizens under the Soviet regime. Clearly, the majority of Russians in the 1990s survived outside the parameters of the market economy, for if they were dependent solely on goods purchased with cash, much of the population would not have been fed.[84] In short, the Russian populace failed to command sufficient aggregate monetary demand to stimulate enterprises.

The expansion of barter relations in Russia from 1995 to 1998 stands as a principal sign of state collapse.[85] The inability of the Russian administration to stabilize use of currency in turn deepened state fragmentation, as regional figures scrambled both to find alternative means for securing economic relations, and lacked incentives to heed many central directives or policies. Feudalization—the growing practice of regional power holders negotiating with one another and a nominal central power while keeping local populations from using ostensibly "national" laws to gain a stake in central governance—spread relentlessly.

What internal production of goods and services oriented to the domestic market did develop remained confined to either the production of luxury goods for Russia's small commercial elites and urban middle class, or to the production of food products, toiletries, and the like. Moreover, imports dominated over domestic production in provisioning Russia's few commercially dynamic cities. Thus by mid-1998, Moscow depended on imports to feed nearly 80 percent of its people.[86]

In retrospect, "loans for shares" shifted the practical weight of economic "policy" to seven oligarchs, while gutting Russia's political order of any institutional stability for years.[87] Trajectory improvisation was thus artificially extended for groups and networks managing to gain some hold on national, regional or sectoral power, while the vast majority of the populace had to adjust trajectories in line with the diktat of whichever group dominated them.

In such circumstance, parliamentary opponents of the president—emasculated by the Yeltsin constitution and playing a largely symbolic role often misrecognized by the public—became more aggressive in skirmish-like attacks on the Russian government, without ever seriously threatening the *faux* Russian presidential system of rule. In many regions, governors acted like laws onto themselves, as a majority of the population and state-owned enterprises descended into elementary barter relationships.[88] In fact, "dual economies"—one an export-oriented, monetized political capitalism, the other a nonmonetized, barter economy—characterized Russia in the 1990s. The two linked politically, through a restricted labor market that only entailed partial deployment of work through wages, by means of sectoral connections.

In the meantime, as proxies displaced the now infrequently seen Yeltsin, Russian high politics appeared a more and more opaque affair, with a virtually powerless Duma engaged in shadow boxing with a virtual president. And yet, conceiving the oligarchs as either rulers or even stable is misleading, as their power in turn rested on a fragile combination of affairs. Violence emerged as central in propping up oligarchies in such conditions.

Organized Violence in 1990s-Era Russia

Measuring the degree of violence in Russia in the 1990s proves difficult for a number of reasons. Unreliable reportage, misleading or contradictory statistical measures, and changes of opaque and unreliable Soviet accounting systems to more open ones all figure here. But preliminary figures can be taken from such sources, for although "the data cannot be substantively accurate" it can be shown "to correctly reflect the general tendency."[89]

Comparing Figure 5.2 to Figure 5.3, a rough idea emerges of how increasing homicide rates in Russia in the 1990s correlated with increasing rates of killings of thieves and bandits (*avtoritety*).

The October 1994 killing of Dmitrii Kholodov signaled the state's impotence—or worse—in protecting journalists who crossed certain boundaries. In the immediate wake of Kholodov's assassination, a local official mentioned that "practically anyone who wished" could monitor personal phones in Moscow without police being able to trace them.[90] All of this signaled the degree of "privatization" of nominal state organs then underway, exposing Russia's nascent free press to new forms of intimidation, as Figure 5.4 (listing violent deaths of Russian journalists in the 1990s) reveals.

Journalistic investigations of various unseemly elements of life remained novel in Russia. That such investigations at times exposed various figures at different levels of officialdom—no matter how disunited with each other on other matters—underscored the extent to which a relatively independent press

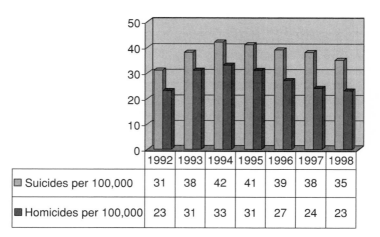

	1992	1993	1994	1995	1996	1997	1998
▨ Suicides per 100,000	31	38	42	41	39	38	35
▪ Homicides per 100,000	23	31	33	31	27	24	23

FIGURE 5.2. Homicide and Suicide Rates in Russia, 1992–1998.
Source: Goskomstat of Russia (1999: 74).

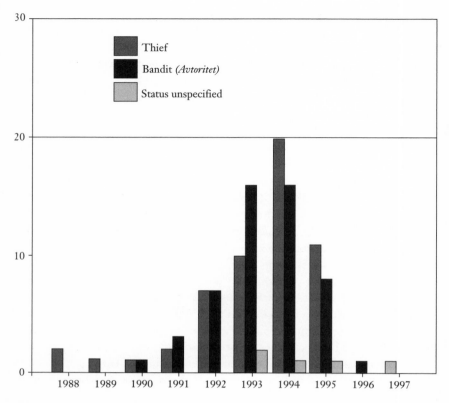

FIGURE 5.3. Assassinations (Successful and Attempted) and Arrests of Crime Group Leaders, Russia, 1986–1997.
Source: Rough calculations on the basis of available data by Volkov (2002: 78).

threatened exposure of unpleasant aspects of actual political rule. Such reporting threatened obscure maneuvering with exposure, spotlighted the indifference of officials to formal laws, brought to light arbitrary relations between practical alliances and elective procedures at distinct levels, and revealed degrees of interpenetration of various fragments of Russian officialdom with nominally "criminal" networks. Thus journalists found that such reporting occasioned various degrees of harassment, including from "official" sources, a dilemma stemming from the absence of any Federal-level "roof" (*krysha*) for investigative journalism in the Russian Federation of the 1990s.[91] Such realities point to the dependence of journalists on the arbitrary diktat of regional power holders for their own safety, indicating how feudalization retarded the development of an independent press in post-Soviet Russia.

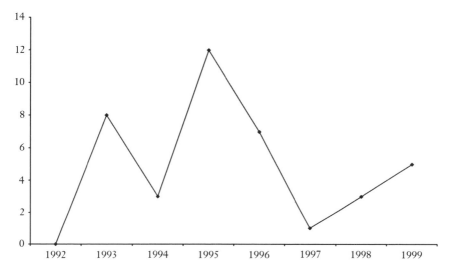

FIGURE 5.4. Violent Deaths of Journalists in the Russian Federation, 1992–1999. *Source:* The *Committee to Protect Journalists*, "Journalists killed in the line of duty in the last ten years," at http://www.cpj.org/killed/Ten_Year_Killed/Intro.html.

Journalistic activity makes starkly visible how the combination of decentralization without any means of regulating the process as whole—either through political organizations, monetary control, or the rule of law—engendered a process of feudalization of regional powers constantly negotiating with one another in an arbitrary and opaque fashion. The parallels between the Soviet disintegration and premodern patterns of dissolving patrimonial power thus stand out, as lack of distinctions between "private" and "public" realms marked both patrimonial and feudal orders in agrarian civilizations. In the postcommunist Russian Federation, such feudalizing tendencies displaced democratic change and underscored the extent to which the post-1993 phase of Yeltsin's government brought a presidential regime highly dependent on regional alliances and emerging oligarchies. Absent any real means of bringing into practice the arcana of often directly contradictory laws, the more and more feudalized authority of Russian governance shifted to the oligarchs by default.

At the same time, the context of the global order—and specifically, the orientation to a transition of some variant of market economy enmeshed with that order—gave rise to political capitalism with outlets to global markets emerging in a dominant position, Moscow *primus inter pares*. The "privatization of power" and the rise of political capitalism linked as means of maintaining the shadow power of the presidential government, preventing any viable national opposition from forming. These two processes reached their zenith—or nadir—in the financial crash of August 1998, seven years to the month after August 1991.

1998 and the Rise of Putin

The spring of 1998 witnessed the appointment of Sergei Kirienko as prime minister. Looking to reassert the political initiative from parliamentary opponents bent on exploiting wage and pension arrears against him, Yeltsin fired his long-time prime minister, Viktor Chernomyrdin in March, appointing the relatively unknown Kirienko to take his place.[92] Kirienko hailed from Nizhnii Novgorod, a city in north-eastern Russia anomalous for its openness and experimentation under former city leader and now top Kirienko aid, Boris Nemstov.

The Russian president ceded more power to Kirienko than granted Chernomyrdin, and Kirienko responded by appointing a team of "young Turks" dedicated to radicalizing the liberalizing measures of previous years. In so doing, the Kirienko government took steps to reign in the tax-evading habits of the financial–industrial groups, steps unprecedented in the Yeltsin period. Kirienko's tenure in office—lasting from spring to August of 1998—thus brought to a head conflicts in the economy growing since shock therapy.[93] Unlike the days of early 1992, however, Kirienko's government remained tied to Yeltsin without DemRossiia or any open linkages to voluntary associations.

Although Russia ran a strong trade surplus in the mid-1990s, in the years just prior to financial collapse, export revenues propped up the hybrid of a barter-based "real" economy of industrial production and a "virtual" economy of high finance driving the commercial boom in Moscow and a few other cities.[94] On the one hand, the oligarchs who controlled Russia's largest FIGs siphoned off much of the capital inflow, either gobbling up Russian assets offered in insider deals as part of privatization, or spiriting it abroad to offshore accounts. Some estimates place the total amount of Russian capital flight between 1990 and 1998 at over 200 billion dollars, dwarfing the combined amount of foreign investment, aid and loans extended Russia since the dissolution of the Soviet Union.[95]

On the other hand, federal and regional governments appropriated revenues from the export of natural resources and plowed them into their yawning budget deficits. Tellingly, almost a quarter of revenue collected by the government in the first half of 1997 came from taxes on oil and natural gas exports, which accounted for over 44 percent of Russia's total exports during the first six months of the following year.[96] About 45 percent of the world's natural gas deposits and 13 percent of its oil reserves lie below Russian soil.[97] Although gas and especially oil production declined through the nineties due to deteriorating physical capital stocks, lack of investment in the energy sector, and poor internal transport, Russia still produced nearly 600 billion cubic meters of natural gas and over 300 million tons of oil in 1997. Indeed, in that year Russia provided roughly 30 percent of Europe's natural gas needs.[98] Russia also stood as a major producer and exporter of nickel, gems, and precious metals.[99]

The relation between export revenue and patronage stands out. Patronage machines on the federal, regional, and local levels redistributed segments of export revenues in traditional Soviet fashion, in the form of salaries, social benefits, and subsidies to state enterprises, with middlemen at all levels lining their pockets along the way. Until early 1998, political bosses and economic managers stabilized these arrangements by haphazardly provisioning workers with handouts of goods and sporadically supplying utilities and social services to local populations. Starved of cash and shunned as an investment opportunity by Russian banks addicted to speculating on high-interest government treasury bills, industrial enterprises public and private kept these arrangements going by the tried and true Soviet method of informal barter deals between enterprise managers, and sometimes between enterprises and importers and exporters.[100]

By March, however, the deterioration of the ability of such Soviet-era methods of provisioning the populace combined with the snowballing problem of wage and pension arrears to generate a wave of strikes, hostage takings of managers, and worker-organized blockages of rail lines across the country. As of April, the International Federation of Chemical, Energy, Mine and General Workers estimated that fully a quarter of the wage force had suffered either delayed wage payments, payments of wages in kind—often in the form of unsaleable merchandise—or a simple refusal by management to pay back wages at all.[101] Similarly, many enterprises stopped paying into pension funds, contributing to the growing problem of pension arrears. By May 30, government and press figures claimed that enterprises owed the government Pension Fund between 17 and 18 billion rubles.[102] Tellingly, privatized state-enterprises— enterprises controlled by FIGs—emerged as the worst offenders in the area of wage and pension arrears.[103]

The spreading rebellions against delinquent wage and pension payments imperiled the stability of the Yeltsin-era hybrid of political capitalism and further "feudalized" territorial and economic powers. The wave of labor unrest and social protest intensified in May 1998 after miners in Cheliabinsk blocked the Trans-Siberian railroad demanding immediate payment of their back wages.[104] Although miners now lacked any Federation-scale social movement to align with—as in the days of DemRossiia—increasing militancy prompted the Kirienko government to intensify its efforts to hold the FIGs more accountable for their tax obligations. Over the summer, however, FIG after FIG successfully resisted Kirienko's measures to increase the effectiveness of tax collections and introduce more competitive bidding into privatization auctions.[105]

The "revolt of the oligarchs" doomed Kirienko's attempt to reassert authority over the FIGs, increase tax collections and thus defuse the growing time-bomb of wage and pension arrears. This failure exacerbated the government's mounting financial predicament, exposing to the whole country the inability of the central government to assert its authority over Russia's new "feudal" powers.

Desperate to stave off outright financial collapse, Kirienko devalued the ruble and defaulted on payments of foreign-held short-term government securities on August 17. The crisis immediately deepened, prompting Yeltsin to fire Kirienko on August 23 and attempt to bring back Chernomyrdin, following heavy pressure openly asserted in the media by Boris Berezovsky, head of LogoVaz, one of the largest of Russia's FIGs and a former deputy prime minister in the Chernomyrdin government.[106] But it was too late, as economic turmoil and political chaos destroyed Yeltsin's ability to maneuver among Russian elites now locked in internecine conflict. Reduced to a near figurehead, Yeltsin in the end agreed to appoint former Soviet Foreign Minister official Yevgenii Primakov as prime minister to avoid a power struggle threatening his ouster.[107]

Since the days of Leonid Brezhnev's rule over the Soviet Union, political elites in Moscow have relied heavily on revenues from raw materials exports to prop up Russia's economy. Yeltsin, like Mikhail Gorbachev before him, proved incapable of reducing Russia's dependence on revenues gained from such exports. Indeed, petro dollars remained the glue that held together both the FIGs of the oligarchs and the barter economy of the regional bosses.[108] In August 1998, however, the government announced that Russian oil and natural gas sales abroad were down 26 percent from the previous year.[109] The fall in the volume of petroleum and gas exports coincided with a steep drop in world oil prices from almost 20 dollars a barrel in October 1997, to about 12 dollars a barrel in by March 1998.[110] These trends cumulatively slashed Russia's export revenues, triggering the implosion of a system already struggling under the pressure of mounting social unrest. But the crisis could never have snowballed into full-scale financial meltdown if the economic order erected under Yeltsin had not been a house of cards ready to buckle under an unfavorable shift in petroleum prices.

In retrospect, the Yeltsin government represented at best a weak power broker at the center of opaque, shifting and highly unstable networks of political bosses and financial kingpins. The dynamics of Yeltsin's arbitrary personal leadership style, the lack of institutional responsibility given the Duma under Yeltsin's new "presidential constitution," and the form of political capitalism described above combined to generate a protracted state of political paralysis between the Yeltsin administration and an obstructionist legislature. Over the years, the ongoing political carnival in Moscow undermined feeble efforts to institutionalize a regulatory and tax framework suitable for extending market relations throughout the Russian hinterlands and encouraging smaller-scale entrepreneurship aimed at satisfying consumer demand. Instead, political figures in Moscow adjusted to the "dual economy" of monetized exports, and nonmonetized barter relations, in part due to a habitus formed in Soviet fields. It is thus not surprising that the FIGs stepped ever more boldly into the political vacuum at the top after 1997, in effect "colonizing" and "privatizing" Russia's government and siphoning monetizable exports from various sectors in the process.

Rather than the drop in world oil prices—the proverbial straw that broke the camel's back—the roots of Russia's 1998 financial meltdown lay in the progressive loss of control by the Yeltsin government over both the FIGs and the resurgent local and regional power centers of the postcommunist period. Recall that prior to 1996, Yeltsin retained the power to appoint and dismiss at least some of the governors of many of Russia's regions. From this year forward, however, all governors gained popular election. This weakened the ability of the central government to control the actions of the governors or entice them to cooperate with the president by threatening a presidential dismissal.

In the last years of the Soviet regime, a combination of "generalized corruption" and "total" state-organized redistribution enabled apparatchiki to appropriate funds for personal use. If anything, this hemorrhaging of revenues became even more pronounced under the Yeltsin government, due to the latter's extreme administrative weaknesses, its inability to reign in corrupt practices, enforce its own laws and decrees, or even issue a Federation-wide currency. The Kirienko interlude demonstrated graphically the extent to which the distinction between "criminal" and "economic" activity disappeared in post-Soviet Russia, for without a state capable of enforcing laws, might makes right in the economic sphere. The sometimes brutal struggle of oligarchs for control of economic turf, punctuated by gangland style assassinations, echoed in a decentralized fashion the history of arbitrary rule under Soviet commissars. Thus the FIGs and their private security services routinely used contract murder, blackmail and bribery of unpaid civil servants to capture the lion's share of revenues from raw materials exports as a hapless central government looked on.[111]

Unable to collect taxes, come to agreement with the Duma over how to lower spending or increase revenue, or impose professional standards of conduct on public officials, the government found itself repeatedly turning to the very FIGs its policies had created in search of cash to finance the federal budget. Indeed, the "loans for shares" scheme emerged as an archetype of the government's long-term strategy for managing its chronically under-funded operations. At crunch times, the oligarchs responded to government entreaties by lending the state money at exorbitant interest rates and by buying high-interest short-term government securities, some paying dividends as high as 150 percent after a very short interval of time. When such securities came due, the government would either turn around and do the same thing over again, or solicit funds from the IMF. Public financing thus took the form of a large-scale Ponzi scheme.[112]

Predictably, a pyramid of public debts soon accumulated, mirrored by a pyramid of illusory private bank assets in the form of short-term government securities and paper debts owed banks by ailing state-enterprises. As large segments of the state-industrial sector had been gobbled up by the oligarchies, many bank assets thus took the form of an extensive web of chits owed by FIGs to each other. Moreover, the windfall profits reaped by banks lending funds to a cash-starved regime created a massive disincentive to consider extending loans to Russian enterprises hoping to recapitalize their decaying plants. After all, why would a banker lend capital at relatively low interest rates to a decrepit enterprise lacking a clear market for its goods when it could make a killing by investing this same money in lucrative short-term government securities?

The government's fiction of sticking to austerity measures mandated in IMF loan conditions further exacerbated the situation. For the government— who were simply mimicking the policy dictates of IMF loan officers at this point—"austerity" meant not paying salaries in the military, state enterprises, mines and the educational and health services. The standard of living of most ordinary Russians—especially those outside of financial centers like Moscow or Nizhnii Novgorod—thus continued to deteriorate as the shoddy social services inherited from Soviet times disintegrated altogether. Indeed, among the most telling statistics of the period from 1987 to 1997 stand the drop in male life expectancy from 64.8 years in 1988 to 57.6 years in 1994—a first in an industrial country—a skyrocketing infant mortality rate, and sharp rises in disease rates of all sorts.[113]

By July of 1998, the federal government could no longer count on the army or the police to obey its orders in much of the Russian Federation. The reasons for this are not difficult to understand. On July 14, the newspaper *Izvestiia* published the results of a survey of military officers in western Russia in which only 18.5 percent claimed they could live off their pay.[114] Among conscripts, the situation was worse, underscoring the inability of the Russian brass to feed its troops.[115] In the summer of that year, an army commander was detained for feeding dog food to enlisted men.[116] On August 21, the government announced that the fiscal breakdown of the state made it impossible to issue outgoing military personnel housing certificates for that year.[117]

Utterly inadequate pay combined with a military culture of hazings of draftees to place hundreds of thousands of young men in desperate straits. According to former Army officer and Duma Defense Committee Chair Lev Rokhlin, there were 1,534 noncombat deaths, including 614 suicides, in the armed forces in 1997 and the first four months of 1998.[118] Rokhlin, who led the initial Russian attack against the Chechen capitol of Grozny and then later became an outspoken critic of the Yeltsin administration, spearheaded the creation of the Movement to Support the Army in September 1997. He was murdered under mysterious circumstances on July 3, 1998.[119]

Local police forces faced a similar state of disarray, as meager and intermittently paid salaries intensified the dependence of law-enforcement personnel on bribes and rendered the police highly susceptible to privatization under the aegis of local bosses and economic oligarchies. In this atmosphere, "violent entrepreneurship" flourished under various "roofs" (*kryshi*), a colloquial Russian term for protection organized through legal or criminal channels. "With the entry of KGB and MVD cadres into the market as private agents, the age of the 'roofs' reached its zenith."[120] On this basis, a number of governors erected virtual dictatorships on a regional basis, co-opting local law enforcement agencies into their regimes.

The authoritarian regime of Kirsan Iliumzhinov in the Republic of Kalmykia, an autonomous region in south-central Russia, stands as perhaps the most egregious example of this trend. Larisa Yudina, a local reporter who exposed some of Iliumzhinov's corrupt practices in the region's only independent newspaper, was brutally murdered on June 9, 1998.[121] On June 19, Yeltsin' studied silence on abuses by regional strongmen prompted "the Apple" (*Yabloko*) parliamentary head, Grigorii Yavlinskii, to denounce Yeltsin's tolerance of the "feudal excesses" of governors who had exchanged support for Yeltsin in return for a virtual free-hand in running their "fiefdoms."[122]

Similar great difficulties plagued Russia's educational and health sectors. In many Russian localities, the always shoddy Soviet health services virtually disintegrated as impoverished clinics and hospitals found it impossible to pay their staffs or buy medicines and supplies. At the same time, teachers organized strikes and work stoppages across the Russian Federation throughout 1998, moving toward an all-Russia teachers' strike in January 1999.[123] The consequences of "feudalized" political capitalism under Yeltsin thus matured not only as financial collapse, but also as the further deterioration of what remained of the central Russian state, namely, the armed forces, the security forces, the courts and the education and health services. Alexander Lebed'— now again a Yeltsin adversary—and other politicians tied to the military used such conditions to spearhead calls to dump Yeltsin altogether and rebuild the Russia state from the bottom up.[124]

Such were the circumstances in which the monetary collapse of August 1998 unfolded. In Russian popular opinion, Yeltsin now hovered near 2 percent, and his name often brought derision and scorn.[125] In this atmosphere, the president kept as low a profile as possible, as proxy groups tried to find a way out.

After the collapse, various elite fragments—some centered in the Yeltsin government—scrambled to somehow stabilize the situation and halt the process of feudalization. An entourage of Yeltsin's personal emissaries and beneficiaries headed by his daughter, Tat'iana Diachenko—now called "the family" (*sem'ia*)—more and more operated as the public face of the president. In the meantime, small fractions of democrats in the parliament haggled about the inequities of ineffective presidential rule, while the term "democrat" in public took on a derisive connotation.

On November 20, 1998, Galina Starovoitova—the early leader of the Moscow Tribune, the only figure appointed for a time to Yeltsin's government who retained any connection with fragments of former DemRossiia activists, and subsequently a leader of a small wing of parliamentarians trying to revive democratization—was assassinated in her St. Petersburg apartment building.[126] Unresolved for years, the shooting death of Starovoitova underscored the rise of "violent entrepreneurs" to prominence in Russia's political life.[127]

By early 1999, with investigations into Yeltsin's monetary affairs beginning in Switzerland, accusations unveiling Boris Berezovsky's use of listening devices threw the oligarchs in disarray.[128] As the first months of the year unfolded, an investigation into Yeltsin's personal culpability in financial illegalities in Switzerland raised the possibility that the Russian president faced the possibility of indictment if he lost power. All of this triggered a still murky attempt to expose the Russian leader of the investigation, Prosecutor General Yurii Skuratov, in a grainy videotape purportedly showing him in bed with two prostitutes in a hotel room.[129] Charges and countercharges flew back and forth between the prosecutor and Yeltsin's immediate group, now known as "the family" (*sem'ia*) in the Russian Press.

As mentioned above, "the family" centered on an informal circle of business operatives and advisors grouped around Yeltsin's daughter, Tat'iana

Diachenko. February and March 1999 witnessed a soap opera of charges leaked from Skuratov's office, and counter smears originating from Diachenko's group and directed at Skuratov, in the Russian press.[130] In this atmosphere, rumors began to circulate widely that "the family" was planning the cancellation of the parliamentary elections scheduled for December and the 2000 presidential elections.

As the situation dragged on into early May, Duma figures hostile to Yeltsin organized an impeachment maneuver against the Russian president. But Yeltsin offset impeachment by replacing Primakov with Sergei Stepashin as prime minister just as the president's many opponents launched the impeachment drive.[131] Within days, Yeltsin survived impeachment.[132] With the failure of impeachmen , the "Skuratov affair" quickly deflated, with Skuratov remaining in office bu backing down from his investigation.[133] It was during this period that the rise of Vladimir Putin to the Minister of Security from the Russian Federal Security Service began to gain notice.[134]

By the summer of 1999, figures in Moscow began to recognize that the financial crisis had less of an effect in many rural and semirural areas, as barter played a central role in provisioning them anyway. The financial crisis generated increasing domestic demand from the cities, as impoverished urban Russians could no longer afford prices of many imported goods—an economic consequence obvious in Keynesian economics, but overlooked by a myopic neoliberal focus on global free trade. Thus the threat of hyperinflation eased in mid-1999 as the aftermath of the financial crisis of 1998 forced urban Russians *en masse* out of the world market, restimulating urban demand in the Russian countryside and thus buffering everyday reliance on barter relationships.[135]

In early August 1999, Chechen terrorists struck in Dagestan. These attacks reignited armed conflict with Federal troops, opening an unexpected exit to Yeltsin and his entourage from the disastrous situation they had found themselves in since the financial crash of 1998. The president quickly elevated Vladimir Putin from minister of security to prime minister, replacing Stepashin, and then renewed war with Chechnya. By August 12, over six thousand Russian troops had been airlifted into Dagestan to fight Chechen rebels. But it was the terrorist bombings in Moscow and other Russian cities in the late summer of 1999 which rallied the population to Putin against the Chechen rebellion.

As the fall of 1999 wore on, Yeltsin, Putin and other Federal political figures organized the "Unity" bloc (*Edinstvo*) as an ad hoc coalition of regional and sectoral groupings distant from the democratic groups of the early 1990s, economists involved with reform in the mid-1990s, and the Communist Party of the Russian Federation. The December 19 elections gave Unity 23 percent of the seats, while fracturing the rest of the vote in ways that left Yabloko as the only pro-democracy group from the early 1990s surviving the 5 percent cut-off for parliamentary representation of political parties or coalitions, with a mere 5.93 percent of the vote.[136] Putin then improvised a temporary reconciliation with the Communist Party to shield Yeltsin's "family" from prosecution and arrange a more stable basis for Russian governance than had existed since 1992.

Such were the circumstances that enabled Yeltsin's sudden resignation from the presidency on December 31, 1999, ceding the position provisionally to Putin. The new Russian president quickly organized an outright victory in direct presidential elections in March 2000, cementing a peaceful transition of power which, just a few months earlier, had appeared impossible. Thus the Yeltsin period in Russia's postcommunist history came to an abrupt close.

The Myth of Democratic Power

As the Putin government consolidated power, the new president turned his attention to reversing the process of feudalization and reasserting Federal authority across the Federation. The campaign against Chechnya stood at the figurational center of this process.[137] Indeed, Putin's popular election, when combined with habituation among Duma deputies to the plebiscitarian order of the 1993 Russian Constitution, gave the new regime the ability to orchestrate politics around the symbolic unity of the Russian Federation and contain further disintegration of Federal powers. In this narrow sense, Putin's rise brought an end to the long interregnum of institutional disintegration seen in Russia since the collapse of Soviet power. And yet, the very process of feudalization had itself brought the possibility of Federation-wide democratic consolidation to a close long before.

The roots of the failure of rapid democratic institutionalization during the early years of political revolution lie in the late-1991 abandonment of the project of transforming DemRossiia into a democratic political party in favor of an economic revolution from above. Yeltsin's attempt to meld a presidency formed in the Soviet-era Russian Republic into an emergency plebiscitarian regime capable of consolidating new political institutions in the independent Russian Federation in part represented an attempt to by-pass certain aspects of "the parade of sovereignties"—feudalization—that helped destroy the Soviet Union. And yet as Yeltsin struggled to maintain the facade of central authority and jump-start an economy stubbornly resistant to the elixir of suggested Washington Consensus policies, feudalization fashioned a motley coterie of "violent entrepreneurs" and more benign marketeers in the big cities from a clay of former party-state apparatchiks, "gray" market dealers and urban professionals and intellectuals able to position themselves in the networks connecting the Russian government to key economic sectors and regional power alignments.[138]

The shards of DemRossiia thus played no significant role in the Yeltsin presidency after the latter's attack against hard-line remnants of Russian Congress of Peoples Deputies in October 1993. This rendered the protracted struggle to institutionalize a presidential regime in the new Russian Federation a remote, internecine struggle between elite fragments in a country lacking the most basic elements of sovereign power, from the rule of law to a functional national currency. The process of trajectory improvisation—the innovation of new political institutions in a situation of institutional breakdown—thus radically narrowed to elite fragments, which struggled for years to somehow "normalize" the situation and establish functional national institutions. The sense of remoteness this fostered among erstwhile members of democratic networks—let alone nominal Russian citizens per se—forced individuals into a process of adjusting life trajectories to regional and local powers indifferent or even hostile to democratic processes.

As a result, the protracted struggle over state power among narrow groups lacking any clear ties to broader social movements greatly accelerated the devolution of sovereignty to regional levels, effectively blocking the emergence of a postrevolutionary civil society. In this sense, Yeltsin's quick turn to a revolution from above in late 1991—absent any call for new elections or use of DemRossiia networks to meld an emergent civil society—represented the worst of both worlds. But this outcome closely reflected the economistic thinking of Yeltsin advisors mesmerized by neoliberal policy, itself blind to the political side of economic equations.

Neoliberalism in the early 1990s—like the Marxist-Leninist Doppelgänger it replaced—represented itself as a universal model applicable to all times and circumstances. To the extent that regional variation figured in neoliberal policy recommendations at all, it played only the role of adjunct. Indeed, the generic, "totalistic" aspects of neoliberal theory help explain its powerful attraction to both former party-state officials and specialists disillusioned with communist ideology. In effect, one totalistic theory displaced another, without forcing a deeper revision of habitus among those who championed it.

But in fact, regional variation in the development of the global order underscores the empirical limitations of any such generic model. The diversity of regional outcomes in a broader global order—what Leninist theorists used to call "combined and uneven development in the world capitalist system"—requires supplanting generic models of "capitalism" and "socialism" with more historically accurate models of the diversity of capitalisms, regimes, and movements to change them. This, in turn, triggers a need for a broader and deeper rethinking of assumptions governing sociology—and the social sciences writ large—operative in the period between the 1840s and the 1990s. Such reflections have motivated Gil Eyal, Iván Szelényi, and Eleanor Townsley to call for a shift from a "classical"—generic—to a neoclassical model of sociology. Here, "the project of neoclassical sociology is to explain . . . diversities of capitalism and the differences in their origins and operations."[139]

In this light, the narrow economistic thinking of Yeltsin's advisors in late 1991 and 1992 marks a shift from one generic, totalistic theory—the Soviet doctrine of Marxism–Leninism—to a second totalistic theory—the neoliberal doctrine of generic capitalism treated simply as an ideology. Certainly, neoliberal doctrine as an "elaborate contraption" of political discourse lacks a totalitarian figurational doctrine similar to the totalitarian ethos of Marxism–Leninism. In this sense, neoliberal doctrine as a totalistic theory simply elides the political from discourse altogether—if at all, treating politics disdainfully, from the perspective of those who "know better" about property rights—rather than combining it with an extensive justification for state-terrorism as in Marxism–Leninism. Nonetheless, the messy realities of social life impede on attempts to implement "pure" neoliberal doctrines, bringing to light the thin, hollowed out utopianism latent in neoliberalism deployed as a simple ideology, an "elaborate contraption" taken off the shelf "whole" from academic settings and put to work in political ways. Indeed, the impossibility of pure neoliberal doctrine to account for large sections of social life, and the tendencies of more perceptive economists working out of this tradition to modify neoliberal abstractions through more empirically intelligible historical accounts of how social orders and geopolitical realities actually effect policy making, stands as a warning against treating neoliberal economics *tout ensemble* as an ideology.[140]

The gap between the vague political vision of DemRossiia in 1990 and 1991—undeveloped as it was due to the movement's "antipolitics"—and the use of a generic "theory" of neoliberalism as an elaborate contraption, a reified ideology, stands out. Indeed, the tendency to transform neoliberalism into an ideological Doppelgänger of Marxism–Leninism among Yeltsin's immediate group figured centrally as Soviet institutions disintegrated and political entrepreneurs attempted to improvise a new trajectory to reorient habitus throughout the population of the new Russian Federation. At the same time, DemRossiia as a social movement played a role that neither the Yeltsin counterelite, nor the movement aktiv, understood, as the habitus of various figures constrained patterns of trajectory improvisation in the context of Soviet institutional collapse.

The confluence of such developmental patterns shaped Russia's nascent postcommunist political order decisively. During the halcyon days of the early 1990s, Yeltsin rode the DemRossiia movement to power and selectively incorporated much of its rhetorical strategy in the early years of political revolution, despite presidential advisors' virtual abandonment of DemRossiia networks in late 1991. In this sense, the shifting Yeltsin entourage of 1990 and ninety-one used networks organized through DemRossiia to undermine the Soviet political order, pushing the process of trajectory adjustment of habitus and institution toward trajectory improvisation by undermining the Soviet Union as an institutional order. That the same Yeltsin entourage quickly abandoned the idea of melding these very networks into an institutional cornerstone of the new Russian Federation marginalized the DemRossiia aktiv and initiated a protracted period of institutional disarray in postcommunist Russia. The Yeltsin group and the DemRossiia core in Moscow rationalized such moves to themselves and others in terms of neoliberalism reduced to an empty ideology. The rationale for this disastrous shift thus lies in the ideological appeal of a simplified neoliberal theory to the new Russian political elite and the DemRossiia core, an appeal marked by the global context of waxing American power in the early 1990s and its regional and local appeal to economic technocrats with little patience for either broader democratic theory, or the often tedious nuts and bolts of grassroots politics.

Yet, despite the abandonment of grassroots politics by Yeltsin advisors with a radically technocratic ethos, the echo of DemRossiia continued to sound in Russian politics long after the dissipation of the networks that constituted the movement in its heyday. Putin finally brought this echo to a close by managing a practical ensemble of statist, authoritarian and democratic themes during his ascent. Aided by the Chechen conflict and a rise in global oil prices, this "reconciliation of opposites" proved capable of stabilizing Russian politics and institutionalizing federal governance in Russia eight years after the collapse of the Soviet regime. This institutional consolidation, however, remains tenuous. At various levels and regions of the Russian Federation, much of the population remains excluded from affairs of governance, and federal institutional power has been rehabilitated on a largely arbitrary and personalistic basis.

Looking back, the importance of the long interregnum of institutional disarray in postcommunist Russia asserted itself once Yeltsin's presidential apparatus was forced into various opaque dealings with remnants of the economic-managerial nomenklatura and traders rising out of the closed commodity brokerages (birzhi) of the early Yeltsin period. Absent any effective public voice in this process following the disintegration of DemRossiia—or even open publicity (*glasnost'*) regarding its unfolding—much of the populace of urban Russia found itself marginalized. With the departure of Galina Starovoitova from Yeltsin's government, most living links between the post-October 1993 presidential apparatus and the democratic movement of 1990–1991—informal in any case—were severed.

In the wake of the parliamentary rebellion against Yeltsin and the forcible suppression of the Supreme Soviet in October 1993, parliamentary democrats and their supporters fractured in multiple differing directions as the inherent contradictions of supporting Yeltsin became explosive. The democratic factions elected to the post-1993 Duma and Council of the Federation—the successors of the Congress of Peoples Deputies and the Supreme Soviet—found themselves unable to work with one another and in a distinct minority in comparison to neo-communist and authoritarian-nationalist groupings.

In retrospect, the miscarriage of Yeltsin's revolution from above led Russia in a direction seen before in the underdeveloped world, where regional power brokers ruling *de facto* "fiefdoms" ensure the perpetuation of weak central government and the continuing disenfranchisement of citizens at the local level. Rather than a market bounded by the rule of law and the mutual observance of contracts, such conditions bred what Max Weber called political capitalism, where former apparatchiki in charge of raw-materials exports and chiefs of trading-based syndicates assumed the role played by caciques and caudillos in Latin America and effendis in the lands of the former Ottoman Empire. Absent the rule of law, such power brokers forced weak central leaders to play by the rules of personal understandings and provisional bargains. Until 1998, the ultimate trump-card of such regional power brokers remained "the declaration of sovereignty" through control of regional bodies, as in the case of Chechnya.

Joel Migdal has dubbed such situations "triangles of accommodation" between strong regional power brokers, on the one hand, and weak central authorities and local citizens, on the other. Such arrangements arise in a situation of relative backwardness in which regional strongmen—too powerful to be subordinated to strict central authority—establish positions as rent collectors and middlemen at the expense of blocking the consolidation of effective national institutions indefinitely and preventing the emergence of effective voluntary associations at the grass roots.[141]

The emergence of powerful regional and local elites undercutting the center from below and strangling reemergent society from above raises fundamental questions about the meaning of labels like "democrat" and "nationalist" in postcommunist Russia. The achievements of the Yeltsin counterelite and the democratic movement—the dismantling of the party-state and the creation of a fragile new ensemble of political symbols linking Russian national identity to democracy—inadvertently helped create a new myth, the myth of democratic power.

And yet almost immediately, the Yeltsin government departed from democracy building, abandoning DemRossiia and relying on a more and more personalistic style of rule to create conditions for a revolution from above. The symbolic commitment to constitutional democracy by significant numbers of Yeltsin appointees and federal deputies in postcommunist Russia does not a democratic power make. The broad institutionalization of the rule of law and the concomitant differentiation of civic and civil spheres of social life—not personal rulership and unregulated corporate pacts—remains the stuff from which democratic polities are made.

In the wake of the 1993 elections and the first Chechen invasion, Yeltsin's government—and the Russian state—became more and more dependent on the formation of sectoral oligarchic groupings linking regions to a greatly weakened center. The sectoralization and regionalization of political power in Russia not only stripped the center of much of its authority, it also greatly weakened the protective cover of reemergent society in relation to patronage politics. For the consolidation of representative democracy at the top presupposes some vibrancy of associations, communities and small-scale market enterprises in localities, as Alexis de Tocqueville recognized long ago. Without such vibrancy, democratic networks whither back toward authoritarian practices, and the habitus of much of the population must adjust—not to regular participation in politics—but to a welter of often opaque groupings and networks striving to control regions and localities. Here, cultivation of local "bosses" emerges as a necessity of survival, and the whole project of reorienting habitus toward the rule of law in a procedural democracy withers on the vine.

Indeed, without vibrant, transparent associations, representative democracy remains vulnerable to gutting in the form of corporatist pacts. At the same time, without the protective cover of a constitutional order—the rule of law—associations, enterprises, and communities are subject to colonization by the patronage networks of sectoral and regional strongmen. The mythical conflation of the consolidation of democratic institutions with the assumption of a limited number of posts in a weak and divided government nominally controlled by democrats obscures such realities.

The myth of democratic power left the activists and political entrepreneurs of the DemRossiia of 1990–1991 disoriented and divided once Yeltsin's revolution from above miscarried. Behind the negative unity of the democrats in 1990–1991—"democracy equals the removal of the communists"—lay very diverse implicit understandings of what democracy meant in terms of positive postrevolutionary programs. The great strengths of antipolitics as a strategic way to unify democratic opposition to the totalistic politics of the party-state quickly turned into a terrible liability once the party-state had been overthrown.

Indeed, beyond processes of marketization and "de-statization" (razgosudarstvlenie) as they unfolded in the forms of shock therapy and then "loans for shares," stands the reality that such programs prefigured the destruction of the specialists as a distinctive type of middle strata rooted in the old order. The specialist strata, after all, depended not on professional certificates licensing the selling of services on a market—a "middle class" in the western sense—but on state distribution of incomes, state allocation of jobs, and subordination to state-designed and -controlled organizations. By breaking up the foundation of partocratic power—a centralized, allocative command economy controlled through a party-state—the specialists inadvertently helped initiate a process of self-liquidation as a distinctive status group.

When the realities, as opposed to the populist slogans, of marketization set-in, many specialists became confused. In one sense, economic disenfranchisement spread as the result of the very reforms they had fought for. That such reforms remained opaque and deeply compromised by an apparat mode of implementation only aggravated the situation At the same time, the reality that the long-cherished hope of marketization—the liquidation of the nomenklatura's monopoly over social and economic life—also meant the destruction of the specialists as a status group with a respected place in society profoundly demoralized and disoriented many erstwhile democratic activists.

For former "60ers" (*shestidesiatniki*) and younger activists they influenced in the democratic movement—intellectuals with roots in the unofficial opposition, the dissident movement, and the *neformalitet* of the late 1980s—democracy meant the realization of "general human values" (*vseobshchie tsennosti*) and the realization of a just and free social order. Alexander Podrabinek—a dissident activist and editor of *Ekspress-Khronika*, the *samizdat* organ of the remnants of the human rights movement in the late 1980s and early 1990s—exemplified such trends. Podrabinek declined to join Dem-Rossiia due to its tendency to compromise with "communists," understood in the vaguest and broadest sense as merely those who had at some point compromised with the party-state in order to get by and get along. He expressed the disappointment of many when, reflecting on the results of August 1991 less than a year later, he pointed out the window during an interview and said "Look around, you'll see that nothing's changed."[142]

From the standpoint of the political sociology of regime disintegration, Podrabinek's observation seemed incongruous. But from the standpoint of everyday life, Podrabinek spoke volumes about the realities on the ground for millions of ordinary Russians. Political enfranchisement remained minimal for the majority, and the symbology of democracy remote. Podrabinek's statement revealed inherent tension between the liminal experience of *déclassé* grassroots protest at the height of the democratic movement, and the professionalizing orientation of pro-democracy political entrepreneurs.

Liminality—the condition of transition between one social status and another[143]—describes the identity-forming yet institutionally ephemeral experiences of solidarity experienced by social-movement participants in revolutionary situations. The temporary dissolution of "status consciousness" felt by participation in a fraternal experience in which established status distinctions temporarily fade into the background creates liminal states of mind that potentially function as defining experiences of identity through a person's subsequent life. A subjective sense of alienation between memories of such experiences, and subsequent representations of them by powerful figures and groups, signal resurgent dissonance between habitus and field, and trigger everything from disenchantment between a grass roots and a former political champion, to a "studied forgetting" of the experience altogether. Here, ranges of adaptation resurge, encompassing everything from a habitus of adjustment—of latent opposition, career adjustment and so forth—to a more disempowered habitus of litany.

> Litanies were ritualistic appeals for overall deliverance: from the cyclical upheavals of Russian life . . . from poverty, from needless suffering, from absurdism. The litany was thus a kind of supplication . . . an almost prayer-like recitation of suffering and loss, directed toward some vague source or possibility of social redemption.[144]

In all such responses, the Soviet legacy persists in many ways and at many levels: from the adaptation to arbitrary and personalized realities of regional power, to the dispositional proclivity of former political entrepreneurs, to extreme factionalism. Some Russian commentators now regard this problem generationally, arguing that the Soviet influence will slowly recede as sections of the managerial nomenklatura form new interests and a post-Soviet generation comes of age.[145]

As the Soviet influence recedes, the question of the place of Russian national identity moves more forcefully to the center of Russian political life. Despite the passing of the Soviet legacy as a basis for a rightist-imperial revival, the democratic legacy of 1989–1993 renders a relatively weak influence on the role of national identity in Russian political life today. The Soviet legacy may thus revive in other ways. After all, national politics in Russia is today only weakly constrained by a democratic disposition in political life. The framing of the "war on terrorism" in the United States after September 1991 further weakened such dispositions, as it privileged a politics of expedience, strengthening the hand of statists in the Putin government both globally, and in the "intra-Federation" context of Chechnya.

The slow deadening of the grassroots legacy of DemRossiia and its selective cooptation by a "moderately" authoritarian government thus remind us of a basic fact. Associational modes of agency characteristic of social movements and a democratic political culture remain "value neutral," for authoritarian movements of nationalism sometimes mobilize in an autonomous fashion along side democratic political associations. Whether or not what Veljko Vujacic has called the "dual revolution of citizenship and nationhood" will continue along parallel tracks remains to be seen.[146]

In the meantime, the resurgence of a statist image of Russian national governance at the end of the 1990s rode an intense reaction to feudalization and the meaninglessness of many laws and regulations. What was really happening in Russian high politics remained excluded from much of the population, now adjusted to getting by and getting along under alternative circumstances, and under the pressure of terrorism and the resurgent conflict in Chechnya. If anything, Putin's rule remained highly personalistic, and attempts to shift Russian life to a state of national law, rooted in universal citizenship, remained but a symbolic figure and rhetorical device. While such symbolic figures constitute one aspect of reality, in themselves they remain institutionally ambiguous. Here, the Soviet Constitution of 1936—"Stalin's Constitution"—stands as a warning: in itself, this document seemed respectful of citizens' rights, but served in reality to legitimate a horrific dictatorship.

Such gaps between practices and their representation are, however, historical commonplaces. These gaps remain central to understanding the complex relation between intellectual discourses and their transformation into the elaborate contraptions of policy. Indeed, such gaps are ubiquitous, as neoliberal pronouncements often have as little to do with "objective" representations of reality as Marxism–Leninism once did. Rather, neoliberal assumptions driving such pronouncements all too commonly emerge as elaborate contraptions which justify rather than analyze. Striving for "objectivity" in postcommunist Russia, then, means turning away from macroeconomic abstractions and toward a close historical analysis of the forms of capitalism and political culture generated by the Soviet collapse and the historically irreducible course of successive Yeltsin governments in the 1990s. And such an analysis must face the reality of feudalization.

As we have seen, feudalization arose as an unintended consequence of Soviet decline and then disintegration, taking initial form as "the war of the laws." DemRossiia championed this as a road to federal Russian power in a

disintegrating, multinational empire for tactical reasons. But a national political tactic must embody some semblance of "governmentality," of how and
where governance shall be established, on what legal principles, and with what
objects of administration.[147] Above all, governmentality entails the formation
of a historical variant of habitus that effectively consolidates broad sentiment
favoring procedural forms of legality and administration, forms that can be
fruitfully engaged as a means for pursuing interests, disputes, and questions of
substantive politics. As ends themselves, such procedural modes remain pale
shadows, and historically their formation has been closely bound up with the
formation of substantive national identities.

The Russian opposition of the late 1980s and early 1990s, however, poorly
understood the national question in an imperial context, and the repressive
character of the Soviet state and its forms of state-engineered stratification
exacerbated the unintended consequences of this. To a large extent, this imag-
inative failure reflected the inability of a managerial and intellectual habitus
formed in the center of an empire to practically grasp what the generation
of national democratic institutions actually entailed. Instead, key figures in
Russia's democratic movement remained marked by the habitus of an "abstract economism" enthralled with changing its shirt from Marxism–Leninism
to neoliberalism. Yeltsin's moves to remain above the movement—jettisoning
it in the immediate aftermath of August 1991—stood as a telling marker
of this habitus. But so then did the remarkably passive acquiescence of the
DemRossiia core to the course of events.

Paths of decentralization unfold in different directions, signaling the danger
of overreliance on a generic concept of representative democracy to capture
such diversity. Robert Dahl and Charles Lindblom introduced the concept of
"polyarchy" as a way of more clearly distinguishing modern forms of representative democracy in nation-states from models of direct democracy, such
as the Athenian city-state of antiquity. Dahl and Lindblom emphasized how
a "plurality of oligarchies" constrained by constitutional norms and elected
bodies opens up possibilities for public will formation from below.[148] Interpreting events in Russia in the immediate post-Soviet period in light of Dahl
and Lindblom, the break up of the monoorganizational structure of the Soviet
order once ruled by the closed estate of senior Communist Party appointees—
the partocratic nomenklatura—created the possibility of unstable polyarchy
emerging. Polyarchy in Russia, however, at best remained only superficially
bound by constitutional principles and popular representation, and lacked any
notion of the nation-state to orient institutional reforms.

The situation of a democratic movement emerging in the center of a multinational empire lacking a history of national politics was a situation unantici-
pated by Dahl and Lindblom. Here, other paths from the juncture of emergent

polyarchy within nominally representative democracy appeared. One way was the partial feudalization of effective authority, a feudalization that fed on the failure of Russian democrats to overcome their habitus and see the "national problem" clearly—or the concomitant danger of not understanding what citizenship entailed as a daily practice. The imperial, multinational, and repressive character of the Soviet state meant that decentralization unfolded along geographic and social lines formed in the Soviet period, urban and specialist-centered, but unattached to any substantive sense of a "national ideal" or "national citizenship" in Russian cultural life. Whereas non-Russian nationalities identified "the Soviet" with "the Russian"—thus preserving in latent forms national identities as oppositional identities—Russia's democratic specialists at the end of the communist era failed to conceive opposition in nationalist terms, except as a tactical afterthought of strategic goals.

As an artifact of Russia's imperial history, then, the Soviet-era intelligentsia did not recognize itself as bearer of an alternative vision of citizenship rooted in an emergent national identity, multiethnic yet unified through Russian idioms and identities. Instead, intelligenty tended to look at nationality through an imperial lens, unable to work out ways to symbolically connect a cultural sense of "Russian-ness" to state identity or to bridge the gap between urban elites and other sectors of the population. The democratic networks of Russian politics in the late 1980s and early 1990s instead realized an ersatz Russian nationality for tactical reasons, aiding the rise of an urban-centered politics subservient to Yeltsin's immediate entourage with its "economistic" obsessions. The often arbitrary character of Soviet law—embodied in the tension between *zakonnost'* (legality) and *partiinnost'* (party-spiritedness)—exacerbated this tendency, as the habitus of those raised under Soviet rule disposed them to view law more as a tactical device than as actual rules of the game, a disposition that undermined the very "economistic" logic championed by pro-democracy specialists.

The experience of feudalization put an end to such strategies, as a mere tactical commitment to nationality without a minimally consistent vision of the rule of law in the early 1990s led to the rule of many, often contradictory and localized "laws" and arbitrary powers—and by extension, a multiplicity of divergent senses of national identity. The shelling of the parliament in October 1993—more than two years after Yeltsin left DemRossiia to fragment and wilt—accelerated rather than stemmed this process, fostering not a democratic civil society, but a distinctive variant of political capitalism realized through "violent entrepreneurship." As the long interregnum wore on, Yeltsin's actual powers shrank, supplanted in large part by "the oligarchs" once the presidential election of 1996 ended the possibility of a Soviet revival. Although this presidential election put an end to the revanchist hopes of those nostalgic for imperial rule through a revived communist movement—a key turn of events—at the same time it failed to consolidate an alternative. Indeed, the presidential election of 1996 can be seen as the last act of antipolitics on the Russian political stage

After the financial collapse of 1998, the vacuum of powers at the Russian federal level overwhelmed even oligarchic blocs, forcing Yeltsin to concede daily governance to a temporary alliance of apparatchiki and "violent entrepreneurs" under new prime minister and former Soviet foreign minister, Yevgenii Primakov. But Primakov's attempt to fashion a stable alignment to rebuild Russian governance proved ephemeral, as Yeltsin used his presidential powers to dismiss the Primakov government and appoint Sergei Stepashin in the spring of 1999, barely surviving an impeachment attempt in the process. Then the renewal of the Chechen campaign allowed the group around the Russian president—his "family"—to assert itself one last time and engineer a successor regime with the ascent of Vladimir Putin. Russians again found themselves under the image of a strong central leader, an image construed by an ersatz of anticommunist, Soviet-like, and nationalist symbology, with little sense beyond stabilizing the situation and reasserting the authority of the Russian Federal state under the patina of "reform" and "stability." Such symbology echoed from above in the habitus of many, diverse groups, displacing the antipolitical—that is, anti-Soviet—identification of a shrunken and fragmented urban stratum of specialists.

Reduced to a shell, representative democracy now stood as one of several vague archetypes around which the leadership tried to mobilize unity, as the Putin presidency struggled to reassert basic functions of a state, from a stable ruble, to minimally serviceable welfare functions, to a more assertive international presence. "Stability," though, in the face of continuing warfare in Chechnya, economically deleterious circumstances, and tremendous political and legal weaknesses, remained fragile and dependent on oil and gas exports. For the time being, the rise in global oil prices over the next few years did provide Putin the leeway of postponing facing this situation. Such stability, however, remained a long way from the democratic dreams of August 1991.

In 2000, the majority in the Russian Federation thus found itself again on the sidelines of a political process that remained to it opaque, as Putin rolled back the partial opening of media—always limited, even in its most open days in the early 1990s, by Moscow powers. Russia's revolutionary passage from Soviet times was at end. Russia's fate—as a nation-state, a social formation, a geographic entity, and a distinctive culture—had avoided feudalization turning into outright disintegration. Yet the failure to consolidate a functioning rule of law and a strong civil society haunts the Russian present.

Appendix: English Translation of Russian Questionnaire Used in the Survey in Chapter One

Sociological Survey of the Leadership, Members, and Active Supporters of the Democratic Russia Movement

This questionnaire represents an integral component of sociological research on the Democratic Russia movement in Moscow from the moment of its inception through November 1991. The aim of this survey is to determine the social base of the movement and the extent of activism of its participants in the indicated period.

This survey is anonymous, and therefore if you decide to participate in it, there is no need to indicate your name. After filling out the questionnaire, please place it in the preaddressed envelope that has been provided and mail it.[1]

Thank you!

1. Date and place of birth:
2. Sex: M/F
3. Nationality (according to your passport):
4. a) Marital status: single/married/divorced
   b) Do you have children: yes/no
      If yes, how many?   1/2/3/more than 3
5. a) Do you consider yourself a religious believer?   yes/no
      If yes, what is your religion?
   b) Did your parents consider themselves religious believers?
      Father: yes/no
      Mother: yes/no

If yes, what was their religion?
>   Father:
>   Mother:
>   c) If you are married or divorced, does you spouse or former spouse con-
>   sider him or herself to be a religious believer?   yes/no
>   If yes, what is his/her religion? ———

6. What level of education have you completed?
   a) primary
   b) middle school
   c) high school
   d) vocational or technical school
   e) attended a university or institute, but did not receive degree
   f) associate or bachelor's university degree
   g) postgraduate degree[2]

   NOTE: This question was repeated in identical form in reference to the
   respondent's father, mother, and—if married or divorced—spouse.

7. Please write out your profession as it corresponds to your education:
   ———

8. In which of the following social groups would you place yourself as belonging prior to August 1991?
   a) representative of a state or a governmental agency
   b) director or assistant director of an enterprise, social organization, or
      other official institution
   c) entrepreneur or director of a cooperative
   d) specialist with a graduate, university, or institute education in the sphere
      of science, culture, education, medicine, or law
   e) specialist with a technical profile with a graduate, university, or in-
      stitute education [usually engineers, chemists, and other "applied
      scientists"]
   f) cultural worker (teacher, librarian, museum staff member, and so on)
   g) employee [*sluzhashchii*] with a technical or office profile (typist, labo-
      ratory worker, record keeper/file clerk [*uchetnik*], nurse, and so on)
   h) skilled worker
   i) retail clerk, janitorial work, and so on [*rabotnik sfery obsluzhivaniia*]
   j) unskilled worker
   k) university or graduate student
   l) none of the above[3]

   NOTE: This question was repeated in identical form in reference to the
   respondent's father, mother, and—if married or divorced—spouse.

9. What was the monthly per capita income in your household in
   1986–97:
   1988–89:
   1990–91:
10. Do you consider yourself a member of the Russian intelligentsia, that is, do
    you have a feeling of social responsibility, do you strive for constant spir-
    itual self-improvement and the dissemination of universal human values
    in all aspects of your activity?   *yes/no*
11. Had you traveled abroad prior to August 1991?   *yes/no*
12. Do you know or have you seriously studied a foreign language?   *yes/no*
13. Did you listen regularly to western radio broadcasts prior to perestroika?
    yes/no
    If no, did you listen regularly to western radio broadcasts prior to August
    1991?   *yes/no*
14. Did you read *samizdat* literature in the indicated times?
    a) before 1986
    b) after the onset of perestroika
15. Were you ever a member of the CPSU?   *yes/no*
    If yes, please indicate the approximate date you joined the party:
16. If you were ever a member of the CPSU, then did you exit this organization
    before August 1991?   *yes/no*
17. When did you begin to feel disillusioned with the Soviet system?
    a) always felt disillusioned
    b) before 1986
    c) after the onset of perestroika
18. At what time did you become politically active?
19. a) Do you live close to a metro (i.e., Moscow subway) station?   *yes/no*
    b) If yes, please write the name of this station:
20. Did you participate in the following activities in the indicated periods?[4]
    a) letters to newspapers and/or appeals to Soviet or Party bodies?
    b) sign collective appeals, petitions, or protest statements?
    c) participate in the work of informal political organizations?
    d) distribute samizdat literature or unofficial newspapers?
    e) distribute or post leaflets or announcements of upcoming political
        protests?
    f) participate in street protests or walk pickets?
    g) participate in strikes?
21. Did you actively participate in election campaigns in
    a) 1989?   *yes/no*
    b) 1990?   *yes/no*

Notes

Introduction

1. For the December 1993 Russian Constitution, see *Rossiiskaia gazeta* (Dec. 25, 1993).

2. Ironically, following Stepashin's appointment to prime minister—less than four months earlier, on May 12, 1999—Putin's rise to prominence began to be noted in the Russian press; see "Kto sil'nee segodnia v Rossii?" [Who's Stronger Today in Russia?] in *Nezavisimaia gazeta* (May 15, 1999: 2).

3. See *Izvestiia* (May 18, 1999: 1).

4. Electoral procedures for Duma deputies are given in Section Five of the 1993 Constitution, available online at: http://www.cityline.ru/politika/doc/krf.html#g5.

5. In Russian, "v tualete poimaem—my ikh v sortire zamochim," reported in S. Repor and M. Boldyrin, "Politika: Luzhkovu meshaiut prishel'tsy," *Argumenty i fakty*, No. 39 (Sept. 29, 1999: 2).

6. Three days after the elections, *Nezavisimaia gazeta*'s headline proclaimed "Vladimir Putin stal glavnoi politicheskoi figuroi" [Vladimir Putin Becomes the Central Political Figure] (*Nezavisimaia gazeta*, Dec. 22, 1999: 1). Arrangements between Putin and the CPRF crystallized in the early weeks of the New Year.

7. For Putin's succession to the presidency and his immunity decrees on Dec. 31, 1999, see *Izvestiia* (Jan. 5, 2000: 1–3) and *Nezavisimaia gazeta* (Jan. 6, 2000: 1, 3, 8).

8. "No matter the number of victims, Putin's strategy is not to remain modestly quiet, but to the contrary, to make Chechnya a national example." Kremlin sources cited in "Vladimir na shee," *Kommersant-Vlast'*, No. 7 (Feb. 22, 2000), available online at: http://dlib.eastview.com/sources/article.jsp?id=3201168.

9. Posted on the Putin campaign Web site, www.putin2000.ru, in Feb. 2000.

10. See, for instance, longtime Russian human rights activist Sergei Kovalev's bleak assessment of Putin's rise (Kovalev 2001).

11. The etiology of *longue durée* in recent French thought lies in Fernand Braudel's focus on the persistence of social patterns over long historical periods; see, for instance, his remarks on the "ancient and no doubt...incurable" divide between poverty and wealth in "world economies" (Braudel 1984: 26). Braudel, it should be noted, tended to downplay the importance of events in relation to social patterns in ways at variance with many explanatory strategies in the social sciences (Roth 1979).

12. See Gorbachev's own call for realizing "world technological standards" in his early account of the many goals of the reform program (Gorbachev 1988: 78–81).

13. Interview with *DemRossiia* leader Il'ia Zaslavskii.

14. See Walker (2003) for the centrality of the breakdown of Soviet federal institutions in the communist collapse.

15. Heller and Nekrich (1986: 151–157). Such principles persevered through subsequent Soviet constitutions.

16. For strategy behind the "shock therapy" slogan in Russia, see Murrell (1993). For an insider overview of the Washington Consensus, see Stiglitz (2002).

17. See James Ferguson's notion of development discourse as an elaborate contraption that has effects in the world (Ferguson 1990).

18. The analysis of semantic frames as "cultural tool kits" here follows Swidler (1986).

19. Lotman and Uspenski (1985: 31).

20. "Neoliberalism" is here used heuristically to describe a policymaking discourse. In this sense, the "elaborate contraption" of neoliberal policymaking should be clearly distinguished from the much more diverse and contested meanings of the term neoliberal in academic circles, here set aside. See Ferguson (1990) for the distinct orientations of policymaking and academic discourses.

21. See Eyal, Szelényi, and Townsley (1998: 46–85).

22. Ken Jowitt's analysis of "Soviet neotraditionalism" in significant part inspired the analysis of feudalization and Soviet collapse offered here. Indeed, the background for understanding the complex roots of feudalization in late-communist Soviet society lies in Jowitt (1992: 121–157).

23. See Furet (1989).

24. Citation from Cantor (1993: 202). In recent years, the feudal analogy has been widely applied to postcommunist Russia; see, for instance, Ericson (2000), Humphrey (2002), and Verdery (1996). At the same time, feudal analogies became common in Russian speech; see, for instance, Yeltsin's political foe Ruslan Khasbulatov's reference to "feudal regionalism" (*feodal'noe regionalizm*) in commentary on his adversary's resignation (*Nezavisimaia gazeta*, Jan. 6, 2000: 3).

25. "The early communist system has been called 'feudal socialism' because loyalty to patrons and faith in the proper world-view recall the logic of feudal rank order and clientelism. Notwithstanding the fact that socialism was a thoroughly modern ideology, this analogy is useful because it highlights how the top of the state-socialist social hierarchy was like a 'ruling estate' . . . based on patron-client relations" (Eyal, Szelényi, and Townsley 1998: 28).

26. See Weber (1978: 1006–1015, 1020–1022, 1070–1085).

27. Handelman (1995) exemplifies the prevalence of "mafia" metaphors in analyses of 1990s Russia.

28. See Volkov (2002).

29. See David Woodruff's analysis of "money unmade" and the expansion of barter relations in the 1990s (Woodruff 1999).

30. Although Tocqueville framed political revolution in such terms, his work figures here only as a source for an initial definition. While Tocqueville explained "the Great Revolution" in France as the "necessary" outcome of a protracted historical process, his analysis preceded much modern social theory, and thus can only be retrospectively placed in terms of later developments, such as "relative deprivation" theories of social movements (Henslin 1999: 609). Such retrospective framings remain problematic and require careful qualification.

31. The best account of the Soviet collapse as a "revolution from below" remains Urban (1997), though "below" here refers to relatively privileged Russian professionals.
32. The "revolution from above" framing is presented starkly by Kotz (1997: 6): "the ultimate explanation for the surprisingly sudden and peaceful demise of the Soviet system was that it was abandoned by most of its own elite, whose material and ideological ties to any form of socialism had grown weaker and weaker as the Soviet system evolved.... [The downfall of communism] was a revolution from above."
33. While Fish (1995) privileges "antipolitics" as central to understanding networking among Russian professionals and intellectuals in his multilevel account of the Soviet collapse, he misses its symbiotic relation to networking in the Yeltsin counterelite.
34. See Skocpol (1979: 5–6, 14–18, 33–40, 284–293) as well as Goldstone's summary of the Skocpolian approach to the comparative study of revolutions (Goldstone 1994). For critical treatments of Skocpol relevant to the present discussion, see Abbott (1991) and Sewell (1996). Skocpol (1994) contains a rebuttal of some of Sewell's argument in response to an earlier piece by Sewell (1994). The Sewell–Skocpol exchange reveals a certain degree of mutual misunderstanding rooted in the elusiveness of Skocpol's original methodological statements. Somers (1996) is also of interest, as she discusses her own development from a Skocpolian position to a position closer to the one developed herein.
35. Fitzpatrick (1994: 2).
36. Here, social order in the external sense of patterns of interaction appears simply as an "observable regularity of social life" (Weber 1978: 29–31).
37. The concept of institution here converges with Weber's concept of "legitimate social order," a situation in which conformity to authoritative prescriptions issued by sanctioned authorities is "objectively probable" (Weber 1978: 29–38). "For highly institutionalized acts, it is sufficient for one person simply to tell another that this is how things are done. Each individual is motivated to comply because otherwise his actions and those of others ... cannot be understood ... [T]he fundamental process is one in which the moral becomes the factual" (Zucker 1991: 83).
38. "A man who raises his hat in greeting is unwittingly reactivating a conventional sign inherited from the Middle Ages, when ... armed men used to take off their helmets to make clear their peaceful intentions" (Bourdieu 1981: 305). Michael Polanyi stressed the centrality of tacit, customary varieties of knowledge in human life (Polanyi 1983).
39. See Yurchak (1997: 171–174).
40. "Even that which is most codified ... has as its principle not explicit, objectified and thus themselves codified principles, but practical models" (Bourdieu 1990a: 77). Note also that institutions and organizations are not coterminus, as the former can govern a wide variety of the latter as well as steer interaction both inside and outside of formally organized contexts (Bellah et al. 1990: 10–12).
41. Bendix (1977: 127–174).
42. See Sharlet (1977) for the distinction between *zakonnost'* and *partiinost'*. The corruption of *partiinost'* in the Soviet era gave rise to "Soviet neotraditionalism" (Jowitt 1992: 121–157).
43. See the analysis of "plan-bargaining" in Soviet-type economies (Kornai 1992).
44. Ledeneva (2002).
45. Ken Jowitt's work on "Soviet neotraditionalism" formed an important exception to this tendency in Western scholarship. In an essay originally published in 1983,

Jowitt wrote that the "Soviet regime is best seen as an institutionally novel form of charismatic political, social, and economic organization undergoing routinization in a neotraditional direction ... Soviet regime corruption stems from the Party's refusal fundamentally to alter its view of itself as a heroic transforming principle and its corresponding claim to exclusive political status in a situation where it appears unable to identify an ideologically correct and strategically feasible social combat task" (Jowitt 1992: 127).

46. "For a Leninist party, organizational integrity means the competence to sustain a combat ethos among political officeholders who act as disciplined, deployable agents" (Jowitt 1992: 122).

47. For the origin of tendencies here called feudalization in the Soviet era, see Jowitt's analysis of the roots of "neotraditionalization" (1992: 121–158).

48. For the concepts of habitus and field used throughout, see Bourdieu (1981; 1984: 169–175, 244–256; 1990b).

49. The pattern of obscuring the persistence of the old through its symbolic negation is common in Russian history. Referring to the much earlier formation of Russian Christianity, for instance, Iurii M. Lotman and Boris A. Uspenskii note that "the 'new culture', which conceived of itself as the negation and complete annihilation of the 'old', was in practice a powerful means of preserving the latter. The 'new culture' included both inherited texts and past forms of behavior, whose functions had become a mirror image of what they were before. In sum, the everyday practice of orthodoxy is an undervalued source for the reconstruction of the Eastern Slavic pagan cult" (Lotman and Uspenskii 1985: 39–40).

50. See Elias (1978: 13–32) for the concept of figurations and Mouzelis (1995: 69–80) for how the agentic figuration of events can complement the observational analysis of institutions.

51. Sociological terminology often reduces arrays of institutions in social fields to simply "structures," both obscuring how human agency reproduces and disorganizes institutions, and casting such institutions and the fields in which they operate as somehow "external" to human behavior and socialization. For an overview of the many problems resulting from such "structure–action" dualisms in sociological thought, see Alexander (1987) and Mouzelis (1995).

52. For an elaboration of the concept of international demonstration effect—the concept on which transnational demonstration effect is modeled—see Bendix (1984: 114–119) and Janos (1986: 84–95). The supplanting of "international" by "transnational" here reflects the practical distinction between the international as mediated by institutions grounded in a national context, such as the United Nations, and the transnational as those social forms operating in several national contexts simultaneously and yet independently from specific national or international institutions, such as the Greenpeace movement.

53. "Glocalization" has been widely used in recent years to map "the interpenetration of the global and the local, resulting in unique outcomes in different geographical areas" (Ritzer 2003: 193). Playing on this, Ritzer goes on to conceptualize transnational corporatist policies as "grobalization," stemming from such transnational entities' interest "in seeing their power, influence and (in some cases) profits *grow*" (p. 194; emphasis in original). Thus tensions between localizing and transnational-corporatist

tendencies can be recast between "glocalization" and "grobalization" within globalization as a whole. Much of this converges with earlier analyses of demonstration effects.

54. "Stalin's industrialization...was conceived as a great leap from a relatively backward country to an ultramodern industrial power" (Kuromiya 1988: xi–xii).

55. The specification of the federal-national and the world levels are well understood in many contemporary accounts of social movements; see, for instance, Tarrow (1998: 176–195) on the *longue durée* of movement cycles.

56. For archetypal examples of postwar functionalist, psychologistic, and utilitarian theories of social mobilization and revolution, see respectively Kornhauser (1959), Gurr (1972), and McCarthy and Zald (1973). McAdam (1982: 5–35) summarizes critiques of these approaches. McCarthy and Zald subsequently moved toward a political process approach; see McAdam, McArthy, and Zald (1996).

57. See Jean L. Cohen's discussion of tensions between "strategic" and "identity-oriented" social movement theory for many examples of the latter (Cohen 1985).

58. Melucci (1989: 46).

59. Christian Joppke thus calls for a "contextualized political process perspective" (Joppke 1993a: 12–18).

60. The following adapts McAdam (1982: 36–59) and Tarrow (1998) in ways compatible with both Cohen and Joppke.

61. See Cohen (1985) for an extended analysis of how agents' identities mediated processes of mobilization in Western peace, feminist, and ecological movements in the 1980s. The developing political process model, the growth of postmodernist theories of identity, and Cohen's own preoccupation with larger theories of civil society all eclipsed her call for a theory of "new social movements." For the ways that postmodernism led to a variegated terminology for writing about essentially similar movement processes, see the ethnographic studies in Burawoy et al. (2000).

62. See Bourdieu (1991: 107–116, 163–202), Gamson et al. (1992), Snow et al. (1986), and Snow and Benford (1988).

63. "The words 'Leningrad People's Front' have certain connotations for people ... The noun 'front' is associated in Russian with a combative and offensive task, and with confrontation and the consolidation of forces. The mobilizing mythos of the term is obvious, representing an appeal for unifying all forces against ... the common enemy" (Zdravomyslova 1996: 132).

64. Again, "chaos" is here understood technically. Full institutional breakdowns of political orders, of which political revolutions stand as a subtype, thus parallel the tipping into chaos observed when turbulence arises in fluid flows. "Turbulence in a fluid was a behavior ... never producing any single rhythm to the exclusion of others. A well-known characteristic of turbulence was that the whole broad spectrum of possible cycles was present at once. Turbulence is like white noise, or static. Could such a thing arise from a simple, deterministic set of equations?" (Gleick 1987: 138). The parallel here is obvious: when political institutions fully disintegrate, "order" no longer steers behavior at a national level, and the disintegration of such political steering entails the eruption of a vast array of contending directions toward which agency may orient.

65. "There is a dialectical interaction between habitus and institutional position ... which underlies the process of social change: the new positions change the habitus of individuals, but individuals who are recruited into those positions also affect

the way institutions operate." It thus follows "that we disagree strongly with those who think that if the 'right' institutions are implemented, the 'appropriate' behavior will inevitably emerge . . . [R]ather . . . institutions and incumbents of institutional positions shape each other in unpredictable ways" (Eyal, Szelényi, and Townsley 1998: 8, 44).

66. See Joppke (1993a: 4–18).

67. See Weber (1949: 95–103), which also—unhappily—includes Weber's misleading distinction between "generic" and "genetic" ideal types. The former are indeed heuristic and generalized models, while the latter represent empirical models— not "genetic ideal types"—derived from careful historical accounts of actual processes. For an exegesis of why, given Weber's epistemological assumptions, ideal types are always "generic," and his problematic conflation of ideal types and empirical models, see Burger (1987: 115–140, 154–167).

68. See Giddens (1984: 284) on the "double hermeneutic" of the social sciences: "The appropriateness of the term derives from the double power of translation or interpretation involved. Sociological descriptions have the task of mediating the frames of meaning within which actors orient their conduct. But such descriptions are interpretive categories which also demand an effort of translation in and out of the frames of meaning involved in sociological theories."

69. For phenomenology, see Berger and Luckmann (1966); for content analysis, see Krippendorff (1980); for genealogy, see Foucault (1972). Interest analysis is ubiquitous in the social sciences, though Weber and Bourdieu distinguished material (economic) from ideal (symbolic) interests.

70. In certain situations, "conduct remains unintelligible unless you bring into the picture habitus and its specific inertia, its hysteresis. The situation I observed in Algeria, in which peasants endowed with a precapitalist habitus were suddenly uprooted and forcibly thrown into a capitalist cosmos, is one illustration" [Bourdieu quoted in an interview with Loïc Wacquant] (Bourdieu and Wacquant 1992: 130).

71. See Ringer (1997: 150–155) for an overview of the Weberian use of the concept of interests as an interpretive device.

72. Bourdieu (1993).

73. For methods observers use to check their own reifications, see Ringer (1997: 106–110).

74. Habermas (1987: 126–128, 328–331).

75. "Sociology has to include a sociology of the perception of the social world, that is, a sociology of the construction of the world-views which themselves contribute to the construction of this world" (Bourdieu 1990b: 130). Further, " 'symbolic systems' fulfill their political function . . . by bringing their own distinctive power to bear on the relations of power which underlie them and thus by contributing, in Weber's term, to the 'domestication of the dominated' " (Bourdieu 1991: 167).

76. So long as symbolic forms are conceptualized as emergent properties of "reality," the acknowledgement of the causal efficacy of symbolic forms in no way entails an "idealistic" methodology, despite the claims of some like Blau (1998).

77. See Garcelon (1997b: 55–58).

78. "Commercial classes arise in a market-oriented economy, but status groups arise within the framework of organizations which satisfy their wants through monopolistic liturgies, or in feudal or in *ständisch*-patrimonial fashion. Depending on the prevailing mode of stratification, we shall speak of a 'status society' or a 'class society' "

(Weber 1978: 306). Bourdieu's ill-advised generalization of "market" to designate just about any strategically employable symbolic form detaches markets from money and mars an otherwise useful set of distinctions (Bourdieu 1991: 52–57).

79. See Bourdieu (1986) for a statement of the typology of capitals developed here. For the genetic relationship between the concepts of economic and social capital in recent American sociology, see Woolcock (1998).

80. See Mouzelis (1995: 201) for the former and Bourdieu (1987) for the latter.

81. "The distribution of the different types and subtypes of capital at a given moment in time represents the . . . set of constraints, inscribed in the very reality of . . . [a social] world" (Bourdieu 1986: 242).

82. "Professional and intellectuals could not only appeal to symbolic resources latent in the domestic realm, but could also bring to bear symbolic resources *from outside*, from the West" (Garcelon 1997a: 328; emphasis in the original).

83. Reproduction is here used very broadly, for some degree of agentic innovation occurs all the time in stable institutional contexts and modify the latter. In this sense, I am treating patterns of incremental change in stable institutions here as cases of reproduction. How agency contributes to such patterns of such incremental change is thus bracketed and left aside. Nee and Lian (1994) represent a "rational actor" approach to how to model such long-term processes, an approach which can be reworked in terms of trajectory adjustment.

84. The trajectory correction model of social change aims to adapt Bourdieu's sociology for purposes of the comparative study of secular processes of social change (Eyal, Szelényi, and Townsley 1998: 8–9, 44–45). Of course, "model" here means a heuristic device rather than a predictive-algorithmic schema. The trajectory correction model entails a suite of assumed necessary conditions of social change used to frame actual case studies, as in the identity oriented political process model of social movements and revolutions outlined above.

85. Habitus ties agents to institutions in fields "and in this interactive process, *both are likely to be altered*" (Eyal, Szelényi, and Townsley 1998: 44; emphasis in original).

86. Kellert (1993: 114) writing on the significance of chaos theory in the natural sciences. As the physicist Jeffrey Dunham emphasized to me during a conversation, chaos theory—unlike more problematic notions like "catastrophe theory," "complexity theory," and the like—is as rock solid as $2 + 2 = 4$.

87. Some physicists and biologists consider all social systems "chaotic" ("dissipative or "nonlinear"), as opposed to "conservative" or "entropic" (nondissipative or Hamiltonian) systems encountered at times in physics. The recourse to statistical methods ubiquitous in the social sciences is seen as a prime indicator of this; see Kellert (1993: 41–42).

88. Weber's distinctions between status, markets, status groups, and classes (Weber 1978: 302–307) are here modified in light of network theory. Granovetter (1985) initiated the latter, albeit in a more limited "economistic" form than employed here. Fuchs (2001: 251–292) defines networks as the most general level of human sociation, though his reduction of agents to "observers" (pp. 17–40) serving as "nodes" of networks (pp. 251–253) remains problematic.

89. Weber (1978: 926–940).

90. Evans (1995).

91. "The different types of capital can be distinguished according to their reproducibility or, more precisely, according to how easily they are transmitted . . . Everything

which helps to disguise the economic aspect also tends to increase the risk of loss...Thus the (apparent) incommensurability of the different types of capital introduces a high degree of uncertainty" (Bourdieu 1986: 253).

92. Putnam (1993).

93. See Ledeneva (1998) for an extended treatment of *blat* in Soviet daily life. Jowitt (1992: 224) describes such behavior as an emergent "booty economy" in the ostensibly socialist context of late-Soviet society.

94. "Stickiness" is here loosely adapted from Evans (1995).

95. Arrow (1998: 97–98).

96. Value neutrality here stems from Weber (1978: 1001, 1112), who used the term in a neo-Kantian and not a positivist sense.

97. Woolcock (1999).

98. Harvey (1990: 125–140).

99. Kuromiya (1988: 103–104).

100. See Jowitt (1992: 220–223) for an overview of the developmental stages of twentieth-century Leninist regimes.

101. See Weber (1949: 100–103) as well as Roth (1971: 109–128).

102. Weber (1978: 1006–1110).

103. Weber (1978: 356–384).

104. Thus "the political realm as a whole is approximately identical with a huge princely manor" (Weber 1978: 1013).

105. See Weber's discussion of what he calls "the most elementary types of traditional domination," gerontocracy, patriarchalism, and patrimonialism (Weber 1978: 231–232).

106. See Eric Wolf's synthesis of the Weberian theory of the origins of the state with a neo-Marxian political economy of agrarian civilization in his analysis of the transition from "kinship" to "tributary" modes of production (Wolf 1982: 73–100).

107. See the discussion of Tsarism as patrimonialism, cast in explicitly Weberian terms, in Pipes (1995: 22–24).

108. "The structure of *feudal relationships* can be contrasted with the wide realm of discretion and the related instability of power positions under pure patrimonialism...The personal duty of fealty has here been isolated from household loyalties, and on its basis a cosmos of rights and duties has come into being" (Weber 1978: 1070).

109. "Everywhere the vassal...had to be a free man, not subordinate to the patrimonial power of a lord" (Weber 1978: 1081).

110. The complex array of possibilities here forms the basis of much of Weber's analysis of "traditional authority" (Weber 1978: 215–241, 1006–1110).

111. Pipes (1995: 281–318).

112. Selznick (1960) analyzed the "combat-military" ethos driving Soviet socialism at length. Jowitt (1992: 43–46) refined this into the concept of the party-state as an "impersonal hero organization," which substituted "charismatic for procedural impersonalism" as an alternative to Western representative democracies.

113. Jowitt's emphasis on "routinization" in the transition from the Stalin to the post-Stalin leadership keys his analysis of the declining saliency of Leninism as an impersonal yet heroic ideology. If the "distinctive quality of Leninist organization is the enmeshment of status...in the framework of an impersonal-charismatic organization" (Jowitt 1992: 16), then the routinization of a Leninist party dictatorship "led to the

emergence of a parasitical Communist Party ... not subject to effective central discipline, not able to distinguish between the particular interests of its elite members and the general interests of the Party and country, and insensitive to the distasteful social ethos and threatening political climate it was creating in the Soviet Union" (224–225).

114. See Kuromiya (1988).

115. Relations between ideal types and historical models are clarified at length in Burger (1987).

116. The concept of state-engineered stratification comes from Zaslavsky (1991).

117. Jowitt (1992: 245) framed this secular decline as the growing inability of the Party leadership to subordinate "the particular interests of its cadres to the Party's general interests."

118. Jowitt (1978) developed the ideal type of Leninist revolutionary oligarchy as an "impersonal hero organization" structured by the *modus operandi* of democratic centralism and unified by the ethos of a self-appointed "vanguard."

119. For early examples of the patrimonial-Soviet analogy, see Bauman (1974) and Roth (1968). More recently, Ken Jowitt and—following Jowitt—Andrew G. Walder proposed the neotraditional model of Leninist authority, albeit Jowitt in more "degenerationist" (developmentalist) terms; see Jowitt (1983) and Walder (1986). Lupher (1996) has written a provocative comparative history of Russian and Chinese communism centered on the concept of patrimonialism. Finally, Russian scholars like Umov (1993) have spoken of "totalitarian feudalism," or the hierarchical order of "supplying-redistributive social estates and status groups" (Starikov 1990).

120. "The party maintained a 'cell' in every institution, and party administrations at all levels had departments paralleling those of the state ... As a result, although all lower-level organizations were subordinated to upper ones in a pyramid, the parallelism of the party-state pyramids and the multiplicity of the state itself created overlapping jurisdictions" (Kotkin 1995: xix).

121. The complex and tangled history of the concept of totalitarianism gave rise to two main variants: figurational and institutional. Among the most important figurational commentators on totalitarianism stand Arendt (1958) and Milosz (1955), while Fainsod (1964) and Friedrich and Brzezinski (1956) developed models of totalitarianism as an institutional order. The descriptive power of the former remains central to understanding the Nazi, fascist, and communist movements of the twentieth century. As an institutional concept, however, totalitarianism fails to describe more than the absolutist instincts, terrorist proclivities, and extremism of movement leaders.

122. Stalin became General Secretary of the Communist Party during the Party's Eleventh Congress on April 2, 1922 (Schapiro 1977: 338). For the origins of the *nomenklatura* system of centralized appointments at this time, see Hosking (1992a: 88–89).

123. The program of officialdom "can be summed up in three points: to increase its power, to increase its privileges, and to enjoy both in tranquility. Khrushchev violated these rules" (Heller and Nekrich 1986: 609).

124. See Heller and Nekrich (1986: 603–620) for the close relationship between senior officials' "collective desire" for security of office and Brezhnev's appointment as General Secretary. Alexander J. Motyl emphasized how Brezhnev's policies created "ideal conditions—horizontal fragmentation and vertical segmentation—for regional officials to engage in localized empire building ... The state, in a word, 'decays' "; cited in Lupher (1996: 272).

125. For a detailed analysis of the crystallization of the *nomenklatura* in the Brezhnev period, see Zaslavsky (1994: 44–90). For evidence of de facto hereditary privilege transfer under Brezhnev, see Hanley, Yershova, and Anderson (1995) and Zaslavsky and Luryi (1979). Fehér, Heller, and Markus (1983) emphasize the feudal-like character of *apparat* privilege in the post-Stalin "Soviet-type societies" of Central and Eastern Europe.

126. In the mid-1970s, György Konrád and Ivan Szelényi conceptualized the ubiquitous rent-seeking tendencies of officials under "state socialism" as "the principle of maximizing the amount of surplus product which flows into the redistribution process"; see Konrád and Szelényi (1979: 154).

127. Weber (1978: 232–233) stressed the selective appropriation of administrative powers by staffs and individuals in his description of the transition from patrimonial to estate-type domination (*ständische Herrschaft*).

128. Lane (1992: 162–166).

129. For the problem of distinguishing the official Soviet *intelligentsia* from its nineteenth-century namesake as both a social form and cultural ideal, see Malia (1961) and Nahirny (1983).

130. "The language of authority never governs without the collaboration of those it governs, without the help of the social mechanisms capable of producing this complicity based on misrecognition, which is the basis of all authority" (Bourdieu 1991: 113).

131. Goskomstat (1990a: 21–35).

132. The very specific Weberian definition of "class situation" ties class to "a probability which derives from the relative control over goods and skill and from their income-producing uses"; in contrast, "status groups [typically] arise within the framework of organizations which satisfy their wants through monopolistic liturgies, or in feudal or *ständisch*-patrimonial fashion" (Weber 1978: 302, 306). Weber defines "social class" as an intermediate analytic category between typical class and status situations: "The status group comes closest to the social class and is most unlike the commercial class" (306–307); the latter is constituted by "the marketability of goods and services" (302). Although Weber places "the propertyless intelligentsia and specialists" under the category social class (305), the context implies specialists under conditions of substantial marketization. Although I employ Bourdieu extensively in this work, I favor Weber's more precise use of the concepts of status and class. Indeed, Bourdieu uses the term "class" so broadly at times as to render it coterminous with "group" per se.

133. See Balzer (1996) and Jones and Krause (1991).

134. Konrád and Szelényi (1979: 146) noted the "feudal character" of the middle strata in Soviet-type societies, at one point describing them as "vassals."

135. See Balzer (1996: 300–303).

136. See Weber (1978: 302–307) for the distinction between status and class society.

137. The phrase "the stratification of places" has been adapted from Logan (1978). See Ferguson (1990) for the idiosyncratic effects of South African passports in the tiny region of Lesotho.

138. For the history of the Soviet passport system, see Garcelon (2001). For additional material, see Brubaker (1994), Khobotov and Zheludkova (1990), Liubarskii (1994), and Matthews (1993).

139. In 1989, nearly 36% of Moscow's employed population were tertiary degree holders, as opposed to just over 15% of the employed populace in the Russian Socialist Federated Soviet Republic; see Goskomstat (1990a: 21–35; 1990b: 46–47).

140. See Kerblay (1983: 203–229), Lane (1992: 162–176), Millar and Wolchik (1994), and Sevast'ianov (1989).

Chapter One

1. See the General Secretary's own account of the early months of *perestroika* (Gorbachev 1988: 3–45).

2. For an extended treatment of the dynamic between Gorbachev's reform program and the Soviet federal system, see Walker (2003).

3. "The Soviet Union may be termed a mono-organizational society, since nearly all social activities are run by hierarchies of appointed officials under the direction of a single overall command" (Rigby 1977: 53).

4. Zaslavsky (1994: 107–108, 124).

5. See Abrahamian (1998).

6. The sub-republican "autonomous republics"—officially, *Avtonomnye sovetskie sotsialisticheskie respubliki* (ASSRs)—and other "autonomous regions" emerged as central sites of constitutional conflict, and thus feudalization, in both the late 1980s and in post-Soviet Russia; see Walker (1992). For the origination of such "sub-republican republics" and other "autonomous zones" in the early Soviet Union, see Hosking (1992a: 114–118).

7. See the *Konstitutsiia*, published in Izvestiia Sovetov narodnykh deputatov SSSR (1988: 7). In this amended, 1988 version, the 1977 "Brezhnev Constitution" declares that "All power in the USSR belongs to the people. The people realize state power through the Soviets of Peoples Deputies, which constitute the political foundation of the USSR. All other state bodies are under the jurisdiction of, and accountable to, the Soviets of Peoples Deputies . . . The organization and activities of the Soviet state are based on the principle of democratic centralism [which entails that] . . . the decisions of higher bodies are obligatory for lower bodies" (Izvestiia Sovetov narodnykh deputatov SSSR 1988: 6).

8. Luk'ianov et al. (1984: 76).

9. Izvestiia Sovetov narodnykh deputatov SSSR (1988: 7).

10. Upon Gorbachev's accession to CPSU General Secretary, the Politburo numbered only nine full (voting) members (Winston 1991: 5).

11. "Voting was conducted more publicly than secretly. Voters who intended to vote for the candidate on the paper ballot proceeded directly to the ballot box and inserted their papers. Booths set up for exercising the right of secret ballot were often located some distance from the ballot boxes, so voters who used this facility [for purposes of marking their ballots 'no'] immediately revealed their intentions" (Lentini 1991: 70).

12. Heller and Nekrich (1986: 287–301) emphasize the role of fictive voters' rights in the Soviet regime's ritual presentation of itself as an embodiment of "the masses." Typical of Soviet officialdom stood the nearly 400-page fictive presentation on "Soviet democracy" in Luk'ianov et al. (1984).

13. Savas and Kaiser (1985: 29–34).

14. For a concise discussion of how Party and economic management were fused in the administrative structures directly subordinated to the Council of Ministers, see Gregory and Stuart (1986: 9–16).

15. The third section of Gorbachev's long opening speech to the 27th Party Congress, delivered on February 25, 1986, emphasized the need to strengthen "socialist legality"; to respect the "freedom and social, political and personal rights" of Soviet citizens; and to implement "socialist self-government" in administrative bodies, local soviets, social organizations, unions, and so forth; see Kommunisticheskaia partiia Sovestskogo soiuza (1986: 77–83).

16. At the January 1987 plenum, Gorbachev stressed that the Party leadership "largely due to subjective reasons had failed to evaluate the necessity of change in a timely manner." He then connected this leadership failure to the "serious deformations of Leninist principles" stemming from the "absolutist practices" and "dogmatic approaches" established during the period of "socialist consolidation" in the 1930s and 1940s. Finally—and most importantly—the General Secretary went on to emphasize the need for a thoroughgoing "democratization of the process of selection of responsible cadres ... on the basis of the general application of electoral principles." ("O perestroike i kadrovoi politike partii," *Izvestiia*, Jan. 28, 1987: 1–5.)

17. In 1992, Yakovlev wrote an account of the Soviet collapse (Yakovlev 1992).

18. See Brubaker (1994), Slezkine (1994), and Zaslavsky (1994: 91–129).

19. See Walker (1992).

20. For the scale of corruption in the late-communist Soviet Union, see Afanas'ev (1997) and Ledeneva (1998). For insight into everyday cynicism in the 1970s and the 1980s, see Yurchak (1997). Ries (1997) maps the ubiquity of practices of public lamentation in *perestroika*-era Russia in her ethnographic study of "Russian talk."

21. For the historical characteristics that distinguished the nascent public realm of late-communist society in Soviet Russia from the public sphere in Canada, the European Union, and the United States in the 1980s, see Garcelon (1997a).

22. Suny (1993).

23. "Translation became one of the major Soviet industries as well as the main source of sustenance for hundreds of professional writers. The 'friendship of the peoples' thesis required that all Soviet nationalities be deeply moved by the art of other Soviet nationalities" (Slezkine 1994: 447).

24. For the role of the Estonian rebellion as a model for Russian urban democratic networking, see Dunlop (1993: 9–66).

25. For the origins of the Westernizer–Slavophile dispute in the 1840s and its subsequent impact on various strands of Russian political thought, see Billington (1970: 320–328).

26. For instance, in the nineteenth century Russian provincial town of Petrovskoe, "there was not a spirit of community, but a conjunction of interests and a collusion of authority. Life was highly integrated, but not well integrated or harmonious" (Hoch 1986: 160).

27. For an overview of the power struggle between Gorbachev and more conservative partocrats that occurred during this time, see Bialer (1989: 203–215). Gorbachev finally resolved the struggle at the pinnacle of the CPSU in favor of deepening reforms at a special session of the Party's Central Committee held on Sept. 30 and 31, 1988; see *Izvestiia* (Oct. 1, 1988: 1) and (Oct. 2, 1988: 1–2).

28. Party Conferences were "mini-congresses" called to deal with pressing orga-nizational or ideological matters, and had not been called for decades; the Eighteenth Party Conference, for example, was held in February 1941 (Schapiro 1971: 646).

29. See Lentini (1991: 72) for how limited experiments with more open electoral procedures in a few select local districts in 1987 paved the way for more extensive political reforms announced at the Nineteenth Party Conference.

30. See "Ob izmeniiakh i dopolneniia Konstitutsii SSSR" (*Pravda*, Dec. 3, 1988: 1–2) and "O vyborakh narodnykh deputatov SSSR" (*Pravda*, Dec. 4, 1988: 1–3) for the text of these decrees.

31. *Current Digest of the Soviet Press*, No. 48 (1988: 5).

32. Thus the final communiqué of the Conference emphasized the need to conduct by the end of 1988 "open elections within Party organizations in accordance with the decisions of the Conference on the reform of the political system and the democratiza-tion of Party life . . . [To] carry-out . . . a reorganization of the Party apparat, introducing essential changes in its structure in accordance with [the Conference's] decisions to sep-arate the functions of the Party and the soviets" (*Izvestiia*, July 2, 1988: 1–2).

33. Khrushchev's fall proved critical, as it solidified the formation of the *nomen-klatura* as a benefice holding stratum by establishing *de facto* lifetime tenure through Brezhnev's "stability of cadres" policy; see Jowitt (1992: 141–144).

34. The degree of general skepticism regarding Gorbachev's "new elections" became evident to pro-reform candidate Anatolii Sobchak the evening he secured his nomination, when a taxi driver asked him: "Well, tell me why you need to do this? After all, the whole thing's a game, it's all lies, both Gorbachev and the elections. You'll be badly hurt, and all the same you won't manage to knock this system down" (Sobchak, 1991: 18–19).

35. For an overview of the new, hybrid CPD-USSR, see Chiesa (1993: 14–26). The Nineteenth Party Conference also envisioned the creation of similar, two-tiered legislative structures in the fifteen Soviet Republics, with elections to the Russian Republic's Congresses of Peoples Deputies—as well as to regional and local soviets—tentatively scheduled for the fall of 1989.

36. Besides the electoral law published in *Pravda* on Dec. 3 and 4 (see note 30), the following served as sources for this paragraph: Chiesa (1993), Duncan (1992), Lentini (1991), Levanskii and Bazhanova (1990), and Ol'sevich (1990).

37. M. Steven Fish's comparative analysis of regional sections of the democratic movement and of the miners' strikes of 1989 and 1991 is instructive in this regard (Fish 1995: 137–199).

38. See the extended account in Matlock (1995: 113–119) as well as in Bialer (1989). Yeltsin's account was published in Yeltsin (1990a); it can be viewed in English in Yeltsin (1990b: 177–199). For Yeltsin's speech and Gorbachev's response at the October 1987 plenum, see Gorshkov and Zhuravlev (1992: 21–39). Yeltsin's speech was not published in the official Soviet press for another eighteen months, a fact that backfired: "Since the Kremlin refused the demands that Yeltsin's speech be published, different versions of the speech began to circulate in print around the world—from Moscow *samizdat* [self-published materials] to émigré papers, from *Le Monde* and *Die Ziet* to London's *Observer* and *U.S. News and World Report*" (Solovyev and Klepikova 1992: 70).

39. For the text of Yeltsin's address to the Nineteenth Party Conference, see Gorshkov and Zhuravlev (1992: 75–89). The publication of Yeltsin's speech in *Pravda*

("Vystuplenie tovarishcha El'tsina B. N.," July 2, 1988: 10) and *Izvestiia* ("Rech' to-varishcha El'tsina B. N.," July 9, 1988: 9) signaled more openness in the degree of *glasnost'*.

40. By 1988, only seven regional Party leaders in office in 1982 remained at their posts (Helf 1994: 103). Helf's study presents a definitive account of Gorbachev's sweeping, bloodless purge.

41. "The same democratic reforms of 1987 and 1988 which threatened the system also radically altered the context of both Russian regional leaders and republican leaders, radically shifting their attention away from central politics and toward survival in their respective local political environments" (Helf 1994: 136).

42. The worker, Anatolii Marchenko (1991), wrote a searing account of his experiences as a dissenter, representing just how much more repression dissidents faced if they emerged in the working class proper.

43. For a historical overview of the dissident movement in Russia, see Alexeyeva (1985: 267–397).

44. See Bonnell (1990).

45. "A voluntary association generally has three basic features. It is an organized group 1) that is formed in order to further some common interest of its members; 2) in which membership is voluntary in the sense that it is neither mandatory nor acquired through birth; 3) that exists independently of the state" (Bonnell 1990: 63). See Articles 24 and 50 of the Constitution of the USSR, which grants the right to form such associations to Soviet citizens (*Konstitutsiia*, published in Izvestiia Sovetov narodnykh deputatov SSSP 1988: 12, 20).

46. Izvestiia Sovetov narodnykh deputatov SSSP (1988: 7).

47. Babkina (1991: 27). Beyond the initial symbolic importance of its passage, this law played no significant role in subsequent developments.

48. Lampert (1987: 10).

49. Gorbachev's address to the Plenum emphasized the need for "the maximal democratization of the socialist system ... Only through the consistent development of democratic forms inherent in socialism is the widening of self-management possible ... New social organizations are being created ... which together indicate the growing participation of workers in the social affairs and management of the country" (*Izvestiia*, Jan. 28, 1987: 1–5).

50. Alexeyeva (1990: 136).

51. Sundiev (1989: 61).

52. "The main distinctive feature of the period between the second half of 1987 and the first half of 1988 was that the clubs and groups that managed to get the support of this or that official organization and were allowed access to meeting premises were a success" (Igrunov 1991: 18).

53. Igrunov (1991: 15).

54. A good example of how such problems plagued attempts to organize broader, regional political clubs and voluntary associations is the history of the All-Union Social-Political Club (*Vsesoiuznyi sotsial'no-politicheskii klub*) and the Russian Popular Front (*Rossiiskii narodnyi front*)—two still-born attempts to organize cross-regional networks of informal political groupings (Berezovskii and Krotov 1990: 239–241, 319–322). For a discussion of the concentration of conservative blocs of apparatchiks in particular regions, and especially in rural and agricultural areas, see Helf (1994).

55. Interview with Il'ia Zaslavskii.

56. Alexeyeva (1988).

57. Hosking (1992b: 8).

58. Interview with Vladimir Bokser.

59. Interview with Sergei Stikhiinskii.

60. The enmeshing of rightist informals in the 1980s and the repressive apparat is discussed in Brudny (1989) and Vujacic (1995).

61. Aves (1992).

62. Aves (1992: 58) and Vujacic (1995).

63. For extended empirical treatments of the *neformaly* of 1986–1988, see Alexeyeva (1988, 1990), Berezovskii et al. (1992a, 1992b), Berezovskii and Krotov (1990), Hosking (1990: 50–75; 1992b), Iushenkov (1990), Pribylovskii (1991), and Zhudkova et al. (1988). Zhudkova et al. (p. 95) claim that by 1988, 7–8 percent of the urban population over fourteen years of age had participated at some point in an independent grassroots group.

64. See Hosking (1992b: 16–17). For an overview of the cooperative movement in the late 1980s, see Slider (1993).

65. McFaul and Markov (1993: 1–9).

66. Interview with Alexander Pobrabinek; see also Hopkins (1983).

67. Interview with Vera Kriger.

68. For the organizing of human rights defense groups in 1987–1988 modeled on earlier dissident groups, such as Press Club Glasnost and the Moscow Human Rights Society, see Alexeyeva (1990: 16–27).

69. Alexeyeva (1990: 25–26) and Berezovskii and Krotov (1990: 242–243).

70. Statement issued at the founding of the Union of Constitutional Democrats, held at Civic Dignity's initiative in the fall of 1989; see Koval' (1991: 154).

71. Interview with Vladimir Lysenko.

72. Interviews with Memorial Initiative Group founders Viacheslav Igrunov, Vladimir Lysenko, and Lev Ponomarev.

73. A draft of Memorial's charter published in *Ogonek* in early 1989 stated the association was to "preserve and immortalize the memory of the victims of Stalinism," "reestablish the historical truth about the illegalities of Stalinism," and "study its causes and consequences"; see *Ogonek* (No. 4, 1989: 29).

74. See Hewett and Winston (1991: 507).

75. See Afanas'ev (1988: 277–507).

76. The moralist stance of Memorial and other groups dedicated to the defense of human rights displayed strong affinities with Czechoslovakia's Vaclav Havel and Charter 77 (Havel 1988).

77. Interview with Lev Ponomarev, later a central figure in the *DemRossiia* Coordinating Council.

78. Pribylovskii (1991: 38).

79. Severiukhin (1988).

80. Gleb Pavlovskii and Maxim Meer in *Moskovskie novosti* (Feb. 18, 1990: 8–9).

81. For the social character of these two important clubs, see Berezovskii and Krotov (1990: 263–264, 294–295) and Igrunov (1991).

82. The "functional equivalent to citizenship in Leninist regimes is enfranchisement through the party ... Though, in formal regard, revisionist movements are

equivalent to the citizenship movements in the West, they are 'movements' only in [the] metaphorical sense. Revisionism originates in the political apparatus and the intellectual circles that revolve around it. Very much the lamento about the 'revolution betrayed' . . . revisionism is limited to the intellectual elites" (Joppke 1993b: 15).

83. Interview with Alexander Podrabinek; see alsoKagarlitsky (1990: 195–209).

84. For a history of the "young socialists," as they came to be called, see Alexeyeva (1990: 56–57).

85. Interview with Pavel Kudiukin.

86. Among such figures were Victor and Anna Zolotarev of the Constitutional-Democrats, Victor Aksiuchets of the Russian Christian-Democratic Movement, and Pavel Kudiukin and Oleg Rumiantsev of the Social-Democratic Party (Beliaeva et al. 1991: 113).

87. Berezovskii et al. (1991: 187).

88. See Berezovskii and Krotov (1990: 246) and Hosking (1990: 67).

89. See Flaherty (1990: 91). Ten issues of *Otkrytaia zona* were produced between October 1987 and August 1989 (Berezovskii and Krotov 1990: 248).

90. Hosking (1990: 66).

91. Berezovskii and Krotov (1990: 263–264).

92. Hosking (1992b: 14).

93. Interview with Viacheslav Igrunov.

94. See Berezovskii and Krotov (1990: 246–248).

95. Berezovskii and Krotov (1990: 243).

96. The authorities took a particular dislike to Novodvorskaia's activities, as documented in *Ekspress-Khronika* (Jan. 3, 1988: 4–5).

97. Koval' (1991: 270).

98. Shul'gin (1990: 192).

99. Interview with Yuri Veshninskii.

100. Beliaeva et al. (1991: 114).

101. For an account of the surge of street protest in Moscow in the summer of 1988, see Kagarlitsky (1990: 1–29). Gorbachev himself opened the Nineteenth Party Conference by positively noting the role of "rallies and gatherings" in the reform drive; see Kommunisticheskaia partiia Sovestskogo soiuza (1988: 75).

102. The Moscow Tribune was described as an "elite" group in an interview with Galina Starovoitova.

103. Information concerning the background of a significant segment of the future leadership of *DemRossiia* in these four Moscow-based associations was gleaned from two sources: (1) interviews with Democratic Russia leaders such as Yuri Afanas'ev, Vladimir Bokser, Leonid Bogdanov, Vera Kriger, Vladimir Lysenko, Lev Ponomarev, etc. and (2) public announcements of membership in *DemRossiia's* elected bodies and its affiliate organizations as published in movement documents and other Russian sources.

104. On the mobilization of popular fronts in the Baltics in mid-1988, see Aves (1992: 32–34).

105. A list of these grouplets can be found in Sundiev (1990: 33). Flaherty (1990) provides a thorough summary of the emerging ideology of the "new Russian left" in the period of the Moscow Popular Front.

106. See the *New York Times* (June 26, 1988: 9).

107. Interviews with Vladimir Bokser and Mikhail Schneider.

108. For decree details, see "O prakticheskoi rabote no realizatsii reshenii XIX vsesoiuznoi partiinoi konferentsii," *Izvestiia* (July 30, 1988: 1–3).

109. Sundiev (1990: 33).

110. Duncan (1992: 69–70).

111. In 1989 and 1990, the number of informal groups continued to grow, though some of this growth represented the winking in and out of existence of a multiplicity of transient "tiny circles" (*karlikovye kruzhki*); see Pavlovskii and Meer (*Moskovskie novosti*, Feb. 18, 1990: 8–9).

112. Fadeev (1992: 119).

113. Aves (1992: 51).

114. Sources for this paragraph (as well as the two paragraphs following it) include Berezovskii et al. (1991: 95), Morrison (1991: 89), the *ofitsiosnyi* bulletin *Panorama* (No. 2, 1989: 15), Pribylovskii (1991: 43), and Yeltsin (1990b: 57–60).

115. Sources include the *ofitsioznye* bulletins *Ekspress-Khronika* (March 26, 1989: 1) and *Panorama* (No. 1, 1989: 9, 11), Ol'sevich (1990: 218), and interviews with Vladimir Bokser and Mikhail Schneider.

116. Sources for this, and other material in this and the following paragraph, include Berezovskii et al. (1991: 19, 93), *Moskovskie novosti* (Feb. 12, 1989: 14), and (Feb. 19, 1989: 9), and the *samizdat* bulletin *Grazhdanskoe obshchestvo* (No. 18, Feb. 1989: 1–2).

117. Sakharov quoted in *Moskovskie novosti* (Feb. 19 1989: 9).

118. Interview with Galina Starovoitova.

119. Sources include *Moskovskie novosti* (Feb. 12, 1989: 2) and interviews with Vladimir Lysenko and Galina Starovoitova.

120. Interviews with Viacheslav Igrunov, then active in Memorial, the Popular Front movement, and the Moscow Information Exchange; and Galina Starovoitova.

121. Roxburgh (1991: 128).

122. See *Ekspress-Khronika* (May 28, 1989: 1), (June 4, 1989: 1), and (June 18, 1989: 1), as well as *Panorama* (No. 5, 1989: 2).

123. See Byzov et al. (1991) for a summary of survey data. For an overview of democratization within professional associations after 1985, see Slider (1991: 145–164).

124. For an overview of the extent and scale of radical-reformist networking within officially organized and sanctioned professional associations between 1986 and 1989, see Slider (1991).

125. For an account of the Tbilisi massacre, see "Sobytie v Gruzii," *Ekspress-Khronika* (April 16, 1989: 1–2).

126. Roxburgh (1991: 136).

127. See the article by Leonid Baktin criticizing the "extremely rude" (*grubii*) manner in which Gorbachev treated Sakharov (*Moskovskie novosti*, June 11, 1989: 9).

128. Koval' (1991: 438).

129. See *RFE/RL* (June 9, 1989: 14). For an overview of the roots and depth of Yeltsin's popularity at this time, see Vitalii Tret'iakov's "The Boris Yeltsin Phenomenon" in *Moskovskie novosti* (April 16, 1989: 10).

130. Pribylovskii (1991: 37).

131. Several of these meetings were held at the *neformaly* research center, the Moscow Information Exchange (interview with Viacheslav Igrunov).

132. Two hundred sixty-eight deputies declared themselves members of the Inter-regional Group's first general conference (*obshchaia konferentsiia*) on July 29–30. The data on wavering deputies who sometimes worked with and sometimes against the group is cited in Pribylovskii (1991: 37).

133. Interview with Yuri Afanas'ev.

134. Arkadii Murashev quoted in Morrison (1991: 109). Murashev, a leading figure of the emerging pro-democracy wing of the CPSU, replaced Sakharov as a cochair of the Inter-regional Group following the latter's death in December 1989 (Pribylovskii 1991: 37–38).

135. Remnick (1994: 283).

136. Vujacic (1995).

137. For a game-theoretic explanation of the initial turn to economic reform that conceptualizes demonstration effects in terms of relative advantages, see Nee and Lian (1994).

138. Seniavskii et al. (1984: 182–195).

139. See Kochetov (1988: 9–10) and Sevast'ianov (1989: 171–172).

140. See Lane (1992: 162–176) and Levin (1979: 87–111).

141. Kerblay (1983: 223–225).

142. Pribylovskii (1991: 16).

143. The survey was conducted primarily at two meetings of *DemRossiia*'s Moscow section held on the evenings of May 20 and June 17, 1992. Only questionnaires of respondents who indicated participation in *DemRossiia* prior to August 1991 were used in coding the survey. *DemRossiia*'s leadership consented to the survey and helped facilitate its administration. Approximately 170 persons attended the first meeting and 125 the second (at the second meeting, all potential respondents were asked to fill-out a questionnaire only if they had not done so previously). One hundred twenty-seven usable questionnaires were collected at the first meeting and fourty-one at the second. Eleven questionnaires were also collected from members of the Matveevskoe district-level (*raionyi*) section of *DemRossiia* Moscow, for a total respondent base of 178.

144. See Colton (1990: 285–344) and Hahn (1991).

145. Lane (1992: 164–65).

146. Source of data on CPSU membership are taken from Gorbachev et al. (1990). Survey results of CPSU members in attendance at *DemRossiia*'s First Congress taken from Berezovskii et al. (1991: 228–229) and Koval' (1991: 305).

147. For the "intra-Party clubs" and the origins of the Democratic Platform, see Gladysh (1990) and Vite (1989). Other sources for the above include Beliaeva et al. (1991), Koval' (1991: 99–111), Lipitskii and Vite (1990), Pribylovskii (1991: 67–68), Sekretariat XXVIII s"eszda KPSS (1990), the *ofitsioznyi* news bulletin *Panorama* (No. 12, Oct. 1990: 6), and an interview with Democratic Platform member Vladimir Lysenko.

148. Vujacic (1995: 521–543).

149. Chiesa (1993: 206).

150. Interview with Marta Nadezhnova, a pseudonym for an interviewee who wished to remain anonymous.

151. Millar and Clayton (1987: 56).

152. Above all, relative deprivation theory offers "no explanation of how individual psychological discontent is transformed into organized collective action" (McAdam 1982: 15).

153. For overviews of the magnitude of Soviet economic stagnation in the 1970s and 1980s, see Desai (1987) and Winiecki (1986).

154. See Breslauer (1978).

Chapter Two

1. See Tarrow (1998). For a brief summary of revolutions relevant to the present study, see Goldstone (1994: 315–318).

2. Interview with Vladimir Bokser.

3. Interview with Lev Ponomarev.

4. Starovoitova met Sakharov in the *Moscow Tribune* (interview with Galina Starovoitova).

5. Interview with Viacheslav Igrunov.

6. Interview with Il'ia Zaslavskii.

7. See Pribylovskii (1991: 42–45) and Berezovskii et al. (1991: 95).

8. Berezovskii et al. (1991: 95).

9. "Legitimate imposture succeeds only because the usurper is not a cynical calculator who consciously deceives the people, but someone who in all good faith *takes himself to be* something that he is not" (Bourdieu 1991: 214).

10. Interview with Marta Nadezhnova.

11. *Samizdat* leaflet of the *Matveevskii klub izbiratelei* dated Aug. 3, 1989.

12. Interview with Boris Rakovskii.

13. For the origins of the Russian word *iacheiko* (cell) in the Bolshevik movement, see Selznick (1960: 208).

14. Interview with Vladimir Kutukov.

15. Interview with Aleksei Kashirin.

16. Interview with club member Leonid Sholpo. Information on the neighborhood character of *Narodovlastie* was obtained from interviews with club activists Mikhail Gokhman, Aleksei Kashirin, and Dmitrii Kharitonivich.

17. Interview with Dmitrii Kharitonivich.

18. For the history of some of the groupings that came to naught in such attempts, see Berezovskii and Krotov (1990: 239–241) and Duncan (1992: 78–79).

19. Interview with Leonid Bogdanov.

20. Interview with Yakov Gorbadei, an organizer of the Zelenograd-Tyshino voter club affiliated with the larger Moscow Association, which became a district organization of *DemRossiia*-Moscow.

21. Interview with Sergei Stikhiinskii.

22. For a history of the *Brateevo* association, which mobilized several thousand residents, nominated local candidates, supported Yeltsin in the spring of 1989, and eventually affiliated with *DemRossiia* in 1990, see Berezovskii et al. (1991: 186).

23. See "72 goda strogomu rezhimu," *Ekspress-Khronika* (Nov. 12, 1989: 1–2).

24. Several members of the Moscow Party Club, such as Igor Chubais, were heavily involved in organizing the demonstrations at Luzhniki stadium immediately before and during the First CPD-USSR (Il'ina 1991).

25. Interview with Alexander Podrabinek.
26. McFaul and Markov (1993: 24–25).
27. Interview with Jan Rachinskii.
28. Interview with Vladimir Lysenko.
29. The article "Po stranitsam 'Ekspress-Xroniki' 89" (*Russkaia mysl'*, Sept. 29, 1989: 1–2) contains general information on the Inter-regional Group's attempt to support opposition candidates. This issue also contains Yuri Afanas'ev's speech, "Oformlenie legalnoi oppozitsii" (p. 4), which notes how the Soviet government blocked the Group's attempt to establish a fund for such candidates.
30. See Berezovskii et al. (1991: 95) and "Deviat' dnei iz zhizni Borisa El'tsina," *Positsiia* (No. 1, 1990: 1–2).
31. By the second-half of 1989, higher quality, professional-looking papers and bulletins began displacing poor quality, mimeographed sheets of *samizdat* typical of the dissident movement and the *neformalitet*. Printed professionally in large runs on a semiofficial basis (*ofitsiozno*), such higher quality papers emerged from discrete arrangements between print shop workers, on the one side, and political entrepreneurs and activists on the other. For an overview of the transformation of opposition *samizdat* and the appearance of the semiofficial, i.e., unregistered but tolerated, press, see Tolz, *RFE/RL* (Dec. 14, 1989: 12–14).
32. Besides interviews, other sources of information for the above three paragraphs include Berezovskii et al. (1991: 62, 92–93) and Pribylovskii (1991: 15).
33. "Zabastovka v Vorkute," *Ekspress-Khronika* (Nov. 5, 1989: 1).
34. "Ubiistvo Aleksandra Sotnikova," *Ekspress-Khronika* (Oct. 22, 1989: 1).
35. Time was short, as the new election law decreed by the outgoing RSFSR Supreme Soviet on Oct. 27, 1989 set a deadline of January 2 for filing nomination notices (Colton 1990: 286).
36. Interview with Victor Sheinis.
37. Berezovskii et al. (1991: 93).
38. See Hahn (1991) and Pribylovskii (1991: 15).
39. For some of the Soviet leader's pronouncements at the Congress, see *Izvestiia* (Dec. 13, 1989: 1–5) and Remnick (1994: 283–284). *Izvestiia* continued to publish Gorbachev's Congress statements through December 26.
40. For Sakharov's draft constitution, see Iushenkov (1990: 226–239).
41. From "Sozdan Izbiratelnyi Blok Demokraticheskaia Rossia," *Ogonek* (No. 6, Feb. 3–10, 1990: 17–18).
42. *Moskovskie novosti* (Aug. 6, 1989: 10).
43. *Moskovskie novosti* (Feb. 11, 1990: 8–9).
44. For a summary of actions held on February 25, see *Ekspress-Khronika* (Feb. 27, 1990: 1–2).
45. Interview with Leonid Sholpo.
46. On the eve of the Second Congress of the CPD–USSR, Gorbachev had repeated his long-stated and strong opposition to altering Article 6 in any way (*Pravda*, Dec. 19, 1989: 1). For a detailed account of Gorbachev's sudden abandonment of the cardinal organizing principle of the party-state, see Roxburgh (1991: 155–175).
47. Sources for this and the following two paragraphs include an interview with Andrei Degtiarev; an article on the RSFSR Law on Elections passed by the outgoing RSFSR Supreme Soviet, "On Changes and Additions to the USSR Constitution on the

Question of the Electoral System" in *Izvestiia* (Dec. 23, 1989: 1); Dawn Mann, "The USSR Constitution: The Electoral System" (*RFE/RL Report on the USSR*, Feb. 2, 1990: 10–13); and Duncan (1992).

48. Colton (1990: 286).

49. See *Moskovskie novosti* (March 25, 1990: 4).

50. Interview with Mikhail Shneider.

51. The stratification of audiences adapts Logan (1978).

52. See *Panorama* (No. 10, 1990: 1).

53. See *Positsiia* (No. 3 1990).

54. Interview with Vera Kriger.

55. Interviews with Vladimir Bokser, Vera Kriger, and Mikhail Schneider.

56. Interview with Mikhail Gokhman, an activist from the *Narodovlastie* voter club in the *Cheremushkinskii* district.

57. See Commission on Security and Cooperation in Europe (1990: 100).

58. *Moskovskie novosti* (April 15, 1990: 4).

59. *Pravda* (April 12, 1990: 1–2).

60. See the articles by Yeltsin supporters Stankevich, "Esli obiasnit spokoino," and Velikhov, "Shans viiti iz krizisa," both in *Literaturnaia gazeta* (March 14, 1990: 1); as well as the piece supporting concentration of power in the CPD by Deputy Lopatin, "Nuzhna politicheskaia volia," also in *Literaturnaia gazeta* (March 21, 1990: 1).

61. See Vujacic (1995).

62. For a history of *DemRossiia* voter blocs outside Moscow, see Berezovskii et al. (1992a: 34), Fish (1995: 147–189), and Pribylovskii (1991: 15–18).

63. See, for example, *Izvestiia's* headline "The Main Question—the Institution of the Presidency" (*Izvestiia*, March 13, 1990: 1–2).

64. For an overview of the constitutional changes implemented at the Third CPD-USSR, see White et al. (1993: 67–73).

65. *Izvestiia* (March 16, 1990: 1–2).

66. *Moskovskie novosti* (May 27, 1990: 9).

67. *Pravda* (Oct. 18, 1989: 2).

68. *Izvestiia* (March 17, 1990: 3, 10).

69. See Vujacic (1994).

70. For an analysis that highlights the disintegration of all-Union institutions along federal and ethnic lines during the Soviet collapse and its aftermath, see Walker (2003).

71. See *Moskovskie novosti* (April 22, 1990: 2, 4). The difficulty of pinning down the exact size of the *DemRossiia* bloc in the RSFSR Congress at any given time stems from both the lack of any constraining ties between nominal *DemRossiia* deputies-elect and the voter clubs that helped nominate and elect them. Moreover, the lack of anything resembling party discipline among Congress deputies led to constantly shifting alliances among individual deputies in 1990–1991. In early June, estimates of the size of the democratically oriented bloc in the RSFSR Congress varied between 25 and 27 percent of the CPD-RSFSR's 1,068 deputies (*Moskovskie novosti*, June 3, 1990: 2).

72. Interviews with Lev Ponomarev and Galina Starovoitova.

73. *Moskovskie novosti* (April 22, 1990: 4).

74. Eighty-six percent of the deputies elected to the First RSFSR Congress remained nominal CPSU members (*Pravda*, May 17, 1990: 1).

75. For the Russian Communist Party, its linkages with rightist groups, and the origins of what Zhiuganov would come to call "National Bolshevism," see Vujacic (1995).

76. See *Pravda* (May 19, 1990: 1–2).

77. *Izvestiia* (May 29, 1990: 2).

78. See *Sovetskaia Rossiia* (June 14, 1990: 1) for the official declaration of independence. Voting details and parliamentary commentary can be found on pp. 2–5 of the same issue of this paper.

79. See *Panorama* (No. 7, July 1990: 1–2) and *Positsiia* (No. 5, 1990: 2) for details on the composition of the RSFSR Supreme Soviet.

80. See, for instance, *The Economist* (Oct. 20, 1990: 3–6).

81. *Moskovskie novosti* (June 3, 1990: 5).

82. For the confusion over jurisdictions in the last fourteen months of the Soviet Union, see Levicheva (1991). Lenin introduced the concept of dual power into Russian political discourse in April 1917 (Lenin 1975).

83. *Sovetskaia Rossiia* (June 16, 1990: 1).

84. On Silaev's background and Sverdlovsk connection to Yeltsin, see *Izvestiia* (June 20, 1990: 4) and *Moskovskie novosti* (June 24, 1990: 16).

85. Interview with Galina Starovoitova.

86. Solovyov and Klepikova (1992: 92).

87. *Sovetskaia Rossiia* (July 12, 1990: 4).

88. Published eventually as Shatalin et al. (1990).

89. *Izvestiia* (July 7, 1990: 2).

90. The RSFSR Congress of Peoples Deputies adopted the Decree on Power on June 20 (*Izvestiia*, June 21, 1990: 1).

91. See "Na forume kommunisty Rossii," *Pravda* (June 21, 1990: 1–2).

92. See *Demokraticheskaia Rossiia* (No. 2, Aug. 1990: 1) and *Moskovskie novosti* (June 24, 1990: 4).

93. Sekretariat XXVIII s"eszda KPSS (1990: 129–132).

94. See *Izvestiia* (July 4, 1990: 3) for accounts of both demonstrations.

95. *Izvestiia* (July 13, 1990: 1).

96. *Moskovskie novosti* (July 22, 1990: 6).

97. See *Pravda* (July 6, 1990: 2–5 and July 8, 1990: 2–6) for examples of rightist speeches.

98. See *Izvestiia* (July 11, 1990: 1–2).

99. See the statement at the *DemPlatforma* conference to announce the mass resignation of the Platform from the CPSU ("Sobytie nedeli: Vykhod iz KPSS" *Ekspress-Khronika*, July 24, 1990: 4).

100. *Pravda* (Aug. 14, 1990).

101. For the official announcement of the new Union-wide 500-Day Plan and the intention to draft a new Union treaty, see *Izvestiia* (Aug. 2, 1990: 1).

102. *Literaturnaia gazeta* (Aug. 15, 1990: 9).

103. See Shatalin et al. (1990).

104. Popov emerged out of more narrow academic circles with his description of the Soviet order as an "administrative-command system" in 1987 (Reddaway and Glinski 2001: 105)—terminology that would subsequently become commonplace among democratic reformers and activists. An early sign of this growing influence was the

article "Izvlekaia uroki" (*Moskovskie novosti*, Nov. 22, 1987: 3) The degree to which Popov subsequently became a polarizing figure in democratic circles is marked by divergent Western descriptions of him, ranging from a "radical opposition leader" (Remnick 1994: 282) to an "authoritarian privatizer" (Reddaway and Glinski 2001: 62).

105. *Moskovskie novosti* (April 29, 1990: 1, 4).

106. *Moskovskie novosti* (April 8, 1990: 2 and April 15, 1990: 4).

107. See the June 12, 1990, minutes of the *Mossovet* in *Vedomosti Mossoveta* (No. 1, 1991: 13–14).

108. See Timothy Frye, "The Moscow City Soviet Stakes Its Claim," *RFE/RL Report on the USSR* (Aug. 3, 1990: 16–19).

109. "Napadenie militsii," *Ekspress-Khronika* (June 26, 1990: 1).

110. *Moskovskie novosti* (May 6, 1990: 4).

111. See *Moskovskie novosti* (May 13, 1990: 6) and "Pervomaiskie demonstratsii," *Ekspress-Khronika* (May 8, 1990: 2).

112. For the rationale behind this and other measures detailed in the following paragraph, see Popov's speech "Obrashchenie predsedatelia Mossoveta," Moskovskii gorodskoi sovet (1990: 6–8).

113. *Moskovskie novosti* (June 10, 1990: 10).

114. Stankevich quoted in "Sovety i vlast'," *Pravda* (June 29, 1990: 5). Additional sources for the above two paragraphs include Moskovskii gorodskoi sovet (1990); *Izvestiia* (July 21, 1990: 1); issues of *Moskovskie novosti* from March 25, April 8, April 15, May 6, June 8, and July 10, 1990; and *Vedomosti Mossoveta* (No. 1, 1991: 14–17).

115. For growing tensions between the *Mossovet* leadership and some radical deputies over such issues, see "Sobytie nedeli," *Ekspress-Khronika* (Aug. 14. 1990: 6).

116. See, for instance, coverage of the November 21 picket by a hundred artists against the *Mossovet* leadership's plan to sell their apartments to business concerns ("Moskovskaia nedelia," *Ekspress-Khronika*, Nov. 27. 1990: 2).

117. Popov (1990: 7).

118. Colton (1990: 343).

119. See *Kommersant*" (Sept. 3–10, 1990: 10) and *Panorama* (No. 11, Sept. 1990: 3).

120. *Demokraticheskaia Rossiia* (No. 2, Aug. 1990: 10–11).

121. Remnick (1994: 308).

122. *DemRossiia* candidates for the *raisovety* were poorly organized and nominated (interview with Vladimir Bokser); Zaslavskii's campaign was exceptional in this sense.

123. *Demokraticheskaia Rossiia* (No. 4, Oct. 1990: 1–3).

124. See Zaslavskii, "Archipelag demokratii" in *Ogonek* (No. 26, June 23–30, 1990: 15).

125. From the official newspaper of the October soviet, *Piatnitsa* (No. 1, 1990: 2). Although this issue was undated beyond year of publication, several articles suggest December, 1990, as month of publication.

126. See details in *Kommersant*" (Feb. 11–18, 1991: 12) and (Feb. 18–25, 1991: 12).

127. *Kuranty* (Feb. 20, 1991: 2).

128. The strategy of de-sovietization was developed at length by Popov (1990, 1991).

129. See Travkin's article "Will the Bolsheviks Hand Power to the Soviets?" in *Demokraticheskaia Rossiia* (No. 2, Aug. 1990: 1–2).

Chapter Three

1. Pribylovskii (1991: 15–16).
2. Interview with Vladimir Kutukov.
3. Interview with Leonid Bogdanov.
4. Kasparov was one of the minority of original *Orgkomitet* members who was not a Peoples Deputy (Berezovskii et al. 1991: 91).
5. For a summary of Travkin's previous career, see Beliaeva et al. (1991: 159).
6. The "anti-Travkin" Free Democratic Party of Russia first appeared at a "northwest regional founding conference" held in Leningrad on July 8–9, 1990 (*Kommersant*, July 9–16, 1990: 11).
7. *Demokraticheskaia Rossiia* (July 1, 1990: 5).
8. See *Voprosy ekonomiki* (No. 8, 1990: 152–154).
9. See Duncan (1992: 100) for Sal'e's charge. The spring 1990 split between Travkin and most of the other prominent figures dominating Moscow democratic networks eerily echoed the split between Bolsheviks and Mensheviks over Lenin's centralized conception of leadership at the July 1903 Second Congress of Russia's Social-Democrats; for the latter, see Schapiro (1971: 48–54).
10. Interview with Sergei Stikhiinskii.
11. Additional sources for the above paragraphs include the first issue of the newspaper, *Demokraticheskaia gazeta* (July 1, 1990); and interviews with Leonid Bogdanov, Vera Kriger, Lev Ponomarev, and Il'ia Roitman.
12. *Golos izbiratelia* (No. 12, 1990: 1).
13. "Protocol No. 1 of the *DemRossiia dvizhenie* Organizing Committee" (*samizdat* mimeograph dated July 14, 1990).
14. *Panorama* (No. 13, Dec. 1990: 3) and interview with Mikhail Shneider.
15. Mimeographed *samizdat* sheet entitled "Democratic Russia's Statement of Intention," dated July 11, 1990.
16. *Panorama* (No. 7, July 1990: 4).
17. Several grassroots activists described such individuals as inveterate "splitters" (*raskol'niki*). Interviews with Yakov Gorbadei and Vladimir Ostroglas.
18. For the SPD, see Kudiukin (1990). For the origins and history of the CPSU's *DemPlatforma*, see Gladysh (1990), Koval' (1991: 99–111), and Lipitskii and Vite (1990).
19. *Ekspress-Khronika* (July 24, 1990: 2).
20. *Ekspress-Khronika* (Aug. 7, 1990: 2).
21. *Demokraticheskaia Rossiia* (No. 3, Sept. 1990: 1).
22. See *Panorama* (No. 12, Oct. 1990: 6).
23. See *Demokraticheskaia Rossiia* (No. 3, Sept. 1990: 16).
24. Interview with Vladimir Lysenko.
25. *Ekspress-Khronika* (Oct. 16, 1990: 3).
26. Berezovskii et al. (1991: 228).
27. The Democratic Russia Fund was in fact formed prior to *DemRossiia*'s Founding Conference by USSR, RSFSR, and *Mossovet* deputies. Its Managing Board included key Moscow Association of Voters' figures Lev Ponomarev and Leonid Bogdanov (Pribylovskii 1991: 17).
28. Interview with Mikhail Gokhman.
29. Source *samizdat* mimeograph entitled "Kommiunike No. 2 Orgkomiteta dvizheniia 'Demokraticheskaia Rossiia'," dated Oct. 1, 1990.

30. Sources for attendance at the Founding Congress include "Itogi uchreditel'nogo s"ezda dvizheniia 'Demokraticheskaia Rossiia'," *Demokraticheskaia Rossiia* (No. 5, Nov. 1990: 1); "Konsolidatsiia demokraticheskikh sil," *Demokraticheskaia Rossiia* (No. 1[6], Jan. 1991: 1); and *samizdat* documents of *DemRossiia dvizhenie* located in the archives of the Moscow Information Exchange and the Democratic Russia Sociological Service.

31. Survey results reported in Berezovskii et al. (1991: 228–229) and Koval' (1991: 305).

32. Survey figures from *DemRossiia*'s Second Congress appeared in a mimeographed *samizdat* bulletin released by the Democratic Russia Fund's Sociological Service (*DR-Sotsio*) dated Nov. 1991.

33. Interviews with Leonid Bogdanov, Vladimir Bokser, and Lev Ponomarev.

34. *Samizdat* mimeograph of "Ustav DemRossiia dvizhenie" [Charter of the *DemRossiia* movement], dated as accepted by the Founding Congress on Oct. 21, 1990.

35. See *Panorama* (No. 13, Dec. 1990: 1, 13) and Pribylovskii (1991: 14).

36. *Samizdat* leaflet entitled "Deklaratsiia dvizheniia 'Demokraticheskaia Rossiia'," dated Oct. 22, 1990.

37. See "Dokument N 16: Resoliutsiia Uchreditel'nogo s"ezda Dvizheniia 'Demokraticheskaia Rossiia'," in Berezovskii et al. (1992a: 35–36).

38. Interview with Lev Ponomarev.

39. *Demokraticheskaia Rossiia* (No.1[6], Jan. 1991: 1, 3).

40. Organizational details from documents of *DemRossiia dvizhenie* located in the archives of the Moscow Information Exchange and the Democratic Russia Sociological Service; *Demokraticheskaia Rossiia* (No. 1[6], Jan. 1991: 1, 3); and Berezovskii et al. (1992a: 12; 34–44). By the end of March 1991, membership in the Coordinating Committee reached forty-eight persons, a number that remained stable for the rest of the year.

41. See *Panorama* (No. 13, Dec. 1990: 3).

42. *Nezavisimaia gazeta* (Dec. 28, 1990: 1).

43. Interview with Galina Starovoitova.

44. Interview with Yuri Afanas'ev.

45. Interview with Il'ia Zaslavskii.

46. *Panorama* (No. 10, Sept. 1990: 1).

47. On November 29, for example, a Moscow Association of Voters activist who had been severely beaten the previous day died, but the event got little attention, despite the direct appeal of the DR *orgkomitet* that Yeltsin and Popov take charge of the investigation (*Ekspress-Khronika*, Dec. 11, 1990: 2).

48. Term adapted from Logan (1978).

49. See Igor Kliamkin, "Partiia 'my'—partiia 'oni'?" in *Demokraticheskaia Rossiia* (No. 1[7], March 22, 1991: 8–9). In March 1991, this paper switched to a weekly from a monthly format. The first issue of 1991 was thus the last monthly issue (Jan.), marked "No. 1" but followed by a bracketed [6]. The paper did not issue again until March 22, also as "No. 1" but with a bracketed [7]. This change was connected with organizational disputes within the paper; see Gleb Pavlovskii, "Svoia obez'iana," *Nezavisimaia gazeta* (April 23, 1991: 8) for one view of this squabble.

50. *Sovetskaia Rossiia* (Sept. 4, 1990: 1).

51. *Pravda* (Sept. 18, 1990: 1–2).

52. See Yeltsin's speech in *Sovetskaia Rossiia* (Oct. 18, 1990: 2).

53. Quoted in Gorshkov and Zhuravlev (1992: 255).
54. *Izvestiia* (Sept. 25, 1990: 2).
55. *Pravda* (Sept. 26, 1990: 2).
56. *Ekspress-Khronika* (Oct. 16, 1990: 1–2).
57. *Izvestiia* (Oct. 18, 1990: 2).
58. *Komsomol'skaia Pravda* (Nov. 4, 1990: 2).
59. *Nevskii kur'er* (No. 17, Nov. 18, 1990: 2).
60. Popov (1990, 1991).
61. See *Izvestiia* (Nov. 7, 1990: 6) and *Komsomol'skaia Pravda* (Nov. 8, 1990: 1).
62. Quoted in *Izvestiia* (Nov. 15, 1990: 1).
63. Roxburgh (1991: 198–200).
64. See *Izvestiia* (Nov. 24, 1990: 1–2).
65. See *Sovetskaia Rossiia* (Nov. 21, 1990).
66. *Pravda* (Nov. 29, 1990: 1).
67. *Izvestiia* (Dec. 3, 1990: 3).
68. *Pravda* (Dec. 13, 1990: 1, 3).
69. *Ekspress-Khronika* (Dec. 4, 1990: 2).
70. *Ekspress-Khronika* (Dec. 11, 1990: 2).
71. Shevardnadze's speech is reproduced in Dallin and Lapidus (1991: 698–699).
72. *Pravda* (Jan. 15, 1991: 1).
73. For counterelite thinking in early January, see the long article "Demokratich-eskaia perspektiva—91," *Moskovskie novosti* (Jan. 13, 1991: 8–9).
74. *Izvestiia* (Jan. 10, 1991: 1).
75. *Izvestiia* (Jan. 12, 1991: 1).
76. See *Ekspress-Khronika* (Jan. 15, 1991: 1–2), (Jan 22, 1991: 1, 4), and (Jan. 29, 1991: 2). *Moskovskie novosti* (Jan. 20, 1991: 1) labeled the events "Bloody Sunday" [Krovavoe voskresen'e], echoing the shooting of hundreds of unarmed demonstrators by Tsarist police on Jan. 19, 1905. For the significance of the term "Bloody Sunday" in Russian politics, see Bonnell (1983: 106–110) and McDaniel (1988: 104–108). The following week, *Moskovskie novosti* (Jan. 27, 1991: 1) ran a front page panoramic photograph of a huge protest against the "Baltic events" in Moscow. The Latvian Committee of National Salvation appeared several days after its Lithuanian predecessor (see *Izvestiia*, Jan. 16, 1991: 1, 3).
77. *Izvestiia* (Jan. 15, 1991: 2).
78. *Izvestiia* (Jan. 16, 1991: 1, 3) and (Jan. 18, 1991: 2).
79. See *Nezavisimaia gazeta* (Jan. 15, 1991: 1–3).
80. Interview with Aleksei Kashirin.
81.   From the ofitsioznyi circular *Dvizheniie "Demokraticheskaia Rossiia"—informatsionnyi biulleten'* (No. 2, Jan. 1991: 1).
82. *Dvizheniie "Demokraticheskaia Rossiia"—informatsionnyi biulleten'* (No. 3, Feb. 1991: 1).
83. See *Express-Khronika* (Jan. 22, 1991: 4). *Movskovskie novosti* (Jan. 27, 1991: 1) estimated the number of demonstrators as between 700,000 and 800,000; *Nezavisimaia gazeta* (Jan. 22, 1991: 1) reported over half a million. The great disparity of figures cited in both the Soviet and Western presses make it difficult to estimate the size of the rally, though a number of interviewees cited it as the largest of the Gorbachev period.

84. *Kuranty* (Jan. 23, 1991: 1–2).

85. *Pravda* (Jan. 23, 1991: 2).

86. See *Komsomol'skaia pravda* (Jan. 23, 1991: 1).

87. For Gorbachev's decree, see *Izvestiia* (Jan. 23, 1991: 1). For typical democratic criticisms of the currency reforms, see the articles under the page headline "Reform protiv reforma" [Reform against reform], *Moskovskie novosti* (Feb. 3, 1991: 4).

88. *Kuranty* (Jan. 30, 1991: 1, 4).

89. For the price decree, see *Izvestiia* (Feb. 15, 1991: 1–2).

90. For the texts of both Yeltsin and Lukianov's statements, see *Argumenty i fakty* (No. 8, Feb. 1991: 2).

91. See the reactions of various deputies to Yeltsin's speech in *Izvestiia* (Feb. 21, 1991: 2).

92. For the *DemRossiia* rally, see *Kommersant"* (No. 8, Feb. 18–25, 1991: 12); for the RSFSR Supreme Soviet vote, see *Izvestiia* (Feb. 22, 1991: 2).

93. Interview with Mikhail Shneider.

94. *Kuranty* (Feb. 9, 1991: 4).

95. *Ekspress-Khronika* (Jan. 29, 1991: 4).

96. From "Zaiavlenie o sozdanii Demokraticheskogo Kongressa" in the *ofitsioznyi* circular *Dvizheniie "Demokraticheskaia Rossiia"—informatsionnyi biulleten'* (No. 5, Feb. 1991: 1).

97. For the initial wording of the referendum, see *Izvestiia* (Jan. 18, 1991: 3).

98. *Ekspress-Khronika* (Feb. 12, 1991: 1).

99. The question of creating a new Russian presidency had been discussed at both the First and Second Congresses of Peoples Deputies of the RSFSR in the spring and fall of 1990 (Urban 1992: 188–189).

100. See *Kuranty* (March 5, 1991: 1) and *Moskovskie novosti* (March 10, 1991: 2).

101. *Moskovskie novosti* (Feb. 10, 1991: 2).

102. *Izvestiia* (Feb. 22, 1991: 2).

103. See *Demokraticheskaia Rossiia* (No. 1[7], March 22, 1991: 8–9).

104. See *Izvestiia* (March 11, 1991: 2) and *Pravda* (March 11, 1991: 4).

105. Interview with Vladimir Bokser.

106. For a summary of referendum results, see White et al. (1993: 88–89).

107. For the course of the Kuzbass strikes prior to March 17 and a list of the miners' demands, see *Ekspress-Khronika* (March 12, 1991: 4).

108. *Kommersant"* (No. 12, March 18–25, 1991: 11).

109. For the initial threat posed by the Third CPD-RSFSR to the democratic movement, see the ridicule of the rightist Communist Ivan Polozkov's speech in *Izvestiia* (March 11, 1991: 3).

110. See *Izvestiia* (March 22, 1991: 1) and (March 26, 1991: 1).

111. Gorbachev's action suspending the *Mossovet* jurisdiction over police functions both attempted to curb dual power, and rebuffed nine *Mossovet* deputies on hunger strike to protest the USSR Interior Ministry's refusal to confirm the city soviet's appointment of pro-reform General Komissarov as Chief of Police; see *Izvestiia* (March 23, 1991: 6).

112. For the first, see *Kuranty* (March 23, 1991: 1), and for the second, see *Komsomol'skaia pravda* (March 26, 1991: 3).

113. *Izvestiia* (March 28, 1991: 1).

114. Interview with the Social-Democratic Party's Pavel Kudiukin.

115. See *Izvestiia* (March 28, 1991: 1) and (March 29, 1991: 1).

116. The work of developing the constitutional amendments governing the new presidency was turned over to the RSFSR Supreme Soviet and the Fourth CPD-RSFSR was scheduled to be convened on May 21 to ratify them; see *Izvestiia* (April 6, 1991: 1, 3).

117. *Izvestiia* (March 21, 1991: 3).

118. *Kommersant"* (March 25–April 1, 1991: 3).

119. See *Izvestiia* (April 4, 1991: 1–2).

120. See "Zaiavlenie Plenuma Soveta Predstavitelei dvizhenia DemRossiia o Kruglom Stole politicheskikh sil," dated April 13, in *Kuranty* (April 16, 1991: 2).

121. See *Ekspress-Khronika* (April 16, 1991: 3).

122. For laws relevant to the Russian presidency passed by the Supreme Soviet, see *Kommersant"* (April 22–29, 1991: 2); for regulations on filing presidential nominations, see *Kommersant"* (May 13–20, 1991: 12).

123. *Nezavisimaia gazeta* (April 25, 1991: 2).

124. *Izvestiia* (April 24, 1991: 1).

125. *Kommersant"* (April 22–29, 1991: 12).

126. Democratic Russia's leading figures put as positive a spin as possible on these developments in their accounts, summarized in a number of articles in *Demokratich-eskaia gazeta* (No. 7, May 10, 1991).

127. For miners' support of Yeltsin's candidacy, see *Nezavisimaia gazeta* (May 5, 1991: 1). For the call to suspend the strike, issued on May 8, see *Ekspress-Khronika* (May 14, 1991: 1). For the Gorbachev–Yeltsin anticrisis program, see *Izvestiia* (April 24, 1991: 1).

128. *Pravda* (April 26, 1991: 1).

129. *Nezavisimaia gazeta* (May 12, 1991: 1).

130. See *Izvestiia* (April 22, 1991: 1–2), which summarizes the Soiuz bloc's moves without naming Alksnis, and *Moskovskie novosti* (April 21, 1991: 7).

131. *Nezavisimaia gazeta* (May 12, 1991: 1, 3).

132. *Izvestiia* (May 11, 1991: 3).

133. Popov (1991: 52).

134. Interview with Il'ia Roitman of the Democratic Party of Russia.

135. Interview with Dmitrii Khanov of the Russian Christian-Democratic Movement (RKhDD).

136. From "Zaiavlenie riada kollektivnykh chlenov dvizheniia 'Demokraticheskaia Rossiia'," *samizdat* leaflet dated April 14, 1991.

137. From "Deklaratsiia konstruktivno-demokraticheskogo bloka 'Narodnoe soglasie'," *samizdat* leaflet released in Moscow and dated April 19, 1991.

138. *Nezavisimaia gazeta* (April 27, 1991: 2).

139. *Demokraticheskaia Rossiia* (No. 7, May 10, 1991: 1).

140. Interview with Yakov Gorbadei.

141. From *Dvizheniie "Demokraticheskaia Rossiia"—informatsionnyi biulleten'* (No. 11, July 1991: 1).

142. See *Nezavisimaia gazeta* (May 7, 1991: 1).

143. For Popov's economic proposals during the campaign, see *Moskovskie novosti* (June 9, 1991: 12).

144. By May 14, for instance, 54 percent of respondents reported a favorable attitude toward the idea of Popov as mayor; see *Nezavisimaia gazeta* (May 14, 1991: 1).

145. *Samizdat* leaflet dated July 7, 1991. This leaflet was signed by Coordinating Committee members Gleb Yakunin and Lev Ponomarev.

146. Interview with Victor Sheinis.

147. *Komsomol'skaia pravda* (May 18, 1991: 6).

148. For the suspiciousness with which many grassroots activists viewed Rutskoi, see *Panorama* (No. 1/28, July 1991: 1–2).

149. See *Moskovskie novosti* (June 2, 1991: 2) and *Nezavisimaia gazeta* (June 4, 1991: 2).

150. See, for instance, the interview with Nikolai Bogaenko, a member of Burbulis' staff, in *Kommersant"* (June 2–10, 1991: 12).

151. For the explosion at DR's headquarters, see *Kuranty* (May 18, 1991: 1), *Nezavisimaia gazeta* (May 18, 1991: 1), and *Kommersant"* (May 13–20, 1991: 13).

152. The old headquarters had been obtained by Il'ia Zaslavskii in his capacity as head of the October district soviet (interview with Il'ia Zaslavskii).

153. *Kommersant"* (May 20–27, 1991: 2).

154. See *Izvestiia* (June 19, 1991: 1) and (June 20, 1991: 1) for final tallies in the presidential race. For results of the election in Moscow and Leningrad, see *Kommersant"* (June 10–17, 1991: 6).

155. *Demokraticheskaia Rossiia* (No. 8, May 17, 1991: 7).

156. See *Panorama* (No. 1/28, July 1991: 2).

157. The above account draws from the weekly *Kommersant*, which covered Popov's Moscow closely. See *Kommersant"* (June 17–24, 1991: 6), (June 24–July 1, 1991: 8), (July 8–15, 1991: 9), (July 15–22, 1991: 10), and (July 22–29, 1991: 12).

158. *Kommersant"* (July 15–22, 1991: 1).

159. For a history of the first months of Popov's movement, see V'iunitskii (1991).

160. See *Dvizhenie "Demokraticheskaia Rossiia"—informatsionnyi biulleten'* (No. 12, July 1991: 1).

161. Interviews with Vladimir Bokser and Il'ia Zaslavskii. Popov and Travkin hailed the "de-party-zation" decree, which was published in *Izvestiia* (July 24, 1991: 1). For partocratic condemnation of the decree, see *Izvestiia* (July 23, 1991: 1) and *Nezavisimaia gazeta* (July 23, 1991: 1).

162. See the conservative daily *Sovetskaia Rossiia* (July 23, 1991: 1).

163. On the Fifth CPD-RSFSR and the stalemate over electing a Chairman of the Russian Supreme Soviet, see the series of relevant articles in *Izvestiia* (July 10, 12, 16–17, 1991).

164. See Mitrokhin (1991).

165. Interviews with Il'ia Roitman, Pavel Kudiukin, Vladimir Lysenko, and Dmitrii Khanov.

Chapter Four

1. For the full text of "Postanovlenie No. 1 Gosydarstvennogo komiteta po chrezvychainomy polozheniiu v CCCP" [Resolution No. 1 of the State Committee for the State of Emergency of the USSR], see Voiskunskaia et al. (1991: 26–28). The text was distributed by the *TASS* news service and published on the front page of *Sovetskaia Rossiia* on August 20. Besides Yanaev, the GKChP included KGB head Vladimir Kriuchkov, Interior Minister Boris Pugo, Defense Minister Dmitrii Yazov, Prime

Minister Valentin Pavlov, Chairman of the USSR Military Defense Council Oleg Baklanov, Chair of the Peasant's Union Vasilii Starodubtsev, and Alexander Tiziakov, president of the Association of State Enterprises and Industrial Groups in Production, Construction, Transportation and Communications. A short biography of State Committee members can be found in Belousova and Lebedev (1992: 33–37).

2. See Gorbachev's account, as reproduced in Bonnell, Cooper, and Freidin (1994: 161–169) and Remnick (1994: 452–459).

3. Central Soviet television broadcast Lukianov's statement, "Zaiavlenie predsedatelia verkhovnogo soveta SSSR," at 8 in the morning on August 19; see "A Coup Chronology: The First Two Days" compiled by the editors of *The Current Digest of the Soviet Press* (Sept. 18, 1991: 15). Dated August 16, the statement was published on August 20 in both *Pravda* and *Sovetskaia Rossiia*; see Nikol'skii (1991: 31–32).

4. From "Obrashchenie k sovetskomy narody," dated August 18 and published by *Pravda* (Aug. 20, 1991: 1).

5. *Sovetskaia Rossiia* (Aug. 20, 1991: 2).

6. The texts of the three documents are in Nikol'skii (1991: 35–38).

7. Interview with Vladimir Bokser.

8. *Izvestiia* (Aug. 24, 1991: 4).

9. See Karpukhin's explanation in *Literaturnaia gazeta* (August 28, 1991: 5).

10. See Bonnel, Cooper and Freidin (1994: 12–13).

11. See the interview given by rightist Alexander Prokhanov in *Komsomol'skaia Pravda* (Sept. 3, 1991: 4).

12. See transcripts of the interrogations of Kriuchkov, Pavlov, and Yazov in *Izvestiia* (Oct. 10, 1991: 7)

13. Sources for the next three paragraphs include Belousova and Lebedev (1992); Bonnell, Cooper and Freidin (1994); *Ekspress-Khronika* (Aug. 27, 1991: 1, 2); Rossiiskoe informatsionnoe agentstvo (1991); Luzhkov (1991); Nikol'skii (1991); Voiskunskaia et al. (1991); "A Coup Chronology: The First Two Days," *Current Digest of the Soviet Press* (Aug. 22, 1991: 15–26); and various other newspaper and journalistic accounts.

14. After Yelstin fired his longtime senior bodyguard, Alexander Korzhakov, in the spring of 1996, Korzhakov retaliated by publishing an "inside account" of Yeltsin's days as Russia's leader, which claimed the President was drunk the evening of August 19. This report has not been independently confirmed. See Mark Franchetti, "Bodyguard Tells All on Boozing Boris" in the *Times* (London Sunday Edition, June 22, 1997), available at http://web.lexis-nexis.com/universe/document?_m=c9cfe918183fc5c14beeec63afc67-d7f&_docnum=14&wchp=dGLbVtb-zSkVA&_md5=b0d746b6259bb30dab7ea8cde1c 208e9.

15. Many of these statements are reproduced in Voiskunskaia et al. (1991).

16. Interview with Vladimir Kutukov.

17. *Pravda* (Aug. 20, 1991: 1).

18. Such mimeographed papers included issues of *Argumenty i fakty, Kuranty, Kommersant", Komsomol'skaia pravda, Megapolis ekspress, Moskovskii komsomolets, Nezavisimaia gazeta, Rossiiskaia gazeta, Rossiiskie vesti, Sobesednik,* and *Stolitsa.*

19. See "Demokratiia dolzhna umert' zashchishchat'sia" [Democracy ought to struggle to the death in self-defense], the lead story in the first issue of *Obshchaia gazeta 11* (Aug. 20, 1991: 1).

20. See Bonnel and Freidin (1993).
21. Nikol'skii (1991: 43–62) includes a transcript of the press conference.
22. *Nezavisimaia gazeta* (June 4, 1991: 2).
23. Interview with Il'ia Zaslavskii.
24. Interview with Leonid Bogdanov.
25. Interview with Marta Nadezhna.
26. Interview with Alexei Kashirin, a member of *Narodovlastie*.
27. Interviews with Vladimir Bokser and Mikhail Shneider.
28. Interview with Viacheslav Igrunov.
29. For a picture of this flag, see the front page of the evening edition of *Izvestiia* (Aug. 20, 1991: 1).
30. Figures condensed from various newspaper accounts, as well as *Ekspress-Khronika* (Aug. 27, 1991: 1–3).
31. *Izvestiia* (Aug. 22, 1991: 2).
32. *Vecherniaia Moskva* (Aug. 23, 1991: 1).
33. A summary of Gorbachev's press conference can be found in *Izvestiia* (Aug. 23, 1991: 2).
34. By the time of his symbolic demotion in front of Yeltsin, Gorbachev was reduced to praising the role of the Russian President in the August events (Gorshkov and Zhuravlev 1992: 385–386).
35. *Nezavisimaia gazeta* (Aug. 24, 1991: 1).
36. *Ekspress-Khronika* (Aug. 27, 1991: 2).
37. For Gorbachev's decree suspending the Soviet Communist Party, see *Izvestiia* (Aug. 26, 1991: 1–2).
38. For this committee and its early history, see *Kommersant"* (Aug. 26–Sept. 2, 1991: 2).
39. *Nezavisimaia gazeta* (Aug. 27, 1991: 1).
40. *Nezavisimaia gazeta* (Sept. 7, 1991: 1).
41. *Kommersant"* (Sept. 16–23, 1991: 3).
42. For Yeltsin's statement on the possible redrawing of Russia's borders, see *Nezavisimaia gazeta* (Aug. 27, 1991: 1).
43. For the Rutskoi's negotiations in Ukraine, see *Moskovskie novosti* (Sept. 8, 1991: 7).
44. *Izvestiia* (August 26, 1991: 2–3).
45. See *Kommersant"* (Sept. 2–9, 1991: 2).
46. *Nezavisimaia gazeta* (Sept. 10, 1991: 1).
47. See *Rossiiskaia gazeta* (Sept. 13, 1991: 1) for the full text of this decree.
48. *Rossiiskaia gazeta* (Sept. 18, 1991: 1).
49. *Kommersant"* (Sept. 30–Oct. 6, 1992: 2).
50. *Moskovskie novosti* (Sept. 29, 1991: 1).
51. *Kommersant"* (Sep. 30–Oct.6 1991: 2).
52. White et al. (1993: 91).
53. Sources for the above include articles in *Rossiiskaia gazeta* (Sept. 20, 21, 24, 26, 28, and Oct. 2, 1991) and *Moskovskie novosti* (Sept. 22 and 29, 1991).
54. *Moskovskie novosti* (Sept. 29, 1991: 9).
55. *Rossiiskaia gazeta* (Oct. 30, 1991: 1).

56. Igor Kliamkin cited in *Demokraticheskaia Rossiia* (No. 20, Aug. 9–16, 1991: 4).

57. The reservations of many DR leaders toward the treaty are presented in two issues of *Demokraticheskaia Rossiia* (No. 20, Aug. 9–16, 1991: 8) and (No. 21, Aug. 16–22, 1991: 8–9).

58. Sources include *Agentstvo novostei i informatsii* (No. 172, Aug. 19, 1991: 5), a mimeographed "special issue" (*ofitsioz*) produced during the August events, and *Panorama* (No. 2/29, Sept. 1991: 5).

59. *DemRossiia* first presented its comprehensive proposal for remaking Russian institutions in the mimeographed circular, *Dvizheniie "Demokraticheskaia Rossiia"— informatsionnyi biulleten'* (No. 14, Aug.–Sept. 1991: 1).

60. Sources for the following two paragraphs include *Ekspress-Khronika* (Sept. 10, 1991: 7) and (Sept. 24, 1991: 4), *Kommersant* (Sept. 2–9, 1991: 3), *Kuranty* (Sept. 7, 1991: 3), and *Vedomosti Mossoveta* (No. 5, 1991: 4–14).

61. See *Nezavisimaia gazeta* (Sept. 14, 1991: 1, 2) and (Sept. 21, 1991: 1, 2).

62. Interview with Yakov Gorbadei.

63. *Ekspress-Khronika* (Sept. 10, 1991: 7).

64. *Nezavisimaia gazeta* (Sept. 21, 1991: 2).

65. See *Kommersant"* (Sept. 16–23, 1991: 14).

66. *Kuranty* (Sept. 25, 1991: 1).

67. *Nezavisimaia gazeta* (Sept. 26, 1991).

68. Interview with Mikhail Shneider.

69. Interview with Volodimir Ostroglas.

70. *Nezavisimaia gazeta* (Sept. 17, 1991: 1).

71. *Samizdat* flyer signed by Yuri Afanas'ev, Arkadii Murashev, Lev Ponomarev, Gleb Yakunin, and Kirill Ignat'ev, dated Sept. 18, 1991.

72. For the origins of this Association in the summer of 1991 and the role of the Komissarov affair in pushing it into opposition to Popov, see Pribylovskii (1991: 41).

73. See Zaslavsky (1994) for an extended discussion of the institutional significance of the *propusk* in Soviet society.

74. *Ekspress-Khronika* (Oct. 15, 1991: 1).

75. *Samizdat* leaflet entitled "Resolution of the City Conference of the Democratic Russia Movement," dated fall 1991.

76. The November 12 "scandal" surrounding the Second Conference of the Moscow City Organization of Democratic Russia is recounted at some length in *Panorama* (No. 3/30, Dec. 1991: 4–5).

77. *Samizdat* leaflet issued by the Political Coordinating Committee of the Christian-Democratic Movement, dated October 1991.

78. From page 4 of a Democratic Party of Russia *samizdat* leaflet entitled "Moskovskaia gorodskaia organizatsiia: Polozhenie v Moskve i pozitsiia DPR" [The Moscow City Organization: The Situation in Moscow and the Position of the DPR] located in a folder of materials from October and November 1991, at the Moscow Information Center (*Informatsionnyi tsentr Moskva-BIO*), an archive of *samizdat* and *ofitsioz* previously known as the Moscow Bureau of Information Exchange, the Russian initials for which are MBIO.

79. The draft constitution was published as a four-page insert on October 11, 1991, in *Rossiiskaia gazeta*.

80. For an overview of the failure of Rumiantsev's constitution to be placed on the agenda of the Fifth Russian CPD, see Walker (1992).

81. Interview with Lev Ponomarev.

82. See *Nezavisimaia gazeta* (Oct. 29, 1991: 1).

83. *Rossiiskaia gazeta* (Nov. 2, 1991: 1). For an overview of the proposed new Russian government, see *Kommersant"* (Nov. 4–11, 1991: 24–25).

84. *Rossiiskaia gazeta* (Nov. 1, 1991: 1).

85. *Rossiiskaia gazeta* (Nov. 5, 1991: 1).

86. *Rossiiskaia gazeta* (Nov. 7, 1991: 1). For a complete list of Yeltsin's first governing group, see *Kommersant"* (Nov. 11–18, 1991: 18).

87. See Walker (1992).

88. On events in Checheno-Ingusetiia and the Russian government' initial response to them, see *Ekspress-Khronika* (Nov. 12, 1991: 1) and *Rossiiskaia gazeta* (Nov. 7, 1991: 1) and (Nov. 12, 1991: 1).

89. *Ekspress-Khronika* (Oct. 1, 1991: 1–2) and (Nov. 5, 1991: 1, 4 and 5).

90. *Kuranty* (Nov. 13, 1991: 1).

91. Afanas'ev's remarks cited in Bogdanov et al. (1991: 3).

92. For a more detailed exposition of the position that the breakup of the RSFSR would not necessarily hinder reform, see Afanas'ev's article "United but Divisible" [Edinaia, no delimaia] in *Demokraticheskaia Rossiia* (No. 33, Nov. 23, 1991: 1).

93. See the 1990 article entitled "Why Russia's Democratic Movement 'Fears' the National Idea" by Marina Sal'e, the Leningrad-based *DemRossiia* figure and Afanas'ev ally known among many activists as "the mother of the Revolution" for an early expression of *intelligenty* mistrust of Russian nationalism (*Leningradskii literator* No. 4/9, Sept. 2, 1990: 2–4). Sal'e's title contains a double entendre, as the Russian verb *stesniat'sia* can mean either "to be afraid of" or "to be ashamed of."

94. For Astaf'ev and Roitman's speeches, see Bogdanov et al. (1991: 10–11, 23–24).

95. See the Democratic Party of Russia's post-Second Congress statement explaining its departure in *Demokraticheskaia gazeta* (No. 25/28, Dec. 2, 1991: 5–6). Similar explanations were offered by Astaf'ev (*Moskovskaia pravda*, Nov. 23, 1991: 2) and the Christian-Democratic leadership (*Put'*, No. 10/13, 1991: 2–3).

96. See the article by Igor Kharichev (*Kuranty*, Sept. 5, 1991: 4) that presents the reasoning behind the core's position on a moratorium on border disputes.

97. "Rezoliutsiia II s"ezda dvizheniia 'Demokraticheskaia Rossiia' o kurs Prezidente RSFSR na provedenie korennykh reform," *samizdat* leaflet dated Nov. 10, 1991.

98. Internal *DemRossiia* documents and *samizdat* mimeographs located in the *neformaly* archive, the Moscow Information Center (*Informatsionnyi tsentr Moskva-BIO*), served as sources for the above synopsis of the Social Committee for Russian Reforms, whose Russian initials were OKRR. These documents include "Ustav OKRR," "Proekt OKRR," and several DR Coordinating Committee memos.

99. "Rezul'taty golosovaniia po vyboram sopredsedatelei Soveta Predstavitelei" and "Rezul'taty golosovaniia po vyboram chlenov Kordinatsionnogo Soveta," *samizdat* leaflet dated Nov. 11, 1991.

100. Sources include DR memo noting Coordinating Committee attendance in 1991 as well as a *samizdat* mimeograph circulated by Republican Party member V. Luchin entitled "Kakim byl i kakim dolzhen byt' koordinatsionnyi sovet" [What the Coordinating Committee Has Been and What It Must Become], dated Jan. 9, 1992.

101. See *Kuranty* (Nov. 13, 1991: 4) and *Nezavisimaia gazeta* (Nov. 12, 1991: 2).

102. *Nezavisimaia gazeta* (Oct. 2, 1991: 1).

103. *Nezavisimaia gazeta* (Nov. 26, 1991: 1)

104. *Nezavisimaia gazeta* (Dec. 10, 1991: 1).

105. For an overview of the early history of the Commonwealth, see White et al. (1993: 92–97).

106. See the article by Anatolii Salutskii on the prospects for an anti-Yeltsin coalition of monarchists, nationalists, and communists that appeared in the now-revived, post-CPSU *Pravda* (Dec 2, 1991: 1, 3).

107. Vujacic (1994, 1995).

108. *Nezavisimaia gazeta* (Jan. 3, 1992: 1).

109. Interview with Yuri Afanas'ev.

110. Sources for this and the next paragraph include DR memos; a series of mimeographed exchanges between the Afanas'ev minority and the core located in the archive of the Moscow Information Exchange; and interviews with Yuri Afanas'ev, Vladimir Bokser, Kirill Ignat'ev, and Lev Ponomarev.

111. Interview with Vladimir Lysenko.

112. *Rossiiskaia gazeta* (Feb. 10, 1992: 1).

113. The Russian press figures for this demonstration vary considerably, with the pro-reform daily *Nezavisimaia gazeta* reporting sixty thousand participants at the pro-Yeltsin rally, while approximating demonstrators at the anti-Yeltsin demonstration at forty thousand (Feb. 11, 1992: 1). *Izvestiia* (Feb. 11, 1992: 1) reported rough equality between the pro- and anti-Yeltsin rallies, though giving no numbers, while *Sovetskaia Rossiia* (Feb. 11, 1992: 1–2) seems to have followed the Ministry of Internal Affairs in grossly exaggerating the size of the anti-Yeltsin rally, citing 120,000 demonstrators.

114. *Express-Khronika* (Feb. 17–24, 1992: 1) reported the anti-Yeltsin riot of February 23 drawing thirty thousand participants, while the *New York Times* reported only five thousand (see Serge Schmemann, "Anti-Yeltsin Demonstrators Clash with Moscow Police," *New York Times*, Feb. 24, 1992: 1–2).

115. Khasbulatov dubbed Burbulis and Gaidar "boys in pink pants" at this Congress. Sources for this paragraph include issues of *Rossiiskaia gazeta* issued between April 6 and 24 (1992) as well as *Kommersant"* (April 13–20, 1992: 18) and (April 20–27, 1992: 1, 20).

116. For Popov's interview, see *Argumenty i fakty* (No. 14, April 1992: 1). He announced his resignation on June 5; see *Nezavisimaia gazeta* (June 6, 1992: 1–2).

117. Author's eyewitness estimate.

118. *Nezavisimaia gazeta* (May 30, 1992: 1).

119. *Nezavisimaia gazeta* (May 26, 1992: 2).

120. The Russian sociologist and political commentator Oleg Vite (1992) called this configuration "the August bloc."

Chapter Five

1. Shevtsova (1992: 117).

2. For the notion of governmentality as a means of describing the rise of modern nation-states, see Foucault (1991: 87–104).

3. By the Sixth Congress, some proto-parties and other splinters formerly allied with *DemRossiia* stridently insisted on the government's resignation; see "Nuzhen sil'nyi politicheskii tsentr" (*Demokraticheskaia gazeta*, 16(46), April 4, 1992: 2), a small paper

issued by Travkin's Democratic Party of Russia, which itself still searched for some sort of modus vivendi between fractions. For an overview of "shock therapy," see Murrell (1993).

4. *Izvestiia* (Oct. 9, 1992: 1).

5. *Nezavisimaia gazeta* (Oct. 30, 1992: 1).

6. *Izvestiia* (Oct. 16, 1992: 2).

7. See *Moskovskie novosti* (No. 49, Dec. 6–13, 1992: 1, 4) for an overview of Zorkin's attempt at compromise between Yeltsin and former party-state groups in the Congress. Zorkin's reasoning is difficult to fathom in legal terms: "The President is right to a great extent; however, we [the Constitutional Court] must also say he is in equal measure wrong."

8. *Moskovskie novosti* (No. 51, Dec. 20–27, 1992: 4). For the course of the conflict between the President and the Seventh Congress, see *Nezavisimaia gazeta* (Dec. 11, 12, and 15, 1992). The numerical outline of the Russian Congress can be viewed at http://www.cityline.ru/politika/gos/ndrs.html.

9. Chernomyrdin gained the office of prime minister with 721 votes (*Moskovskie novosti*, No. 51, Dec. 20–27, 1992: 5).

10. Radically different interpretations of what such a referendum could entail aroused intense disagreement between Khasbulatov and Yeltsin within weeks of the Seventh Congress; see *Moskovskie novosti* (No. 4, Jan. 21, 1993: 1).

11. See "Sem' punktov 'demokraticheskogo vybora' " [Seven points of "democratic choice"] in *Nezavisimaia gazeta* (Jan. 13, 1993: 2) and "Demokraty ozabocheny poiskami preemnika El'tsina" [Democrats are anxious about the search for Yeltsin's successor] in *Nezavisimaia gazeta* (Feb. 25, 1993: 2), for the origins of the referendum drive in the rump DemRossiia core and the uneasy relationship between the President and the core in the early period of organizing the referendum drive.

12. *Nezavisimaia gazeta* (Jan. 12, 1993: 1).

13. *Segodnia* (March 10, 1993: 1).

14. *Nezavisimaia gazeta* (March 16, 1993: 1).

15. For referendum specifics decreed by the presidency, see *Moskovskie novosti* (No. 13, March 26, 1993: 4).

16. Figures between 50,000 and 100,000 were cited in the Russian press for this rally; see *RFE/RL* (March 29, 1993). For an optimistic assessment of this demonstration, see Brudny (1993: 167–168).

17. See, for instance, the leading article in *Segodnia* (March 23, 1993: 1) on these events, subtitled "Bor'ba podyshkami prodolzhaet v partere" ["The Pillow Fight Continues in the Orchestra"]. For the concept of "routinization," see Weber (1946: 297), in which he failed to sufficiently differentiate formal rules from informal norms.

18. See Andranik Migranian, "Osnovye itogi IX s"esda" in *Nezavisimaia gazeta* (April 10, 1993: 2).

19. See the June 1992 article (Ivanov-Smolenskii, "Tri Rossiiskie partii sozdaiut umerennyi tsentristskyi blok," *Izvestiia* [June 12 1992]: 2) on the formation of the Civic Union (*Grazhdanskii soiuz*) for early ambitions that such a pacted compromise could be arrived at among parliamentary and executive wings.

20. *Segodnia* (June 4, 1993: 1).

21. For an overview of the conflict in the branches of Russian federal governance over the Conference, see "Konstitutsionnoe soveshchanie: El'tsin poka dovolen—Khasbulatov poka net," *Nezavisimaia gazeta* (June 10, 1993: 1).

22. See the August 1993 interview with Constitutional Court head Valerii Zorkin for his perspective on the spring and summer 1993 conflict in *Nezavisimaia gazeta* (Aug. 24, 1993: 5).

23. See Kochetov (1993: 67–68) and Umov (1993: 33–34).

24. Lilia Babaeva, "Rossiiskii predprinimatel': mezhdu vchera i zavtra" ["The Russian Entrepreneur: Between Yesterday and Tomorrow]," *Segodnia* (Jan. 4. 1994: 10).

25. Interview with Marta Nadezhna.

26. Lane and Ross (1995).

27. Irina Savvateyeva, "Does the new elite derive from the old nomenklatura? About those who rule us," *Current Digest of the Post-Soviet Press* (46, June 15, 1994: 8). Hanley, Yershova, and Anderson (1995) provide statistical evidence of a "power bloc" of former state-enterprise managers, who constituted 37.3 percent of "the new state elite" in the post-1992 Russian administration.

28. A comprehensive survey of two thousand members of Russia's old and new elites completed between 1990 and 1993 provides a wealth of statistical evidence confirming the reproduction of the managerial *nomenklatura* and the ascent of the economic-managerial apparat in the early postcommunist period. Carried out by a research team including Szelényi et al. (1995), the results of this survey were presented in a special issue of *Theory and Society*. This survey demonstrates that 92.1 percent of managers of state-enterprises in 1993 had been either *nomenklaturshchiki* (66.6 percent) or managers or administrators directly below the nomenklatura rank (25.5 percent) in 1988. Further, in 1993, 79.6 percent of managers in the nascent "private sector" (discussed later) had been either nomenklaturshchiki (37.6 percent) or managers or administrators directly below the nomenklatura rank (42 percent) circa 1988 (Hanley, Yershova, and Anderson 1995). Hanley and associates call the ascent of the managerial apparat after 1991 "the revolution of the deputies," that is, the revolution of apparat-plenipotentiaries against the top partocratic elite.

29. See Eyal, Szelényi, and Townsley (1998: 113–176) for a precise overview of this problem and enumeration of nomenklaturshchiki in several countries of the former Soviet bloc, including Russia.

30. See summary in *Nezavisimaia gazeta* (Sept. 22, 1993: 1).

31. Just prior to Yeltsin's disbanding of these bodies, Rumiantsev and others working on draft constitutions in the Congress and Supreme Soviet still strove to work out a compromise with Yeltsin's Constitutional Committee on the basis of "ironic support" (*ironicheskaia podderzka*); see *Nezavisimaia gazeta* (Sept. 15, 1993: 1).

32. See separate statements against Yeltsin issued by Memorial and Oleg Rumiantsev, as well as a statement by pro-democracy Moscow intellectuals that "Yeltsin himself has led the country to the brink of civil war," in *Nezavisimaia gazeta* (Sept. 30, 1993: 1–2), to get the flavor of such pro-democracy dissent from the president.

33. See front-page articles in *Izvestiia* and *Nezavisimaia gazeta* (Oct. 5, 1993). "Hard rightist" here signifies Stalinists from reactionary groups in the old CPSU, as well as other rightist-irredentist groupings, though Russian official and journalistic language already was inverting toward more standard western use of the right–left distinction. For additional sources for this and the following paragraph, see Reddaway and Glinski (2001: 418–429) and Urban (1997: 285–290).

34. As stipulated in Article 111, Section 6 (*Stat'ia 111, Glava 6*) of the December 1993 Russian Constitution, published in *Rossiiskaia gazeta* (No. 237[853], Dec. 25, 1993).

35. Direct appointment to these posts appeared originally as a provisional measure adopted in early 1992, but extended until completion of the gradual reintroduction of elections to such posts by December 1996; see the official history of government bodies published by the Russian Federation at http://www.cityline.ru/politika/fs/sf.html#is.

36. For the latter, see Ginsborg (2003).

37. See Jowitt (1992: 21–22) for "charismatic impersonalism" as a central aspect of the distinctively Leninist variation on modernism. For Jowitt, the corruption of Leninism entails "neotraditionalism" (121–158).

38. For early results, see *Nezavisimaia gazeta* (Dec. 28, 1993: 1). Final results can be viewed at http://www.cityline.ru/politika/fs/gd1rezv.html. Under the current constitution, adopted after the October 1993 disbanding of the Russian Supreme Soviet, the Duma consists of 450 members, half of which are elected by "party lists," the other half on an "individual" basis. Though many individually elected members were identified by party association for this election, fully 130 of members elected on an individual basis remained nominally nonaligned.

39. After then-Constitutional Court head Valerii Zorkin's Nov. 30, 1992, ruling authorizing communist reorganization, Yeltsin did not challenge the reappearance of communists on the Russian electoral scene, so long as they did not try to reconstitute the CPSU. For the founding of the CPRF in January and February 1993, see *Pravda* (Feb. 13, 1993: 1–2) and (Feb. 16, 1993: 1).

40. For the attempt to organize this failed party, see the front page and subsequent materials in *Demokraticheskaia Rossiia* (No. 4, June 1994).

41. Interview with Albert Tsevtkov.

42. See Katsenelinboigen (1977) for a conceptualization and analysis of the range of informal "markets" in the late-communist Soviet Union. Such "markets," in various modified forms, served as the basis for many emergent economic arrangement in post-communist Russia.

43. Only 6 respondents out of 178 identified themselves as "entrepreneurs" in the survey taken of DemRossiia *aktiv* on May 20 and June 17, 1992 (see Tables 1.1 and 1.2 in Chapter 1).

44. Murrell (1993).

45. For the role the threat of hyperinflation played in urban Russia in 1992 and 1993, see "Diagnos: khronicheskiia infliatsiia" ["Diagnosis: Chronic Inflation"], *Moskovskie novosti* (Sept. 1993: 1) and "Giperinfliatsiia: kto postavit diagnoz" ["Hyperinflation: Who Supplies the Diagnosis?"], *Nezavisimaia gazeta* (April 13, 1993: 4).

46. Conversion of rubles into hard currencies—currencies whose value floated on international monetary exchanges—obtained official sanction on Feb. 10, 1993, though new organizations in fact operated such exchanges from Jan. 9, 1992, just a few days after the launching of shock therapy; see http://www.micex.ru/currency/history.html. The birzhi opened by presidential decree on Oct. 6, 1992; see *Kommersant"—Daily* (Oct. 7, 1992: 1).

47. For an overview of the situation on the "lost illusions" (*utrachinye illusii*) surrounding birzhi at the beginning of 1993, see the various accounts collected in *Kommersant"—Daily* (Jan. 9, 1993: 5)

48. Burawoy and Krotov (1992: 35–36).

49. "While economic transactions are increasingly governed by the pursuit of profit through trade, they leave production more or less unchanged." (Burawoy and Krotov 1993: 52.)

50. See the illuminating account of relations between gaming interests and Luzhkov in *Kommersant"—Daily* (Oct. 2, 1996: 1).

51. *Izvestiia* (Oct. 19, 1994: 1). See also Grachev's statement that he would resign if linked to Kholodov's death (*Izvestiia* Oct. 25, 1994: 5).

52. *Nezavisimaia gazeta* (Jan. 12, 1994: 1, 3).

53. *Izvestiia* (March 3, 1994: 1, 2).

54. For an early account of Grachev's purge of senior military figures, see *Moskovskie novosti* (No. 49, Dec. 9–15, 1994: 1).

55. *Moskovskie novosti* (No. 52, Dec. 30, 1994 – Jan. 5, 1995: 2).

56. *Moskovskie novosti* (No. 24–25, June 30–July 6, 1995: 2).

57. See *Kommersant"—Daily* (Jan. 21, 1995: 6), which includes a listing of halting steps toward "voucherization" of Gazprom in preceding months, including the distribution to sixty-one Russian regions of Gazprom shares the preceding June.

58. See "Kto-to igraet v ruletky 'M-M-M', a rasplachivat'sia eto predlagaiut vsem" [Only some played roulette at M-M-M, but everyone is ordered to pay] in *Izvestiia* (Oct. 13, 1995), available at http://dlib.eastview.com/sources/article.jsp?id=3187617.

59. From "Vauchery provoslavnykh kristian sokhraneny," *Radonezh* (No. 2, March–April 1995: 33).

60. See the optimistic account of "Our Home is Russia" in *Moskovskie novosti* (No. 34, Sept. 1–7, 1995: 1), with a picture of a smiling Moscow Mayor Yuri Luzhkov seated next to Prime Minister Chernomyrdin.

61. The rump of Russia's Choice, Russia's Democratic Choice, failed to officially register for the vote and garnered only six seats from the election; see http://www.cityline.ru/politika/fs/gd2frac.html.

62. For an overview of election results, see http://www.cityline.ru/politika/fs/gd2frac.html.

63. Splits among groups of Yeltsin advisors over canceling the elections outright are detailed in Commission on Security and Cooperation in Europe, *Report on Russia's Presidential Election: June 16 and July 3 1996* (Aug. 1996: 3–4).

64. The blatant favoritism Yeltsin suddenly enjoyed in the mass media before the election is documented in Commission on Security and Cooperation in Europe, *Report on Russia's Presidential Election: June 16 and July 3 1996* (Aug. 1996: 10).

65. See McFaul (1997: 48).

66. Confirmation and some detail regarding Yeltsin's hospitalization over a heart attack did not become widely available until September; see *Pravda: spetsial'nyi vypusk gazety* (Sept. 13–20, 1996: 1).

67. *Nezavisimaia gazeta* (Jan. 18, 1996: 1–2) outlines reasons for Chubais' removal a few weeks before it occurred.

68. See http://www.corbina.ru/~rost/oknaro/chubais.html and http://ww.sem40.ru/famous/polit20.shtml for complete listings of various posts held by Chubais in the 1990s.

69. *Moskovskie novosti* (No. 26, July 17–31, 1995: 7) reported that though "almost 117,000 out of 240,000 state-owned enterprises stand now at different stages of privatization," the economic results had been marginal.

70. First introduced by Weber in relation to the later Roman Empire, Karl (1997) refined the concept of political capitalism to analyze oil-exporting arrangements in twentieth century "petrol states" in ways adapted here.

71. The concept of "shareholder" capitalism as a characterization of the historical variant of capitalist economy seen in the United States in the 1990s is adapted from Peter Evans "The Politics of Economic Governance in a Globalized Political Economy" (Presented at the session "The Global Political Economy and Third World Inequality," 93rd Annual Meeting of the American Sociological Association, San Francisco, Aug. 23, 1998).

72. Dinello (1997) presents a summary overview of the FIGs.

73. By the second half of 1995, the Federal administration registered chronic 30–40 percent revenue shortfalls (*Moskovskie novosti*, No. 36, Sept. 15–21, 1995: 9).

74. See Walker (1993) for how Yeltsin failed to "incentivize" the Duma.

75. The political consequences of such moves quickly emerged: "It is no exaggeration to say that in the event of a Yeltsin win, the government will have to settle first of all with the banks that helped win votes" (*Moskovskie novosti*, No. 26, July 4–11, 1996: 7).

76. The 1995 creation and sale of Sibneft for 100 million dollars is documented in *Argumenty i fakti* (July 24, 2002), available at http://www.russiamonitor.org/en/main.asp?menu_id=1_a_1468_38.

77. See the account of Chernomyrdin's holdings in *Kommersant"—Daily* (Jan. 13, 1998: 1, 9).

78. See the misuse of public funds detailed in *Moskovskie novosti* (No. 46, Nov. 21–27, 1996: 7).

79. For details, see the analysis "El'tsin: po stupeniam vverkh i vniz" [Yeltsin: Up and down the stairs] in *Sankt-Peterburgskie vedomosti* (Oct. 31, 1998), available at http://dlib.eastview.com/sources/article.jsp?id=2170349.

80. In late 1996, Duma Deputy Sviatoslav Fedorov went so far as to warn enterprises that they must offer workers physical output and stakes in enterprises in lieu of cash; see *Moskovskie novosti* (No. 46, Nov. 21–27, 1996: 7).

81. Regions in the text (Afanas'ev et al. 1995) include *respubliki, kraia, okruga* (excluding *avtonomnaia okruga*), and the cities of Moscow and St. Petersburg.

82. See Afanas'ev et al. (1995: 180). My thanks to Peter Stavrakis for compiling a working table abstracted from this book, which points this out clearly.

83. Sorting out wage levels and poverty levels in Russia between 1995 and 2001 is difficult for a number of reasons. Among the most problematic of these was that the government used different standards at different times when collecting statistics and that nominal wage levels failed to reflect the explosive growth of unpaid wages. Thus A. E. Surinov records both that the percentage of the population receiving less than poverty-level wages decreased from 32.5 percent in April 1995 to 23.9 percent in April 2001; while the percentage of the poor actually grew from 32.1 to 40 percent during the same period (Surinov 2003: 86, 187).

84. The virtual absence of the "domestic economy" from western economic figures compounds difficulties westerners have in understanding this phenomenon; see Block (1990: 46–74).

85. See Woodruff (1999: 110–176).

86. *Business Week* (Sept. 7, 1998: 28).

87. See Jensen (1998).

88. "Until the central government has corrected its line ... it is necessary maximally to retreat from monetary circulation on the territory of the province, that is, to

strengthen the mutual ties of enterprises, and try to carry out such payments in kind [*tovarnye vzaimoraschety*]"; from an interview conducted by Woodruff (1999: 133).

89. Volkov (2002: 77).

90. *Izvestiia* (Oct. 21, 1994: 2).

91. "Outside Moscow, journalists in many of Russia's 89 regions suffered physical attacks, and harassment from local authorities. Newspapers and broadcast stations in the hinterland are heavily dependent on local administrators for essential services such as access to printing presses and leasing of premises. Regional officials across the federation use this leverage to retaliate against media outlets that cover them in an unflattering way. In the Primorye territory, for example, authoritarian governor Yevgeny Nazdratenko jailed the editor of an opposition weekly for five days for publishing telephone transcripts that appeared to implicate the governor himself and other officials" (from the Committee to Protect Journalists' web site at: http://www.cpj.org/attacks00/europe00/Russia.html).

92. Kirienko's confirmation by the Duma took a month and reportedly occurred with 251 of 450 members not participating in a secret session; see *Nezavisimaia gazeta* (April 25, 1998: 1).

93. Kirienko resigned as Prime Minister on August 23 (*Izvestiia* Aug. 25, 1998: 1).

94. This terminology plays with the formulations in Clifford Gaddy and Barry Ickes, "Russia's Virtual Economy," *Foreign Affairs* 77 (Sept./Oct. 1998). Gaddy and Ickes value Russian production conventionally, in line with IMF and World Bank standards. For a critique of the latter, see Woodruff (1999: 175–176).

95. *The Economist* (May 23, 1998: 66).

96. See "Resursnye platezhi nakanune peremen" [Resource payments on the eve of changes] in *Ekonomika i zhin'* (Sept. 6, 1997), available at http://dlib.eastview .com/sources/article.jsp?id=2764368. For the total volume of Russian oil and natural gas exports in the first half of 1998, see "Vneshniaia torgovlia Rossii," *Ekonomika i zhizn'* (Aug. 22, 1998), at http://dlib.eastview.com/sources/article.jsp?id =2760393.

97. Figures cited by Veronika Sivkova in *Argumenty i fakty* (April 9, 2003), available at http://dlib.eastview.com/sources/article.jsp?id=4836863.

98. See "Rossiiskomu gazu net al'ternativy" in *Rossiiskaia gazeta* (May 27, 1998), available at http://dlib.eastview.com/sources/article.jsp?id=1855765.

99. Conversely, military hardware stands as the only category of industrial goods that Russia manufacturers exported on a significant scale during this period. See Vadim Solov'ev, "Rossiia demonstriryet agressivnyi stil'," *Nezavisimaia gazeta* (Aug. 26, 1998), available at http://dlib.eastview.com/sources/article.jsp?id=36349.

100. See Sergei Tsukhlo, "Ekonomicheskii analiz narodnoe khoziaistvo," *Ekspert* (March 6, 2000, available at http://dlib.eastview.com/sources/article.jsp?id=2794006) for the centrality of barter in the Russian economy in the mid- to late-1990s. The role of barter exchanges in lieu of payment in enterprise exchanges is examined by Aleksandr Bekker in *Segodnia* (April 5, 1996, at http://dlib.eastview.com/sources/article .jsp?id=2002443). For an overall view of the role of barter in Russia in the 1990s, see Woodruff (1999).

101. See http://www.icem.org/campaign/no_pay_cc/situation_9810.html.

102. See Oksana Dmitrieva, "Robin Gud v iubke," *Moskovskii komsomolets* (May 30, 1998), available at http://dlib.eastview.com/sources/article.jsp?id=97694.

103. See the analysis by Svetlana Il'ina in *Nezavisimaia gazeta* (June 11, 1998), available at http://dlib.eastview.com/sources/article.jsp?id=313234.

104. Reports on these actions can be found in "13 Maia—'chernyi' den' dlia shakhterov," *Sankt-Peterburgskie vedomosti* (May 14, 1998), available at http://dlib.eastview.com/sources/article.jsp?id=2164770 and "'Rel'sovaia voina': v zalozhnikakh u shakhterov okazalas' vsia strana," *Krasnaia zvezda* (May 23, 1998), available at http://dlib.eastview.com/sources/article.jsp?id=3340686.

105. For a summation of the government's tax policies and their failures between 1992 and the end of July 1998, see "Primenie nalogovogo zakonadatel'stva. Arbitrazhnaia praktika" [Application of tax legislation. Practical experience of arbitration.] in *Ekonomika i zhizn'* (Aug. 8, 1998), available at http://dlib.eastview.com/sources/article.jsp?id=2760209. Resistance to Kirienko's policies on privatization emerged early in the summer; see "Duma otkazalas' ot programmy privatizatsii" [Duma to reject privatization program] in *Kommersant"—Daily* (June 26, 1998), available at http://dlib.eastview.com/sources/article.jsp?id=3752995. Just before his dismissal as prime minister, Kirienko tried to negotiate with the oligarchs over tax and other policies; see "Pravitel'stvo gotovo na sgovor s oligarkhami" [The government is prepared for negotiations with the oligarchs], *Kommersant"—Daily* (Aug. 7, 1998), available at http://dlib.eastview.com/sources/article.jsp?id=3755238.

106. For the role of Berezovsky in the aborted attempt to reappoint Chernomyrdin as prime minister, see Aleksandr Budberg, "Staryi kon' v novoi borozde" [Old horse in a new furrow], *Moskovskii komsomolets* (Aug. 25, 1998), available at http://dlib.eastview.com/sources/article.jsp?id=99646.

107. *Rossiiskaia gazeta* (Sept. 11, 1998: 1).

108. Karl (1997) analyzes in some detail how dependence on oil exports lead to forms of political capitalism dominating national and regional political and economic alliances in a great diversity of national contexts.

109. "Vneshniaia torgovlia Rossii," *Ekonomika i zhizn'* (Aug. 22, 1998), available at http://dlib.eastview.com/sources/article.jsp?id=2760393.

110. "Kak upal neftianoi rynok," *Kommersant"—Vlast'* (Aug. 4, 1998), available at http://dlib.eastview.com/sources/article.jsp?id=3203971.

111. Volkov (2002: 126–154).

112. For the magnitude of political fallout from the disclosure of the sorry state of government financing in August 1998, see "Ot 'chernogo vtornika' do 'chernogo ponedel'nika'" [From "black Tuesday" to "black Monday"], *Sankt-Peterburgskie vedomosti* (Aug. 17, 1999), available at http://dlib.eastview.com/sources/article.jsp?id=2180161.

113. For a summary of some of these grim figures, see "V demograficheskom nokaute" ["A demographic knockout"], *Sankt-Peterburgskie vedomosti* (Oct. 5, 2002), available at http://dlib.eastview.com/sources/article.jsp?id=4405535. The figure for male life expectancy in 1994 comes from this article, while the figure for male life expectancy in 1988 is taken from Goskomstat SSSR (1990a: 28). According to "V demograficheskom nokaute," the average death rate of males had recovered somewhat, to 60.8 years, by 1997.

114. *Izvestiia* (July 14, 1998: 2).

115. *Kommersant"—Daily* (July 10, 1998: 5).

116. "Armiiu kormili sobach'imi konservami," *Kommersant"—Daily* (July 10, 1998), available at http://dlib.eastview.com/sources/article.jsp?id=3753788.

117. "Voennosluzhashchikh vnov' podstavilil," *Nezavisimaia gazeta* (Aug. 25, 1998), available at http://dlib.eastview.com/sources/article.jsp?id=316263.

118. *Segodnia* (May 30, 1998), reported in *RFE/RL*, http://www.friends-partners. org/news/omri/1998/06/980601I.html.

119. *Izvestiia* (July 4, 1998: 1–2).

120. Volkov (2002: 139).

121. *Izvestiia* (June 10, 1998: 1–2).

122. Yavlinskii's speech, "Otkrytoe pis'mo prezidentu Rossii," was excerpted in *Nezavisimaia gazeta* (June 19, 1998: 1, 3).

123. In January 1999, Radio Free Europe reported "Applications to participate in the all-Russia strike action have so far been submitted by 38 oblasts, republics, and krais from 6,600 educational institutions, according to Vladimir Yakovlev, chairman of the Central Committee of the Education and Science Workers Union"; see *RFE/RL* (Jan. 20, 1999), available at http://www.rferl.org/newsline/1999/01/200199.asp.

124. Lebed' perished in a plane crash on April 28, 2002; see *Izvestiia* (April 30, 2002: 1 and 3).

125. See "Novye dannye VTsIOM," *Nezavisimaia gazeta* (Oct. 21, 1998), available at http://dlib.eastview.com/sources/article.jsp?id=318187, which summarizes polling at this time by the most prestigious sociological institute in postcommunist Russia.

126. The Starovoitova assassination shook what was left of the democratic wing of Russian politics; see *Nezavisimaia gazeta* (Nov. 24, 1998: 1–3).

127. As distinct from Soviet-era "thieves in law" (*vory v zakone*), essentially bandits, violent entrepreneurs emerged directly from feudalization as substitutes for collapsed state sovereignty, varying widely in their conduct and organizational modes across regions; see Volkov (2002: 74–77).

128. See stories on the private investigative agency *Atoll* and how they aroused interest in the prosecutor general's office in *Moskovskii komsomolets* (Jan. 20 and 22, 1999).

129. The first excerpts from the videotape were shown on March 17 (*Moskovskii komsomolets*, March 18, 1999: 1).

130. In late March, the Communist Party of the Russian Federation claimed that "the Skuratov affair" had become a "provocation" (*Nezavisimaia gazeta* March 20, 1999: 3). The "Skuratov affair" intensified after Yeltsin tried to remove him from office (*Nezavisimaia gazeta* April 3, 1999: 3).

131. *Izvestiia* (May 13, 1999: 1).

132. On the failure of impeachment, see "Partiinaia distsipliona ne vyderzhala ispytaniia impichmentom," *Izvestiia* (May 18, 1999: 1).

133. See *Nezavisimaia gazeta* (May 19, 1999: 3) and (May 28: 1999: 1).

134. The Russian press began to notice the seriousness of Putin as a power player about the time of the failed impeachment drive against Yeltsin in May; see "Kto sil'nee segodnia v Rossii?" [Who is More Powerful Today in Russia?], *Nezavisimaia gazeta* (May 15, 1999: 2)

135. In the first two weeks of September 1998, inflation neared 50 percent a month, the conventional benchmark of hyperinflation. See "Rossiia na poroge giperinfliat-sii," *Moskovskie novosti* (Sept. 15, 1998), available at http://dlib.eastview.com/sources/article.jsp?id=145893.

136. Recall that the 1993 election law split the 500 Duma seats down the middle, with election of 250 seats by party lists and 250 seats by individual candidates. For

party list seats, the final tally was 24.29 percent for the Communist Party of the Russian Federation; 23.32 percent for Unity; Fatherland/All Russia (a bloc of apparat reformers around former Prime Ministers Primakov and Chernomyrdin, and Moscow Mayor Luzhkov), 13.33 percent; the Union of Rightist Forces (a bloc of pro-market economists with few ties to the early 1990s democratic movement), 8.52 percent; Zhironovsky's bloc, 5.98 percent; and Yabloko, 5.93 percent; from the *Interfax* news agency in Russia, cited in "Final Duma Election Results Announced, *BBC Summary of World Broadcasts* (Dec. 30, 1999), at http://web.lexis-nexis.com/universe/document?_m= 5486c0de8fc277a1a037bbfd5432a93d&_docnum=3&wchp=dGLbVzb-zSkVb&_md5 =8836c3610bfab0e5560d52c805ad8d39.

137. "Chechnya has been suppressed for the national cause. It seems that both Machiavelli and Margaret Thatcher were right. Keep the population ready for war, and the State will be more integrated and stable" (Harrison 2003: 15–16).

138. The notion of "gray" marketeers is used provisionally where state power—understood in Weberian terms as the monopoly of the legitimate use of violence—tends to break down (Volkov 2002: 16—26).

139. Eyal, Szelényi, and Townsley (1998: 188).

140. For a more empirically realistic modification of neoliberal thought, see Stiglitz (2002). The economist Krugman (1999) has warned against the dangers of treating neoliberal assumptions as an ideology.

141. Migdal (1988: 238–277).

142. Interview with Alexander Podrabinek.

143. The concept of liminality is adapted to modern contexts from Turner (1977), who used it to describe status transitions in pre-statist societies.

144. Ries (1997: 112). This only touches on one of the many facets of litanies analyzed by Ries as daily practices, markers of habitus, in Russian social life.

145. For instance, Shevtsova (1998: 330) observed that "Appeal to this term [nomenklatura] serves mainly as a means of intra-clan [*vnutriklanovyi*] struggle. The old ruling class split apart some time ago, and its individual fragments acquired new interests."

146. Vujacic (1994).

147. For the origins of the concept of "governmentality" used here, see Foucault (1991).

148. See Dahl (1989: 213–298) and Lindblom (1977: 131–143).

Appendix

1. As indicated in Chapter 1, the vast majority of survey respondents filled out questionnaires at two general meetings of *DemRossiia dvizhenie* held in the *Mossovet*. Oral instructions for respondents to return completed questionnaires on their way out were given before the meetings commenced, with the assent of Democratic Russia's Coordinating Committee. A small number of respondents (11 out of 178) mailed back questionnaires delivered to organizers of two district-level DR associations in Moscow: (1) the *Narodovlastie* voters club and (2) the *Matveevskii* district association.

2. As the Russian school and university systems are quite different than the American pattern, I have here translated the spirit and not the letter of the questionnaire by rendering the questions in their rough American equivalents. This question was actually broken into two sub-sections, the second of which asked the respondent to specify which type of educational institution he or she last attended, i.e., (1) public school,

(2) vocational school, (3) academic institute, (4) a university or college, or (5) graduate school.

3. This list is in itself testimony to the extent to which individuals not belonging to the working class, the peasantry—collective farmers (*kolkhozniki*)—or the *nomenklatura* proper saw themselves more in terms of discrete status groups, rather than as part of a broader "middle class." See Yanowitch (1977: 7) for similar lists of occupations used in Soviet social science in the 1960s and 1970s.

4. For each activity listed under this question, respondents were asked to check off spaces marked "regularly," "from time to time," and "never" for the following periods: (1) before 1986, (2) in 1986–1987, (3) in 1988–1989, and (4) in 1990–1991.

Bibliography

List of Interviewees

Afanas'ev, Yuri (member of *DemRossiia* Coordinating Committe, hereafter DR CC)
Beliaeva, Nina (political scientist; legal advisor to pro-democracy activists)
Bogdanov, Leonid (member of DR CC)
Bokser, Vladimir (member of DR CC)
Degtiarev, Andrei (political scientist)
Gokhman, Mikhail (DR activist; journalist)
Gorbadei, Yakov (DR activist)
Ignat'ev, Kirill (member of DR CC)
Igrunov, Viacheslav (Memorial activist)
Kashirin, Alexei (DR activist)
Khanov, Dmitrii (RKhDD member; DR activist)
Kharitonivich, Dmitrii (DR activist)
Kriger, Vera (member of DR CC)
Kudiukin, Pavel (SPD member; member of DR Council of Representatives, hereafter DR CR)
Kutukov, Vladimir (DR activist)
Lysenko, Vladimir (RPR member; member of DR CR; member of DR bloc in parliament)
Nadezhnova, Marta (pseudonym of DR activist)
Ostroglas, Vladimir (pseudonym of DR activist)
Podrabinek, Alexander (former dissident; editor of *samizdat* bulletin *Ekspress-Khronika*)
Ponomarev, Lev (member of DR CC; member of DR bloc in parliament)
Rachinskii, Jan (Memorial activist; DR activist)
Rakovskii, Boris (DR activist)
Roitman, Il'ia (DPR member; member of DR CR)
Sheinis, Victor (member of DR bloc in parliament; member of DR CR)
Shneider, Mikhail (member of DR CC)
Sholpo, Leonid (DR activist)
Starovoitova, Galina (member of DR CC; member of DR bloc in parliament; Yeltsin advisor 1991–1992)
Stikhiinskii, Sergei (pseudonym of DR activist; *Brateevo* activist)
Tsevtkov, Albert (DR candidate at level of Moscow city districts in 1990 elections)
Veshinskii, Yuri (geographer)

Zaslavskii, Il'ia (member of DR CC; Chairman of October District Soviet in Moscow)

Note: All the interviews were conducted by the author in Moscow between February and July 2002, exceptions being the interviews with Viacheslav Igrunov and Galina Starovoitova, which were conducted in Berkeley, CA, in October 1993, and with Andrei Degtiarev, which was conducted in Moscow in June 1995.

Russian Periodicals and News Bulletins Cited

Argumenty i fakty (Arguments and Facts)
Demokraticheskaia gazeta (Democratic Gazette)
Demokraticheskaia Rossiia (Democratic Russia)
Ekspert (Expert)
Ekspress-Khronika (Express Chronicle)
Ekonomika i zhizn' (Economics and Life)
Golos izbiratelia (Voice of the Voter)
Grazhdanskoe obshchestvo (Civil Society)
Izvestiia (Information)
Kommersant"—Daily (Man of Commerce Daily, initially the weekly *Kommersant"*; *Daily* is in English in this otherwise Russian language paper)
Komsomol'skaia pravda (Komsomol Truth)
Kuranty (Chimes)
Krasnaia zvezda (Red Star)
Leningradskii literator (Leningrad Man of Letters)
Literaturnaia gazeta (Literary Gazette)
Moskovskii komsomolets (Moscow Komsomoler)
Moskovskie novosti (Moscow News)
Moskovskaia pravda (Moscow Truth)
Nevskii kur'er (Neva Courier)
Nezavisimaia gazeta (Independent Gazette)
Obshchaia gazeta 11 (Joint Gazette of the Eleven)
Ogonek (Little Flame)
Piatnitsa (Friday)
Panorama (Panorama)
Positsiia (Viewpoint)
Pravda (Truth)
Put' (Path)
Rossiiskaia gazeta (Russian Gazette)
Rossiiskie vesti (Russian News)
Russkaia mysl' (Russian Thought)
Sankt-Peterburgskie vedomosti (St. Petersburg Bulletin)
Segodnia (Today)
Sovetskaia Rossiia (Soviet Russia)
Stolitsa (The Capital)
Vecherniaia Moskva (Evening Moscow)
Vedomosti Mossoveta (Bulletin of the Moscow City Soviet)

Articles, Books, and Reports

Abbott, Andrew. 1991. "History and Sociology: The Lost Synthesis." *Social Science History* 15:201–238.

Abrahamian, Levon H. 1998. "Mother Tongue: Linguistic Nationalism and the Cult of Translation in Postcommunist Armenia." Berkeley Program in Soviet and Post-Soviet Studies Working Paper Series, University of California, Berkeley.

Afanas'ev, Yuri N., ed. 1988. *Inogo ne dano*. Moscow: Progress.

Afanas'ev, M. H. et al., eds. 1995. *Rossiiskie regiony nakanune vyborov—95*. Moscow: Iuridicheskaia literatura.

Afanas'ev, Mikhail N. 1997. *Klientelizm i Rossiiskaia gosudarstvennost'*. Moscow: Tsentr konstitutsionnykh issledovanii.

Alexander, Jeffrey C. 1987. "Action and Its Environments." In J. C. Alexander et al., eds., *The Micro-Macro Link*, pp. 289–318. Berkeley: University of California Press.

Alexeyeva, Ludmilla. 1985. *Soviet Dissent: Contemporary Movements for National, Religious, and Human Rights*. Middletown, CT: Wesleyan University Press.

———. 1988. "Independent Youth Groups in the USSR." *Across Frontiers* 4(3):4–5, 32.

———, ed. 1990. *Nyeformaly: Civil Society in the USSR*. New York: Helsinki Watch Committee.

Arendt, Hannah. 1958. *The Origins of Totalitarianism*, rev. ed. Cleveland OH: Meridian Books.

Arrow, Kenneth J. 1998. "What Has Economics to Say About Racial Discrimination?" *Journal of Economic Perspectives* 12:91–100.

Aves, Jonathan. 1992. "The Evolution of Independent Political Movements after 1988." In Geoffrey A. Hosking et al., eds., *The Road to PostCommunism: Independent Political Movements in the Sovit Union, 1985–1991*, pp. 29–66. London: Pinter Publishers.

Babkina, M. A., ed. 1991. *New Political Parties and Movements in the Soviet Union*. Commack, NY: Nova Science Publishers.

Balzer, Harley D. 1996. "Conclusion: The Missing Middle Class." In H. Balzer, ed., *Russia's Missing Middle Class: The Professions in Russian History*, pp. 293–319. Armonk, NY: M. E. Sharpe.

Bauman, Zygmunt. 1974. "Officialdom and Class: Bases of Inequality in Socialist Society." In Frank Parkin, ed., *The Social Analysis of Class Structure*, pp. 129–148. London: Tavistock Publications.

Beliaeva, Nina et al. 1991. "Mnogopartiinost' v Rossii, 1917–1990 gg." *Problemy vostochnoi evropy* 31/32:79–163.

Bellah, Robert N., Richard Madsen, William M. Sullivan, Ann Swidler, and Steven M. Tipton. 1990. *The Good Society*. New York: Vintage.

Belousova, Galina A., and Vladimir A. Lebedev. 1992. *Partokratiia i putch*. Moscow: Izdatel'stvo respublika.

Bendix, Rheinhard. 1977. *Nation-Building and Citizenship*, rev. ed. Berkeley: University of California Press.

———. 1984. *Force, Fate, and Freedom: On Historical Sociology*. Berkeley: University of California Press.

Berezovskii, Vladimir N. et al. 1991. *Rossiia: partiia assotsiatsii soiuzy kluby: sprovochnik*, 2 knigi. Moscow: Pay-Press.

———. 1992a. *Rossiia: partii assotsiatsii soiuzy kluby: sbornik materialov i dokumentov*, kniga 2. Moscow: Pay-Press.

————. 1992b. *Rossiia: partii assotsiatsii soiuzy kluby: sbornik materialov i dokumentov*, kniga 5. Moscow: Pay-Press.

Berezovskii, Vladimir N., and Nikolai I. Krotov, eds. 1990. *Neformal'naia Rossiia*. Moscow: Molodaia gvardiia.

Berger, Peter L., and Thomas Luckmann. 1966. *The Social Construction of Reality: A Treatise in the Sociology of Knowledge*. New York: Anchor Books.

Bialer, Seweryn. 1989. "The Yeltsin Affair: The Dilemma of the Left in Gorbachev's Revolution." In S. Bialer, ed., *Politics, Society and Nationality inside Gorbachev's Russia*, pp. 91–119. Boulder, CO: Westview Press.

Billington, James H. 1970. *The Icon and the Axe: An Interpretive History of Russian Culture*. New York: Vintage.

Blau, Peter M. 1998. "Culture and Social Structure." In Alan Sica, ed., *What Is Social Theory? The Philosophical Debates*, pp. 265–275. Malden, MA: Blackwell.

Block, Fred L. 1990. *Postindustrial Possibilities: A Critique of Economic Discourse*. Berkeley: University of California Press.

Bogdanov, Leonid A. et al., eds. 1991. *Materialy II s"ezda dvizheniia "Demokraticheskaia Rossiia."* Moscow: DR-Press.

Bonnell, Victoria E. 1983. *Roots of Rebellion: Workers' Politics and Organizations in St. Petersburg and Moscow, 1900–1914*. Berkeley: University of California Press.

————. 1990. "Voluntary Associations in Gorbachev's Reform Program." In George W. Breslauer, ed., *Can Gorbachev's Reforms Succeed?*, pp. 63–76. Berkeley, CA: Center for Slavic and East European Studies.

Bonnell, Victoria E., and Gregory Freidin. 1993. "Televorot: The Role of Television Coverage in Russia's August 1991 Coup." *Slavic Review* 52:810–838.

Bonnell, Victoria E., Ann Cooper, and Gregory Freidin, eds. 1994. *Russia at the Barricades: Eyewitness Accounts of the August 1991 Coup*. Armonk, NY: M. E. Sharpe.

Böröcz, József, and Akos Róna-Tas. 1995. "Small Leap Forward: Emergence of New Economic Elites." *Theory and Society* 24:766–772.

Bourdieu, Pierre. 1981. "Men and Machines." In K. Knorr-Cetina and A. V. Cicourel, eds., *Advances in Social Theory and Methodology: Toward an Integration of Micro- and Macro-Sociologies*, pp. 304–317. Boston: Routledge and Kegan Paul.

————. 1984. *Distinction: A Social Critique of the Judgement of Taste*. Cambridge, MA: Harvard University Press.

————. 1986. "The Forms of Capital." In John G. Richardson, ed., *Handbook of Theory and Research for the Sociology of Education*, pp. 240–258. New York: Greenwood Press.

————. 1987. "Legitimation and Structured Interests in Weber's Sociology of Religion." In Scott Lash and Sam Whimster, eds., *Max Weber, Rationality and Modernity*, pp. 119–136. London: Allen and Unwin.

————. 1990a. "Codification." In *In Other Words: Essays Toward a Reflexive Sociology*, pp. 76–86. Stanford, CA: Stanford University Press.

————. 1990b. "Social Space and Symbolic Power." In *In Other Words: Essays Toward a Reflexive Sociology*, pp. 123–139. Stanford, CA: Stanford University Press.

————. 1991. *Language and Symbolic Power*. Cambridge, MA: Harvard University Press.

————. 1993. "The Field of Cultural Production, Or: The Economic World Reversed." In *The Field of Cultural Production: Essays on Art and Literature*, pp. 29–73. New York: Columbia University Press.

Bourdiey, Pierre, and Loïc J. D. Wacquant. 1992. *An Invitation to Reflexive Sociology*. Chicago: University of Chicago Press.

Braudel, Fernand. 1984. *The Perspective of the World*. Vol. 3, *Civilization and Capitalism 15th–18th Century*. New York: Harper and Row.

Breslauer, George W. 1978. "On the Adaptability of Soviet Welfare-State Authoritarianism." In Karl W. Ryavec, ed., *Soviet Society and the Communist Party*, pp. 3–25. Amherst: University of Massachusetts Press.

Brubaker, Rogers. 1994. "Nationhood and the National Question in the Soviet Union and Post-Soviet Eurasia: An Institutional Account." *Theory and Society* 23:47–78.

Brudny, Yitzhak M. 1989. "The Heralds of Opposition to Perestroyka." *Soviet Economy* 5:162–200.

———. 1993. "The Dynamics of 'Democratic Russia', 1990–1993." *Post-Soviet Affairs* 9(2):141–170.

Burawoy, Michael et al. 2000. *Global Ethnography: Forces, Connections, and Imaginations in a Postmodern World*. Berkeley: University of California Press.

Burawoy, Michael, and Pavel Krotov. 1992. "The Soviet Transition from Socialism to Capitalism: Worker Control and Economic Bargaining in the Wood Industry." *American Sociological Review* 57:16–38.

———. 1993. "The Economic Basis of Russia's Political Crisis." *New Left Review*, no. 198:49–69.

Burger, Thomas. 1987. *Max Weber's Theory of Concept Formation: History, Laws and Ideal Types*, expanded ed. Durham, NC: Duke University Press.

Byzov, L. G. et al. 1991. "Reflections of Sociologists on the Political Reforms." *Soviet Sociology* 30:26–42.

Cantor, Norman F. 1993. *The Civilization of the Middle Ages*. New York: HarperCollins.

Chiesa, Giulietto. 1993. *Transition to Democracy: Political Change in the Soviet Union, 1987–1991*, with Douglas Taylor Northrop. Hanover, NH: University Press of New England.

Cohen, Jean L. 1985. "Strategy or Identity: New Theoretical Paradigms and Contemporary Social Movements." *Social Research* 52(Winter):663–716.

Colton, Timothy J. 1990. "The Politics of Democratization: The Moscow Election of 1990." *Soviet Economy* 6:285–344.

Commission on Security and Cooperation in Europe. 1990. *Elections in the Baltic States and Soviet Republics: A Campendium of Reports on Parliamentary Elections Held in 1990*. Washington, DC: Commission on Security and Cooperation in Europe.

Dahl, Robert A. 1989. *Democracy and Its Critics*. New Haven: Yale University Press.

Dallin, Alexander, and Gail W. Lapidus, eds. 1991. *The Soviet System in Crisis: A Reader of Western and Soveit Views*. Boulder, CO: Westview Press.

Desai, Padma. 1987. *The Soviet Economy: Problems and Prospects*. Oxford: Basil Blackwell.

Dinello, Natalia. 1997. "Financial-Industrial Groups and Russia's Capitalism." Institute on East-Central Europe, available at http://ciaonet.org/conf/ece01din.html.

Duncan, Peter J. S. 1992. "The Rebirth of Politics in Russia." In Geoffrey Hosking et al., eds., *The Road to PostCommunism:Independent Political Movements in the Soviet Union, 1985–1991*, pp. 67–120. London: Pinter Publishers.

Dunlop, John B. 1993. *The Rise of Russia and the Fall of the Soviet Empire*. Princeton, NJ: Princeton University Press.

Economist staff. 1998. "A Guide to Offshorny Banking." *The Economist*, May 23:66.

———. 1999. "Russia's Economic Quagmire." *The Economist*, April 24:69–70.

Elias, Norbert. 1978. *What Is Sociology?* New York: Columbia University Press.

Ericson, Richard E. 2000. "The Post-Soviet Russian Economic System: An Industrial Feudalism?" In Tuomas Komulainen and Iikka Korhonen, eds., *Russian Crisis and Its Effects*, pp. 133–166. Helsinki: Kikimora Publications.

Evans, Peter B. 1995. *Embedded Autonomy: States and Industrial Transformation.* Princeton, NJ: Princeton University Press.

Eyal, Gil, Iván Szelényi, and Eleanor Townsley. 1998. *Making Capitalism without Capitalists: The New Ruling Elites in Eastern Europe.* London: Verso.

Fadeev, Valerii V. 1992. *Ocherk 88 goda.* Moscow: Russkoe slovo.

Fainsod, Merle. 1964. *How Russia Is Ruled.* Cambridge, MA: Harvard University Press.

Fehér, Ferénc, Agnes Heller, and Gyorgy Markus. 1983. *Dictatorship over Needs.* Oxford: Basil Blackwell.

Ferguson, James. 1990. *The Anti-Politics Machine: "Development," Depoliticization, and Bureaucratic Power in Lesotho.* Cambridge: Cambridge University Press.

Fish, M. Steven. 1995. *Democracy from Scratch: Opposition and Regime in the New Russian Revolution.* Princeton, NJ: Princeton University Press.

Fitzpatrick, Sheila. 1994. *The Russian Revolution*, 2nd ed. Oxford: Oxford University Press.

Flaherty, Patrick. 1990. "The Making of the New Soviet Left." *Telos*, no. 84:88–114.

Foucault, Michel. 1972. *The Archaeology of Knowledge.* New York: Pantheon Books.

———. 1991. "Governmentality." In Graham Burchell, Colin Gordon, and Peter Miller, eds., *The Foucault Effect: Studies in Governmentality*, pp. 87–104. Chicago: University of Chicago Press.

Friedrich, Carl J., and Zbigniew K. Brzezinski. 1956. *Totalitarian Dictatorship and Autocracy.* Cambridge, MA: Harvard University Press.

Fuchs, Stephan. 2001. *Against Essentialism: A Theory of Culture and Society.* Cambridge, MA: Harvard University Press.

Furet, Francois. 1989. "Feudal System." In F. Furet and Mona Ozouf, eds., *A Critical Dictionary of the French Revolution*, pp. 684–693. Cambridge, MA: Harvard University Press.

Gamson, William A., David Croteau, William Hoynes, and Theodore Sasson. 1992. "Media Images and the Social Construction of Reality." *Annual Review of Sociology* 18:373–393.

Garcelon, Marc. 1997a. "The Shadow of the Leviathan: Public and Private in Communist and Post-Communist Society." In Jeff Weintraub and Krishan Kumar, eds., *Public and Private in Thought and Practice: Perspectives on a Grand Dichotomy*, pp. 303–332. Chicago: University of Chicago Press.

———. 1997b. "The Estate of Change: The Specialist Rebellion and the Democratic Movement in Moscow, 1989–1991." *Theory and Society* 26:39–85.

———. 2001. "Colonizing the Subject: The Genealogy and Legacy of the Soviet Internal Passport." In Jane Caplan and John Torpey, eds, *Documenting Individual Identity: The Development of State Practices in the Modern World*, pp. 83–100. Princeton, NJ: Princeton University Press.

Giddens, Anthony. 1984. *The Constitution of Society: Outline of the Theory of Structuration.* Berkeley: University of California Press.

Ginsborg, Paul. 2003. "The Patrimonial Ambitions of Silvio B." *New Left Review* 21: 21–64.

Gladysh, Y. 1990. "Ot partiinogo kluba k 'demokraticheskoi platforme'." *Narodnyi deputat*, no. 6:59–62.

Gleick, James. 1987. *Chaos: Making of a New Science.* New York: Penguin.

Goldstone, Jack A. 1994. "Revolutions in World History." In J. Goldstone, ed., *Revolutions: Theoretical, Comparative and Historical Studies*, pp. 315–318. New York: Harcourt Brace.

Gorbachev, Mikhail. 1988. *Perestroika: New Thinking for Our Countryand the World.* New York: Harper and Row.

Gorbachev, Mikhail et al. 1990. "Informatsiia i khronika." *Izvestiia TsK KPSS*, no. 4:112–15.

Gorshkov, M. K., and V. V. Zhuravlev, eds. 1992. *Gorbachev—El'tsin: 1500 dnei politicheskogo protivostoianiia.* Moscow: Terra.

Goskomstat SSSR. 1990a. *RSFSR v tsifrakh v 1989 g.* Moscow: Finansy i statistika.

———. 1990b. *Uroven' obrazovaniia naseleniia SSSR po dannym vsesoiuznyi perepesi naseleniia 1989 g.* Moscow: Finansy i statistika.

Goskomstat of Russia. 1999. *Russia in Figures: Concise Statistical Handbook*, English ed. Moscow: State Committe of the Russian Federation on Statistics.

Granovetter, Mark S. 1985. "Economic Action and Social Structure: The Problem of Embeddedness." *American Journal of Sociology* 91:481–510.

Gregory, Paul R., and Robert C. Stuart. 1986. *Soviet Economic Structure and Performance*, 3rd ed. New York: Harper and Row.

Gurr, Ted R. 1972. "The Calculus of Social Conflict." *Journal of Social Issues* 28:27–47.

Habermas, Jürgen. 1987. *Lifeworld and System: A Critique of Functionalist Reason.* Vol. 2, *The Theory of Communicative Action.* Boston: Beacon Press.

Hahn, Jeffrey W. 1991. "Continuity and Change in Russian Political Culture." *British Journal of Political Science* 2:493–512.

Handelman, Stephin. 1995. *Comrade Criminal: Russia's New Mafiya.* New Haven, CT: Yale University Press.

Hanley, Eric, Natasha Yershova, and Richard D. Anderson. 1995. "Russia—Old Wine in a New Bottle? The Circulation and Reproduction of Russian Elites, 1983–1993." *Theory and Society* 24:657–667.

Harrison, J. Frank. 2003. "Russian Federalism Today." *Studies in Post-Communism: Occasional Paper*, no. 1:1–16, http://www.stfx.ca/pinstitutes/cpcs/studies-in-post-communism/Harrison2003.pdf).

Harvey, David. 1990. *The Condition of Postmodernity: An Enquiry into the Origins of Cultural Change.* Cambridge, MA: Blackwell.

Havel, Vaclav. 1988. "AntiPolitical Politics." In John Keane, ed., *Civil Society and the State: New European Perspectives*, pp. 381–398. London: Verso.

Helf, Gavin. 1994. *All the Russias: Center, Core and Periphery in Soviet and Post-Soviet Russia.* Ph.D. dissertation, University of California, Berkeley.

Heller, Mikhail, and Aleksandr M. Nekrich. 1986. *Utopia in Power: The History of the Soviet Union from 1917 to the Present.* New York: Summit Books.

Henslin, James M. 1999. *Sociology: A Down-to-Earth Approach*, 4th ed. Boston: Allyn and Bacon.

Hewett, Ed A., and Victor H. Winston, eds. 1991. *Milestones in Glasnost and Perestroyka: Politics and People.* Washington, D.C: The Brookings Institute.

Hoch, Steven L. 1986. *Serfdom and Social Control in Russia: Petrovskoe, a Village in Tambov.* Chicago: University of Chicago Press.

Hopkins, Mark. 1983. *Russia's Undergroud Press: The Chronicle of Current Events.* New York: Praeger Publishers.

Hosking, Geoffrey A. 1990. *The Awakening of the Soviet Union.* London: Heinemann.
——. 1992a. *The First Socialist Societ: A History of the Soviet Union from Within,* 2nd enlarged ed. Cambridge, MA: Harvard University Press.
——. 1992b. "The Beginnings of Independent Political Activity." In G. Hosking et al., eds., *The Road to PostCommunism: Independent Political Movements in the Soviet Union, 1985–1991,* pp. 1–28. London: Pinter Publishers.
Humphrey, Caroline. 2002. *The Unmaking of Soviet Life: Everyday Economies after Socialism.* Ithaca, NY: Cornell University Press.
Igrunov, Viacheslav. 1991. "Public Movements: From Protest to Political Self-Consciousness." In Nina Belyaeva and Brad Roberts, eds., *After Perestroika: Democracy in the Soviet Union. Significant Issues Series* XIII, no. 5 , pp. 14–31. Washington, DC: The Center for Strategic and International Studies.
Il'ina, Tatiana. 1991. "'My vse pereboleli KPSSom...'." *Obshchestvennie nauki i sovremennost'* 4:68–76.
Iushnekov, Sergei N., ed. 1990. *Neformaly: sotsial'nye initsiativy.* Moscow: Moskovskii rabochii.
Izvestiia Sovetov narodnykh deputatov SSSR. 1988. *Konstitutsiia (osnovnoi zakon) Soiuza sovetskikh sotsialistucheskikh respublik.* Moscow: Izvestiia Sovetov narodnikh deputatov SSSP.
Janos, Andrew C. 1986. *Politics and Paradigms: Changing Theories of Change in Social Science.* Stanford, CA: Stanford University Press.
Jensen, Donald N. 1998. "The Big Seven: Russia's Financial Empires." *Transition* 9(1):15–17.
Jones, Anthony, and Elliott A. Krause. 1991. "Professions, the State, and the Reconstruction of Socialist Societies." In A. Jones, ed., *Professions and the State: Experts and Autonomy in the Soviet Union and Eastern Europe,* pp. 233–253. Philadelphia, PA: Temple University Press.
Joppke, Christian. 1993a. *Mobilizing Against Nuclear Energy: A Comparison of Germany and the United States.* Berkeley: University of California Press.
——. 1993b. "Some Characteristics of Social Movements in Leninist Regimes." Unpublished manuscript, University of Southern California, Los Angeles.
Jowitt, Ken. 1978. *The Leninist Response to National Dependency.* Berkeley: Institute of International Studies, University of California.
——. 1983. "Soviet Neotraditionalism: The Political Corruption of a Leninist Regime." *Soviet Studies* 3:275–97.
——. 1992. *New World Disorder: The Leninist Extinction.* Berkeley: University of California Press.
Kagarlitsky, Boris. 1990. *Farewell Perestroika: A Soviet Chronicle.* London: Verso.
——. 2000. "Stsenarii. S terroristami ne razgovarivaem. No pomogaem? Versiia vzryvov domov v Rossii." *Novaia gazeta,* Jan. 24, No. 3.
Karl, Terry L. 1997. *The Paradox of Plenty: Oil Booms and Petro-States.* Berkeley: University of California Press.
Katsenelinboigen, Aron. 1977. "Colored Markets in the Soviet Union." *Soviet Studies* 29:62–85.
Kellert, Stephen H. 1993. *In the Wake of Chaos: Unpredictable Order in Dynamical Systems.* Chicago: University of Chicago Press.
Kerblay, Basile. 1983. *Modern Soviet Society.* New York: Pantheon.

Khobotov, Anatolii N., and Tamara I. Zheludkova. 1990. *Iz istorii stanovleniia i razvitiia pasportnoi sistemy v SSSR (oktiabr' 1917–1974 gg.)*. Moscow: Akademiia MVD SSSR.

Kochetov, Aleksei N. 1988. "Novye tendentsii v sovershenstvovanii sotsial'noi struktury sovetskogo obshchestva (1980-e gody)." *Istoriia SSSR*, no. 6:9–10.

———. 1993. "Istoki 'novoi' sotsial'noi struktury." *Svobodnaia mysl'*, no. 9:67–68.

Koenker, Diane. 1981. *Moscow Workers and the 1917 Revolution*. Princeton, NJ: Princeton University Press.

Kommunisticheskaia partiia Sovestskogo soiuza. 1986. *XXVII s"ezd kommunisticheskoi partii Sovetskogo Soiuza: stenograficheskii otchet. Tom 1*. Moscow: Izdatel'stvo politicheskoi literatury.

———. 1988. *XIX vsesoiuznaia konferentsiia kommunisticheskoi partii Sovetskogo Soiuza, 28 iiunia—1 iiulia 1988 goda: stenograficheskii otchet*, Vol. 1. Moscow: Izdatel'stvo politicheskoi literatury.

Konrád, György, and Ivan Szelényi. 1979. *The Intellectuals on the Road to Class Power: A Sociological Study of the Role of the Intelligentsia in Socialism*. New York: Harcourt Brace Jovanovich.

Kornai, János. 1992. *The Socialist System: The Political Economy of Communism*. Princeton, NJ: Princeton University Press.

Kornhauser, William. 1959. *The Politics of Mass Society*. Glencoe, IL: The Free Press.

Kotkin, Stephen. 1995. *Magnetic Mountain: Stalinism as a Civilization*. Berkeley: University of California Press.

Kotliakov, V. M. 1990. *Vesna 89: Geografiia i anatomiia parlamentskikh vyborov*. Moscow: Progress.

Kotz, David. 1997. *Revolution from Above: The Demise of the Soviet System*, with Fred Weir. London: Routledge.

Koval', B. I., ed. 1991. *Rossiia segodnia: politicheskii portret v dokumentakh 1985–1991*. Moscow: Mezhdunarodnye otnosheniia.

Kovalev, Sergei. 2001. "The Putin Put-On." *The New York Review of Books* 48(Aug. 9): 29–32.

Krippendorff, Klaus. 1980. *Content Analysis: An Introduction to Its Methodology*. Beverly Hills, CA: Sage Publications.

Krugman, Paul. 1999. *The Accidental Theorist and Other Dispatches from the Dismal Science*. New York: W. W. Norton.

Kudiukin, Pavel M. 1990. "Sotsialdemokraty: istoki i tsel'." *Dialog*, no. 9:45–48.

Kuromiya, Hiroaki. 1988. *Stalin's Industrial Revolution: Politics and Workers, 1928–1932*. Cambridge: Cambridge University Press.

Lampert, Nick. 1987. "Russia's New Democrats: The Club Movement and Perestroika." *Détente*, nos. 9/10:10–11.

Lane, David. 1992. *Soviet Society under Perestroika*, rev ed. London: Routledge.

Lane, David, and Cameron Ross. 1995. "The Changing Composition and Structure of the Political Elites." In Lane, ed., *Russia in Transition: Politics, Privatization and Inequality*, pp. 52–75. London: Longman.

Ledeneva, Alena V. 1998. *Russia's Economy of Favors: Blat, Networking and Informal Exchange*. Cambridge: Cambridge University Press.

———. 2002. "How Russia Really Works," http://www.opendemocracy.net/themes/ article.jsp?id=6&articleId=253 (accessed Jan. 16, 2002).

Lenin, Vladimir I. 1975 [1917]. "The Dual Power." In Robert C. Tucker, ed., *The Lenin Anthology*, pp. 301–304. New York: W. W. Norton.

Lentini, Peter. 1991. "Reforming the Electoral System: The 1989 Elections to the USSR Congress of People's Deputies." *The Journal of Communist Studies* 7:69–94.

Levanskii, V., and E. Bazhanova. 1990. "Obshchestvennye predpochteniia: analiza massovogo soznaniia v period vyborov narodnykh deputatov SSSR." *Narodnyi deputat*, no. 3:36–43.

Levicheva, Valentina. 1991. "Kto delaet politiku?" *Narodnyi deputat*, no. 14:95–101.

Levin, A. I. 1979. *Nauchno-tekhnicheskii progress i lichnoe potreblenie*. Moscow: Mysl'.

Lindblom, Charles E. 1977. *Politics and Markets : The World's Political Economic Systems*. New York: Basic Books.

Lipitskii, Vasilii S., and O. T. Vite. 1990. "Demplatforma ukhodit...kto vmesto nee?" *Dialog*, no. 14:37–39.

Liubarskii, Kronid. 1994. "Pasportnaia sistema i sistema propiski v Rossii." *Rossiiskii biulleten' po pravam cheloveka*, no. 2:14–26.

Logan, John R. 1978. "Growth, Politics, and the Stratification of Places." *American Journal of Sociology* 84:404–416.

Lotman, Iurii M., and Boris A. Uspenski. 1985. "Binary Models in the Dynamics of Russian Culture (to the End of the Eighteenth Century)." In Alexander D. and Alice Stone Nakhimovsky, eds., *The Semiotics of Russian Cultural History*. Ithaca, NY: Cornell University Press.

Lupher, Mark. 1996. *Power Restructuring in Russia and China*. Boulder, CO: Westview Press.

Luk'ianov, A. I. et al. 1984. *Sovety narodnykh deputatov: spravochnik*. Moscow: Politizdat.

Luzhkov, Yurii. 1991. *72 chasa agonii: avgust 1991. Nachalo i konets kommunisticheskogo putcha v Rossii*. Moscow: Magisterium.

Malia, Martin. 1961. "What is the Intelligentsia?" In Richard Pipes, ed., *The Russian Intelligentsia*, pp. 1–18. New York: Columbia University Press.

Marchenko, Anatolii. 1991. *Moi pokazaniia*. Moscow: Moskovskii rabochii.

Marx, Karl. 1974 [1869]. "The Eighteenth Brumaire of Louis Bonaparte." In David Fernbach, ed., *Karl Marx: Surveys from Exile, Political Writings Volume II*. New York: Vintage.

Matlock Jr., Jack F. 1995. *Autopsy on an Empire: The American Ambassador's Account of the Collapse of the Soviet Union*. New York: Random House.

Matthews, Mervyn. 1993. *The Passport Society: Controlling Movement in Russia and the USSR*. Boulder, CO: Westview Press.

McAdam, Doug. 1982. *Political Process and the Development of Black Insurgency, 1930–1970*. Chicago: Univesity of Chicago Press.

McAdam, Doug, John D. McCarthy, and Mayer N. Zald. 1996. "Introduction: Opportunities, Mobilizing Structures, and Framing Processes—Toward a Synthetic, Comparative Perspective on Social Movements." In McAdam, McCarthy, and Zald, eds., *Comparative Perspectives on Social Movements: Political Opportunites, Mobilizing Structures, and Cultural Framings*, pp. 1–20. Cambridge: Cambridge University Press.

McCarthy, John D., and Mayer N. Zald. 1973. *The Trend of Social Movements in Americ: Professionalization and Resource Mobilization*. Morristown, NJ: General Learning Press.

McDaniel, Tim. 1988. *Autocracy, Capitalism, and Revolution in Russia*. Berkeley: University of California Press.

McFaul, Michael. 1997. *Russia's 1996 Presidential Election: The End of Polarized Politics*. Stanford, CA: Hoover Institution Press.

McFaul, Michael, and Sergei Markov. 1993. *The Troubled Birth of Russian Democracy: Parties, Personalities, and Programs*. Stanford, CA: Hoover Institution Press.

Melucci, Alberto. 1989. *Nomads of the Present: Social Movements and Individual Needs in Contemporary Society*. Philadelphia, PA: Temple University Press.

Migdal, Joel S. 1988. *Strong Societies and Weak States: State-Society Relations and State Capabilities in the Third World*. Princeton, NJ: Princeton University Press.

Milanovic, Branko. 1998. *Income, Inequality, and Poverty during the Transition from Planned to Market Economy*. Washington, DC: The World Bank.

Millar, James R. 2002. "Normalization of the Russian Economy: Obstacles and Opportunities for Reform and Sustainable Growth." *The National Bureau of Asian Research Analysis* 13(April):5–43.

Millar, James R., and Elizabeth Clayton. 1987. "Quality of Life: Subjective Measures of Relative Satisfaction." In J. Millar, ed., *Politics, Work and Daily Life in the USSR*. Cambridge: Cambridge University Press.

Millar, James R., and Sharon L. Wolchik. 1994. "Introduction: The Social Legacies and the Aftermath of Communism." In J. Millar and S. Wolchik, eds., *The Social Legacy of Communism*, pp. 1–28. Cambridge: Cambridge University Press/the Woodrow Wilson Center Press.

Milosz, Czeslaw. 1955. *The Captive Mind*. New York: Vintage Books.

Mitrokhin, Sergei. 1991. "Fenomen protopartii." *Vek XX i mir*, no. 10:24–28.

Morrison, John. 1991. *Boris Yeltsin: From Bolshevik to Democrat*. London: Dutton.

Moskovskii gorodskoi sovet. 1990. *Materialy pervoi sessii Mosskovskogo gorodskogo soveta nardnykh deputatov RFSFR: Dvadtsat' pervogo sozyva (tret'ia chast' 27 iiunia—6 iiulia 1990 g.)*. Moscow: Informatsionnyi sektor.

Mouzelis, Nicos. 1995. *Sociological Theory: What Went Wrong? Diagnosis and Remedies*. London: Routledge.

Murrell, Peter. 1993. "What is Shock Therapy? What Did It Do in Poland and Russia?" *Post-Soviet Affairs* 9(April–June):111–140.

Nahirny, Vladimir C. 1983. *The Russian Intelligentsia: From Torment to Silence*. New Brunswick, NJ: Transaction.

Nee, Victor, and Peng Lian. 1994. "Sleeping with the Enemy: A Dynamic Model of Declining Political Commitment in State Socialism." *Theory and Society* 23: 253–296.

Nikol'skii, A. V., ed. 1991. *Avgust-91*. Moscow: Izdatel'stvo politicheskoi literatury.

Ol'sevich, T. A., ed. 1990. *Vesna 89: geografia i anatomiia parlamentskikh vyborov*. Moscow: Progress.

Pipes, Richard. 1995. *Russia under the Old Regime*, 2nd ed. New York: Penguin.

Polanyi, Michael. 1983. *The Tacit Dimension*. Gloucester, MA: Peter Smith.

Popov, Gavriil. 1990. "Perspektivy i realii: o strategii i taktike demokraticheskikh sil na sovremennoi etape." *Ogonek* , no. 50:6–8 and no. 51:5–8.

———. 1991. *Chto delat'?* Moscow: Pozitsiia.

Pravosudov, Sergei. 2000. "Bloka OBR voobshche moglo ne byt'." *Nezvisimaya gazeta*, Jan. 14, No. 5.

Pribylovskii, Vladimir. 1991. *Slovar' novykh politicheskikh partii i organizatsii Rossii*. Moscow: Panorama.

Putnam, Robert D. 1993. *Making Democracy Work: Civic Traditions in Modern Italy.* Princeton, NJ: Princeton University Press.

Reddaway, Peter, and Dmitri Glinski. 2001. *The Tragedy of Russia's Reforms: Market Bolshevism against Democracy.* Washington, DC: United States Institute of Peace Press.

Remnick, David. 1994. *Lenin's Tomb: The Last Days of the Soviet Empire.* New York: Vintage.

Ries, Nancy. 1997. *Russian Talk: Culture and Conversation during Perestroika.* Ithaca, NY: Cornell University Press.

Rigby. T. H. 1977. "Stalinism and the Mono-Organizational Society." In Robert C. Tucker, ed., *Stalinism: Essays in Historical Interpretation*, pp. 53–76. New York: W. W. Norton.

Ringer, Frtiz. 1997. *Max Weber's Methodology: The Unification of the Cultural and Social Sciences.* Cambridge, MA: Harvard University Press.

Ritzer, George. 2003. "Rethinking Globalization: Glocalization/Grobalization and Something/Nothing." *Sociological Theory* 21:193–209.

Rossiiskoe informatsionnoe agentstvo. 1991. *Khronika putcha: chas za chasom.* Leningrad: Leningradskoe otdelenie Rossiiskogo informatsionnogo agentstva.

Roth, Guenther. 1968. "Personal Rulership, Patrimonialism, and EmpireBuilding in the New States." In Reinhard Bendix, ed., *State and Society: A Reader in Comparative Political Sociology*, pp. 581–591. Boston: Little, Brown and Company.

———. 1971. "Sociological Typology and Historical Explanation." In Reinhard Bendix and G. Roth, eds., *Scholarship and Partisanship: Essays on Max Weber*, pp. 109–128. Berkeley: University of California Press.

———. 1979. "Duration and Rationalization: Fernand Braudel and Max Weber." In G. Roth and Wolfgang Schluchter, eds., *Max Weber's Vision of History: Ethics and Methods*, pp. 166–193. Berkeley: University of California Press.

Roxburgh, Angus. 1991. *The Second Russian Revolution: The Struggle for Power in the Kremlin.* London: BBC Books.

Savas, E. S., and John A. Kaiser. 1985. *Moscow's City Government.* New York: Praeger.

Schapiro, Leonard. 1971. *The Communist Party of the Soviet Union*, 2nd ed. New York: Vintage.

———. 1977. *The Origin of the Communist Autocracy: Political Opposition in the Soviet State First Phase: 1917–1922*, 2nd ed. Cambridge, MA: Harvard University Press.

Sekretariat XXVIII s"eszda KPSS. 1990. "II vsesoiuznaiia konferentsiia 'Demokratich-eskoi platformy v KPSS'." *Izvestiia TsK KPSS*, no. 8:129–132.

Selznick, Philip. 1960. *The Organizational Weapon: A Study of Bolshevik Strategy and Tactics.* Glencoe, IL: The Free Press.

Seniavskii, S. L. et al. 1984. *Aktual'nye problemy istorii razvitogo sotsializma v SSSR.* Moscow: Mysl'.

Sevast'ianov, A. N. 1989. "Intelligentsia: chto vperedi?" In Anatolii G. Vishnevskii, ed., *V chelovecheskom izmerenii*, pp. 170–179. Moscow: Progress.

Severiukhin, A. 1988. "The New Left: From Discussion to Action." *Across Frontiers* 4(1): 6–7, 30–31.

Sewell, William H., Jr. 1994. "Ideologies and Social Revolutions: Reflections on the French Case." In T. Skocpol, ed., *Social Revolutions in the Modern World*, pp. 169–198. Cambridge: Cambridge University Press.

————. 1996. "Three Temporalities: Toward an Eventful Sociology." In Terrence J. McDonald, ed., *The Historic Turn in the Human Sciences*, pp. 245–280. Ann Arbor: University of Michigan Press.

Sharlet, Robert. 1977. "Stalinism and Soviet Legal Culture." In Robert C. Tucker, ed., *Stalinism: Essays in Historical Interpretation*, pp. 155–179. New York: W. W. Norton.

Shatalin, C. C. et al. 1990. *Perekhod k rynku: kontseptsiia i programma*. Moscow: Arkhangel'skoe.

Shevtsova, Liliia. 1992. "Vlast' v Rossii." In Y. Byrtin, ed., *God posle Avgusta: gorech' i vybor*, pp. 117–128. Moscow: Literatura i politika.

————. 1998. "Rossiia: Logika politicheskikh peremen." In L. Shevtsova, ed., *Rossiia politicheskaia*. Moscow: Moskovskii Tsentr Karnegi.

Shul'gin, Nikolai. 1990. "DS: besstrashie svobody." In Sergei N. Iushenkov, ed., *Neformaly: sotsial'nye initsiativy*, pp. 190–197. Moscow: Moskovskii rabochii.

Skocpol, Theda. 1979. *States and Social Revolutions: A Comparative Analysis of France, Russia, and China*. Cambridge: Cambridge University Press.

————. 1994. "Cultural Idioms and Political Ideologies in the Revolutionary Reconstruction of State Power: A Rejoinder to Sewell." In *Social Revolutions in the Modern World*, pp. 199–210. Cambridge: Cambridge University Press.

Slezkine, Yuri. 1994. "The USSR as a Communal Apartment, or How a Socialist State Promoted Ethnic Particularism."*Slavic Review* 53:441–452.

Slider, Darrell. 1991. "The First Independent Soviet Interest Groups: Unions and Associations of Cooperatives." In Jim Butterfield and Judith B. Sedaitis, eds., *Perestroika from Below: Social Movemens in the Soviet Union*, pp. 145–164. Boulder, CO: Westview Press.

————. 1993. "Gorbachev's First Reform Failure: Work-place Democratization." *Journal of Communist Studies* 9:62–83.

Snow, David A., E. Burke Rochford Jr., Steven K.Worden, and Robert D. Benford. 1986. "Frame Alignment Processes, Micromobilization, and Movement Participation." *American Sociological Review* 51:464–481.

Snow, David A., and Robert D. Benford. 1988. "Ideology, Frame Resonance, and Participant Mobilization." *International Social Movements Research* 1:197–217.

Sobchak, Anatolii. 1991. *Khozhdenie vo vlast'*, izdanie vtoroe, dopolnennoe. Moscow: Novosti.

Solovyov, Vladimir, and Elena Klepikova. 1992. *Boris Yeltsin: A Political Biography*. New York : Putnam.

Somers, Margaret R. 1996. "Where is Sociology after the Historic Turn? Knowledge, Cultures, Narrativity, and Historical Epistemologies." In Terrence J. McDonald, ed., *The Historic Turn in the Human Sciences*, pp. 53–90. Ann Arbor: University of Michigan Press.

Starikov, Evgenii. 1990. "'Ugrozhaet' li nam poiavlenie 'srednego klassa'?" *Znamia*, no. 10:192–96.

Stark, David. 1992. "Path Dependence and Privatization Strategies in East Central Europe." *East European Politics and Society* 6(1):17–51.

Stiglitz, Joseph E. 2002. *Globalization and Its Discontents*. New York: W. W. Norton.

Sundiev, Igor Y. 1989. "Samodeiatel'nye ob"edineniia molodezhi." *Sotsiologicheskie issledovaniia*, no. 2:56–62.

Sundiev, Igor Y. 1990. "Nashestvie marsian…?" In Sergei Iushenkov, ed., *Neformaly: sotsial'nye initsiativy*, pp. 4–43. Moscow: Moskovskii rabochii.

Suny, Ronald Gregory. 1993. *The Revenge of the Past: Nationalism, Revolution, and the Collapse of the Soviet Union*. Stanford, CA: Stanford University Press.

Surinov, A. E. 2003. *Uroven' zhizni naseleniia Rossii: 1992—2002 gg*. Moscow: IITs "Statistika Rossii."

Swidler, Ann. 1986. "Culture in Action: Symbols and Strategies." *American Sociological Review* 51:273–286.

Szelényi, Iván et al. 1995. "Reproduction vs. Circulation of Elites During the Post-communist Transformation of Eastern Europe." *Theory and Society* 24:615–802.

Tarrow, Sidney. 1998. *Power in Movement: Social Movements and Contentious Politics*, 2nd ed. Cambridge: Cambridge University Press.

Turner, Victor. 1977. *The Ritual Process: Structure and Anti-structure*. Ithaca, NY: Cornell University Press.

Umov, V. I. 1993. "Rossiiskii srednii klass: sotsial'naia real'nost' i politicheskii fantom." *Politicheskie issledovaniia*, no. 4:26–40.

Urban, Michael E. 1992. "Boris El'tsin, Democratic Russia and the Campaign for the Russian Presidency." *Soviet Economy* 44(2):187–207.

———. 1997. *The Rebirth of Politics in Russia*, with Vyacheslav Igrunov and Sergei Mitrokhin. Cambridge: Cambridge University Press.

Verdery, Katherine. 1996. *What Was Socialism, and What Comes Next?* Princeton, NJ: Princeton University Press.

Vite, Oleg T. 1989. "Aktivnost' vne reglamenta: chto stoit zauchastiem chlenov KPSS v neformal'nykh organizatsiiakh." *Politicheskoe obrazovanie*, no. 13:7–11.

V'iunitskii, Vladimir I. 1991. "Manifest 'deviatki': priglashenie k razvodu?" *Dialog*, no. 13:69–75.

Voiskunskaia, Natella et al. 1991. *Korichnevyi putch krasnykh Avgust '91*. Moscow: Tekst.

Volkov, Vadim. 2002. *Violent Entrepreneurs: The Use of Force in the Making of Russian Capitalism*. Ithaca, NY: Cornell University Press.

Vujacic, Veljko. 1994. "The Russian Right: 1989–1993." In Carol A. Timko, ed., *Russia after the Elections: A Conference Report*, pp. 41–54. Berkeley, CA: The Berkeley-Stanford Program in Soviet and Post-Soviet Studies.

———. 1995. *Communism and Nationalism in Russia and Serbia*. Ph.D. dissertation, University of California, Berkeley, CA.

Walder, Andrew G. 1986. *Communist NeoTraditionalism: Work and Authority in Chinese Industry*. Berkeley: Universtiy of California Press.

Walker, Edward W. 1992. "The New Russian Constitution and the Future of the Russian Federation." *The Harriman Institute Forum* 5(10, June):1–16.

———. 1993. "Politics of Blame and Presidential Powers in Russia's New Constitution." *East European Constitutional Review* 2:116–119.

———. 2003. *Dissolution: Sovereignty and the Breakup of the Soviet Union (The Soviet Bloc and After)*. Lanham, MD: Rowman & Littlefield.

Weber, Max. 1946. *From Max Weber: Essays in Sociology*. Edited by H. H. Gerth and C. Wright Mills. New York: Oxford University Press.

———. 1949. "'Objectivity' in Social Science and Social Policy." In *The Methodology of the Social Sciences*. New York: The Free Press.

———. 1978. *Economy and Society: An Outline of Interpretive Sociology*. Edited by Guenther Roth and Claus Wittich, 2 vols. Berkeley: University of California Press.

White, Stephen et al. 1993. *The Politics of Transition: Shaping a Post-Soviet Future.* Cambridge: Cambridge University Press.

Winiecki, Jan. 1986. "Are Soviet-type Economies Entering an Era of Long-Term Decline?" *Soviet Studies* 38: 325–348.

Winston, Victor H. 1991. "The Early Years of the Gorbachev Era: An Introduction." In Ed a. Hewett and V. H. Winston, eds., *Milestones in Glasnost and Perestroyka: Politics and People*, pp. 3–10. Washington, DC: The Brookings Institution.

Wolf, Eric R. 1982. *Europe and the People without History.* Berkeley: University of California Press.

Woodruff, David. 1999. *Money Unmade: Barter and the Fate of Russian Capitalism.* Ithaca, NY: Cornell University Press.

Woolcock, Michael. 1998. "Social Capital and Economic Development: Toward a Theoretical Synthesis and Policy Framework." *Theory and Society* 27:151–208.

———. 1999. "Managing Risks, Shocks, and Opportunities in Developing Economies: The Role of Social Capital." Develpment Research Group papers, published by the World Bank.

Yakovlev, Aleksander. 1992. *Predislovie—Obval—Posleslovie.* Moscow: Novosti.

Yanowitch, Murray. 1977. *Social and Economic Inequality in the Soviet Union.* White Plains, NY: M. E. Sharpe.

Yeltsin, Boris N. 1990a. *Ispoved' na zadannuiu temu.* Moscow: Chas pik.

———.1990b. *Against the Grain: An Autobiography.* Translated by Michael Glenny. New York: Summit Books.

Yurchak, Aleksei. 1997. "The Cynical Reason of Late Socialism: Power, Pretense, and the Anekdot." *Public Culture* 9:161–188.

Zaslavsky, Victor. 1991. "Rossiia na puti k rynku: gosudarstvennozavisimye rabotniki i populizm." *Politicheskie issledovaniia*, no. 5:65–79.

———. 1994. *The Neo-Stalinist State: Class, Ethnicity, and Consensus in Soviet Society*, 2nd ed. Armonk, NY: M.E. Sharpe.

Zaslavsky, Victor, and Yuri Luryi. 1979. "The Passport System in the USSR and Changes in Soviet Society." *Soviet Union/Union Sovietique* 6(Part 2):137–153.

Zdravomyslova, Elena. 1996. "Opportunities and Framing in the Transition to Democracy: The Case of Russia." In Doug McAdam, John D. McCarthy, and Mayer N. Zald, eds., *Comparative Perspectives on Social Movements: Political Opportunites, Mobilizing Structures, and Cultural Framings*, pp. 122–137. Cambridge: Cambridge University Press.

Zhudkova, I. et al. 1988. "Samodeiatel'nye initsiativy. Nefromal'nyi vzgliad." *Kommunist*, no. 9:95–106.

Zucker, Lynne G. 1991. "The Role of Institutionalization in Cultural Persistence." In Walter W. Powell and Paul J. DiMaggio, eds., *The New Institutionalism in Organizational Analysis*, pp. 83–107. Chicago: University of Chicago Press.

Index

Marc Garcelon is an Assistant Professor in the Department of Sociology and Anthropology at Middlebury College.